FATHERS, HUSBANDS AND LOVERS

Legal Rights and Responsibilities

SANFORD N. KATZ
MONROE L. INKER

MELBA MCGRATH
Editorial Associate

A Publication
of the
American
Bar Association
Section of
Family Law

Cover design by Terry Haas

Produced by the ABA Press
Library of Congress Catalog Card No. 79-84397
ISBN: 0-89707-000-3

CONTENTS

Note: The double pagination on each page occurs because the articles have been reproduced from the original volumes of the *Family Law Quarterly.* Retaining the original pagination allows quick access to cross-references in the footnotes.

The page number in the upper corner of each page is from the original volume. The number at the bottom of each page reflects this book's pagination.

Acknowledgements

We wish to acknowledge with gratitude the editorial assistance of Jonny J. Frank and Jeffrey D. Ginzberg, both members of the Class of 1980 at Boston College Law School.

Melba McGrath was intimately involved in the planning and preparation of the manuscript and we value her contribution. Special thanks are due Hope Bulger for her assistance in guiding the book through publication.

Sanford N. Katz
Monroe L. Inker

Introduction

SANFORD N. KATZ
MONROE L. INKER

Human history has placed man in the driver's seat of the family, with mate and offspring in the back seat traveling the road their driver chose. The driver has had to supply and maintain the vehicle and provide provender for the female and children. But the passengers have had no choice in direction or goal, and there was always a chance the driver might become bored and leave them stranded by the roadside or become infuriated by their presence and beat up on them. Sometimes only the woman would be ditched and the man would ride on triumphantly with his children. Sometimes the man would decide that being hemmed in by the laws of marriage was an unnecessary drag, in which case ditching the female, with or without offspring, became even simpler.

All that is changing in the Western world, most notably for us in the United States. Though ERA has not (yet) been federally adopted, women, with their children, have come a long way toward dual driving. There are now paternity tests close to complete accuracy that are making men responsible for the support of illegitimate children they have claimed were not theirs. There are inheritance and social security and Workmen's Compensation laws that apply equally to legitimate and illegitimate offspring. There are laws and programs that track a man from state to state when he tries to escape the costs of rearing his children. When man and mate separate, there is a whole new approach to the division of accumulated property which takes into consideration the monetary value of the woman's contribution to the man's success, to homemaking and child rearing. And this, almost regardless of whether the twain have been legally joined. There is even doubt whether the old verse, "Whither thou goest I will go," is still viable. There are reliefs for the victims of furious fathers, husbands and lovers and there are attempts to get to the psychological and social sources of the fury and ameliorate or extirpate it. The articles in this book are concerned with the driver. He is no longer alone in the front seat. More and more often he has a fully licensed co-driver: his mate.

Establishment of Paternity

This book, a collection of articles that have appeared in the *Family Law Quarterly*, begins, as it were, *ab ovo*: Who is a father? Of course the husband of a legitimately married couple is legally assumed to be the father of resulting offspring; but recent figures disclose that almost one-third of births in this country are the result of a nonlegalized relationship. There are urban areas where illegitimates account for more than 50 percent of live births. In many of these cases the man declared by the mother to have sired her child is unwilling to admit paternity, and in other cases several men may have had relationships with the mother and paternity is uncertain. Changing life-styles have somewhat reduced the social stigma of illegitimacy, but the child's right to a legal relationship with his father is still often ignored. The problem may be identification.

In 1976 the *Family Law Quarterly* published guidelines jointly established by the American Medical Association and the American Bar Association (the latter represented by Harry Krause) on the current status of serologic testing for parenthood. It was the first report developed jointly by both associations and the first joint statement on the science and art of blood typing in disputed paternity cases. Its purpose was to provide a definition of the current state of capabilities and some certainty in a field of rapidly evolving scientific developments as to what is practically possible.

Traditionally, in common law the illegitimate child had no father; he was viewed as the child of his mother only. But the tradition is ending. In 1968 the United States Supreme Court began to decide a series of cases on the basis of the Equal Protection Clause which established as a principle the legal equality of the illegitimate with the legitimate child in all significant substantive areas except inheritance. Nevertheless, largely because of outdated and defective paternity ascertainment procedures, it is still only a minority of illegitimate children who achieve legal relationships with their fathers. Gains in substantive rights are meaningless without improvement in procedures for ascertaining paternity. Reform is needed to provide the illegitimate child with a responsible father and, equally important, to protect men falsely convicted of parenthood in what is anachronistically viewed by some states as a criminal prosecution. A new procedural framework for the paternity action is necessary, and medical evidence must play the lead within that framework. The Uniform Parentage Act created that framework for the utilization of medical evidences.

Dr. Chang Ling Lee discusses the current medical status of paternity testing, which is based on increasingly sophisticated laboratory tests of the detectable properties of blood components. For many years the solution of paternity problems was based on a small number of blood tests which gave only about a 50 percent chance for a man falsely named to be excluded. Many more such tests are now available, and by the use of all possible current tests the theoretical chance of exclusion is over 99 percent, although in reality it is unnecessary and unnecessarily expensive in most cases to conduct all of the tests. Many of the newer tests are far more complicated than the older ones, and it often requires technical experts to conduct and evaluate them correctly. But the use of the more numerous and more complex tests greatly enhances the likelihood that the named man is in fact the father of the child. Such tests are widespread in Europe and are increasingly used in this country to assist in the final decision of the courts.

Of course there are limitations: The more tests that are made, the more genetic variations are found in many systems. Although some variants are rare, they should be considered before a final conclusion is made. An exclusion from paternity cannot be 100 percent certain, but through the statistically high results from the tests, estimation of exclusion or likelihood of paternity could provide the courts with a valuable tool for a valid judgment and could reduce the cost to taxpayers by making sure the true father fulfills his child support obligation.

Artificial Insemination and Test Tube Babies

Another type of problem with fatherhood arises from artificial insemination, a process used for centuries in animal husbandry and in this century fairly common for women whose husbands are sterile. This area has recently gone through remarkable physical and legal changes, culminating in 1978 with the birth of two infants, one in England and one in India, resulting from fertilization of the mother's egg by the father's sperm outside the uterus. For this volume Mary Ann Oakley has made major revisions in her original *Family Law Quarterly* article on test tube babies.

The first legal case involving semen from a donor other than the husband arose in Canada more than fifty years ago. American courts have ruled variously on the legitimacy of infants thus conceived. But beginning in 1964, when Georgia passed a statute legitimizing children conceived by artificial insemination (if both husband and wife consent in writing), other states either judicially or by statute have followed suit. Ms. Oakley believes that the legal problems arising from artificial insemination can be resolved by statutory legitimization of the children in question. The statute should provide that any child born after the artificial insemination of its mother is the legitimate child of that mother and her spouse, whether or not the husband consented. Hospital records and birth certificates should name the mother's husband as the child's father, and the donor should be anonymous to both spouses and the spouses to the donor, who should have no known genetic defects at the time (not more than one week before donating his semen) of a complete physical examination.

Other problems arise with *in vitro* fertilization, which involves the union of the sperm with the ovum outside the body and the transplantation of the embryo into the uterus. Where the husband provides the sperm and the wife the ovum, the resulting child is the biological offspring of the spouses; where a donor provides the sperm used in the *in vitro* fertilization, again there should be statutory coverage to protect the child's legitimacy. But when the ovum also comes from a donor; or if the ovum is a donor's and the sperm the husband's; or if, most difficult of all, the wife cannot bear a child, but her ovum is fertilized by her husband's sperm *in vitro* and the embryo transferred into a "hostess" who goes through the pregnancy and bears the child, the situation may become exceedingly complex. Again, clearly defining statutes covering all such complexities, including the possibility that the "hostess" may decide on an abortion, must be written into law.

Unwed Father's Procedural Rights

With the enormous increase in illegitimate births and with the new sophisticated techniques for establishing paternity, the impact of the *Stanley* case has created seemingly endless repercussions and—coincidentally—confusion. Whereas in the past unwed fathers had been ignored almost completely in adoption and custody proceedings, the decision of the United States Supreme Court in 1972 in *Stanley* declared that such fathers were entitled to notice in these proceedings, thus in this respect equalizing the rights of parents irrespective of their sex or legal status.

Jerome Barron discusses the impact of *Stanley* in "Notice to the Unwed Father and Termination of Parental Rights." Difficulties arose almost immediately after the decision. While Stanley himself had lived with his children and their mother for years, many unwed fathers were not only averse to raising their illegitimate offspring but were not even aware of their existence. On the other hand, compliance with the notice requirement seemed, under the Supreme Court decision, essential for a valid termination of parental rights decree. How was the social service agency or the court to proceed when the whereabouts and even the identity of the father were unknown? Should the mother be compelled to identify him? Should termination and adoption proceedings be bogged down for months or even years by the search for the father, with possibly severe effects on the child?

Many states have still not amended their statutes to comply with *Stanley*. The new legislation that does exist either prescribes diligent efforts to give notice to the unwed father or backs away from the problem by assuming such obligation only when the father is known, either by his own acknowledgement or through identification by the mother. Compelling the mother to provide this information may infringe on her constitutional rights, and some states have already declared such action unconstitutional. Relying on service by publication to the unwed father when even his name is unknown is obviously futile, unless, at the court's discretion, the mother's name is included in the publication notice even though she may not consent. The latter approach is a compromise between ignoring *Stanley* where the father is unknown and compelling the mother to identify the father. In spite of the arguments against service by publication, it is still better than no notice. Yet, publication is useless unless it contains some information which can alert the unwed father to the imminence of a termination proceeding.

Nevertheless, the Supreme Court seems to have foreseen that a measure of flexibility would be necessary in regard to notice to the unwed father in the context of adoption and custody. Professor Barron concludes that the question of whether or not notice by publication should be required should, in the final analysis, be left to the sound discretion of the court which has inquired into the matter: an approach also taken by the Uniform Parentage Act, which balances the due process rights of the natural parent and the practical necessities of adoption.

Support and Abortion

In the next article Martin Levy and Elaine Duncan make a constitutional analysis of *Roe v. Wade*'s impact on paternal support and affirm the father's duty of support, particularly in cases of illegitimacy, when the mother consciously decides not to abort. Their argument is based on the fact that the purpose of the child support statutes is to place the burden of support on those responsible for the birth and that a rational relationship or nexus exists between the father's act of intercourse and the birth of the child. From this they conclude that, to make the statutes consistent with equal protection, an implicit requirement for paternal support has been established. If the father is not held responsible, there is a high degree of possibility that the burden of support, including birth costs, education and years of nurture will fall on the state when the child is illegitimate. The statutes are thus not intended as punishment for the father's indiscretion but to prevent the state's suffering for the "sins of the fathers."

But *Roe* aroused doubts about the validity of paternal support decisions. It placed the determination regarding abortion solely with the mother and her physician, making it unilaterally the woman's choice and thus raising the question as to whether her decision preempts conception as the cause of birth, or acts as an intervening causation of birth and thus makes her alone responsible for the actual birth of the child. Viewed in this light, the father's legal connection to his unborn child is that of a helpless bystander, and his constitutional rights would be violated by paternal support statutes which force him to support a child born because the mother, breaking the nexus between the father's act of intercourse and the child's birth, consciously decided to bear and not to abort. Recent decisions, in *Jones v. Smith* and *Doe v. Doe* for instance, do lend some support to this viewpoint.

Levy and Duncan, examining the nexus between conception and birth from tort, contract and criminal law analogies, argue that the nexus is not broken by the impact of *Roe,* and that there can thus be no valid challenge to paternal support statutes under the Equal Protection Clause. They do believe that the duty of support should be imposed equally on both parents, and that current paternal support statutes based on this premise should be upheld.

Father's Right to Custody

The requirement that both parents are responsible for the support of their children is a small territorial gain in the steady erosion of absolute empire held by husbands and fathers for almost nine hundred years—until, in fact, the women's rights movement began in the nineteenth century. In "Life with Father: 1978," Henry Foster and Doris Jonas Freed write about the changes that have taken place in spousal and parental relationships since feudal times, when the wife was not even legally a person and a father was always assumed to have full custodial rights over his child. Today his traditional prerogatives are practically anachronisms, and with the rise of the movement for children's as well as women's rights, the nuclear family is likely to consist of all chiefs and no Indians.

Foster and Freed discuss the ferment in family law which is leaving no tradition secure. Their particular focus is on child custody. From the beginning of our history the father's right to custody was probably not feudally absolute in the United States—early decisions, though referring to the father's natural rights, often took into consideration particular circumstances. Gradually the "tender years" doctrine came to prevail and the mother was usually awarded custody, especially of young children. But only if she were a "fit" mother. If she were adulterous, "loose" in her morals—sexual, of course—or addicted to the bottle, the father would often be the preferred custodian. Even though "the good of the child"—our present "best interests"—was supposedly the major consideration in determining custody, there was an underlying animus against a woman who had refused the obligations of marriage without apparent cause, or had strayed from the straight path of double-standard Victorian morality. Many a judge in today's courts is still implicitly basing parental fitness on the sexual morality of the mother. Lesbianism is a new if unstated ground for a woman being unfit as a mother.

Nevertheless, in the majority of cases the sentimental image of the woman as the tender, nurturing, God-appointed guardian angel for her children still prevails. This is true, surprisingly, even in states which have ERA provisions. Nevertheless, the "tender years" doctrine is slowly but increasingly being condemned as sex discrimination, violative of due process and equal protection provisions of the Constitution. There has been recent recognition that the father may be the parent with whom the children have the closest relationship; and even though the mother is not condemned as unfit, the father may be awarded custody as probably ministering best to the long-range future of the children.

This study of a father's custodial rights concludes with a series of charts covering three facets of current laws and decisions in all American jurisdictions: is tender years doctrine in effect?; relevant statutes; and significant decisions. There are some surprises.

Wife Beating

Once it was man's God-given—or at least law-given—right to beat his wife and children. The trail of misery winds through all the pages of recorded history and through every class, creed, color and culture of the world. Today the thousands of reported cases of wife-battering are but crude maps which leave the thousands of unreported cases uncharted and unseen. Michael Freeman writes about what the French call the English vice (pot and kettle certainly) and the law's treatment of wife-battering in England, Canada and the United States. It is a fact that we do not know how much violence is inflicted upon wives today—there is, to be sure, also some battering of husbands by wives, but in minute proportion, if only because of the male's greater physical strength—or whether such violence is increasing. We do not know the causes of wife-battering, though there are recent theories which view the violent husband as the victim of violence in his childhood or as one of the army of unemployed who, often "under the influence," vent their frustrations on their nearest. There is an old theory, or myth, that wives long to be beaten.

It is generally accepted today that violent people are tormented and unhappy, but there is no consensus as to how we are to cure their torment. As in so many of the horrors raging through the world, every evil appears inextricably bound with another. It may seem to us that until the whole structure of society is changed, or perhaps until original sin has been eradicated, nothing can be improved and no one helped.

But piece by piece and case by case, there are some remedies in law for the battered wife. She may bring charges of assault and battery. In England any attack by a husband causing his wife any actual bodily harm, though the harm may not be serious, constitutes a criminal offense. There have even been cases recently where wives who killed their abusing husbands received suspended sentences or were acquitted. Nevertheless, in general, wives are reluctant to report marital assault to the police. They are ashamed; they half-consciously feel they have "brought it on" themselves; they have an unfortunately well-founded fear that police attitudes are sympathetic to the male and scornful of the woman; and finally, pragmatically, if they should go through with court proceedings and the husband is jailed, there will be a drastic loss of income in the home and the woman may suffer even worse violence when the husband is released.

Some practical help is becoming available. More and more refuges for terrorized wives with their children are being set up all over the Western world. In these refuges attempts are being made to deal with the violence and to strengthen the family bonds that are being torn apart. Beyond the crisis refuge, a movement originating in Holland (called Triangel there) is spreading to provide living quarters and treatment for the whole unhappy family, even to improve their outside working conditions and to encourage physical well-being through exercises and games.

Alimony and Assignment of Property

With or without violence, more and more families are coming apart. In this country a conservative estimate shows one out of three marriages ending in divorce. Recent statutory changes by a number of states are providing improved systems of financial adjustment upon divorce, in some cases to prevent a wife who has spent thirty years helping her husband and rearing their children from being turned penniless into a world she is unprepared to face, and in others to prevent a husband from being fleeced by a wife "accustomed" after a year of marriage to a high-flying lifestyle she claims is now necessary to her physical and psychological health. In "Alimony and Assignment of Property," the authors describe the new statutory scheme in Massachusetts which amends the law for alimony and property division. It is a significant reform which changes the historical basis for alimony awards and empowers the court to adjust the division of all property of the spouses.

Although the husband, particularly in long-standing marriages, is still very often the sole financial supporter and the wife devotes herself to the physical, mental and social needs of the family, alimony awards are being affected by the rapidly growing trend toward economic independence for women, married or not. There is also an increasing awareness in court awards that even where the wife has not worked outside the home, she has contributed to her husband's financial status by her management of the home and should be considered his partner. Recognizing the marital partnership concept, Massachusetts and other noncommunity property states have passed laws that enable courts to divide the property of the spouses upon divorce, in addition to granting alimony to the wife. Length of the marriage is one critical consideration; and though it is argued that fault should not be considered in property division, the courts must balance all the equities and weigh the achievement of one spouse against the possible disloyalty, dishonesty or cruelty of the other. It is important that the courts maintain the distinction between alimony, based on the common law duty of the husband to support his wife, and property which is derived from the joint contribution of both spouses to their marital partnership.

Alimony and Short-Term Marriages

The laws on alimony as well as on property division are changing rapidly and now require the courts to consider the needs of both spouses and their individual ability to be self-supporting. In "Alimony Orders Following Short-Term Marriages," the authors discuss these issues. Divorce after a short marriage is an inevitable by-product of the rise in the national divorce rate, with more and more people willing to call it quits after a brief attempt at wedded bliss. The laws, however, have not kept pace with this recent trend, and there is confusion even about the principles to be applied in setting alimony and the division of property after short-term marriage; case law is scattered and contradictory.

The very term, short-term marriage, is used without analysis of the criterion to be applied, but, in general, six years or less is the cut-off point. But should the marriage be dated from the time when the parties began living together, or only from the precise day of the ceremony? Again, should the length of the marriage be determined by the date of physical separation or from when, although the spouses are still living together, the marriage is no longer physically or emotionally viable?

Whatever the decision on the length of the marriage, it is only one of many factors courts consider in awarding alimony, and as a rule there is no comment on the relative importance of the factors. In practice, courts seem to place the greatest emphasis on the financial circumstances of the parties. Here the majority view is that sufficient alimony should be awarded to allow the spouse, if able-bodied and when there are no minor children, to train herself in marketable skills—but with a cut-off point so that she does not become merely a parasite. Age and health of the spouse are, of course, important considerations: A woman with health problems, or in her fifties without a continuing work record, would almost automatically be unable to find a position. The standard of living, important in long-standing marriage, is usually not a factor where the marriage has been brief; although where there are children the court may base the alimony on the family's previous lifestyle so that the children will not suffer. The wife's contribution to the marriage, just as in property division, is also a major factor, whether that contribution has been financial or back-up service in the home. Failure to contribute has sometimes justified a small alimony award, while evidence of misconduct, particularly in the case of physical cruelty, may enter into the consideration of a larger award as a punitive measure against the aggressor. It is obvious that a definition of terms and a uniform approach toward the relative weight of all the factors must be sought to prevent unjust disparity.

The danger of unjust disparity is particularly striking in cases of unstructured domestic unions, which have now become widespread. Some derive from cultures with long histories of informal families, some from a distaste for traditional marriage, and still others from a kind of radical chic; in addition to the monogamous heterosexual union, they now include group living and homosexual ménages. The great majority of those who forgo formal marriage for a "free" union have no awareness of the economic consequences of their choice. Couples are rarely sophisticated enough to formalize their personal or legal expectations, and when there are crises like sickness, unemployment, death or separation, one of the partners can find himself in a highly vulnerable situation.

Property Rights of *De Facto* Spouses

The growing number of such relationships, in spite of labels like meretricious and illicit, means that the law can no longer ignore their existence and must make provision for the harm they may cause to one of the partners. Carol Bruch discusses some of the legal solutions and options that are being or should be used to protect the property rights of *de facto* spouses. She analyzes the prior impediments to the use of standard legal doctrines in such cases, among them refusal by some courts to assign economic value to personal services—which even in cases of legal spouses are only recently being recognized. Most courts, faced with a number of distinctive relationships, have restricted their use of general legal principles in the case of *de facto* spouses and as a result have been hindered from granting relief.

Bruch offers several general legal and equitable doctrines which may and should be applied to nonmarital domestic relations, and presents an argument for placing upon individuals the burden of a clear statement that they wish to arrange for inequitable results, rather than imposing such results upon the many persons who live together with no stated division of financial responsibility. Otherwise the law will support by implication an unconscionable contract, where one party renders important services for years and when the relationship ends must return to the job market without skills or resources while the other retains all the wealth and increased earning power acquired through and during the unlegalized relationship. It is clear that the standards of good faith and fair dealing must be recognized in this area as well as in commercial and interpersonal economic transactions if palpable injustice is to be avoided.

There are no more knights of the open road, carrying or abandoning mate and offspring according to mere whim. Once a man has become a member of the wedding, whether through a legal ceremony or a private agreement, even if not formally articulated; once he has become a father, no matter through how fleeting a connection, he is responsible in law to his partner and to his offspring. He is accountable. He has become part of the great chain of human relationships, with its ineluctable dependencies.

Joint AMA-ABA Guidelines: Present Status of Serologic Testing in Problems of Disputed Parentage*

American Medical Association, Committee on Transfusion and Transplantation, Drs. Jack P. Abbott and Kenneth W. Sell, Chairmen, and American Bar Association, Section on Family Law, Committee on Standards for the Judicial Use of Scientific Evidence in the Ascertainment of Paternity, Harry D. Krause, Chairman, (Principal draftsmen: J. B. Miale, M.D., E. R. Jennings, M.D., W. A. H. Rettberg, M.D., K. W. Sell, M.D., and H. D. Krause).

Preface

In 1971, the American Bar Association's Section on Family Law approached the American Medical Association requesting that a joint committee be formed to study the implications of scientific advances in blood typing tests to determine (non)paternity and make appropriate recommendations.

This report brings to successful conclusion five years of close collaboration between members of the medical and legal professions.

It represents the first "official" statement concerning the science and art of blood typing in cases of disputed paternity since the

*Approved by the American Medical Association and by the Section on Family Law, American Bar Association. (In accordance with their policy against taking positions concerning technical reports involving non-legal subject matter, the House of Delegates of the American Bar Association has not taken a position on this report.)

reports of the AMA's Committee on Medicolegal Problems in 1952 and 1957 (Ref. 1, 2). It also is the first such report that was developed jointly by individuals working with both professional associations. With the endorsement of the AMA and ABA, the report is intended to provide guidance to the legislator, the judge and the practicing lawyer as well as to medical personnel engaged in this specialty. The purpose throughout has been to provide an understandable, though not oversimplified, definition of the current state of capabilities. The report will provide a measure of certainty where rapid recent scientific developments have created uncertainty as to what has become scientific fact and what remains hypothesis, and as to what is practically possible and what remains performable only under highly specialized conditions.

While the report identifies certain systems as useful for routine testing, there is no intent to exclude anything that can be shown to produce useful results. Indeed, even while this report was being discussed, new developments, especially in the HLA sector, began to overshadow more traditional approaches, and further progress may be anticipated. On the legal side, it is expected that this report will lead to further work and specific legislative proposals, particularly regarding the law of evidence. In short, this report is intended as the beginning of a continuing process.

Many have helped bring us to this stage. Special thanks are due to John B. Miale, M.D., the principal draftsman on the medical side, as well as to Drs. Elmer R. Jennings, William Dolan and William Rettberg, subcommittee members and Dr. Herbert F. Polesky. On the legal side, thanks are due to Judge Orman Ketcham, Harry Fain, Esq., and Lawrence H. Stotter, Esq., who provided valuable comments on the numerous drafts through which this report was put. A great many thanks also go to the members of the original AMA's ad hoc committee consisting of Drs. Alexander S. Wiener, Chang Ling Lee and John B. Miale who originally undertook to study the medical side and who, after two years of fruitful and enlightening discussion greatly enhanced the depth and scope of this report. Much gratitude, finally, is due to Dr. Joseph B. Jerome of the AMA staff whose help and dedication were crucial to the successful completion of this report.

JACK P. ABBOTT
Chairman (1974-75)
Committee on Transfusion and Transplantation
American Medical Association

KENNETH W. SELL
Chairman (1976-)
Committee on Transfusion and Transplantation
American Medical Association

HARRY D. KRAUSE
Chairman, Ad Hoc
Committee on Standards for the Judicial Use of Scientific Evidence in the Ascertainment of Paternity and
Council member, Section on Family Law,
American Bar Association

I. Introduction

A. *The Facts and Law of Illegitimacy*

Despite declining birth rates, the problem of illegitimacy remains at the level of a national crisis. The ten years from 1961 to 1970 saw enough new illegitimate children to populate a city the size of Los Angeles; the last five years, a city the size of Detroit. More than three hundred and ninety-eight thousand illegitimate children were added in 1970, 360,000 in 1969, 339,000 in 1968, 318,100 in 1967, 302,000 in 1966, for a total exceeding 1,700,000 in just these five years. Moreover, not only has there been an increase in the absolute number of illegitimate births, but the rate has been accelerating and now exceeds ten percent of all births. In many urban areas illegitimacy stands at forty percent and in some it exceeds fifty percent. Neither the "pill" nor liberalized abortion has fulfilled early expectations that the end of illegitimacy may be at hand. On the contrary, while births in general have fallen off, the growing acceptance of "new lifestyles" and the reduced social stigma of illegitimacy seem to have combined to produce the highest proportion of births out of wedlock on the American record. Law and legal practice need to be adapted to changing and unchanged social facts—changing in terms of the increasing acceptability of illegitimacy, but unchanged in terms of each child's right to and need of a legal relationship with his father.

In the eyes of the common law, the illegitimate child had no father at all. Although the mother and child relationship has long been equalized by law, most states have continued to discriminate heavily in the substantive relationship between father and illegitimate child. Discrimination extends to rights of support, inheritance, custody, name, and claims under father-related welfare statutes, such as workmen's compensation, wrongful death, and various federal acts. In short, our law has seen the illegitimate child as the child of his mother and traditionally has all but denied the existence of his father.

This tradition is coming to an end. Beginning in 1968, the United States Supreme Court decided a series of cases on the basis of the Equal Protection Clause of the Federal Constitution which establish the principle that the illegitimate child is entitled to legal equality with the legitimate child in most substantive areas of the law. Numerous state statutes discriminating against illegitimate children have been declared unconstitutional, and the bulk of the remaining legislation on this subject is under severe constitutional doubt.

In one of many decisions favoring the illegitimate child, the United States Supreme Court said:

> The status of illegitimacy has expressed through the ages society's condemnation of irresponsible liaisons beyond the bonds of marriage. But visiting this condemnation on the head of an infant is illogical and unjust. Moreover, imposing disabilities on the illegitimate child is contrary to the basic concept of our system that legal burdens should bear some relationship to individual responsibility or wrongdoing. Obviously, no child is responsible for his birth and penalizing the illegitimate child is an ineffectual—as well as an unjust—way of deterring the parent. Courts are powerless to prevent the social opprobium suffered by these hapless children, but the Equal Protection Clause does enable us to strike down discriminatory laws relating to status of birth where—as in this case—the classification is justified by no legitimate state interest, compelling or otherwise.

The fair conclusion to be drawn from these cases is that state and federal law may not discriminate between legitimate and illegitimate children in any significant substantive area other than inheritance.

Nevertheless, the gulf between the abstract principle and the realization of legal equality between legitimate and illegitimate children continues to loom wide. Owing largely to defective and antiquated paternity ascertainment procedures, only a very small fraction of illegitimate children now achieve legal relationships with their fathers. All gains in substantive rights will mean little or nothing if our procedures for ascertaining paternity are not improved.

Enacted in 1975, Pub. L. 93-647 has injected federal funds and interest into this area. Each state is required to develop an appropriate plan, in accordance with HEW standards, for the ascertainment of paternity (and child support enforcement) within the framework of the A.F.D.C. program. The applicability of the federal legislation, however, is *not* limited to the welfare area and extends to all disputed paternity cases.

Given the substantive legal equality mandated by the United States Supreme Court and Pub. L. 93-647, fundamental reform of the paternity action has become the most pressing task in the area of illegitimacy. Reform is needed to provide a responsible parent for the illegitimate child as well as to protect men who are falsely convicted in what some states anachronistically continue to view as a criminal prosecution. (The cost of even relatively extensive blood typing procedures is dwarfed by the potential cost of child support for eighteen years or more).

Reform must come on two levels: We need a new procedural framework for the paternity action improving both quality and volume and, within that new framework, medical evidence must play the cardinal role. The new procedural framework has been created by the Uniform Parentage Act, adopted by the National Conference of Commissioners on Uniform State Laws in 1973 and approved by the American Bar Association in 1974. Providing an appropriate framework for the utilization of medical evidence is the function of this report.

B. *This report has been prepared with the following goals:*

1. To make available an authoritative guide to all parties who deal with the medicolegal problems of disputed parentage: physicians, attorneys, the courts, legislatures and federal and state health agencies. Accordingly, this report is concerned equally with medical and legal aspects.
2. To survey the total and potential role of serologic testing, as a guide to expanded application in the future.
3. To recommend the present-day application of a limited

number of serologic systems which are believed to be cost-efficient, reliable and noncontroversial.

4. To present data indicating probabilities of exclusion of paternity given various combinations of test systems.
5. To recommend expanded application of serologic data in the estimation of probability of paternity and to discuss and provide guidance concerning the determination of "likelihood of paternity," a concept in common use in Germany and the Scandinavian countries but so far little used in the United States.
6. To recommend the adoption of standard procedures with regard to identification of the involved parties, the collection and identification of specimens, and acceptable laboratory quality control.
7. To make recommendations to the AMA and ABA as to goals to be achieved in the future.
8. To recommend legislation clarifying and simplifying the admissibility in evidence of test results and the effect thereof, including the evidentiary value of the estimation of "likelihood of paternity."

II. Systems Potentially Applicable in Disputed Parentage

As many as 62 immunologic and biochemical systems are potentially applicable (Table 1 page 253). The application of all known systems would establish nonpaternity for about 98 percent of falsely accused men. However, such extensive testing is neither feasible nor recommended, for the following reasons:

1. Antisera for all serologic systems are either not available or in some cases individual antisera are available only in one or very few laboratories.
2. The probability of exclusion in some of the serologic systems is very low, because there are "high frequency" factors found in a large portion of the population.
3. Biochemical systems are being applied to disputed parentage problems in other countries and by some investigators in this country. Where available they can be used to supplement the blood group systems. The ones most useful are the protein

Table 1
Mean Probability of Exclusion of Non-Fathers for Potentially Useful Systems *

Genetic Marker or System	Mean Probability of Exclusion of Non-Fathers		
	Black	White	Japanese
ABO	.1774	.1342	.1917
Auberger	.0105	.0186	. . .
Cartwright (Yt)	.0069	.0395	. . .
Colton	0	.0266	. . .
Cs	. . .	.0006	. . .
Diego	.0030	0	.0304
Dombrock	.0661	.0518	. . .
Duffy	.0420	.1844	.1159
Henshaw	.0151	0	. . .
Hunter	.0170	.0026	. . .
Kell	.0049	.0354	0
Kidd	.1545	.1869	.1573
Lewis[1]	.0262	.0024	.0193
Lutheran	.0368	.0311	0
MNSs	.3206	.3095	.2531
P	.0026	.0266	.0809
Penney	0	.0109	0
Rh	.1859	.2746	.2050
Sd	. . .	.0052	. . .

***From reference 3, modified and with additions. Probabilities of exclusion of non-fathers are calculated from gene frequencies from various authors quoted in the reference, and are considered representative.**

[1]Exclusion of paternity using Lewis cannot be made unless it is combined with secretor testing.

Table 1 (Continued)

Genetic Marker or System	Mean Probability of Exclusion of Non-Fathers		
	Black	White	Japanese
Secretor	.0305	.0296	.0238
St	. . .	.0006	.0283
Sutter	.0667	0	. . .
U	.0001	0	. . .
Vel	0	.0184	0
Xg[2]	.1615	.0965	.1344
Acetylcholinesterase	. . .	.1153	. . .
Acid phosphatase	.1588	.2323	.1340
Adenosine deaminase	.0283	.0452	.0291
Adenylate kinase	.0059	.0428	0
Ag(x)	. . .	.0813	. . .
Alcohol dehydrogenase (locus 2)	. . .	.0452	. . .
Alcohol dehydrogenase (locus 3)	. . .	.1824	. . .
α-acid glycoprotein	.1834	.1773	.1583
α_1-antitrypsin	.0180	.0806	.0170
Amylase (urinary)	.0411	.0399	. . .
Ceruloplasmin	.0504	.0059	.0214
Complement, third component	.0819	.1523	.0192

[2]These are sex-linked systems and are only useful in female children.

systems (Gm, haptoglobin, Gc, Km), the red cell enzymes (AcP, PGM, ADA, EsD), and hemoglobin (beta-chain variants in Blacks).

4. The recommendation made in Section III affords a potentially very high chance of exclusion utilizing only seven test systems at a reasonable cost, whereas the utilization of all known

Table 1 (Continued)

Genetic Marker or System	Mean Probability of Exclusion of Non-Fathers		
	BLACK	WHITE	JAPANESE
Diaphorase	. . .	.0085	. . .
Esterase D	. . .	.0913	. . .
Galactose-A-phosphate-uridyl-transferase	. . .	.0626	. . .
Glucose-6-phosphate dehydrogenase[2]	.0932	0	0
Glutamic oxaloacetic transaminase (soluble)	0	0	.0113
Glutamic pyruvic transaminase (soluble)	.1285	.1875	.1826
Glutathione reductase	.2071	.2016	. . .
Gm, serum groups	.2071	.2275	.1873
Group-specific component	.0731	.1661	.1560
Haptoglobin	.1873	.1834	.1596
Hemoglobin β	.0453	0	0
HLA	.78-.80	.78- 80	.78-.80
Km, serum group (Inv)	.2366	.0601	.1664
Malic enzyme (NADP) soluble	.1258	.1681	. . .
Parotid basic protein	.1163	.0050	0

[2]These are sex-linked systems and are only useful in female children.

systems would cost disproportionately more with only a slight increase in probability of exclusion. No definite statement of cost of quality testing is possible since this may vary regionally. All parties should note that this is an area of special com-

Table 1 (Continued)

Genetic Marker or System	Mean Probability of Exclusion of Non-Fathers		
	Black	White	Japanese
Pepsinogen	.0126	.0126	0
Peptidase A	.0747	.1635	. . .
Peptidase C	.0665	.0102	. . .
Peptidase D	.0459	.0108	. . .
Phosphoglucomutase (locus 1)	.1344	.1457	.1476
Phosphoglucomutase (locus 3)	.1740	.1554	.1306
Properdin Factor B	. . .	.1443	. . .
Pseudocholinesterase (locus 1)	.0052	.0158	0
6-phosphogluconate dehydrogenase	.0335	.0229	.0586
Transferrin	.0410	.0064	.0079
Xm, serum group	.1757	.1625	. . .

petence and the assignment of testing should not be based on the lowest price available.

5. It is not the intent to recommend in all medicolegal problems of disputed parentage that the entire set of tests is mandatory. It is often possible to establish exclusion with the basic blood group systems (ABO, Rh, and MNSs). When these basic tests do not allow exclusion, extended testing may be done (using Kell, Duffy, and Kidd systems) to increase the mean probability of exclusion to the 63-72 percent level. In the event no exclusion is produced at that stage, additional testing using the HLA system (if necessary, by referral) may be done to raise the mean probability of exclusion to at least the 90 percent level. The discussion in this paragraph is in terms of the specific recommendations made in this report and is not intended to exclude the use of other systems (see III).

III. Systems Recommended for Current Use in Exclusion of Paternity or Parentage

Seven serologic systems are recommended for routine investigations (Table 2, page 257).

This recommendation is based on the following considerations: (1) antisera for the six blood group systems are available and reliable, (2) each system provides a reasonably high probability of exclusion in relation to cost, (3) the six blood group systems provide a cumulative probability of exclusion of 63-72 percent, depending on race, (4) the addition of only one other system (HLA) increases the probability of exclusion to 91-93 percent as compared with a probability of exclusion of about 98 percent for 62 systems.

This recommendation is not intended to exclude the use of additional systems (i.e., haptoglobins, hemoglobin variants, etc.) when an investigator has special expertise in these systems. (See II, 3, page 252).

Table 2
The Seven Test Systems Recommended

System	Mean Probability of Exclusion of Non-Fathers		
	Black	White	Japanese
1. ABO	.1774	.1342	.1917
2. Rh	.1859	.2746	.2050
3. MNSs	.3206	.3095	.2531
4. Kell	.0049	.0354	0
5. Duffy	.0420	.1844	.1159
6. Kidd	.1545	.1869	.1573
7. HLA	.78-.80	.78-.80	.78-.80

Table 2 gives the individual probabilities for each system. Cumulative probabilities when several systems are used are not simply the sum of each probability, since in many instances there might be exclusion in more than one system. Calculation of cumulative probabilities is based on the determination of non-exclusion for each system and then applying the formula:

Cumulative Probability = $1 - (1-P_1)(1-P_2) \ldots (1-P_n)$, where P_1, P_2, and P_n are probabilities of individual exclusions. This formula is used to calculate cumulative probabilities for seven recommended systems (Table 3 page 258). It should be noted that this calculation gives the cumulative probability that at least one of these tests will exclude paternity of a falsely accused man.

Table 3

Cumulative Probability of Exclusion of Non-Fathers

Systems*	Cumulative Probability of Exclusion(%)		
	BLACKS	WHITES	JAPANESE
1	17.44	13.42	19.16
1 + 2	33.03	37.19	35.74
1 + 2 + 3	54.50	56.63	52.0
1 + 2 + 3 + 4	54.72	58.17	52.0
1 + 2 + 3 + 4 + 5	56.63	65.88	57.56
1 + 2 + 3 + 4 + 5 + 6	63.37	72.26	64.24
1 + 2 + 3 + 4 + 5 + 6 + 7	91.21	93.34	91.42

*1 = ABO; 2 = Rh; 3 = MNSs; 4 = Kell; 5 = Duffy; 6 = Kidd; 7 = HLA.

IV. Types of Exclusion

A. *Exclusion of Paternity*

Five types of equally acceptable and definite exclusion of a non-father are possible:

1. The classic type, in which the putative father is lacking a specificity which is present in the child and is absent in the mother so that the specificity found in the child must have been inherited from another father (i.e., child is K+, mother and putative father are K-).
2. Exclusion when the child lacks both specificities found in the putative father (i.e., child is group O, putative father is group AB).
3. The child is homozygous with respect to a specificity not present in both parents (i.e., child is *KK,* mother is *Kk* or *KK,* father is *kk*).
4. The child lacks a specificity for which the putative father is homozygous (i.e., child is *kk,* putative father is *KK*).
5. Indirect exclusion where the study of the parents of the mother and putative father or the latters' siblings more clearly define their genetic makeup. For example, a person of phenotype (group) A_1 is either of genotype A_1A_1 or of genotype A_1O. The two genotypes cannot be distinguished by serologic studies on the given person. However, since the two genes are inherited one from each parent, parents of genotypes A_1A_1 and A_1A_1 cannot have a child of genotype A_1O.

B. *Exclusion of Maternity*

As noted in the following sections, it is possible to exclude maternity in certain serologic patterns involving a given mother-child-putative father set. For example, a woman of group A_2 cannot be the mother of a child of group A_1B, regardless of the group of the father.

In addition to situations involving disputed paternity, the question of excluding maternity arises in cases of alleged child exchange, when the exclusion or probability of maternity is of primary importance.

C. *Importance of Genetic Mutation*

The possibility of mutation, invalidating the normal inheritance pattern, is very small, estimated to occur once in 40,000 persons. This is so infrequent that it can be ignored in the interpretation of the serologic findings.

V. The Likelihood of Paternity

In order to increase the utility of serologic testing it is desirable to estimate the likelihood of paternity in cases when the putative father is not excluded. Such estimates are admissible evidence in many foreign countries.

In some special situations, as when there is genetic conformity between the child and putative father for an extremely rare specificity (not present in the mother), for example subgroup A_3 or the rare phenotype M^g, the likelihood of paternity is extremely high and obvious without resort to special calculations. Although such situations are not absolute proof of paternity the court can give this evidence due weight.

Usually the situation is not so simple. The serologist has to deal with various circumstances:

1. Calculation of likelihood of paternity in "one-man" cases, i.e., only one man has been named the putative father and he is not excluded. In this case the computation estimates the likelihood that the one man is in fact the father when compared to a random man.
2. Calculation of likelihood of paternity in "multiple men" cases, where more than one man is suspected or known to be involved, has been tested, and has not been excluded. In this case the computation estimates the likelihood of paternity for each of the involved men and the relative probabilities submitted in evidence. In multiple men cases when the man or men other than the accused are not available for testing there is no alternative at this time than to apply the random man formula.

The great majority of situations fall under the first category.

One simple but mathematically valid estimation of the likelihood of paternity is that when extended testing providing a very high probability of exclusion fails to exclude an accused man there is a high probability that he is in fact the father. The likelihood of paternity can be better estimated using gene frequencies.

In "one-man" cases Hummel (4, 5) has proposed the application of the equation of Essen-Mőller (6). The plausibility of paternity, *W,* is calculated from:

$$W = \frac{1}{1 + \left(\frac{Y_1}{X_1} \cdot \frac{Y_2}{X_2} \cdot \frac{Y_3}{X_3} \cdot \cdots\right)}$$

Where Y is the frequency of various blood group phenotypes of men among the normal male population and X is the frequency of corresponding phenotypes of true fathers in the given mother-child combination.

The calculation can be carried out from tables of genotype frequencies, but Hummel (5) has prepared tables based on logarithms which facilitate the estimation of probability of paternity.

Example: In a given child-mother-putative father combination the putative father is not excluded. The phenotypes are:

Child: A_1; Rh_0rh (cDe/cde); NN; K^+; Fy(a+)
Mother: A_1; Rh_0rh (cDe/cde); MN; K^-; Fy(a-)
Man: A_1; Rh_1rh (Cde/cde); MN; K^+, Fy(a+)

Calculation (using tables of Hummel (5))

1. $\Sigma \log \frac{Y}{X} + 10$ for the blood group systems tested:

A-B-O	9.8739
Rh	9.9477
MN	9.9604
K	8.8865
Fy	9.8176
	48.4861

2. Subtract 10 (n-1), when n = number of systems used

48.4861
-40.0000
8.4861

3. Value for *W* = about 97 percent
4. Therefore, paternity is very likely (Table 4).

Table 4
Verbal Predicates, According to Hummel (5) for Different Likelihoods of Paternity (*W*), Comparing the Phenotype Frequency of the Putative Father to That of A Random Man With the Same Blood Group Phenotype

W	LIKELIHOOD OF PATERNITY
99.80 - 99.90	Practically proved
99.1 - 99.75	Extremely likely
95 - 99	Very likely
90 - 95	Likely
80 - 90	Undecided
< 80	Not useful

It must be noted that the calculations proposed by Hummel (5) are based on the comparison of the putative father to a random man, i.e., based on gene frequencies in a given population. This is open to criticisms which are however not serious. *First,* the comparison of the putative father with a "random" man may be criticized inasmuch as a comparison of the putative father with a non-random man might better approximate the true situation. However, it is just as unsound to choose a non-random man as it is to rely on general population frequencies. *Second,* the data of Hummel (5) are for gene frequencies for Caucasians in Germany. While it is predictable that gene frequencies can vary slightly for Caucasians in other areas the differences are so small that the estimates of likelihood of paternity would not vary significantly. Where there is in fact a marked difference in gene frequencies, as in some other racial groups, the tables worked out by Hummel (5) would not necessarily apply. In such situations the new gene frequencies should be substituted into the original formula. *Third,* the formula is based on a comparison of the putative father with one other non-excluded random man who is presumed to have had equal access to the mother. While this will not correspond to the facts in most cases of disputed paternity, it is a useful working hypothesis.

The difficulty judges, juries, and lawyers may experience in interpreting statistical evidence correctly, and possible due process issues under the Fourteenth Amendment of the U.S. Constitution arising in the light of the assumptions just discussed, raise questions regarding the indiscriminate use of such evidence. As indictated in the Recommendations, (See page 283), the matter should be studied further and appropriate safeguards need be developed to guard against possible misinterpretation of calculations of "likelihood of paternity." It may also be noted that the relatively high exclusion rates that will be produced by the application of the recommended systems will reduce substantially the need for this type of evidence.

VI. Individual Systems

A. *ABO (A_1A_2BO) Blood Group System*

Tests performed on subjects' red blood cells and serum with appropriate antisera and lectins and cells of known blood group allow all subjects to be classified as belonging in one of the following categories: type O, type A_1, type A_2, type B, type A_1B, or type A_2B. The inheritance pattern is well established and allows a tabulation of phenotypes possible or not possible in children from a given mating (Table 5 page 264). In some combinations of serologic factors determined from the mother-child-father combination it is possible to exclude maternity (Table 5 page 264).

The following special serologic features of this system should be noted:

1. Subgroups of A are often incompletely developed at birth, may be adequately developed by three months of age and are usually fully developed by one year of age.
2. Subgroups of A give weak reactions with potent anti-**A** sera and stronger reactions with Anti-**AB**, and may be missed entirely if the antiserum is weak.
3. There is an extremely rare genetic type called cis-AB (Reviron and Salmon, Ref 8) or AB* (Salmon, Ref 9) where the transmissions of blood type AB appears to be by a single rather than two separate chromosomes, so that a cis-AB person can then be the parent of an O child and an O person

Table 5

Exclusion of Paternity and Maternity by the A_1A_2BO System

(If the phenotype of the putative father appears in the box corresponding to the child-mother pair the putative father is excluded. If ME appears in the box there is maternal exclusion.)

Phenotype of Mother	Phenotype of Child					
	O	A_1	A_2	B	A_1B	A_2B
O	A_1B,A_2B	O,A_2,B,A_2B	O,B,A_1B	O,A_1,A_2	ME	ME
A_1	A_1B,A_2B	None	A_1B	O,A_1,A_2	O,A_1,A_2	O,A_1,A_2
A_2	A_1B,A_2B	O,A_2,B,A_2B	A_1B	O,A_1,A_2	ME	O,A_1,A_2
B	A_1B,A_2B	O,A_1,B,A_2B	O,B,A_1B	None	O,A_2,B,A_2B	O,B,A_1B
A_1B	ME	None	ME	None	O,A_2	O,B,A_1B
A_2B	ME	O,A_2,B,A_2B	A_1B	None	O,A_2,B,A_2B	O

can be the parent of a cis-AB child. Cis-AB also reacts weakly with anti-**B**, and more strongly with anti-**B** from A_2 blood than with anti-**B** from A_1 blood. In cis-AB individuals who are secretors no B substance is demonstrable in their saliva, and the A substance may also be affected.

4. In the rare "Bombay" type the red cells contain no A, B, or H agglutinogens and may be typed as type O. However, the serum contains anti-**A**, anti-**B** and anti-**H**.
5. In an occasional leukemic or preleukemic subject there is a change in the reactivity of the red cells which simulates an actual change in blood type, i.e., red cells of a known type A or B person may simulate the reactions of type O cells. Acquired agammaglobulinemia, in leukemia and other diseases, may be characterized by the absence of isoagglutinins in the serum.
6. Change of red cell type has also been reported in subjects with colitis or carcinoma of the stomach, characterized by the red cells acquiring weak B characteristics, i.e., a person of type A_1 reacts as if the group were A_1B. This is called "acquired B." Acquired B should be suspected clinically, from the weak reaction with anti-**B** and from the presence of anti-**B** isoagglutinin in the serum.
7. Failure to demonstrate the expected isoagglutinins in the serum may be due to: (1) acquired or congenital agammaglobulinemia, (2) a weak receptor as in persons of subtype A_4 or A_{el}, 3) the rare blood chimera situation.

B. *The Rh Blood Group System*

This system is more complicated than the ABO system and knowledge has progressed from the first basic distinction between Rh+ and Rh- to the characterization of 40 phenotypes.

Because of its complexity the genetics and serologic principles of the system have come to be expressed by two quite dissimilar concepts, the CDE/cde nomenclature of Fisher and Race and the genetic and serologic principles expressed by the Rh-hr nomenclature of Wiener. A review of the differences between the two is given elsewhere (Miale, Ref. 10). Experts in this field use both interchangeably, though some prefer one or the other. As applied to disputed parentage, both lead to the same conclusion. A comparison of the two is given in Table 6 page 266).

When six antisera are used: anti-**Rh**$_0$ (anti-D), anti-**rh′** (anti-C), anti-**rh″** (anti-E), anti-**rh**^{W} (anti-C^{W}), anti-**hr′** (anti-c), anti-**hr″** (anti-e), plus anti-**hr** (anti-f) to distinguish between a few selected phenotypes, 28 phenotypes can be distinguished corresponding to 55 genotypes. Having determined the phenotype and genotype, or possible genotypes (Miale, Ref. 11), of the child-mother-putative father situation, exclusion or non-exclusion of paternity or exclusion of maternity is decided by standard genetic diagrams.

Example: Child's genotype: $r'r$ (Cde/Cde)
Mother's genotype: R^1r' (CDe/Cde)
Putative father's genotype: rr (cde/cde)

Children of the given mother and putative father must have a genetic makeup which reflects the inheritance of one gene from

Table 6
Comparison of CDE/cde and
Rh-hr Nomenclatures

Genes		Antisera	
WIENER	FISHER-RACE	WIENER	FISHER-RACE
r	cde	Anti-**rh′**	Anti-C
r'	Cde	Anti-**Rh**	Anti-D
r^{w}	C^{W}de	Anti-**rh**	Anti-E
r''	cdE	Anti-**rh**^{W}	Anti-C^{W}
r^{y}	CdE	Anti-**hr′**	Anti-c
R^{o}	cDe	Anti-**hr″**	Anti-e
R^{1}	CDe	Anti-**hr**	Anti-f
R^{1w}	C^{W}De		
R^{2}	cDE		
R^{z}	CDE		

each parent. Accordingly, the only children possible from this mating must have one of the following genotypes: R^1r (CDe/cde) or $r'r$ (Cde/cde). Since the child in this example is of genotype $r'r'$ (Cde/Cde) the putative father is excluded.

Tables of exclusion have been constructed based on the more common genotypes of the child-mother-putative father combination (see Wiener and Nieberg, Ref. 12; Miale, Ref. 13; Erskine, Ref. 14), but should not be used to the exclusion of the application of standard genetic diagrams as in the example above.

The following special serologic features of the Rh system should be noted:

1. Many commercial antisera labelled anti-**rh**′ (anti-C) contain both anti-**rh**′ (anti-C) and anti-$\mathbf{rh}_i$ (anti-Ce) and may in fact contain a preponderance of anti-$\mathbf{rh}_i$ (anti-Ce). Anti-$\mathbf{rh}_i$ (anti-Ce) differs from anti-**rh**′ (anti-C) in its inability to agglutinate cells having the rare agglutinogens rh_y (CdE) and RH_Z (CDE) (very rare in Whites, less rare in Mongols). In the rare genotype Rh_Zrh (CDE/cde) the cells react with anti-**rh**′ (anti-C) but not with anti-$\mathbf{rh}_i$ (anti-Ce).
2. Many rare specificities exist in the system. These define extremely rare genotypes but do not affect the basic pattern.
3. In some individuals the D antigen may fail to react with saline anti-RH_0 though a positive reaction is found with incomplete anti-Rh_0 used in conjunction with an antiglobulin reagent or when slide or rapid tube sera is used. This phenotype, known as D^u, can be caused by interactions with genes on the paired chromosome or in individuals lacking part of the D antigen mosaic. Before excluding parentage of an Rh_0(D) positive child when both alleged parents are Rh_0(D) negative, tests for a weak D or D^u must be done.

C. *The MNSs Blood Group System*

This system is superficially simple, based on two pairs of codominant allelic genes (*M* and *N*) and three phenotypes (M, MN, and N) associated with a second pair of codominant allelic genes (*S* and *s*) determining phenotypes S, Ss and s. Transmission is by gene couplets *MS, Ms, NS,* and *Ns.* In addition, the agglutinogen U, present in all Whites but absent in some Blacks, is associated with both S and s. Therefore 4 antisera (anti-**M**, anti-**N**, anti-**S**, and anti-**s** determine nine phenotypes.

The combinations of phenotypes in the child-mother-putative father combination leading to exclusion of paternity or maternity are shown in Table 7. This is based on testing with all four antisera, which gives the highest possible chance of exclusion (about 30 percent). If only three antisera are used (anti-**M**, anti-**N**, and anti-**S**) the chance of exclusion drops to about 24 percent. Table 8 gives the children possible in a given mother-putative father combination when only three antisera are used. The possibilities of establishing maternal exclusion are limited to two situations: a MS woman cannot be the mother of a NS child and a NS woman cannot be the mother of a MS child.

The following special features should be noted:

1. An exception to the rules that M parents cannot have an N child, or that N parents cannot have an M child, occurs in the rare (about 1:40,000, not to be confused with the rate of spontaneous mutation) instances where one of the pair of genes is M^g. Gene M^g determines an agglutinogen lacking M specificity, so the apparent exclusion in case of a putative father who is N with a child who is M might not hold if the father were M^gN and the child MM^g. *Anti*-$\mathbf{M^g}$ serum is not always available, but where exclusion is based only on the MN system all efforts should be made to test for M^g. In fact, should gene M^g be present in both the father and the child, this would be very strong indication of paternity.
2. The rare allele M^k inhibits the expression of the MN as well as the Ss locus.
3. In Blacks, the He (Henshaw) factor should be taken into account. It is present in about 3 percent of Blacks and absent in Whites. Anti-**He** may be present in anti-**M** serum so that an N+ and He+ individual might mistakenly be typed as MN.
4. S^u, an allele that produces neither S nor s antigen, occurs in about 23 percent of Blacks. No antiserum defining a product of this gene has been found. S^u must be taken into consideration when there is an apparent exclusion of parentage of a Black individual who tests as homozygous S or s.
5. Agglutinogen U should also be considered in Blacks. It is

Table 7

Exclusion of Paternity (and Maternity) by the MNSs System from Nine Phenotypes Determined by Four Antisera

(If the number of the phenotype of the putative father appears in the box corresponding to the child-mother pair the putative father is excluded. If ME appears in the box there is maternal exclusion.)

Phenotype of Mother	Phenotype of Child								
	1 MS	2 Ms	3 MSs	4 NS	5 Ns	6 NSs	7 MNS	8 MNs	9 MNSs
1. MS	2, 4, 5 6, 8	ME	1, 4, 6 6, 7	ME	ME	ME	1, 2, 3 5, 8	ME	1, 2, 3 4, 7
2. Ms	ME	1, 4, 5 6, 7	2, 4, 5 6, 8	ME	ME	ME	ME	1, 2, 3 4, 7	1, 2, 3 5, 8
3. MSs	1, 4, 5 6, 7	2, 4, 5 6, 7	4, 5, 6	ME	ME	ME	1, 2, 3 5, 8	1, 2, 3 5, 8	1, 2, 3
4. NS	ME	ME	ME	1, 2, 3 5, 8	ME	1, 2, 3 4. 7	2, 4, 5 6, 8	ME	1, 4, 5 6, 7
5. Ns	ME	ME	ME	ME	1, 2, 3 4, 7	1, 2, 3 5, 7	ME	1, 4, 5 6, 7	2, 4, 5 6, 8
6. NSs	ME	ME	ME	1, 2, 3 4, 7	1, 2, 3 4, 7	1, 2, 3	2, 4, 5 6, 8	1, 4, 5 6, 7	4, 5, 6
7. MNS	2, 4, 5 6, 8	ME	1, 4, 5 6, 7	1, 2, 3 5, 8	ME	1, 2, 3 4, 7	2, 5, 8	ME	1, 4, 7
8. MNs	ME	1, 4, 5 6, 7	2, 4, 5 6, 8	ME	1, 2, 3 4, 7	1, 2, 3 5, 8	ME	1, 4, 7	1, 5, 8
9. MNSs	2, 4, 5 6, 8	1, 4, 5 6, 7	4, 5, 6	1, 2, 3 5, 8	1, 2, 3 4, 7	1, 2, 3	2, 5, 8	1, 4, 7	None

Table 8
Exclusion of Paternity by the MNSs System When Only Three Antisera Are Used (anti-M, and Anti-N, and anti-S)

MATING	CHILDREN POSSIBLE
MS X MS	MS, M
MS X M	MS, M
M X M	M
MS X MNS	MS, MNS, M, MN
MS X MN	MS, MNS, M, MN
M X MNS	MS, MNS, M, MN
M X MN	M, MN
MS X NS	MNS, MN
MS X N	MNS, MN
M X NS	MNS, MN
M X N	MN
MNS X MNS	MS, M, NS, N, MNS, MN
MNS X MN	MS, M, NS, N, MNS, MN
MN X MN	M, N, MN
MNS X NS	MNS, MN, NS, N
MNS X N	MNS, MN, NS, N
MN X NS	MNS, MN, NS, N
MN X N	MN, N
NS X NS	NS, N
NS X N	NS, N
N X N	N

present in all Whites but absent in a small percentage of Blacks. Blacks who are U negative also lack both S and s. Testing with anti-**U** serum can be helpful in interracial child-mother-putative father combinations, but only when one is U-negative.

D. *The Kell Blood Group System*

There are many specificities in this system, but only two are useful in disputed parentage, K and k. The use of two antisera, anti-**K** and anti-**k** defines three phenotypes, K, k, and Kk, corresponding to genotypes *KK, kk,* and *Kk.* This makes a simple system that needs no further elaboration, exclusion being along classic lines.

The following special features should be noted:

1. Use of both anti-**K** and anti-**k** when testing Whites provides a chance of exclusion of about 3.5 percent. Since very few people are *KK,* testing with only anti-**K** reduces the chance of exclusion by only a few tenths of one percent.
2. The incidence of agglutinogen K is extremely small in Blacks and is zero in Chinese and Japanese. In these racial groups no exclusion can be expected on the basis of this blood group system. On the other hand, in an interracial situation the detection of K positively could provide strong likelihood of paternity.

E. *The Duffy Blood Group System*

Two antisera, anti-**Fy^{a}** and anti-**Fy^{b}**, define four phenotypes, Fy(a+b-), Fy(a+b+), Fy(a-b+) and Fy(a-b-), determined by allelic genes *Fy^{a}*, *Fy^{b}*, and *Fy.* Gene *Fy* has a high incidence in Blacks (about 78 percent) but has only rarely been identified in Whites, so that in Whites only the first three phenotypes are possible. Exclusion is along classic lines.

The following special features should be noted:

If a person fails to react with either anti-**Fy^{a}** or anti-**Fy^{b}** (assuming no technical errors), this would be strong evidence that he or she is Black.

F. *The Kidd Blood Group System*

Two antisera, anti-**Jk^{a}** and anti-**Jk^{b}** define three phenotypes, Jk (a+b-), Jk(a+b+), and Jk(a-b+), determined by the pair of genes *Jk^{a}* and *Jk^{b}*. Exclusion is along classic lines.

The following special features should be noted:

A third gene has been postulated, *Jk,* determining a fourth phenotype, Jk(a-b-). This phenotype has been found in only one family of European Whites, and only in single instances in a Filipino woman, a Chinese, and a Hawaiian-Chinese.

G. *The HLA System*

It has been known for some time that in man there exists a major histocompatability system (HLA) of great complexity, composed of a series of many closely linked genes. Originally the serologically defined specificities of the HLA system were assigned to two linked loci, each with multiple alleles. These two loci are now designated HLA-A and HLA-B. More recently a third locus, HLA-C, was identified although its individual specificities are not easily identified in typing laboratories in the United States. A fourth locus, HLA-D, has also been identified by mixed lymphocyte culture reactions but is not yet readily detected by serological means. The specificities (or the antigens) which are controlled by genes at each of these four loci are now identified by numbers. When the specificity is first recognized, this is indicated by placing a lower case w in front of the number. Later, when general consensus has been reached and the specificity firmly established by the World Health Organization Nomenclature Committee, the w is dropped and the number retained.

A "blank" in a genotype might indicate either homozygocity for a single specificity at a locus or, alternatively, it might indicate an inability to identify an antigen. This is usually clarified by family studies. At present, the majority of antigens in the HLA-A and the HLA-B series are known.

The HLA system is one of genetic dominance. Therefore, two antigens or specificities are possible for each segregating locus. At present, as many as eight tissue antigens can be identified in each individual. More practical limitations of tissue typing today, however, include only the specificities of HLA-A and HLA-B (see Tables 9 and 10 pages 273-74). A total of thirty-nine specificities are now recognized within these two loci. Currently available tissue typing trays (for transplantation only) provided by the National Institutes of Health to each of over 120 typing laboratories in the United States allow for identification of 32 of the genotypic specificities.

Table 9
Gene Frequencies of HLA-A Antigens (18)

	Caucasoid	Mongoloid	American Indian	African Black
HLA-A1	.11	.02	.01	.05
A2	.24	.18	.48	.19
A3	.12	.01	.01	.08
A9	.13	.41	.25	.13
A10	.05	.07	.00	.08
A11	.09	.13	.01	.08
A28	.05	.02	.09	.09
A29	.02	.01	.00	.05
Aw23	.03	.02	.00	.08
Aw24	.10	.34	.25	.05
Aw25	.01	.03	.00	.01
Aw26	.05	.07	.00	.07
Aw30	.04	.02	.02	.16
Aw31	.01	.00	.09	.02
Aw32	.04	.00	.00	.04
Aw33	.04	.07	.04	.07
"Blank"	.04	.06	.02	.06
Aw34*				
Aw36*				
Aw43*				

*Included within frequencies calculated for "blank".

"**NOTE:** Gene frequencies for each racial group add to more than one because Aw23 and Aw24 are newly described splits or sub-components of A9, and Aw25 and Aw26 are splits or sub-components of A10. Therefore, the gene frequencies for each of these more recently described antigens are included twice in the Table; that is, both are represented with the individual genes and then represented in a combined total as the gene frequency for the A9 and A10 antigen. If the gene frequencies for A9 and A10 are subtracted from the total, then the sum of gene frequencies approach the theoretical value of 1.0 more closely."

Table 10
Gene Frequencies of HLA-B Antigens (18)

	Caucasoid	Mongoloid	American Indian	African Black
HLA-B5	.01	.09	.11	.08
B7	.11	.02	.01	.12
B8	.07	.01	.00	.04
B12	.11	.03	.01	.12
B13	.02	.04	.00	.01
B14	.03	.00	.01	.03
B18	.07	.01	.01	.03
B27	.04	.04	.03	.00
Bw15	.07	.16	.15	.04
Bw16	.03	.05	.12	.01
Bw17	.06	.03	.01	.21
Bw21	.03	.00	.04	.01
Bw22	.02	.13	.00	.01
Bw35	.10	.06	.23	.06
Bw40	.05	.24	.13	.06
"Blank"	.11	.12	.16	.15
Bw37*				
Bw38*				
Bw39*				
Bw41*				
Bw42*				

*These antigen frequencies are included within the figure given for "blank" for each of the ethnic groups.

Using these trays, more than 255 haplotypes can be recognized with as many as 65,025 genotypes. The number of antigens in the system (Table 11) makes it apparent that the HLA typing system offers the single most potent method for exclusion.

HLA typing is currently evolving so that the specificity of individual test sera must be considered in establishing the

Table 11
Recognized HLA Specificities*

New	Previous	New	Previous
HLA-A1	HL-A1	HLA-B5	HL-A5
HLA-A2	HL-A2	HLA-B7	HL-A7
HLA-A3	HL-A3	HLA-B8	HL-A8
HLA-A9	HL-A9	HLA-B12	HL-A12
HLA-A10	HL-A10	HLA-B13	HL-A13
HLA-A11	HL-A11	HLA-B14	W14
HLA-A28	W28	HLA-B18	W18
HLA-A29	W29	HLA-B27	W27
HLA-Aw19	Li		
HLA-Aw23	W23	HLA-Bw15	W15
HLA-Aw24	W24	HLA-Bw16	W16
HLA-Aw25	W25	HLA-Bw17	W17
HLA-A26	W26	HLA-Bw21	W21
HLA-Aw30	W30	HLA-Bw22	W22
HLA-Aw31	W31	HLA-Bw35	W5
HLA-Aw32	W32	HLA-Bw37	TY
HLA-Aw33	W19.6	HLA-Bw38	W16.1
HLA-Aw34	Malay 2	HLA-Bw39	W16.2
HLA-Aw36	Mo*	HLA-Bw40	W10
HLA-Aw43	BK	HLA-Bw41	Sabell
		HLA-Bw42	MWA
HLA-Cw1	T1	HLA-Dw1	LD 101
HLA-Cw2	T2	HLA-Dw2	LD 102
HLA-Cw3	T3	HLA-Dw3	LD 103
HLA-Cw4	T4	HLA-Dw4	LD 104
HLA-Cw5	T5	HLA-Dw5	LD 105
		HLA-Dw6	LD 106

*The previously reserved specificities W4(4a) and W6(4b) remain w4 and w6. These specificities are closely associated with the B locus.

reliability of the test results. Tissue typing laboratories are widely distributed throughout the country and their facilities could be available for paternity testing. Bulk sera are currently available to qualified individuals upon application to NIAID. Selected antisera are also commercially available. HLA typing has already been used in Europe for paternity exclusion and has been successful in many cases where red cell typing has failed to exclude paternity (15, 16, 17).

As in other genetic systems, HLA sometimes shows an unusually high association between antigens which constitute a single haplotype. This is referred to as genetic dysequilibrium. Often such associations are very selective for certain ethnic groups or subpopulations within various geographic regions of the world. There is a considerable amount of data available on haplotype frequencies (Ref. 18, 19, 20). However, even larger numbers of special groups must be typed to provide the statistical basis for analysis of their HLA inheritance. Even when all haplotype frequencies are known, the HLA typing laboratory will still require a determination of the racial and geographic origin of the subjects in order to calculate the probability of exclusion of paternity.

EXCLUSION

The calculation of probabilities for either exclusion or identification of a putative father is complicated by our inability to assign a haplotype designation to the father, even when we have identified all four HLA (A and B) antigens. If a putative father is shown to have both HLA antigens which constitute the paternal haplotype inherited by the child, he still could be excluded if studies of the putative father's father and mother revealed that he had inherited the antigens singly; that is, one from each parent.

Using gene frequencies, it is possible to ascribe a general probability of exclusion by using the formula $(1\text{-}P)^4P$ (Ref. 17). The sum of these "probabilities of exclusion" then will give the total probability of exclusion. Using a smaller number of antigen specificities than are generally known today, it was possible to predict that HLA typing would exclude between 76 percent (Ref. 18) to 81 percent (Ref. 17) of men falsely accused of paternity.

LIKELIHOOD OF PATERNITY

The calculation of the statistical likelihood that an accused man is the real father is an even more complicated problem. Here we must calculate the possibility that a man who has both antigens of the suspected paternal haplotype of a child may have inherited these antigens independently, one from each parent (a "Trans" configuration). If they indeed have been inherited together as a true haplotype, they are said to be "Cis" in nature and could have been inherited by a child. If the exact haplotype of the child that has been inherited from the father can be determined, then only those men who have both antigens could possibly be the father. If they have both antigens, the probability that they are in Cis position is $2P\text{-}P^2$ (Ref. 16). The probability of Trans configuration of the antigens can also be calculated.

These calculations are made knowing that the two antigens in question have been detected in a putative father. However, they ignore the possibility that the other two antigens have also been identified. If all four HLA antigens are known, then a more precise calculation of Cis or Trans posssibilities can be made using haplotype frequency tables. Unfortunately, haplotype frequencies are now known only for the common haplotypes. Until all haplotype frequencies have been identified, we probably must be satisfied with simple calculation of serotype frequencies of antigens to determine the likelihood of paternity. Fortunately, the current data commonly allows for the ready identification of antigen frequencies after serologic identification using lymphocytotoxicity tests. Using antigen frequencies, it is possible to determine the likelihood that a man in the random population would possess both antigens which have been identified as paternal HLA antigens of the child in question. In the case of the rarer antigens, this likelihood can be minimized (often less than 1 percent). However, with some common haplotypes, such as HLA-A3 HLA-B7, the general population demonstrates almost a 7.6 percent frequency. Family studies, of course, would be helpful in confirming that the putative father did indeed inherit the antigens in a Cis configuration and therefore would be the most likely to be the father. However, it is difficult to see how the cooperation of family members could be obtained to allow family testing which would result in identification of paternity as opposed to exclusion.

As for some of the very rare blood group subgroups there are very rare HLA specificities (i.e., HLA-Aw35 or HLA-B14) which, if present in both the child and putative father but absent in the mother would indicate a very high probability of paternity.

Example:

	HLA Antigens Present	Possible Haplotypes
Mother	A2, A9, B5, B12	A2 B 5 A 9 B12 A2 B12 A 9 B 5
Child	A2, A11, B7, B12	A2 B 7 A11 B12 A2 B12 A11 B 7

This child inherited the A2 B12 Haplotype from this mother. Therefore, the real father must have A11 B7 as one of his HLA Haplotypes.

Indentification of Putative Father
A3 A11 B7 B5

This male could have the A11 B7 as one of his Haplotypes. So he is not excluded as a possible father. The frequency of B7 in Caucasions is .11 and A11 is .09. The likelihood of these two antigens occurring randomly in the population together is .0099, or about one in a hundred. This would suggest that a putative father who contained these two antigens, that is, A11 B7, would be wrongly identified as the father, approximately one time in a hundred.

Exclusion of Putative Father
A3 A11 B5 B_w15

This man cannot have A11 B7 haplotype and so is excluded as the father.

Finally, the possibility of recombination between antigens of the various allelic series of the HLA complex must be considered by the laboratory which performs the tissue typing. For instance, the recombination rate between antigens of the A and B loci is approximately 0.8 percent (Ref. 21).

H. *Serum Protein and Red Cell Enzyme Systems*

Numerous polymorphic serum protein and red cell enzyme systems (See Table 1) have been well defined by appropriate family studies

(Ref. 22). The genetics of these systems makes it possible to use them in determining exclusions as outlined in Section IV. Many of these systems are stable in frozen samples. Thus, stored hemolysates or serum can be used when other tests fail to provide an exclusion (Ref. 23).

GROUP SPECIFIC COMPONENT

Electrophoresis on a single polyacrylamide gel can simultaneously distinguish the phenotypes of the Group Specific Component, Transferrin and Albumin systems (Ref. 24). Though only the Gc is routinely useful, the other systems can provide additional data on rare occasions.

HAPTOGLOBIN

Haptoglobin, a serum protein system with an exclusion probability of .18, can be determined simultaneously with ceruloplasmin on polyacrylamide gels stained with an ortho-dianisidine substrate (Ref. 24).

Gm AND Km

Human immunoglobulins contain numerous allotypes which have varying racial distribution. These markers (Gm, Am and Km-formerly known as Inv) can be detected by serologic systems (Ref. 25). Their use is limited in children under six months of age whose markers may not be completely developed and in rare individuals with immunodeficiency states.

ACID PHOSPHATASE

Overnight electrophoresis on starch gel followed by reaction with an appropriate substrate makes it possible to determine the phenotype of the red cell enzyme acid phosphatase which has an exclusion probability of .23 in Whites. Simultaneously the less useful isoenzymes of adenylate kinase, adenosine deaminase and 6-phosphogluconate dehydrogenase can be established from the same gel by reaction with other substrates (Ref. 23).

PHOSPHOGLUCOMUTASE

This stable enzyme found in erythrocyte hemolysates like the previous systems is useful both in determining non-paternity and probabilities of paternity when gene frequencies for the test population are established. Isoenzyme patterns in this system, as in most of the other systems, can be recorded on photographs.

VII. Procedures and Forms Relating to the Introduction of Evidence

To satisfy the requirements of the law of evidence and to facilitate the introduction of evidence into the courts, it is recommended that standard procedures, including forms, be adopted. The full series of events relating to the testing procedures, beginning with the court's order (or other request) that samples be taken and tests made, covering the laboratory's procedures and ending with the expert's report to the court, must be documented.

It is recommended that only requests for tests from the court, an officer of the court, or an attorney be honored. All parties should appreciate and preserve the confidentiality of the test results. Test results should be provided only to the requesting agency, court, or party or parties unless there is written authorization from the court, or party or parties concerned, for other distribution.

While it may be desirable to develop and encourage universal adoption of standard forms which satisfy all applicable legal requirements, it is probably sufficient to agree on a standard content of forms, along the lines here expressed.

A. *The Initial Request*

The initial request that blood and other samples be obtained and tested should identify the court or other requesting party, the case, the parties involved in the case and the purpose of the tests (i.e., exclusion of paternity, exclusion of maternity, etc.). The request should direct the named parties to present themselves to the expert or to a laboratory at a designated place, date and time. Each person to be tested should receive a copy of the request. If the testing is to be done elsewhere than in the laboratory where the samples are obtained, the request should state the name and address of the expert to whom the sampes should be shipped. The initial request should indicate the party or parties to whom the results of the tests and the opinion of the expert should be sent.

B. *Identification of Parties when Testing for Disputed Parentage*

It is essential that the persons to be tested in a case of disputed parentage be identified and the identification documented in such a way that there can be no question of identification in court. This can be achieved in various ways, but the following procedure is followed by most experts.

1. All the persons to be tested should be present at the same time if possible and identify each other. If one of the parties cannot be present at the same time he or she should be properly identified when he or she appears for the taking of the sample.
2. The following identification and documentation of identification should be made on an appropriate form or forms:
   a. Date blood samples are drawn.
   b. Name, address, social security number (if any), driver's license number (if any), and signature of each party, indicating which is the child (or children), which the mother, and which the putative father (or fathers).
   c. Permission of each person to be tested for blood and other samples to be obtained, including a statement that he or she understands the purpose of the tests. Typically, the mother or legal guardian will give permission for children or minors.
   d. Right thumb print of each party.* If the baby is less than one year old a properly prepared footprint or palm print is probably better than a thumbprint.†
   e. Separate Polaroid photographs of each party, dated and signed on the back and countersigned by a witness. The baby's photograph is signed by the mother.
   f. If blood samples are drawn elsewhere the above procedures should still be followed it at all possible, as the responsibility for identifying the parties involved rests with the person who obtains the blood samples. It is recommended that the specimens be shipped by registered mail.

---

*The Sirchie system (Sirchie Laboratories, P.O. Box 23845, Pleasant Hill, California 94523), is convenient.

†The Hollister Disposable Footprinter (Hollister, Inc., 211 E. Chicago Avenue, Chicago, Illinois 60611), is convenient.

C. *Identification of Specimens*

1. Anticoagulated (sodium citrate or ACD solution) and clotted venous blood is obtained from each party. Five to ten ml. of each should be obtained from adults and older children. In infants and small babies capillary blood can be used, collected with micropipettes.
2. Each tube should be capped, labeled with the name of the donor and his or her relationship to the others (baby, mother, putative father) and initialed by the phlebotomist and the physician responsible for the taking of the sample.
3. Samples drawn elsewhere should be identified in the same way, then countersigned by the person receiving them and the physician responsible for the testing.
4. If saliva is collected the above rules of identification also apply.

VIII. Guidelines for the Expert

It is assumed that no specific technical instructions are necessary for an investigator who is qualified as an expert. Specific caveats are given in each section dealing with test systems. The following guidelines are designed to insure procedural uniformity.

1. Tests should be performed in duplicate, using a different source of blood grouping reagents for each, and each read independently by two observers.
2. An appropriate working form should be used to record the test results and appropriate controls. The form should show the date the tests were performed and the names of the technologists or physicians who performed the tests or read the results.

IX. The Report of the Expert

Based on the test data, the expert sends a written report of his findings and conclusions to the attorneys representing the parties, or to the court if the testing was ordered by the court. All original data and documentation remain in the expert's files. The report should be sufficiently detailed as to the findings and the expert's opinion based on the findings as to minimize questions. If the test shows a strong likelihood of paternity (as defined in Table 4) this evidence should be given to the court along with a description of the method used for calculating likelihood of paternity.

The report shall be received in evidence by stipulation of the parties or by order of the court.

X. Identification of Qualified Laboratories

It is the opinion of the committee that those laboratories which desire to be "accredited" for this purpose should be required to meet rigorous standards of performance. For the purpose of recognition and accrediting of qualified laboratories the committee believes that qualified accrediting agencies can follow past patterns which have proved effective. Standards should be established regarding personnel, space, equipment, reagents and records. A proficiency testing program should be developed that could be offered, through the Center for Disease Control, the College of American Pathologists or other accrediting agencies. It is the opinion of the Committee that all those laboratories which are capable of performing these tests in a satisfactory manner should be permitted to offer this service and be eligible for reimbursement under the several Federal and State programs.

XI. Recommendations

1. It is recommended that this report be adopted by the AMA Board of Trustees and by the American Bar Association.
2. It is recommended that this report be published jointly by the AMA and ABA, in the Journal of the American Medical Association and in the Family Law Quarterly or other journal designated by the ABA.
3. It is recommended that steps be taken to obtain such Federal, State, or other support as to enable widespread inclusion of HLA studies in the battery of tests used in cases of disputed parentage. This should include not only making available reliable HLA antisera but also provisions for education and continuing education.
4. It is recommended that the National Conference of Commissioners on Uniform State Laws develop new uniform legislation or amend the "Uniform Parentage Act" and the "Uniform Blood Test Act" to (1) clarify judicial authority to order blood tests and (2) simplify the admissibility in evidence of test results and the probative effect thereof, including the evidentiary value of estimations of "likelihood of paternity".

5. It is recommended that the Department of Health, Education and Welfare and the appropriate agencies on the state and local levels adopt and utilize the findings and recommendations of this report in the administration and implementation of P.L. 93-647 as it relates to the establishment of paternity.
6. It is recommended that the AMA and ABA establish procedures to monitor medical and legal developments in this field to facilitate continuing revision and updating of this report as may at any time appear necessary.

REFERENCES

1. *Medicolegal Application of Blood Grouping Tests,* Bureau of Legal Medicine and Legislation. JAMA *149:699-705,* 1952.
2. *Medicolegal Applications of Blood Grouping Tests,* Committee on Medicolegal Problems. JAMA 164:2036-2044, 1957.
3. Chakraborty R. Shaw M, Schull W J: *Exclusion of paternity: The Current State of the Art.* AM. J. HUM. GENET, *26*:477-488, 1974.
4. Hummel, K et al: *Biostatistical Opinion of Parentage, Based Upon the Results of Blood Group Tests,* Vol. 1, 1971; VOL. 2, 1972, Stuttgart, Gustav Fischer Verlag.
5. Hummel, K: Die medizinische Vaterschaftsbegutachtung mit biostatistischem Beweis, 1961, Stuttgart, Gustav Fischer Verlag.
6. Essen-Möller E: Die Beweiskraft der Ähnlichkeit im Vaterschaftsnachweis; theoretische Grundlagen. Mitt Anthrop Ges (Wien) *68*:368, 1938.
7. Mayr W R: Grundlagen zur Berechnung der Vaterschaftswahrscheinlichkeit im HL-A-System. Z Immunitaetsforsch *144*:18-27, 1972.
8. Reviron J, Jacquet A, Salmon C: Un exemple de chromosome "CIS A_1B". Étude immunologique et génétique du phénotype induit. Nouv Rev Fr Hematol *8*:323-338, 1968.
9. Salmon C: Immunogenetique des antigénes ABH, Nouv Rev Fr Hematol *11*:850-862, 1971.
10. Miale J B: LABORATORY MEDICINE-HEMATOLOGY, 1972, (Fourth Ed.), St. Louis, C.V. Mosby Co., p 677-681.
11. Miale J B: LABORATORY MEDICINE-HEMATOLOGY, 1972, (Fourth Ed.), St. Louis, C.V. Mosby Co., Table 9-34, p 682.
12. Wiener A S and Nieberg K C: Exclusion of parentage by Rh-Hr blood tests: revised table including blood factors RH_0, rh′, rh″, hr′ hr″, and hr. J Forensic Med *10*:6, 1963.
13. Miale J B: LABORATORY MEDICINE-HEMATOLOGY, 1972, (Fourth Ed.), St. Louis, C.V. Mosby C., p 686.
14. ERSKINE A G: THE PRINCIPLES AND PRACTICE OF BLOOD GROUPING, 1973, St. Louis, C.V. Mosby Co., p 174.
15. Speiser P: Das HL-A-System im Paternitätsprozess mit Berücksichtigung des Beweiswertes. Wien Klin Wochenschr *87*:321-326, 1975.
16. Soulier J P, Prou-Wartelle O, Muller J Y: Paternity research using the HL-A system. Haematologia (Budapest) *8*:249-265, 1974.
17. Jeannet M, Hässig A, Bernheim J: Use of the HL-A antigen system in disputed paternity cases. Vox Sang *23*:197-200, 1972.
18. DAUSSET J AND COLOMBANI J: HISTOCOMPATIBILITY TESTING 1972, 1973, Baltimore, Williams and Wilkins Company.

19. Mayr W R: Die Genetik des HL-A Systems. Populations und Familienuntersuchungen unter besonderer Berücksichtigung der Paternitätsserologie. Humangenetik *12*:195-243, 1971.
20. Dausset J, Colombani J, Legrand L and Fellows M: Genetics of the HL-A System: deduction of 480 haplotypes, p. 53 in Terasaki PI (ed) Histocompatibility Testing 1970, Baltimore, Williams and Wilkins Co.
21. Amos, D.B., Ward, F.E.: *Immunogenetics of the HL-A System,* Physiol. Reviews, *55*:206-246, 1975.
22. Dykes, Dale: *Serum Proteins and Erythrocyte Enzymes in Paternity Testing in a Seminar on Polymorphisms in Human Blood,* pp 27-42, AABB Washington D.C. 1975.
23. Dykes, Dale and Polesky, Herbert F.: *The Usefulness of Serum Proteins and Erythrocyte Enzyme Polymorphisms in Paternity Tests,* AJCP *65*:816-820, 1976.
24. Polesky, H.F., Rokala, D., Hoff, T.: Serum Proteins in Paternity Testing, Ed. H.F. Polesky, pp 30-44. ASCP, Chicago 1975.
25. Schanfield, M.S., Polesky, H.F. and Sebring, E.S.: *Gm and Inv Typing in Paternity Testing,* Ed. H.F. Polesky, pp 45-53. ASCP, Chicago 1975.
26. Wiener, A.S. and Socha, W.W.: *Methods Available for Solving Medicolegal Problems of Disputed Parentage*. J. Forensic Sci. *21*(1):42-64, 1976.
27. Paternity Testing by Blood Grouping. Second Edition, Ed.L. Sussman, C. Thomas, Springfield, Illinois 1976.

Current Status of Paternity Testing*

CHANG LING LEE, M.D.†

Introduction

For many years only a small number of blood tests have been used in solving paternity problems, and have given only about a 50% chance for a man falsely named as the father to be excluded. Recently, with the progress in medical sciences, many more blood tests are available for paternity cases. The larger the number of tests, the greater the chance of exclusion; by the use of all the currently available blood tests, the theoretical chance of exclusion is over 99%. However, it is unrealistic to conduct all the tests because it is unnecessary in many cases and is too costly.

The procedures for many of the newer tests are far more complicated than those for the older tests. Also, as the number of tests increased, genetic and other variants have been revealed; a classical exclusion may prove to be false if additional careful examinations are carried out. Consequently, experts are often required, not only to conduct the tests but also to interpret the test results correctly.

Customarily, when a man named as father is not excluded by blood tests and there is no other evidence against his paternity, he

*This paper was developed from presentations made at the Annual Meeting of the American Bar Association, August 1974, Honolulu, and at HEW-sponsored workshops in Chicago and San Francisco, March 1975. The author wishes to acknowledge the critical review of the manuscript by Professor Harry D. Krause and the editorial assistance of Ms. Ann Pearl Owen of the College of Law, University of Illinois.

†Director, Charles Hymen Blood Center, Mount Sinai Hospital Medical Center, Scientific Director, Mid-America Regional Red Cross Blood Program, Professor of Medicine and Pathology, Rush Medical College, Chicago, Illinois.

may be mandated to support the child. The use of a larger number of tests makes it possible to estimate with greater confidence the chance that the named man is in fact the father of the child. Thus, the likelihood of paternity is being used in European countries to provide the court with additional support for the final decision.

To discuss these advances intelligently, one must know: first, the principle of paternity testing; second, the blood tests currently used for paternity problems; and finally, the evaluation of results of paternity testing.

Principles of Paternity Testing

Genetic Markers

DEFINITION

Blood tests for paternity problems are based on the existence of genetic markers which are personal characteristics inherited from the parents and controlled by genes on a pair of chromosomes. Personal characteristics can be physical, such as the color of hair, eyes and skin, or detectable properties of the blood components. While the former may occasionally be helpful in arriving at a decision, the latter exhibit a wide variety of differences which are scientifically identifiable and thus become the most useful tool for solving parentage problems.

BLOOD COMPONENTS

The blood consists of red and white blood cells, platelets, and liquid plasma. Each component contains a number of genetic markers (See Table I). More than 260 genetic markers, known as isoantigens, and over 50 called isoenzymes for red blood cells have been reported. Nearly 100 markers are known for plasma protein. For white blood cells, 50 markers known as HLA isoantigens are well established and many more described. Platelets share many HLA isoantigens with leukocytes in addition to having their own specific antigens.

Genetic markers which are inherited as part of a group at the same location on a pair of chromosomes are designated as a system. The genetic markers A, B, and O are in the ABO system, as M, N, S, and s are in the MNSs system. In this way, more than 455 listed genetic markers of blood components have been grouped into 51 systems.

TABLE I

Blood Group Genetic Markers Used In Parentage Problems

Blood Components	Genetic Markers #Known	Genetic Markers #Used	Groups or Systems #Known	Groups or Systems #Used
Red blood cell isoantigens	260+	24	24	10
Red blood cell isoenzymes	55+	15	13	7
Plasma protein	90+	16	13	7
White blood cell isoantigens (HLA)	50+	21	1	1
Total	455+	76	51	25

SELECTION OF GENETIC MARKERS

In theory, each person can be identified by the genetic markers in his blood just as by his fingerprints. In practice, it would become much too involved if tests were to be done for all these genetic markers. Not all genetic markers are equally useful. In selecting genetic markers for paternity testing, the following considerations are important:

1. Inheritance—Not all the reported genetic markers are well established, only those which have been well documented through careful study of family members and the general population should be used in paternity testing.

2. Frequency—The incidence of genetic markers in a given population varies widely. Genetic markers with frequencies between 20% and 50% provide a good chance for exclusion from paternity and are thus most useful. Those with low frequencies are useful for the estimation of likelihood of paternity. Those with high frequencies are only of limited value in paternity testing since they seldom allow a differentiation between the alleged father and other men.

3. Practicality—Reagents for testing must be readily available

and reliable. The procedures should be reproducible and give clear-cut results. Cost is another consideration but should not be over emphasized when compared to the cost of supporting the child.

4. Reliability—Attention should be paid to the fact that genetic variants, wide ethnic differences, and variations under different physiologic and pathologic conditions are known to exist for certain genetic markers.

Inheritance

GENES

Many characteristics are controlled by two genes at the same location on a pair of chromosomes. Each human body cell has 23 pairs of chromosomes, while the mature sperms or ova contain only 23 single chromosomes; thus, only one of a pair of genes is present and transmitted from each parent to the offspring. For example, if *a* and *b* are a pair of genes, either *a* or *b* is transmitted to the offspring; it cannot be neither or both (Figure I).

When an ovum is fertilized by a sperm, the 23 chromosomes in each combine to form again 23 pairs of chromosomes. One half of

FIGURE 1

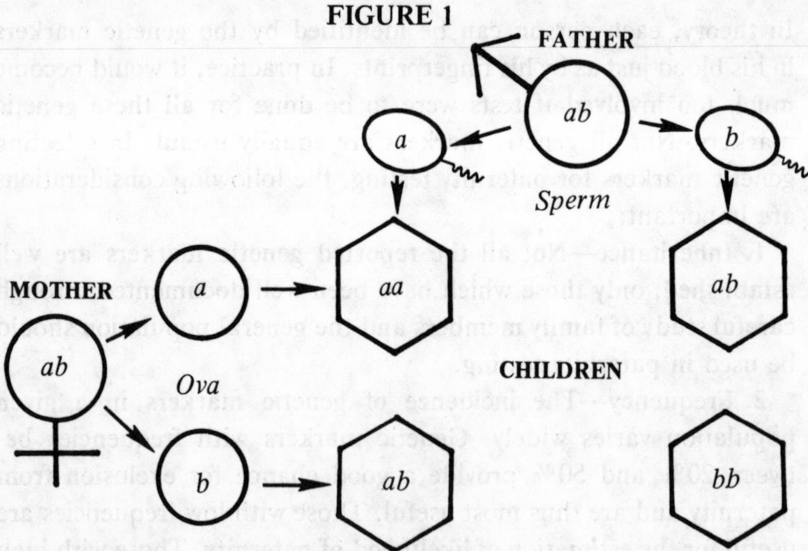

AN EXAMPLE OF INHERITANCE. Sperms and ova carry one of a pair of genes, either *a* or *b*. After fertilization the genes from a sperm and an ovum join to form three possible genotypes; *aa, ab,* and *bb.*

the genes or genetic markers are derived from the father and the other half from the mother. Using the same example as in Figure 1, the children can be only one of 3 types: ***aa***, ***bb*** or ***ab***, depending on whether the ovum and the sperm fertilizing it are carrying the ***a*** or ***b*** gene.

GENOTYPES

The gene combination on a pair of chromosomes, ***aa***, ***bb***, or ***ab*** is called genotype. Persons with genotype ***aa*** or ***bb*** are designated as homozygous (*i.e.*, with identical genes), persons with type ***ab*** as heterozygous (*i.e.*, with different genes).

The genotype of the parents determines the genotype of the children (Table II). If both parents are homozygous for the same gene (***aa*x*aa*** or ***bb*x*bb***), all of their children must be homozygous (***aa*** or ***bb***). If the parents are homozygous for different genes (***aa*x*bb***), all their chidren must be heterozygous (***ab***). If one parent is homozygous (***aa*** or ***bb***) and the other parent heterozygous (***ab***), one half of their children is expected to be homozygous (***aa*** or ***bb***) and the other half heterozygous (***ab***). If both parents are heterozygous (***ab*x*ab***, as in Figure 1), their children can belong to any of the three types (***aa***, ***bb***, ***ab***).

TABLE II

Expected Frequencies of Genotypes of Children of Different Matings

Genotype of Mother		Father	Genotypes of Children *aa*	*ab*	*bb*
aa	X	*aa*	100%		
bb	X	*bb*			100%
aa	X	*bb*		100%	
bb	X	*aa*		100%	
aa	X	*ab*	50%	50%	
ab	X	*aa*	50%	50%	
bb	X	*ab*		50%	50%
ab	X	*bb*		50%	50%
ab	X	*ab*	25%	50%	25%

The genotype *aa*, or *bb* is usually assumed by the absence of the *b* or *a* marker but can be established through the study of family members.

For some characteristics, a third gene may be an alternate at the same location on a pair of chromosomes. The ABO blood group is an example. Without considering the subgroups of A, there are three genes in the group, *A*, *B*, and *O*. Any two of them can be on a pair of chromosomes to form genotypes, while the mature sperm or ovum, having only one of each pair of chromosomes, has only one of the genes. Table III illustrates six possible genotypes, *AA*, *BB*, *OO*, *AB*, *AO*, *BO* and the frequency of each gene or genotype.

At the present time, differentiation of *AA* from *AO* is not possible except by studying the family members. Consequently, both types, *AA* and *AO*, are designated as group A (the phenotype or group to which the individual is assigned on the basis of visible characteristics or laboratory findings). Similarly, the phenotype B consists of *BB* and *BO* genotypes. This is why group A or B parents can have children of group O. In other words, a man of group A or B, who is heterozygous (*AO* or *BO*) may have a child that is neither group A nor group B.

TABLE III

ABO Genotypes of Children of Different Matings*

with their frequencies among whites

GENE ON MOTHER'S OVUM Frequency	GENE ON FATHER'S SPERM Frequency		
	A 0.285	*B* 0.079	*O* 0.636
A 0.285	*AA* 0.081	*AB* 0.023	*AO* 0.181
B 0.079	*AB* 0.023	*BB* 0.006	*BO* 0.050
O 0.636	*AO* 0.181	*BO* 0.050	*OO* 0.404

*Subgroups of A are not taken into consideration

RULES OF INHERITANCE

According to the principle discussed above, the following rules of inheritance can be stated:

1. A child cannot have a genetic marker which is absent in both parents.

2. A child must inherit one of a pair of genetic markers from each parent.

3. A child cannot have a pair of identical genetic markers (*aa*) unless both parents have the marker (*a*).

4. A child must have the genetic marker (*a* or *b*) which is present as an identical pair in one parent (*aa* or *bb*).

Parentage Problems

DISPUTED PATERNITY

Disputed paternity is by far the most important parentage problem. In this situation, the mother is always considered to be the true mother. The genetic markers which are found in the child but are absent in the mother must therefore come from the true father. Exclusion of paternity is normally the primary consideration. Based on the four rules of inheritance above, four types of exclusions from paternity are possible. (See Table IV)

1. The child has a genetic marker (such as blood group A) which is absent in the mother and cannot be demonstrated in the alleged father.

2. In a 3 alternate-genetic marker system (such as ABO), the child (type O) lacks both genetic markers (absence of both A and B in the child) which are demonstrated in the alleged father (type AB).

3. A child is homozygous for a genetic marker (such as *EE*) which is not present in both parents.

4. A child lacks a genetic marker (M-negative) while the alleged father is homozygous for it (*MM*).

The first two types of exclusions are based on the presence or absence of certain genetic markers demonstrable by direct examinations and are known as DIRECT EXCLUSIONS. With extremely rare exceptions (Table IV), these two types of exclusions can be accepted with great confidence.

TABLE IV

Exclusion of Paternity

Types of Exclusion		Mother	Child	Alleged Father	Very Rare Exceptions*
Direct	1	A–	A+	A–	"Bombay"
	2		O	AB	"Cis-AB"
Indirect	3	E+	*EE*	E–	"D––"
	4		M–	*MM*	"M^g"

*Examples for which tests can verify

The third and fourth types of exclusions which are based on the inference of homozygous genotypes determined by a negative reaction in a particular test are known as Indirect Exclusions, and should be accepted with caution. The particular test should be repeated with the same and different reagents or by a different technologist, or in a different laboratory. For some markers, zygosity may be determined by the use of the titration method. The use of other genetic markers may reveal additional exclusions.

OTHER PARENTAGE PROBLEMS

In some cases, the mother or both mother and father may be suspect, such as offspring of immigrants, kidnappings or interchange of babies. Under these circumstances, the alleged mother cannot be assumed to be the true mother and the same principles of inheritance apply for her as for the alleged father.

Genetic Markers Currently Used in Paternity Testing

Since paternity testing is more frequent in Europe than in this country, a survey was conducted abroad. Experts in 24 countries responded to our questionnaires. Their answers show a total of 24 blood group systems, including 74 genetic markers, currently used in paternity testing. Table V lists each of the 25 systems and the 76 genetic markers (one system with 2 markers was added after the survey).

TABLE V

Genetic Markers in 25 Blood Group Systems

currently used in parentage problems

	Systems	Genetic Markers
Red blood cell isoantigens	1. ABO	A_1,A_2,B,O
	2. MNSs	M,N,S,s
	3. Rh	D,C,C^w,c,E,e
	4. Kell	K,k
	5. Duffy	Fy^a,Fy^b
	6. Kidd	Jk^a,Jk^b
	7. P	P_1
	8. Xg	Xg^a
	9. Lutheran	Lu^a,Lu^b
	10. Secretor	Se
White blood cell isoantigens	11. HLA	A1,A2,A3,A9,A10, A11,A28,AW33 B5,B7,B8,B12, B13,B14,B17, B27,B35,B40, BW15,BW21,BW22
Red blood cell isoenzymes	12. Acid phosphotase	AcP^A,AcP^B,AcP^C
	13. Phosphoglucomutase	$PGM_1{}^1$,$PGM_1{}^2$
	14. Adenosine Deaminase	ADA^1,ADA^2
	15. Adenylate Kinase	AK^1,AK^2
	16. 6-Phosphogluconate Dehydrogenase	PGD^A,PGD^C
	17. Glutamic pyruvic transaminase	GPT^1,GPT^2
	18. Esterase D*	EsD^1,EsD^2
	*a recent but useful addition	
Plasma proteins	19. Gm	Glm^a,Glm^x,$G3m^b$
	20. Km	Km^1,Km^3
	21. Haptoglobin	Hp^1,Hp^2
	22. Group specific components	Gc^1,Gc^2
	23. Complement	$C3^1$,$C3^2$
	24. Ag Lipoprotein	Ag^x,Ag^y
	25. Transferrin	Tf^C,Tf^{B2},Tf^{D1}

Figure 2 illustrates the number of countries using different systems or genetic markers for paternity testing, ABO, MNSs, and Rh systems are used in all 24 countries. The markers K, Fy^a, Hp, k, Fy^b, Jk^a, P, Glm^a, Glm^x, $G3m^b$, Gc, Jk^b, Km, Se, AcP and PGM_1 in order of decreasing popularity are used in 22 to 13 countries; Lu^a, Lu^b, Tf, and HLA in 12 to 10 countries; ADA, AK, and Xg^a, in 9 to 6 countries; GPT, C3, PGD and Ag in 4 or less countries. Under special conditions, other genetic markers have also been used in paternity testing, such as S hemoglobin for Blacks and albumin for Amerinds.

FIGURE 2

Number of Countries in Which the Different Genetic Markers Are Used for Paternity Testing*

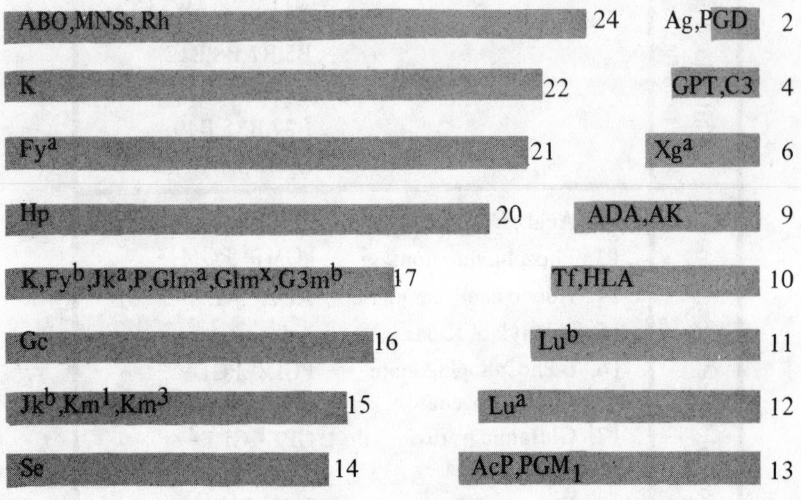

*Laboratories using EsD and other markers were not included in the survey

Figure 3 illustrates the number of systems used in each country. In Austria and West Germany, 22 and 21 systems are used respectively; in Japan and Switzerland, 19 systems; in Belgium, France and East Germany, 18 systems. Only in 6 countries, less than 10 systems are used and in 2 countries, less than 8 systems.

It should be mentioned that this type of survey is rather selective and may not represent the true picture in each country. Nevertheless, since all the respondents are well-known experts in paternity testing, it can be assumed that their criteria for the selection of these genetic markers have been carefully considered. Hence, their answers represent a general up-to-date overall view on this subject.

FIGURE 3

Number of Blood Group Systems Used for Paternity Testing In Different Countries*

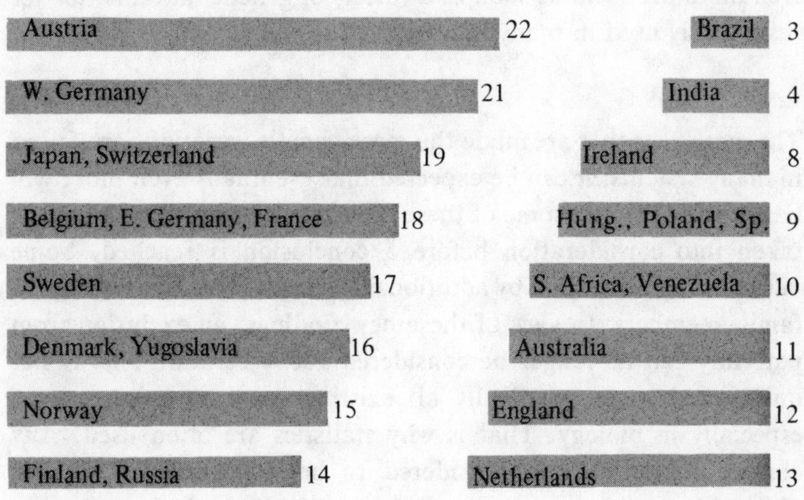

*Based upon responses of a few experts from each country

Evaluation of Test Results

Customarily, the results of a paternity test are reported as "the alleged father is excluded from paternity" or "the alleged father is not excluded from paternity." This seems simple and straightforward and has been generally accepted. However, with progress in science and the increasing demands for better service, this type of reporting may be challenged in at least three aspects.

Reliability of Exclusion From Paternity

PITFALLS

Were blood specimens drawn from the right parties? Were the tests done properly with reliable reagents, suitable instruments, appropriate techniques and by experienced technologists? Were results of the tests correctly interpreted? Has the validity of an indirect exclusion been seriously and carefully examined? Have all the known genetic variations, ethnic differences, as well as physiologic and pathologic conditions been taken into consideration? If any of these aspects are neglected, a true father may be relieved from supporting his child, a true parent may be denied his child, or an immigrant child may be barred from reunion with its true parents. These considerations will become even more pertinent as soon as a variety of genetic markers not yet customarily used in many laboratories are included.

LIMITATIONS

The more tests that are made the more genetic variations are found in many systems; it can be expected that eventually even more will be found. Although some of these variants are rare, they should be taken into consideration before a conclusion is reached. Some variants can be verified by additional testing, others by studying the family members. In view of these new findings, an exclusion from paternity can no longer be considered 100% certain. This is not unexpected since practically all existing rules have exceptions, especially in biology. That is why statistics are often used. Any chance above 95% is considered to be significant. A similar philosophy may have to be applied in paternity exclusion cases, in which the change is usually above 99%. Thus, an appropriate report should read: "According to the current knowledge and our tests results, Mr. X is excluded from paternity of x."

CRITERIA

Direct exclusion by one genetic marker is usually sufficient for an exclusion judgment, provided that all the above pitfalls and limitations have been taken into consideration.

Indirect exclusion by one genetic marker should be verified by additional tests or substantiated by other genetic markers.

In case of any doubt, tests should be repeated by different technologists with different lots of reagents and, preferably, in different laboratories. Should there be any discrepancy in test results from two laboratories, a third laboratory may be asked to resolve the difference. In several European countries, centers for paternity studies have been established to assure the quality and reliability of the test results.

Confidence in a Non-Exclusion

What is the chance of excluding a man wrongfully named as father through tests used in a particular laboratory? The confidence in a non-exclusion depends on the number and the type of genetic markers used in the tests (See Table VI), as well as on the genetic pattern of a mother-child combination (See Table VII).

TABLE VI

Chances for Exclusion of Paternity In 25 Blood Group Systems*

Systems or Genetic Markers	Chances in % Individual	Chances in % Cumulative	Systems or Genetic Markers	Chances in % Individual	Chances in % Cumulative
1. HLA(21 markers)	76	76	14. C3(1,2)	13.8	98.69
2. M,N,S,s	32	84.7	15. EsD(1,2)	9.0	98.81
3. D,C,C^w,c,E,e	29	88.7	16. ADA(1,2)	5.8	98.88
4. AcP(A,B,C)	25	91.3	17. Km(1,3)	5.7	98.90
5. A_1,A_2,B,O	20	93	18. Xg^a	5	99.00
6. Glm^a,Glm^x,$G3m^b$	20	94.4	19. K,k	4	99.03
7. Jk^a,Jk^b	18.7	95.5	20. P_1	4	99.07
8. GPT(1,2)	18.6	96.3	21. Se	4	99.11
9. Fy^a,Fy^b	18.4	97	22. Lu^a,Lu^b	3.6	99.14
10. Hp(1,2)	18	97.5	23. AK(1,2)	3.3	99.17
11. Gc(1,2)	16	97.9	24. PGD(A,C)	2.1	99.19
12. PGM_1(1,2)	14.5	98.23	25. Tf(C,B_2,D_1)	1	99.27
13. Ag(x,y)	14.3	98.48			

*Based on gene frequencies of whites. For many genetic markers, only minor differences exist among various white populations.

TABLE VII
An Example of Chance of Exclusion for a Given Mother-Child Combination (Based on frequencies in the white population)

	Mother	Child	Chance of a Man Being Not excluded	Chance of a Man Being Excluded
	K–	K+	K+(8%)	K–(92%)
Genetic Markers	M–	M+	M+(80%)	M–(20%)
	B–	B+	B+(11%)	B–(89%)

Cumulative chance of NOX-EXCLUSION = 8% X 80% X 11% = 0.7%
Cumulative chance of EXCLUSION = 100% - 0.7% = 99.3%

With this combination, 993 innocent men in 1,000 could be excluded

CHANCE OF EXCLUSION BY THE TYPE OF GENETIC MARKERS

Each genetic marker or system of genetic markers provides different chances of exclusion as listed in Table VI. The white blood cell isoantigen system alone provides a 76% chance of exclusion. The next 13 systems provide from 32% to 13.8% chance of exclusion. By using the first 4 systems, a cumulative chance of over 90% is reached; by the first 7 systems, a 95% chance; and by all systems, a chance of 99.27%. In practice, only a limited number of laboratories presently have the capability of testing nearly all these genetic markers. The amount of involvement may not be justified by the small increase in chance of exclusion. The selection of genetic markers by various countries as illustrated in Figure 3 may serve as a practical guide. In the United States, tests with a chance of 70% of exclusion can be carried out by a number of laboratories. If demand and interest increase, the capability of conducting tests with a 90% or higher chance of exclusion could be reached in a short time.

CUMULATIVE CHANCE OF EXCLUSION

The cumulative chance of exclusion is not equal to the sum of individual chances. Its calculation is given in the following example: The MNSs system provides a 32% chance of exclusion; the ABO system, 20%; thus, 32% x 20% = 6.4% of men in a given population will be excluded by both these systems. Since a person cannot be excluded more than once, the cumulative chance of exclusion by both systems is the sum of the exclusions in both systems minus their product, *i.e.*, 32% + 20% — 6.4% = 45.6%. An alternate method of computation would be to obtain the product of non-exclusions (100% — 32%) (100% — 20%) = 54.4% and deduct it from 100% (100% — 54.4%) = 45.6%. This method is simpler if more than two systems are involved.

CHANCE OF EXCLUSION BY THE NUMBER OF GENETIC MARKERS USED

The chance of exclusion from paternity varies with the number of genetic markers used with each system (Figure 4). In the MN system, the use of 2 markers (M and N), provides an 18.7% chance; of 3 markers (M, N and S), a 23.9%; of 4 markers (M, N, S and s), a 32% chance. In the ABO system, the use of 3 markers (A, B and O), provides a 16.5% chance; of 4 markers (A_1, A_2, B and O), a 20% chance. In the Rh system, the use of 1 marker (D) provides only a 1.8% chance; of 4 markers (D, C, E and c), a 25.6%; of 6 markers (D, C, E, c, e and C^W), a 29% chance. Consequently, there are three different chances for an innocent man to be excluded from paternity: Laboratory #1, using only 6 markers, provides a 33% chance; laboratory #2, using 11 markers, a 54.7%; laboratory #3, using 14 markers, a 61.4% chance.

FIGURE 4

Three Levels of Chance of Exclusion of Paternity
According to the number of genetic markers used in each system

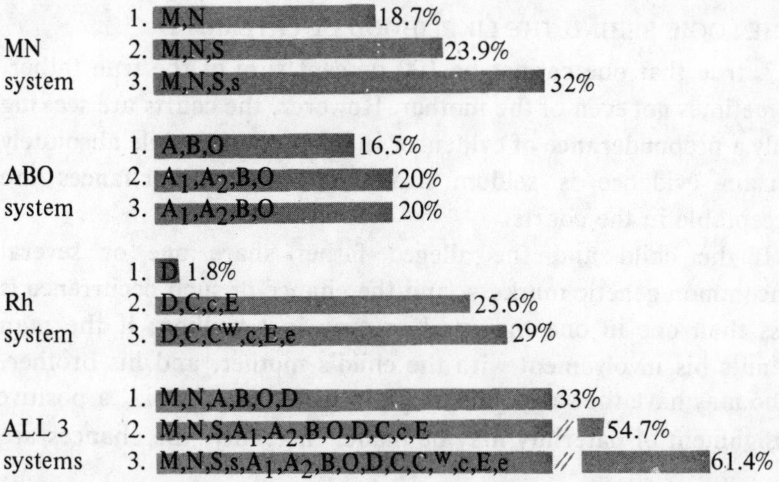

MN system	1. M,N	18.7%
	2. M,N,S	23.9%
	3. M,N,S,s	32%
ABO system	1. A,B,O	16.5%
	2. A_1,A_2,B,O	20%
	3. A_1,A_2,B,O	20%
Rh system	1. D	1.8%
	2. D,C,c,E	25.6%
	3. D,C,C^W,c,E,e	29%
ALL 3 systems	1. M,N,A,B,O,D	33%
	2. M,N,S,A_1,A_2,B,O,D,C,c,E	54.7%
	3. M,N,S,s,A_1,A_2,B,O,D,C,C^W,c,E,e	61.4%

CHANCE OF EXCLUSION FOR A GIVEN MOTHER-CHILD COMBINATION

The chance of exclusion may also depend on a given mother-child combination. (See Table VII) In this example, the mother is negative for 3 genetic markers (K, M, B), her child is positive for all of them. If the alleged father is not excluded, he must be positive for all 3 markers. The chance of finding a random man with these 3 markers is 8% x 80% x 11% = 0.7% or 7 out of 1000 persons. Thus, the cumulative chance of exclusion is 100% — 0.7% = 99.3%. This means that in this particular mother-child combination there is a 99.3% chance for the average innocent man to be excluded from paternity by the use of only 3 genetic markers. This type of combination is uncommon, but it does indicate the importance of genetic patterns of a given mother-child combination.

A PRACTICAL APPROACH

In some cases, the alleged father can be excluded by a minimal number of tests and additional tests would serve no useful purpose. In case there is no exclusion, additional tests should be done to provide at least a 70 percent chance of exclusion in order to be fair. If the man named as father or the court is not satisfied with the results, further tests can be conducted. Thus, it may be practical to adopt the three step test system, a preliminary test, a standard test and an extended test.

Likelihood of Paternity

THE LOGIC BEHIND THE LIKELIHOOD OF PATERNITY

It is true that one cannot be 100 percent sure of the true father, sometimes not even of the mother. However, the courts are seeking only a preponderance of evidence. In other words, while absolutely certain evidence is seldom available, calculated chances are acceptable in the courts.

If the child and the alleged father share one or several uncommon genetic markers, and the chance of such occurrence is less than one in one thousand or even in a million; if the man admits his involvement with the child's mother, and his brother, who may have the same genetic pattern, has an "alibi," a positive assignment of paternity may be made. In reality, the chances are usually greater than one in a thousand and can be evaluated in two ways:

1. *By The Genetic Pattern of a Given Mother-Child Combination* (*Table VII*). If the child has 3 genetic markers (K, M, B) which are absent in the mother, then the alleged father, in order not to be excluded from paternity, must have all 3 genetic markers. The chance of finding a person in the population with all 3 genetic markers is only 7 in a thousand or 1 in 143. Therefore, such an alleged father is likely to be the true father, provided there is no other stronger evidence against this assumption.

2. *By Comparison between the Alleged Father and a Random Man for Being the True Father.* A comparison is made between the chances of the sperms of the alleged father and a random man carrying the genetic markers required for being the true father in a given mother-child combination. For this type of calculation, one must know the frequencies of genes and genotypes of each genetic marker. (See Table III for an example of gene frequencies).

The term gene frequency means the chance of finding sperms or ova carrying a specific gene in a given population, such as 0.285, 0.079 and 0.636 for *A, B* and *O* genes, respectively, for Caucasians. That is, out of 100 random men in the population, sperms or ova of 28 carry *A*, 8 carry *B* and 64 carry *O*. The calculation of gene frequencies is beyond the scope of this report.

The genotype frequencies are derived from the gene frequencies. For instance, frequency of genotype *AA* is the product of 0.285 (*A*) x 0.285(*A*) = 0.081 (8.1%). The frequency of *AO* is the product of 0.285(*A*) x 0.636(*O*) x 2 = 0.362 (36.2%). The phenotype frequency of A (determined by direct examination) is the sum of frequencies of *AA* and *AO* which is 0.088 + 0.362 = 0.443 (44.3%). Among the persons of group A, 0.081/0.443 = 18% are AA and 0.362/0.443 = 82% are AO.

By knowing the gene and genotype frequencies of A, the chance of a man's being the father of a child of group A can be estimated under two situations. The accused man could be either the true father who must have the genetic marker required for a given mother-child combination (A) or a random man who may happen to have the required genetic marker (A). Out of 100 random white men, the sperm of 28 would carry A and could be the father of a child of group

A, *i.e.*, the gene frequency of A represents the chance of a random man. On the other hand, if the mother is *O*, 100% of the children must be group A if the father's genotype is *AA*, whereas only 50% of his children would be group A if he is *AO*. Since 18% of group A persons are *AA* and 82% are *AO*, the chance of a group A person being the true father is 100% x 18% + 50% x 82% = 18% + 41% = 59%. Thus, an unexcluded man of group A has a chance of being the true father of a group A child in the ratio of 59%:28%, or approximately 2 times greater than the chance of a random man. A similar type of estimation can be applied to genetic markers other than A.

Figure 5 shows an example of the estimation of likelihood of paternity based on the same mother-child combination as shown in Table VII. The child has genetic markers K, M and B which are absent in the mother and must come from the true father. If the alleged father is not excluded, he must have all three genetic markers. The chance of a man who is positive for K, M and B to transmit them to a child is 18.7% while the chance of a random man

FIGURE 5

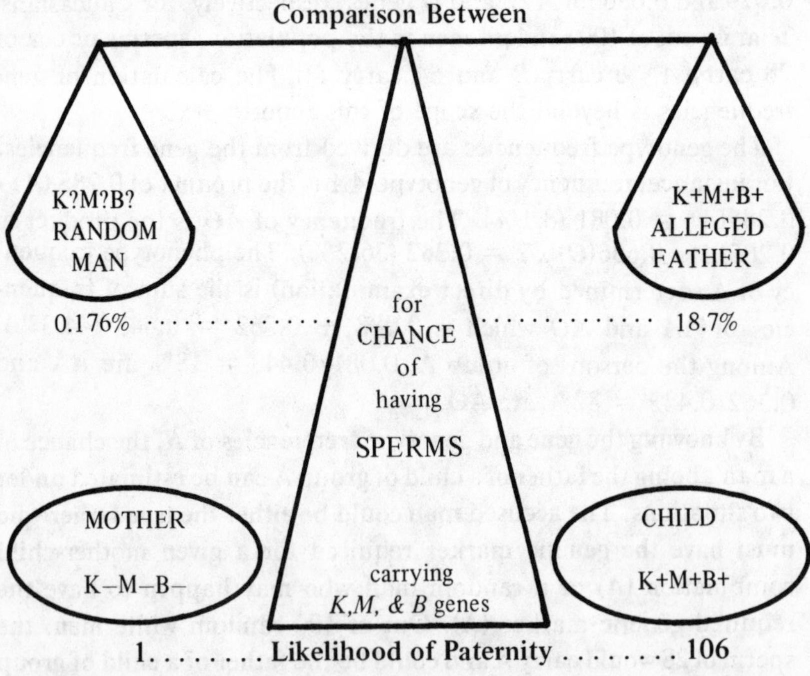

of the same population is 0.176%. Thus, the chance of the alleged father is 18.7%:0.176% or 106 times greater than that of a random man. It is unlikely that during the conception period, another 105 men were involved with the mother of the child. Statistically, odds of 20 to 1 or 95% or better are considered to be significant. Again, other evidence should be taken into consideration.

The second type of estimation not only considers all three parties involved, but also uses the frequencies of genes which are obviously preferable to that of phenotypes as discussed earlier. When two or more men are involved, a similar estimation can be used.

Comments

To protect the right of a man wrongly named as father, the confidence in non-exclusion of paternity should be adequately supported by the number and type of tests used. In the United States it would not be difficult at present to perform tests providing a 70% chance of exclusion. As demands and interest increase, it may be possible in the near future to use tests providing more than a 90% chance of exclusion.

To insure that all tests are carried out correctly and that the test results are properly interpreted, paternity testing should be performed only in laboratories where experts are available.

To make sure that the true father fulfills his obligation to support his child, thus reducing the burden to taxpayers, estimation of likelihood of paternity could provide the courts with a valuable means for arriving at a valid judgment.

Additional research and development in paternity testing are definitely needed: 1) to improve the reliability and reproducibility of the existing tests; 2) to introduce additional genetic markers which may be more valuable than those now in use; 3) to establish the frequencies of different genetic markers in various ethnic groups in the United States and hence to achieve greater precision in statistical evaluation.

Test Tube Babies: Proposals for Legal Regulation of New Methods of Human Conception and Prenatal Development

MARY ANN B. OAKLEY*

Within the present competence of medical science there are three controversial methods of altering the natural process of human conception. One of these methods, artificial insemination,[1] was used with horses as early as the fourteenth century[2] and has become relatively common in this century[3] as a means of enabling women whose husbands are sterile to bear children.[4] The process of *in vitro* fertilization and embryo transfer, although still in the experimental stage, is on the verge of being employed in human beings.[5] Cloning,[6] closely related to embryo transfer in terms of some of the problems it presents, involves far more complex legal and ethical considerations; it has not yet been tested in higher forms of animal life.[7]

---

*Member, Georgia Bar.

1. Artificial insemination is "the introduction of the male semen into the vagina for the sake of procreation by any means other than through the act of copulation." Guttmacher, *Artificial Insemination,* 18 De Paul L. Rev. 566 (1969). This article contains an accurate discussion of the medical aspects of artificial insemination. *See also* McLaren, *Biological Aspects of AID,* in CIBA Foundation, Symposium on Legal and Other Aspects of Artificial Insemination by Donor (A.I.D.) and Embryo Transfer, 3 (1972).

2. Guttmacher, *supra* note 1, at 566. Warring Arab tribes supposedly artificially inseminated the mares of their enemies by inserting into the animals' vaginas, cotton soaked in the semen of inferior stallions. *Id.*

3. *Id.* at 567. Dr. Guttmacher estimates that seven to ten thousand babies are born each year in the United States alone as the result of artificial insemination. The procedure is also common in Japan and England.

4. Other medical problems possibly indicating artificial insemination include impotence, malformation of the penis, and the possibility of genetic defect.

5. Edwards and Steptoe, *Biological Aspects of Embryo Transfer,* in CIBA Foundation, Symposium on Legal and Other Aspects of Artificial Insemination by Donor (A.I.D.) and Embryo Transfer, 11 (1972). *See also* The Washington Post, 28-C (Sept. 1, 1973), for an account of the efforts of Australian doctors to transplant an embryo fertilized *in vitro*. The embryo was aborted after nine days.

6. Cloning is the process of obtaining multiple nuclei from somatic (non-germ) cells and placing a single nucleus into an enucleated ovum. The zygote and subsequent animal would have genetic characteristics identical to those of the donor of the somatic cells.

7. *See* Edwards and Steptoe, *supra* note 5, at 16. In spite of recent "claims" that mammals, even human beings, have been reproduced through cloning, there is no scientific

To many people these processes have an Orwellian connotation;[8] the reaction is to call for at least a temporary ban on all such research[9] and for legislation forbidding these methods.[10] Other people, concerned with overpopulation and its resulting problems, question the necessity or even usefulness of such research.[11] Because the research will probably continue,[12] it seems logical to insure that it is properly controlled and that the legal rights of all persons involved are carefully defined. This paper suggests guidelines, based on current law and legal principles, for defining the legal position of the husband, wife, donor(s), physician, and resulting child in each of these procedures, and to examine the implications of further research. Because artificial insemination has already been the subject of lawsuits and legislation, this study may serve as a model for considering its legal problems and as a basis for analyzing the other two methods from a legal standpoint.

Artificial Insemination and the Law

There are two types of artificial insemination, homologous (AIH), which involves the husband's semen, and heterologous (AID), which involves semen from one or more donors.[13] The former method poses no *legal* problems, because the resulting child is the biological offspring of both husband and wife.[14] There are no ques-

---

evidence that such a development has taken place. *See, e.g.,* Culliton, *Cloning Caper Makes It to the Halls of Congress,* 200 SCIENCE 1250 (June 16, 1978). For an excellent discussion of cloning written for the layperson, *see* Bylinsky, *The Cloning Era Is Almost Here,* FORTUNE (June 19, 1978), 100.

8. "All children were to be begotten by artificial insemination (*artsem,* it was called in Newspeak) and brought up in public institutions." G. ORWELL, 1984, 57 (Signet, ed. 1960).

9. *See, e.g.,* Lappé, *Ethics of In-vitro Fertilization: Risk-Taking for the Unborn,* 2 THE HASTINGS CENTER REPORT 1 (Feb. 1972); H.R. 7724, 93d Cong. 2d Sess. (1974), as amended by the Senate.

10. A resolution introduced into the Ohio legislature in 1955 would have fined those involved in artificial insemination $500 and sentenced them to one to five years' imprisonment. Ohio S. 93 (1955). The resolution was not enacted.

11. Edwards and Steptoe, *supra* note 5, at 16 reject such a belief.

12. *Id.;* McLaren, *supra* note 1, at 8. *See also* note 7, *supra.*

13. AID is used when the husband is totally infertile or carries a known hereditary disease, such as hemophilia. *Id.* at 4. In the United States and Great Britian, 12% of married couples have an infertility problem. In 10-15% of these cases, the husband is solely responsible. *Id.*

14. There is one speculative legal problem, which could arise because it is now technically possible to store semen in sperm banks for many months before using it in an artificial insemination procedure. *See* McLaren, *supra* note 1, at 5-6. If a woman should choose to bear a child by her already deceased husband, whose sperm was frozen before his death, there may be a Rule against Perpetuities problem. The Rule against Perpetuities requires that an interest vest not later than twenty-one years after a life in being at the creation of the interest. Leach, *Perpetuities in a Nutshell,* 51 HARV. L. REV. 638 (1938). However, because sperm

tions of legitimacy. AID, on the other hand, has presented a variety of legal problems since the first case arose fifty years ago.

This early Canadian case[15] held that AID was adulterous, but a close reading of the opinion reveals judicial skepticism that there had been artificial insemination rather than normal sexual intercourse.[16] An unpublished lower court decision[17] in Illinois in 1945 indicated that AID itself would not have been considered adulterous, but the judge refused to accept the wife's statement that she had no sexual contact with the father of the child. A later unreported Illinois lower court decision held that AID was adulterous.[18] The only other court to discuss the relationship of AID to adultery considered the question at length and presented a well-reasoned decision[19] that is much more in line with modern thinking. Under

---

banks are not designed to delay vesting of interests or taking of assets, the purpose is not contrary to the Rule against Perpetuities and the method of conception should not prevent any such interest from vesting. *See* Smith, *Through a Test Tube Darkly: Artificial Insemination and the Law,* 67 MICH. L. REV. 127, 142 (1968). Thies, *A Look to the Future: Property Rights and the Posthumously Conceived Child,* 110 TRUSTS & ESTATES 922 (1971), suggests a Uniform Rights for the Posthumously Conceived Child Act. *See also* VT. STAT. ANN. tit. 27, § 501 (1967). Most states now apply a presumption that a child is legitimate only to one born within three hundred days after the death of the husband or divorce.

15. Orford v. Orford, 49 Ont. L.R. 15, 58 D.L.R. 251 (1921). The case arose from an action for alimony. The plaintiff had come from England to Canada, where she met her husband. After they married, they went to England. A few months later the husband returned to Canada without having consummated the marriage, because the plaintiff experienced great pain (due to a retroflexed uterus) when attempting sexual intercourse. For six years the couple remained apart; when the plaintiff then returned to Canada and the defendant refused to have her as his wife, she sued for alimony. Plaintiff admitted having given birth to a child while she was in England. She had consulted with a physician to find a cure for her retroflexed uterus. The physician suggested surgery, but plaintiff contended that her husband would not give the necessary consent. Because childbirth was the alternative corrective process, she decided to have a baby. She alleged that her neighbor, to whom she told the story, volunteered to be the donor for artificial insemination if she would permit him to adopt the child. She went to the neighbor's flat, where an unnamed physician allegedly anesthetized her. When she awoke, the neighbor informed her that she had been artificially inseminated by his semen. Later, when the same process was repeated, she became pregnant.

16. The judge said:

> [M]y conclusion upon the facts . . . is that her story as to the "artificial insemination" is not to be believed. . . .
>
> I find as a fact that the plaintiff was guilty of adultery in that she had sexual intercourse in the ordinary way with Hodgkinson in the month of May, 1918. . . . [F]rom some time in the latter part of 1917 . . . she had entered upon a course of conduct with Hodgkinson which, if all the facts were known (and I feel that she has failed to disclose them all) would establish that she had become Hodgkinson's mistress.

58 D.L.R. at 255.

17. Hoch v. Hoch, No. 44-C-8307, Cir. Ct. Cook County, Ill. (1945). *See* TIME, Feb. 26, 1945, at 58.

18. Doornbos v. Doornbos, 23 U.S.L.W. 2308 (Super. Ct. Cook County, Ill., Dec. 13, 1954), *appeal dismissed on procedural grounds*, 12 Ill. App. 2d 473, 139 N.E.2d 844 (1956). The husband had consented to AID.

19. MacLennan v. MacLennan, [1958] Sess. Cas. 105, [1958] Scots L.T.R. 12. The hus-

the definition of adultery in *MacLennan v. MacLennan,*[20] it seems unlikely that a present-day court would hold AID adulterous. In fact, courts might have done so in the past since adultery was one of the few acceptable grounds for divorce.[21] Because there have been no criminal prosecutions for AID as adultery in this country,[22] the problem should no longer arise in the courts. The far more critical question is the status of the child conceived as the result of AID.

In those cases in which AID was held an adulterous act, the resulting child was illegitimate. The question of illegitimacy has also arisen apart from any discussion of adultery. A series of such cases in New York began in 1948 with the lower court decision in *Strnad v. Strnad,*[23] a custody battle between the former husband and wife. The husband, who had consented to the artificial insemination of his wife, was held by the court to have "potentially adopted" or "semi-adopted" the child.[24] Thus, he was to be accorded "the same rights as those acquired by a foster parent who has formally adopted a child."[25] The court granted the husband visitation privileges and held that the child was not illegitimate.[26]

The next New York case[27] was a *habeas corpus* proceeding in which the father sought a continuation of custody and visitation rights granted him under a separation agreement with his former wife; the agreement had later been incorporated into a Nevada di-

band sought a divorce on grounds of adultery. The wife claimed that her child was born as the result of AID, to which her husband had never consented.

20. The court defined "adultery" as follows:

> 1. For adultery to be committed there must be the two parties physically present and engaging in the sexual act at the same time. 2. To constitute the sexual act there must be an act of union involving some degree of penetration of the female organ by the male organ. 3. It is not a necessary concomitant of adultery that male seed should be deposited in the female's ovum. 4. The placing of the male seed in the female ovum need not necessarily result from the sexual act, and if it does not, but is placed there by some other means there is no sexual intercourse.

[1958] Sess. Cas. at 113.

21. Such judicial reasoning is anachronistic in this age of no-fault divorce.

22. For a discussion of an Italian case of criminal prosecution for adultery for artificial insemination, see Battaglini, *Artificial Insemination and Adultery in a Recent Italian Trial,* 1961 CRIM. L. REV. at 765. Roman Catholic opposition to artificial insemination is strong. *See* Guttmacher, *supra* note 1, at 578-79.

23. 190 Misc. 786, 78 N.Y.S.2d 390 (Sup. Ct. 1948).

24. 78 N.Y.S.2d at 391.

25. *Id.* at 391-92.

26. "[T]he situation is no different than that pertaining in the case of a child born out of wedlock who by law is made legitimate upon the marriage of the interested parties." *Id.* at 392.

27. People ex rel. Abajian v. Dennett, 15 Misc. 2d 260, 134 N.Y.S.2d 178 (Sup. Ct. 1958).

vorce decree. Everything had been quite satisfactory until the mother remarried and refused to allow her ex-husband to see the children. When he filed the *habeas corpus* action, she, for the first time, alleged that the children were conceived by artificial insemination.[28] The court found that the stipulations of the separation agreement estopped the mother from raising the matter of AID because of potential detriment to the children.[29]

In 1963 a New York court for the first time held that an AID child was illegitimate. In *Gursky v. Gursky*[30] the court found that, even though the husband had consented in writing to AID, "any child whose natural father was not married to its mother irrespective of the marital status of the mother" was illegitimate.[31] Because adoption could be accomplished only in compliance with legal procedures, the court found that the *Strnad* decision could not be logically sustained.[32] Even though the child was held illegitimate, however, the court held the husband liable for its support, on the basis of his consent to AID.[33]

In 1973 another New York court held[34] that the father of a child born after AID with his consent is a "parent" whose consent is necessary for the adoption of that child by the mother's second husband. Refusing to decide the case on the basis of the strong presumption of legitimacy of children born during a marriage,[35] the court rejected *Gursky* as "not persuasive" and as "the only published decision which flatly holds that AID children are illegitimate."[36] The court then focused on the real issue: the child, not the parents, deserved protection. "It serves no purpose what-

28. 134 N.Y.S.2d at 181-82.

29. *Id.* at 182-83. The agreement referred to "issue of the marriage," "the two children of the marriage," "the son," and "the daughter." *Id.* at 180.

30. 39 Misc. 2d 1083, 242 N.Y.S.2d 406 (Sup. Ct. 1963).

31. 242 N.Y.S.2d at 409.

32. *Id.* at 411.

33. *Id.* at 412. It is not clear whether the court found an implied contract to support or applied equitable estoppel.

Gursky v. Gursky was followed in a later case in which a wife moved for temporary alimony and child support. The husband had consented in writing to AID before the birth of both children. The court paid scant heed to the husband's argument that the children were illegitimate and ordered him to pay support. Anonymous v. Anonymous, 41 Misc. 2d 886, 246 N.Y.S.2d 835 (Sup. Ct. 1964).

34. In re Adoption of Anonymous, 74 Misc. 2d 99, 345 N.Y.S.2d 430 (Surrogate's Ct. 1973).

35. 345 N.Y.S.2d at 434. The court preferred to decide the case on the legal issue presented.

36. *Id.*

soever to stigmatize the AID child. . . ."[37] Any child whose parents, during their valid marriage, consented to AID is just as legitimate as a naturally conceived child of that same marriage.[38]

The New York court in this case was influenced by the only decision of an appellate court relating to artificial insemination by a donor, the California criminal case of *People v. Sorensen*.[39] Defendant, by written agreement, consented to the artificial insemination of his wife after fifteen years of childless marriage. After a subsequent divorce, Mrs. Sorensen became ill and unable to work; the district attorney of her county demanded child support payments from defendant. In the ensuing criminal prosecution for nonsupport, Mr. Sorensen pleaded that he was not the father of the child. The California Supreme Court, finding no "natural father," sought the "lawful father."[40] The court said that, although both legitimate and illegitimate minors have a statutory right to support from their parents, primarily the father,[41] "no valid public purpose is served by stigmatizing an artificially conceived child as illegitimate."[42] The court then held defendant to be the lawful father, liable for support of the child.[43]

What California has accomplished judicially, other states have done by statute. Georgia, in 1964, became the first state with a statute legitimizing children conceived by artificial insemination—if both husband and wife consent in writing.[44] Oklahoma[45] passed a similar law in 1967, with an additional requirement that the written consent be filed "under the same rules as adoption papers," not open to the general public.[46] Arkansas law provides that an AID child be treated as the child of its mother and her consenting husband for purposes of intestacy. Consent, under the statute, is presumed unless there is clear and convincing evidence to

---

37. *Id.* at 435.
38. *Id.* at 435-36.
39. 68 Cal. 2d 285, 66 Cal. Rptr. 7, 437 P.2d 495 (1968).
40. 437 P.2d at 498. The court pointed out that, due to sperm banks and the use of frozen semen, the donor could be dead before the artificial insemination took place.
41. *Id.* at 501.
42. *Id.*
43. *Id.* at 501-502.
44. GA. CODE ANN. tit. 74 § 101.1 (1968). The procedure must be done by a licensed physician, who is civilly liable for negligence. *See also* tit. 74, § 9904, providing that anyone other than a physician who performs artificial insemination shall be guilty of a felony.
45. OKLA. STAT. ANN. tit. 10, §§ 551-53 (1973 supp.).
46. *Id.* at § 553. *Accord.* KAN. STAT. ANN. tit. 23 §§ 128-130 (1969 supp.).

the contrary.[47] After the *Sorensen* case, California passed a law legitimizing an AID child when the husband has consented to AID in writing.[48] Recently New York has joined these other states: If a married couple consents in writing to artificial insemination and a doctor certifies the procedure, the child is deemed legitimate for all purposes.[49]

AID: Proposals for Regulation

The problems arising from artificial insemination can be resolved by following the lead of those states which have statutorily legitimized AID children. Any such statute should insure proper medical procedures as well as the legal protection of all parties involved. First, a statute should provide that any child born after the artificial insemination of its mother is the legitimate child of that mother and her husband.[50] To protect the innocent child, this status should be accorded whether or not the husband consented. To enforce the requirement that both husband and wife consent *in writing* to AID,[51] a physician or anyone else who performs AID without the written

47. ARK. STAT. ANN. tit. 61, § 141(c) (1971). The usual questions of inheritance rights and intestacy which occur with any legitimate child may arise in an AID case in a state in which an AID child is considered illegitimate. At common law there could be no inheritance through ties of illegitimacy. Most states provide by statute that an illegitimate child may inherit from his mother and, in the majority of states, from her kindred. T. ATKINSON, HANDBOOK OF THE LAW OF WILLS, § 22 (2d ed. 1953). Although the law in most states on AID children is still uncertain, if an AID child is considered legitimate there will be no problem. No case has been reported which involved inheritance rights, probably because most AID births are known only to the parents and their physician. Certainly all parents of AID children should have wills carefully drafted to prevent probate difficulties in the event the fact of AID becomes known. There may also be questions of what rights the child has to inherit from the donor, or the donor from the child. This situation would never arise if the identity of the donor remains secret—a good argument for complete anonymity. Most donors contribute semen on several occasions. To protect all parties, the donor should sign a waiver of any rights to the child(ren) resulting from his semen.

48. WEST'S ANN. CAL. CODES, CIV. CODE § 216 (1974 Supp.).

49. N.Y. DOM. REL. LAW § 73 (McKinney Supp. 1974). *See also* MD. ANN. CODE, art. 43 § 556 E (Supp. 1974); N.C. GEN. STAT. § 49 A-1 (Supp. 1974).

50. If the mother is unmarried, the usual stigma of illegitimacy would apply. Because the child has no control over what his parents do or who they are, *all* children should be considered legitimate, for legal purposes at the very least. If the father is unknown, the mother alone should have the duty to support. If the father is known, the duty to support the child should be a joint one. *See* De Stoop, *Human Artificial Insemination and the Law in Australia*, 50 AUST. L. J. 298, 304 (June, 1976).

51. AID without consent, while not adulterous, should certainly be grounds for divorce if the husband so desires. Filing the consent form, as in adoption, is required in some states. *See* notes 45-46, *supra*, and accompanying text. This procedure insures preservation of the consent form but curtails the parents' ability to keep the procedure secret.

consent of both spouses should be civilly liable to the nonconsenting spouse.[52]

In order to protect the privacy of all parties, hospital records and birth certificates should name the mother's husband as the father of the child.[53] Furthermore, the donor should be anonymous to both husband and wife, and the recipient couple to the donor.[54] The donor, who should have no known genetic defects should have a complete physical examination not more than one week before donating his semen. Violation of the last safeguard should be *prima facie* evidence of malpractice on the part of the physician who performs AID, in the event that such negligence causes any harm to the mother or the child.[55]

In Vitro Fertilization, Embryo Transfer and the Law

Legal clarification of artificial insemination is a necessary prerequisite for regulating *in vitro* fertilization and embryo transplanting. *In vitro* fertilization basically involves the union of the sperm with the ovum outside of the body.[56] At some stage, the embryo would be transplanted into the female uterus, where it would presumably develop and be born in the usual way at the usual time. The potential variations in this process pose different legal problems.

When the husband provides the sperm and the wife the ovum,[57] the legal situation is analogous to that of homologous artificial insemination: the resulting child is the biological offspring of both husband and wife. This process has been compared with the procedure for facilitating birth by Caesarian section,[58] and was originally

52. *See* Comment, *Artificial Insemination and the Law*, 1968 Ill. L.F. 203, 229 (1968), suggesting that the doctor who performs AID without written consent be chargeable with a misdemeanor.

53. Guttmacher, *supra* note 1, at 571.

54. *Id.* at 570.

55. Section 21.03(b) of the City of New York Health Code (1959) provides that both donor and recipient in AID must have compatible Rh factors. Section 21.05 prohibits donors with venereal diseases, tuberculosis, and congenital disease or defect. Only a licensed physician may perform AID, § 21.01.

56. Edwards and Steptoe, *supra* note 5, at 11, 13.

57. *Id.* at 11, emphasizing that

> embryo transfer will be used almost exclusively for many years to come to alleviate infertility within a marriage, by giving husbands and wives a chance to have their own children. Relatively few women need an oocyte or embryo from a donor to alleviate their infertility; such treatment will be limited to only a small number of patients.

58. Stone, *English Law in Relation to AID and Embryo Transfer*, in CIBA Foundation,

designed to make possible birth of children to married couples in which the wife suffers from a disability such as a tubal occlusion.[59]

A second situation arises if a donor provides the sperm used in the *in vitro* fertilization. Because this situation is so similar to heterologous artificial insemination, the same laws and legal principles should determine the rights of the parties.[60] If the ovum also comes from a donor, or if the ovum comes from a donor and the sperm from the husband, the problem becomes more complex. Never before has there been any question as to the identity of the mother of a child when it is born, because birth itself is conclusive proof of motherhood. When the ovum comes from another source, is fertilized and transferred into the wife's uterus, the question becomes whether contributing the germ cell or carrying and giving birth to the child entitles a woman to claim motherhood. In order to avoid all the problems which have been raised with AID, a state should include within its regulation of embryo transfer a provision that the wife is deemed to be the mother of the child for all legal purposes.[61]

The most difficult situation arises when, for health or other reasons, a woman is unable to bear a child and still desires to have biological offspring. In this hypothetical situation, the wife's ovum would be fertilized by the husband's sperm *in vitro* and the embryo transferred[62] into a third party, or "hostess," who would carry the child for the duration of the pregnancy and then give birth to it. The resulting infant would be biologically the offspring of the woman who contributed the ovum and gestationally the offspring of the "hostess" who bore it. Such a situation may be called "embryonic adoption." To protect the rights of all parties involved, clear regulations need to be established in every state. First, all parties must consent in writing to the procedure. The "hostess" must

---

Symposium on Legal and Other Aspects of Artificial Insemination by Donor (A.I.D.) and Embryo Transfer 69, 73 (1972).

59. *Id.* at 73. Lappé, *supra* note 9, at 2 observes that the need for *in vitro* fertilization and embryo transfer "is in no way diminished, as some have insisted, by the fact that most causes of female infertility stem from venereal infections."

60. *See* notes 50-54, *supra,* and accompanying text.

61. The donor of the ovum, like the donor of semen, should be anonymous and should relinquish all rights to the resulting child. *See* notes 53-54, *supra,* and accompanying text.

62. Embryo transfer could "almost certainly" be performed through the cervix without surgery, probably with 8- or 16-celled embryos, the size at which the embryo usually attaches to the human uterus. Edwards and Steptoe, *supra* note 5, at 15.

agree[63] that the baby will be legally the child of the couple who contribute the germ cells and that her rights to the child will terminate at birth. To protect her health, it must be clearly established that, should the pregnancy in any way endanger the "hostess" physically, an abortion will be performed immediately.[64] To protect the privacy of all concerned, especially that of the resulting child, the "hostess" should remain anonymous to the couple and the couple anonymous to the "hostess." As in the case of AID, only the physician would know the identity of all parties concerned. A new birth certificate would be issued with the names of the biological parents of the child; any hospital records and the original birth certificate with the name of the "hostess" on them should be sealed by law and available only upon a court order.[65]

The variances from the common conception of parenthood in these processes are similar to those of adoption. The couple who rear the child, care for him, support him, and who are legally responsible for him, are his legitimate parents. As in other similar situations, no stigma of illegitimacy should ever attach to the child. For his future welfare, the truth about his birth should be private and revealed to him only by his parents, if and as they wish. It is especially important, therefore, that court challenges similar to those in AID cases, which could have only detrimental effects on the child, be avoided with *in vitro* fertilization and embryo transplanting. Each state should act to legitimize these children *before* human embryo transfer becomes a reality rather than merely an experimental possibility.

Another process related to *in vitro* fertilization and embryo trans-

---

63. This agreement could be in the form of a legal waiver, or a contract between the "hostess" and the physician with the recipient couple as third-party beneficiaries. Any direct contract between the "hostess" and the recipient couple would destroy anonymity.

64. Another problem arises if the "hostess" changes her mind during early pregnancy and wants an abortion. Abortion during the first trimester is a matter to be determined only by the pregnant woman and her physician, Doe v. Bolton, 410 U.S. 179 (1973); Roe v. Wade, 410 U.S. 113 (1973). Only during a period roughly corresponding to the last trimester can the state interfere to protect what is then a potentially viable fetus. *Id.* Even the right of the father of the unborn child is, in this process, uncertain. In a Florida case, the United States Supreme Court affirmed a lower court ruling which held unconstitutional a state requirement for "spousal or parental consent" before an abortion is performed. Gerstein v. Coe, 428 U.S. 901 (1976). It might therefore be difficult for the would-be recipient couple to interfere with such a step by the "hostess" during the first month of pregnancy. There would be, of course, a possible action for damages for breach of contract.

65. This procedure is commonly used for the adoption of a child.

fer is cloning, the method by which the nucleus is removed from an individual's somatic cell and put into an enucleated egg. The resulting child should have the same genetic content as the donor of the nucleus.[66] Therefore, it is theoretically possible for a person to repeat himself many times over. Without discussing the problems of how to regulate who may donate these nuclei, it is important to note that the resulting child should be legitimized and his legal parents clearly defined. One reasonable suggestion is that, of a couple desiring to have a child, the wife who receives the transferred embryo, carries the child throughout pregnancy and gives birth to it is the legal mother; her husband would be the legal father. As in other donor situations, privacy should be protected insofar as is possible. One donor would be avoided if the mother could furnish the enucleated egg.[67]

Risks and Legal Liability

One potential problem with any of the processes discussed above is the liability of the physician involved if the child is born defective in any manner. In light of the knowledge presently available, usual standards of medical malpractice should be applicable. The problem of causation is complicated by the fact that a certain number of conventional births result in defective infants[68] and that it might be difficult to prove that the extraordinary process itself is responsible. If the parents have been informed in advance, in writing, of the risks involved and have consented in an informed manner[69] to the

---

66. *See* Edwards and Steptoe, *supra* note 5, at 16.

67. If either parent were to furnish the somatic cell nucleus, the child would be a genetic copy of that particular parent. Because environment also plays a part in the development of a person, the child and his parent would probably not be exactly the same. One can only speculate on the psychological implications if a human being, because he is a genetic copy of some other human being, loses much of his uniqueness.

68. About 2-3% of all children have defects readily identifiable at birth; if a group of children is followed for the subsequent 10 years, about 10% are eventually determined to be defective. *See, e.g.*, Leck *et al.*, *The Incidence of Malformations in Birmingham, England, 1950-1959,* 1 TERATOLOGY 263 (1968).

69. "Informed consent" is a major problem itself. Recently, it has been suggested that persons who consent to medical procedures or experimentation do so by a two-step procedure:

> The first part would be the current consent form—a statement of purposes, procedures, risks, discomforts, alternatives and rights. The second would be a short list of questions about the information contained in the first part, and its purpose would be to check how well the subject understood the information expressed there.

Miller and Willner, *The Two-Part Consent Form*, 290 NEW ENG. J. MED. 964, 965 (1974).

procedure in face of those risks, the physician has a stronger defense.[70]

To protect the physician more fully, each state should pass a law with a clause similar to that of Georgia's artificial insemination statute:

> [T]he written authorization provided herein shall not relieve any physician or surgeon from any civil liability arising from his or her own negligent administration or performance of [this procedure].[71]

By implication, the physician is relieved of liability for non-negligent defects.

The parents (as well as the physician) are potentially liable—morally if not legally—for consenting to a procedure which might entail an increased risk to their unborn child. Of course, parents consent to risks in relation to the "normal" birth process,[72] and researchers are already claiming that there are no increased risks of defects merely because the child results from *in vitro* fertilization and embryo transfer.[73] Because some of the possible defects, either

---

70. Many physicians would not be fortunate enough to escape on a technicality as did the doctor sued in Gleitman v. Cosgrove, 49 N.J. 22, 227 A.2d 689 (1967). The physician advised a woman who had had rubella (German measles) during the first month of her pregnancy that the disease "would have no effect at all on her child." Although the doctor knew that the risk of damage from rubella at this stage of pregnancy is about 25%, he did not disclose such information because he believed it unjust to abort three healthy fetuses in order to dispose of one defective one. The New Jersey court held that neither the parents nor the severely defective child could sue, because the mother testified that she would have obtained an abortion had she known of the risk. The court concluded that an abortion would have violated the "preciousness of human life." Because the child would not have been born at all had his mother had an abortion, he was foreclosed from suing. The court, rather than grapple with the informed consent problem, refused to find that the physician's conduct was the cause of the child's condition.

71. GA. CODE ANN., tit. 74 § 101.1(c) (1968).

72. *See* Lappé, *supra* note 9, at 2:

> Fertility drugs which induce super-ovulation are used without regard to the likelihood of multiple births and resulting stunting of fetal growth, prematurity, and higher risk of respiratory disease and death. . . . Moreover, this society has sanctioned the use of sex steroids like diethylstilbestrol to help women who are habitual aborters to have their own children, even when the safety of the artificial steroid was incompletely known.

Daughters of some of the women who took this steroid eventually developed vaginal cancer. There are also couples under an increased risk of producing a child with a genetic defect who elect to take that risk.

73. *See* Edwards and Steptoe, *supra* note 5, at 13:

> All the evidence obtained from transfers has consistently pointed to one conclusion: there are no induced anomalies attributable in any manner whatsoever to the culture and transfer of embryos. Neither has there been any indication of an increase in the incidence of malformations of any kind in [mice, rabbits and farm animals]. Rates of implantation were sometimes low compared with natural mating, but improved techniques in mice, sheep and other species have now reduced the difference to small proportions.

in a "normal" pregnancy or in one resulting from an embryo transplant, can be determined during the early weeks[74] of fetal development, the couple might have to confront the need for an abortion. As the ability of medical science to detect defects of the fetus *in utero* becomes more sophisticated, the question will surely arise as to whether or not the parents have the right to refuse to abort an obviously defective fetus. A physician might require the parents to agree to abortion under such circumstances as a precondition of performing the transplant. Under present law, state interference in such matters during the early stages of pregnancy is impermissible.[75]

Ideally, medical science should perfect the *in vitro* fertilization and embryo transfer procedures to the point where the risks involved fall to a socially acceptable level, "presumably . . . one . . . equivalent to the risks normally undertaken in a "natural" pregnancy."[76] However, lowering the risks and perfecting the tech-

---

See also Lappé, *supra* note 9, at 2:

> This has even proven true when the embryos have been subjected to the extreme manipulation of stripping off their protective outer cover and actually fusing them with a second embryo.

74. Chromosomal defects can be discovered by amniocentesis, a procedure by which amniotic fluid is obtained through a needle placed into the pregnant uterus, usually transabdominally. The amniotic fluid contains liquid and fetal cells. A defective fetus can be identified through a study of the cells and/or fluid. For example, the researcher can grow the cells in tissue culture for about three weeks; at that point, one can, by counting and identifying the chromosomes, determine the existence of such chromosomal disorders as Down's syndrome (mongolism). Because it is necessary to wait until the uterus is above the pubic bone, this procedure cannot be employed until about the fifteenth week of pregnancy. The study takes three weeks, and sometimes it must be repeated. Therefore, the pregnancy has advanced very close to the end of the second trimester and to the point where abortion is both a greater risk than early in the pregnancy and may also fall within the period during which the state could intervene to protect a potentially viable fetus. *See* Doe v. Bolton, 410 U.S. 179 (1973); Roe v. Wade, 410 U.S. 113 (1973). In addition there are other problems with amniocentesis. The cells drawn through the needle might be those of the mother rather than of the fetus—or of only one of fraternal twins. There are also dangers of infection, hemorrhage, and of the process itself triggering abortion. *See generally* A. Milunsky, The Prenatal Diagnosis of Hereditary Disorders (1973). Because the embryo is readily available, a similar process could be used in *in vitro* fertilization even before the embryo is transferred into a uterus. A defective embryo, detected at this very early state, would probably be discarded rather than implanted. Legally, such a step seems permissible under Roe and Doe, *supra.* Those persons who cannot morally justify abortion for reasons of genetic defect would probably feel the same way about disposing of the defective embryo.

75. Under Roe v. Wade and Doe v. Bolton, *supra,* the state may not in any way regulate abortion during the first two trimesters of pregnancy, except, during the second trimester, to protect the health of the mother.

76. Lappé, *supra* note 9, at 2. "[T]he moral right of parents to decide to bring their children into the world when they believe there is a reasonable probability of normalcy remains unsullied." *Id.*

niques involved so that the process is both effective and safe in human beings requires human experimentation, raising very difficult moral and ethical—as well as legal—questions.

Research: Whether and How

An American Medical Association editorial has condemned research in *in vitro* fertilization and embryo transplanting because of the belief that medicine should treat only disease and not merely desire to have children.[77] But there is another side to the question:

> The principal justification for attempting *in vitro* fertilization and reimplantation of human embryos (rather than, say, adoption or artificial insemination) has been to afford childless couples a means of having their *own* offspring. (In the United States, there are some two and a half million childless couples, a small proportion of whom would qualify for *in vitro* procedures.) . . . When we speak of justification for medical practice, we are talking simply about a universal obligation to relieve suffering. And childlessness is a particularly acute form of such suffering. There is a deep and pervasive felt need for family lineage and continuity of generations common to all peoples. I believe that human compassion dictates a response to individual couples who strongly sense that need, including the provision of *in vitro* fertilization.[78]

In addition to meeting the deepest desires of childless couples, many researchers in this field point also to the "fall out" benefits of such research in terms of medical knowledge that might help solve other problems.[79]

Even among the advocates of the embryo transfer process, there are persons who propose a moratorium on any research on human beings until more experimentation is done with higher primates and areas of risk are further studied.[80] The problems of control and regulation of such research remain problems which extend far beyond state and even national boundaries.[81] Although health has tradi-

77. Editorial, *Genetic Engineering in Man: Ethical Considerations*, 220 A.M.A.J. 721 (1972).

78. Lappé, *supra* note 9, at 1-2.

79. *See* Edwards and Steptoe, *supra* note 5, at 16-17:

> We are sure that these studies will enhance the understanding of the basis of human conception and may provide valuable data on new clinical approaches to other human problems. We believe that our studies conform with the Hippocratic oath in that they are for the benefit of patients and not for their hurt or for any wrong—indeed we believe they hold out the prospect of widespread benefit.

See also Edwards and Sharpe, *Social Values and Research in Human Embryology*, 231 NATURE 87 (1971).

80. *See, e.g.,* Lappé, *supra* note 9, at 3. *But see* note 5, *supra.*

81. Lappé, *supra* note 9, at 3 observes:

> The moral issue of human embryo manipulation is so great and of such importance to the course of the history of man, that nothing short of a consensus of the scientific

tionally been regarded as within the purview of state police power, the use of federal grants and federal funding of medical research, medical schools and hospitals provides a convenient justification for federal regulation of scientific research in *in vitro* fertilization and embryo transfer.

In 1974 the United States Congress enacted a statute, the National Research Act, regulating research in this area.[82] Title II of the law, designed to protect human subjects of medical research, established within the Department of Health, Education and Welfare a National Commission for the Protection of Human Subjects of Biomedical and Behavioral Research.[83] The eleven-member commission was appointed by the Secretary of HEW "from individuals distinguished in the fields of medicine, law, ethics, theology, the biological, physical, behavioral and social sciences, philosophy, humanities, health administration, government, and public affairs."[84] Five members of the commission are persons who have been or are engaged in biomedical or behavioral research involving human subjects.[85] Charged with investigating and identifying the basic ethical principles in order to establish guidelines for research,[86] the commission issued the part of its report dealing with fetuses and *in utero* fertilization in 1975.[87]

One result of the report was that a moratorium on fetal research imposed in August 1974[88] was lifted.[89] The only recommendation with regard to *in utero* fertilization was that all such research proposals be reviewed by the Ethical Advisory Board and the Institutional Review Board.[90] The explanation from the commission was

---

communities involved would be needed before proceeding. . . . The first step would be a moratorium on experiments leading directly to human egg implantation. The second would be the establishment of an international body to study systematically the scientific bases of *in vitro* manipulation in man. Finally, one can only hope that the first baby fertilized *in vitro* would be produced as the endpoint of a collective and public effort of responsible scientists, and not as the premature experiment of a single physician or scientist.

82. Pub. L. No. 93-348, 93d Cong., 2d Sess. (1974).
83. *Id.* at § 201(a).
84. *Id.* at § 201(b)(1).
85. *Id.*
86. *Id.* at § 202.
87. 40 Fed. Reg. 33526 (Aug. 8, 1975).
88. 39 Fed. Reg. 30962 (Aug. 27, 1974).
89. 40 Fed. Reg. 33526 (Aug. 8, 1975).
90. 45 C.F.R. §§ 46.204, 46.205. The regulations establish two Ethical Advisory Boards, one for the Public Health Service "and its components" and the other for all other HEW

that regulations would be "premature" given the current state of scientific research.[91] From the regulations governing aborted or about-to-be fetuses, it is reasonable to conclude that any regulations issued in the area of *in utero* fertilization will be narrowly drawn.[92]

Neither the statute nor the implementing HEW regulations establish clear policy in this area. There remains the dilemma presented by the need for additional research to assure that the procedures are safe and that the risks are as low as those of ordinary pregnancy. On the other hand, experimentation is necessary to provide such assurances, and such experimentation involves risks to human beings and potential human beings. Society must somehow determine whether these risks are worth the benefits to be gained when the procedures have been perfected. One long-term benefit of *in vitro* fertilization (other than helping childless couples, its primary motivation) would be that human beings could reproduce without the necessity for the mother to go through pregnancy, thereby eliminating the health hazards of pregnancy and childbirth[93] and simultaneously enabling the physician to correct many

---

agencies. These two Boards are "competent to deal with medical, legal, social, ethical, and related issues"; members "include . . . research scientists, physicians, psychologists, sociologists, educators, lawyers, and ethicists, as well as representatives of the general public." Full-time government employees are excluded. 45 C.F.R. § 46.204. In addition an Institutional Review Board at each institution in receipt of HEW grants or contracts governed by these regulations conduct initial and continuing reviews to assure compliance with the regulations. These Boards must have at least five members of varying backgrounds and professional qualifications or perspectives. 45 C.F.R. § 46.106.

91. 40 Fed. Reg. 33527.

92. 45 C.F.R. § 206 provides:

(a) No activity to which this subpart is applicable may be undertaken unless:

(1) Appropriate studies on animals and nonpregnant individuals have been completed;

(2) Except where the purpose of the activity is to meet the health needs of the mother or the particular fetus, the risk to the fetus is minimal and, in all cases, is the least possible risk for achieving the objectives of the activity;

(3) Individuals engaged in the activity will have no part in: (i) any decisions as to the timing, method, and procedures used to terminate the pregnancy, and (ii) determining the viability of the fetus at the termination of the pregnancy; and

(4) No procedural changes which may cause greater than minimal risk to the fetus or the pregnant woman will be introduced into the procedure for terminating the pregnancy solely in the interest of the activity.

(b) No inducements, monetary or otherwise, may be offered to terminate pregnancy for purposes of the activity.

93. Although childbirth and pregnancy are much safer in this era of wonder drugs and advanced surgical techniques than formerly, women still die from complications of pregnancy and childbirth. If pregnancy were unnecessary, these lives would not be lost.

of the birth defects which result in so much tragedy and waste in our society today.[94]

Ultimately society as a whole must determine whether and how such research will go forward, because these decisions are far too consequential to all people to depend on research scientists alone. If the boards and commissions suggested in the proposals consist of widely respected people of different backgrounds and points of view, if members are always appointed with thought and care rather than through political expediency or control, this method for making extremely difficult decisions should be effective. But such boards and commissions must also be sensitive to popular feelings. No society would long tolerate scientific experiments which, when all implications thereof are fully understood, violate the moral sensibilities of that society.

As yet most Americans do not realize the problems and implications of either artificial insemination or *in vitro* fertilization and embryo transfer, much less of the cloning process.[95] The public needs to be informed about what is presently being done and of future potentials, both beneficial and detrimental. For any scientist to avoid informing the public about his work merely because he believes his research would not be accepted is intellectually and morally dishonest. However, many scientists justifiably fear recrimination from a public too unsophisticated to evaluate research properly.[96] An objective board or commission, composed of intelligent and sensitive people of various backgrounds, could help bridge the "communications gap" and provide the necessary evaluation. A public that has been educated can contribute to the decision-making process more effectively.

---

94. *See* Edwards and Steptoe, *supra* note 5, at 11.

95. For an excellent and thorough discussion of the constitutional issues in genetic engineering and these new means of reproduction, *see* Pizzuli, *Asexual Reproduction and Genetic Engineering: A Constitutional Assessment of the Technology of Cloning*, 47 S. CALIF. L. REV. 476 (1974).

96. A physician at the Boston City Hospital was indicted for manslaughter in the death of an aborted fetus. Four other physicians at the same hospital were indicted under an 1814 grave-robbing statute because they used tissues from aborted fetuses for medical research. Dr. Kenneth Edelin, the chief resident in obstetrics and gynecology, was convicted of causing the death of a fetus removed during a second-trimester abortion requested by the mother. The other four doctors had worked for two years on a federally funded experiment to determine which of two drugs might be an alternative to penicillin to treat *in utero* syphilis in fetuses of women with allergies to penicillin. These cases have stirred much comment in the

> [M]an develops his ethics by the method of public discussion, by individual decisions and actions, by public acceptance of what appears to be right and good for man, and by rejection of what appears to be wrong or bad. We agree that it is right and good to reduce misery and improve the quality of life for those who live, by using environmental and social means. We now debate whether it is right and good to use genetic means. Our conceptions of what is ethical, right, and good change in the light of new knowledge and new conditions. What we lack is neither inflexibility of mind nor adventurous spirits, but knowledge and experience. If the future can be judged by the present and the past, we shall get that knowledge and experience and eventually authorize the ethics that permits doing what is believed to be right and good for man.[97]

Conclusion

Because much of the research done in the area of *in vitro* fertilization, embryo transfer, and cloning is the work of scientists in other countries, the international community must finally determine how such research will be conducted and how its effects will be implemented. Even though many months, possibly years, of discussion may be needed to resolve all the moral and ethical problems, it is not too soon for Americans to act to protect the legal rights of all parties concerned. Perhaps a good point of departure is the Uniform Parentage Act,[98] approved by the National Conference of Commissioners on Uniform State Laws in 1973 and the American Bar Association in 1974. This Act defines the relationship between parent and child as a legal relationship between natural or adoptive parents and a child, regardless of the marital state of parents.[99] A man is presumed to be the natural father of a child if he receives the child into his home and holds the child out as his natural offspring.[100]

A child should never be produced until there are "parents" who have donated one or both of the germ cells, or who wish to adopt the

medical and research communities; many have characterized the indictments as response to heavy political pressure from the "right to life" forces which are powerful in Catholic Massachusetts. For further details, *see Grave-Robbing: The Charge against Four from Boston City Hospital*, 186 SCIENCE 420 (Nov. 1, 1974). Dr. Edelin's conviction was overturned on appeal, Commonwealth v. Edelin 4 (Mass. 1976), and a judgment of acquittal entered.

97. Sonneborn, *Ethical Issues Arising from the Possible Uses of Genetic Knowledge*, ETHICAL ISSUES IN HUMAN GENETICS: GENETIC COUNSELING AND THE USE OF GENETIC KNOWLEDGE 1, 5-6 (B. Hilton *et al.*, eds., 1973).

98. 9 U.L.A. Matr. Fam. & Health Laws, 1974.

99. §§ 1 and 2.

100. § 4(a)(4). A husband who consents to artificial insemination, rather than the sperm donor, is the natural and legal father. § 5.

child under the procedure regularly used for adoption in the particular state. Artificial insemination has already been in limbo too long. The suggestions for legal regulation presented herein are aimed at preventing the stigma of illegitimacy and the heartaches of courtroom battles over custody, visitation rights, and support of innocent children. These steps must be taken promptly, even while society determines the allowable limits of scientific research.

Notice to the Unwed Father and Termination of Parental Rights: Implementing *Stanley v. Illinois**

JEROME A. BARRON†

I. The Nature of the Notice Problem

In 1972 in *Stanley v. Illinois*[1] the United States Supreme Court declared that unwed fathers were entitled to notice with respect to adoption and custody proceedings concerning their children. As a result a signal went out to the states, the bar, the courts, and the social service agencies that the termination and adoption process would be unable to proceed, as it mainly had in the past, with carefree indifference to the unwed father. The problem is particularly complicated by the fact that often his identity and whereabouts are unknown.

A new question has now arisen: How *does* one notify the unwed father of a proceeding to terminate his parental rights? Just the asking of this question marks a new chapter in family law in the United States—a chapter that should be titled "The Equalization of Parental Rights."

In a short space of time we have traveled far from the day when the unwed natural father had no rights in his children to this new day where he is said to have the same rights as the unwed mother and the legitimate parents. This equalization of the rights of parents with respect to their children without regard to the parent's

---

*Address before the Family Law Section of the American Bar Association, Annual Meeting, Montreal, Canada, August 13, 1975.

†Professor of Law, George Washington University, Constitutional Law Consultant to Project for Freeing Children for Adoption.

1. 405 U.S. 645 (1972).

sex or legal status is, of course, the teaching of *Stanley,* which made it clear that the right of the unwed father to his children merited constitutional protection. What *Stanley* did not make clear was the form this constitutional protection should take. The case involved an unwed father who had played an important role in raising his children. But the case casts a far wider net, a net which covers unwed fathers who might have no interest in raising their children. Moreover, the net cast by *Stanley* reaches even those who may not be aware of their fatherhood.

As far as the adoption process is concerned, the larger significance of *Stanley* does not derive from the actual holding of the case but from a footnote which has been a source of much study and of much mystification to family lawyers across the country.[2] The Court declared that unwed fathers were entitled to notice with respect to adoption and custody proceedings concerning their children. The Court said that notice of custody and adoption proceedings was vital to the unwed father. How else could he avail himself of the opportunity conferred by *Stanley* for a hearing to make a claim to the custody of his children and a showing of his competence to care for them?

But the difficulty engendered by this single and otherwise quite unobjectionable demand of notice to the unwed father was that all unwed fathers were by no means like Peter Stanley. Many had no desire to raise the illegitimates they had sired. Many were not even aware of the existence of their progeny. Yet under the language of the court, presumably, all unwed fathers had a right to notice. Moreover, compliance with this notice requirement was apparently a *sine qua non* of a valid termination of parental rights decree. The notice problem was intensified by the fact that even if the unwed father had no interest in his children, and had no desire to appear in a termination proceeding, it was often very difficult to reach the father in order for him to acknowledge that indifference. How was the social service agency, or the court, to deal with the situation where notice must be given to the unwed father but his identity and whereabouts are unknown? Should the unwed mother be compelled to identify the father? How long should the termination proceeding be held in abeyance, and the adoption process by delayed, in a quest for the unwed father?

2. Note 1, *supra,* at 657, n. 9.

To what lengths was a state required to go in order to give notice to the unwed father and thus satisfy its due process obligations? If the broadest view of *Stanley* is taken, no termination of parental rights decree is valid unless notice has been given to the unwed father. The Attorney General of Illinois has taken this view of *Stanley.*[3] However, the Illinois practice[4] which insists on notice to

---

3. 1972 Op. Att'y Gen. 542 (Ill.) *See* Note, 61 Ill. Bar. J. 378, 379, n. 54 (1973).

4. The Illinois overreaction to *Stanley*, if that is what it is, is entirely understandable in view of the reaction of the United States Supreme Court to the legal status of the unwed father in Illinois. Thus, in Vanderlaan v. Vanderlaan, 126 Ill. App. 2d 410, 262, N.E.2d 717 (1970), *vacated and consolidated*, 405 U.S. 1051 (1972), the United States Supreme Court granted certiorari, vacated the judgment below, and remanded the case for "further consideration in light of Stanley v. Illinois." In the *Vanderlaan* case, the plaintiff mother sought to modify the provisions of a divorce decree which awarded custody to the defendant father. At the time of the divorce, the couple had one child. Two more children were born to the mother. A court ruled that the defendant was the father of these two children and ordered him to make support payments. Subsequently, the father obtained legal custody of all three children.

The mother then sought to regain custody. The Illinois Appellate Court reversed the lower courts and directed that the lower court grant the custody of all three children to the mother:

> In the instant case, the trial court's orders of August 30,1966, and October 15, 1968, granting the custody of Jeffrey and Randy to defendant were in direct contradiction to the public policy stated in Section 62 of the Paternity Act. (Ill. Dir. Stat. 1967, ch. 106 3/4, § 62). We must *abide by the 'legislative determination that a putative father should have no right to the society of his children born out of wedlock.' . . . Therefore, defendant as the putative father could not be granted custody of the children.* (*See In re* Stanley, 45 Ill. 2d 132, 256 N.E.2d 814.) (Emphasis supplied.)
>
> *Id.* at 720.

Obviously, this 1970 holding of the Illinois Appellate Court could not stand in the light of the declaration of the Supreme Court in 1972 in Stanley v. Illinois, 405 U.S. 645 (1972), that the Illinois statutory scheme which recognized no rights of the natural father to his illegitimate children was unconstitutional:

> The private interest here, that of a man in the children he has sired and raised, undeniably warrants deference, and, absent, a powerful countervailing interest, protection.
>
> *Id.* at 651.

As a result of *Stanley*, Illinois was compelled to recognize the rights of the unwed father. In the light of *Stanley* and *Vanderlaan*, it is not surprising that Illinois whose statutes had long refused to invest the unwed father with the same rights as those of the unwed mother or the legitimate mother and father has now declined to take a view of *Stanley* which would limit the reach of the decision. *See* People ex. Slawek v. Covenant Children's Home, 52 Ill. 2d 20, 284 N.E.2d 291 (1972). In *Slawek*, an illegitimate child was born out of wedlock and placed for adoption through a licensed adoption agency after the natural mother had validly consented. The adoption of the illegitimate child had been finalized without notice to the putative father and without his consent. The natural father argued that Illinois statutes protected the rights of the parents of legitimate children and the natural mother of an illegitimate child in that for such parents notice and consent must be secured before an adoption may proceed. Moreover, such parents are entitled to custody of their children in the absence of a judicial determination of unfitness. The natural father complained that the failure by Illinois to afford these rights to the putative father was unconstitutional. The Supreme Court of Illinois agreed with the natural father:

> We hold that the provisions of the Adoption and Paternity Acts are unconstitutional insofar as they are in conflict with *Stanley, Rothstein* and *Vanderlaan*. In this regard, we direct attention to the United States Supreme Court's remand in the *Rothstein* appeal, in which the issues and facts are similar to those in the instant case. That order, in pertinent part, reads as follows:
>
> [T]he judgment vacated and case remanded . . . for further consideration in light of

all unwed fathers and in obtaining consents from the unwed fathers as a prerequisite to adoption has been criticized by the Child Welfare League of America as having delayed all placements for adoption in Illinois.[5] The league has suggested that implementation

Stanley v. Illinois, 405 U.S. 645, 92 S. Ct. 1208, 31 L. Ed. 2d 551 (1972), with due consideration for the completion of the adoption proceedings and the fact that the child has apparently lived with the adoptive family for the intervening period of time.

Id. at 292.

In the light of the *Slawek* case, which appears to read *Stanley* as requiring notice to all unwed fathers, the Attorney General of Illinois can hardly be criticized for taking a broad rather than a narrow reading of *Stanley*. However, some states have in effect gambled on the constitutional validity of a narrow reading of *Stanley*.

A New York trial court decision has also arguably opted for a more limited view of *Stanley*. In Doe v. Department of Social Services, 71 Misc. 2d 266, 337 N.Y.S.2d 102 (1972), the State Supreme Court in Dutchess County held that one who had previously been adjudicated to be the child's father and who had supported the child for approximately half of her life, while she had been cared for by her paternal grandmother, had a "cognizable and substantial interest" in manner of proposed adoption of the child and had legal status to question or oppose strangers' adopting child:

[3] Section 111(3), Domestic Relations Law (Adoption) expressly provides for the mother's consent only if the child is born out-of-wedlock. In view of *Stanley*, there must now be read into that statute, and it must be so construed, that the mother's exclusive or sole consent suffices only where there has been no formal or unequivocal acknowledgement or recognition of paternity by the father. It is not that the father's consent is now necessary as a condition precedent to adoption, but rather that he be served with "notice" ergo, according the father an opportunity, if he is so advised, to present facts for the court's consideration in determining what is in the best interests of the child. To deny the father any role, however, limited, respecting his child's future life is to treat infants as if they were "choses in action" and to confer upon the adoptive parents a status akin to holders in due course of negotiable instruments. (*Id.* at 107.)

In *Doe*, a New York court read § 111(3), New York Domestic Relations Law, to avoid a construction of that provision which would appear to violate *Stanley*. The court held that the mother's sole consent suffices "only where there has been no formal or unequivocal acknowledgement or recognition of paternity by the father. *Doe* involved a father seeking to stop the placement of his child for adoption." In *Doe* the father was one whose paternity had been adjudicated and who sought a determination of his rights in his child. For such a father, *Stanley* clearly requires notice. There was no reason in *Doe* to rule on the notice due an unknown unwed father. However, the case does raise the question of whether the sole consent of the mother to adoption authorized in § 111(3) becomes operative once again if the natural father's identity is not known. Or must a state make an effort at notice under *Stanley* even to the unknown father where paternity is not to be adjudicated? I incline toward the latter view. I rather think § 111(3) would not be valid under *Stanley* unless some reasonable effort has been made to identify and notify the natural father with respect to a pending termination and adoption of his child.

However, a recent development in New York involving a case decided after this presentation was first prepared must now be reckoned with. In *In re Adoption of Malpica-Orsini,* 36 N.Y.2d 568 (1975), the New York Court of Appeals held that a natural father who had notice of a petition for adoption and who appeared by counsel at the hearing was not denied the equal protection of the laws by a New York statute which requires the natural mother's consent but not the natural father's consent for adoption of an illegitimate child. *Orsini* was critical of the new recognition *Stanley* gives to the natural father. *Orsini* was also critical of extending any new rights in adoption proceedings to natural fathers who acknowledged paternity because of the difficult and continual problems of search and inquiry that would then arise. Whether other state supreme courts will take as hostile a view of the notice mandate in *Stanley* remains to be seen.

5. *See* Reeves, Comment, ***Protecting the Putative Father's Rights After Stanley v. Illinois: Problems In Implementation,*** 13 J. of Family Law 115 at 132, n. 91 (1973).

of a notice and hearing procedure for unwed fathers prior to adoption be limited to those who have either been adjudicated fathers or who have acknowledged their paternity.[6]

Most states have not yet amended their statutes to comply with *Stanley.* The reasons for caution and delay in this regard are considerable. After all, the comments in *Stanley* on the notice to the unwed father appear only in a footnote. The facts of the *Stanley* case itself did not involve the adequacy of notice to an unwed father vis-a-vis termination or adoption. As a result it is difficult for the state, or for any of us, to assess exactly how broadly or how narrowly the Court intended these comments.

The Court pointed out that the Illinois statute governing procedure in juvenile court cases provides for notice "to unknown respondents under the style of 'All Whom It May Concern.' " But how is a respondent to know he is concerned if the mother's name is not included in the notice by publication? It should be remembered that including the mother's name in this notice against her wishes certainly raises a difficult right of privacy problem. A problem of similar difficulty, already mentioned, is whether we may, for purposes of complying with the notice mandate of *Stanley* (if that is what it is), compel the mother to identify the unwed father. If both these issues are decided in favor of the privacy interest which is undoubtedly involved, it would seem that notice by publication becomes even more of an empty legal formalism, absolutely incapable of reaching its intended audience.

None of these issues was briefed to the Court in *Stanley.* Nor was the Court made aware that its requirement of notice to the unwed father would delay the adoption process and cause children to remain in the custody of social services agencies because of the new time-consuming and largely futile duty.

The *Stanley* Court surmised that "the incidental cost of offering unwed fathers an opportunity for individualized hearings on fitness appears to be minimal." Similarly, the Court did not appear to think that notifying the unwed father prior to affecting his rights to his children vis-à-vis "a custody or adoption proceeding" would create any constitutional or procedural obstacle. Has, in fact, the cost of giving due process stature to the interest of the unwed father

6. 1 Child Welfare League Newsletter 6 (Fall-Winter 1972).

in his children been minimal? Are there, in fact, procedural and constitutional obstacles to "foreclosing those unwed fathers" who are not inclined to rear their illegitimate children? In his opinion for the Court in *Stanley* Mr. Justice White's optimism on both these points appears to be somewhat unjustified.

II. The Legislative Response

Some states have enacted new legislation designed to respond to the notice problem raised by *Stanley*. This new post-*Stanley* legislation may be broken down into two classes of statutes, those which make some sort of diligent effort to give notice to the unwed father and those which do not. One set of new statutes represents an effort by the state to assume at least some affirmative obligation to give notice to the unwed father with respect to a pending termination of parental rights proceedings. The other approach is for the state not to assume any obligation of notice to the unwed father unless he is either known, identified by the mother, or has acknowledged the child.

In 1973, South Dakota, for example, enacted a statute of the latter class.[7] The new South Dakota statute is revealingly

7. In 1973, South Dakota enacted the following post-*Stanley* statute with respect to notice to the unwed father:

25-6-1.1 Father of illegitimate child not entitled to notice unless acknowledged.—Notwithstanding any other provision of law or court rule the father of an illegitimate child shall, as a requirement of due process, have no rights to the service of process in adoption, dependency, delinquency, or termination of parental rights proceedings unless he is known and identified by the mother or unless he, prior to the entry of a final order, in any of the three proceedings, shall have acknowledged the child as his own by affirmatively asserting paternity, within sixty days after the birth of the child,

(1) as outlined in § 25-6-1, or,

(2) by causing his name to be affixed to the birth certificate as provided by § 34-24-13.2, or,

(3) otherwise by commencing a judicial proceeding claiming parental rights.

Source: SL 1974, ch. 176.

S.D. COMPILED LAWS ANN. § 25-6-4 (Supp. 1973).

Certainly the South Dakota statute set forth above is a practical approach to the difficult problem of notifying the unwed father. The statute simply assumes that notice to the unwed father who cannot easily be identified is unnecessary. But is such an assumption warranted under *Stanley*? Has the unidentified father had that "opportunity for hearing" to assert, if he chooses, a "claim to competence" for the care of his children as required by *Stanley*? Certainly, there is an argument that such an unwed father has not had notice.

It is true that the Supreme Court may ultimately say that the burden of making inquiry concerning the birth of any progeny should be the responsibility of the father. Such an approach would relieve the burden of identifying the father from the mother and the state. So far, however, no decision has been forthcoming from the Supreme Court which would indicate that the South Dakota statute, however practical as far as the adoption process is concerned, is or is not constitutional.

captioned: "Father of illegitimate child not entitled to notice unless acknowledged." The South Dakota statute provides that the unwed father shall have no rights to service of process in adoption, dependency, delinquency or termination proceedings unless he is known and identified by the mother and unless he acknowledges the child. Similarly, a recent Michigan statute only requires notice to the unwed father if he has filed a notice of intent to claim paternity or has lived with or married the mother after the birth of the child.[8] In a new statute, Minnesota also has insisted on some kind of support or acknowledgement before the state has an obligation to give notice to the unwed father with respect to termination or adoption proceedings.[9] A new Colorado statute is to

---

The implicit policy judgments made by the South Dakota legislature with respect to its new notice to the unwed father statute are clear: the mother should not be compelled to identify the father and the state adoption process is not to be halted at the expense of a futile effort to reach an unknown unwed father through notice by publication.

8. MICH. COMP. LAWS ANN. § 710.3(a) (Supp. 1973).

9. Minnesota, like Michigan, has decided not to worry overmuch about giving notice of termination or adoption to an unidentified natural father of an illegitimate. Thus, amendments to the new 1974 Minnesota adoption law, MINN. STAT. ANN. § 259.26 provide that "notice of the hearing upon a petition to adopt a child shall be given to":

. . .

(3) the parent of an illegitimate child if

(a) The person's name appears on the child's birth certificate, as a parent, or

(b) The person has substantially supported the child, or

(c) The person either was married to the person designated on the birth certificate as the natural mother within the 325 days before the child's birth or married that person within the ten days after the child's birth, or

(d) The person is openly living with the child or the person designated on the birth certificate as the natural mother of the child, or both, or

(e) The person has filed an affidavit pursuant to section 259.261.

This notice need not be given to any above named person whose parental rights have been terminated, whose notice of intention to retain parental rights filed pursuant to section 259.261 has been successfully challenged, who have consented to the adoption or who have waived notice of the hearing. The notice of the hearing may be waived by a parent, guardian or other interested party by a writing executed before two competent witnesses and duly acknowledged. Such waiver shall be filed in the adoption proceedings at any time before the matter is heard.

With respect to retention of parental rights M.S.A., § 259.261, provides as follows:
259.261 Retention of rights

Subdivision 1. Notice by illegitimate parent. Any person not entitled to notice under section 259.26, shall lose his parental rights and not be entitled to notice at termination, adoption, or other proceedings affecting the child, unless within 90 days of the child's birth or within 50 days of the child's placement with prospective adoptive parents, whichever is sooner, that person gives to the division of vital statistics of the Minnesota department of health an affidavit stating his intention to retain parental rights.

Subd. 2. Notice, contents. Such affidavit shall contain the claimant's name and address, the name and the last known address of the other parent of the child and the month and year of the birth of the child, if known.

Subd. 3. Notice, effect. Upon receipt of the aforementioned affidavit the division of vital statistics of the Minnesota department of health shall notify the other parent of same within seven days. This notice to the parent shall constitute conclusive evidence of parenthood

the same effect.[10] Essentially Colorado like Minnesota has put some of the burden of securing notice of a pending termination or adoption proceeding on the unwed father.[11]

---

for the purposes of this statute, unless within 60 days of its receipt, either the notified parent or some other interested petitioner denies that claimant is the parent of the child and files a petition pursuant to chapter 260 to challenge such notice of parenthood. Added by Laws 1974, c. 66, § 1.

Finally, MINN. STAT. ANN. § 259.24 dispenses with consent to adoption of an illegitimate child by the natural parent who has not complied with 359.61, *i.e.*, given an affidavit of intention to retain parental rights to the division of vital statistics of the Minnesota department of health. MINN. STAT. ANN. § 259.24(a) states in pertinent part:

259.24 Consents

Subdivision 1. Exceptions. No child shall be adopted without consent of his parents and his guardian, if there be one, except in the following instances:

(a) Consent shall not be required of the parent of an illegitimate child not entitled to notice of the proceedings under either section 259.26 or section 259.261.

10. The new Colorado statute, 1973 COL. REV. STAT. § 19-1-103(21), provides:

. . . The father of an illegitimate child shall have no parental rights to the child unless he, prior to entry of a decree of adoption, has acknowledged the child as his own by affirmatively asserting paternity as follows:

(a) Causing his name to be affixed to the birth certificate of the child; or

(b) Paying medical or hospital bills associated with the birth of the child; or

(c) Paying support for the child; or

(d) Otherwise asserting his paternity in writing.

The burden of coming forward in Colorado is on the natural father, not the state. It is true that Colorado law is consistent with *Stanley* in that it defines a "parent" as the "natural parent of a legitimate child" as well as "a natural parent of an illegitimate child, or a parent by adoption." 1973 COL. REV. STAT. § 19-1-103. But the new Colorado statutes do nothing to attempt to reach the unwed father unaware of a pending termination proceeding or even of his fatherhood.

11. The narrow interpretation some states have accorded the notice requirements of *Stanley* is illustrated by Alaska. In 1966, the Alaska adoption law was amended to provide as follows:

Consent for adoption is not required

(7) from the natural father if the person to be adopted is a minor of illegitimate birth, not subsequently legitimatized, and notice need not be given him.

Alaska Statutes, § 20.10.070 (1966)

In 1974, the state adoption law was revised:

Unless consent is not required under § 50 of this chapter, a petition to adopt a minor may be granted only if written consent to a particular adoption has been executed by

(2) the father of the minor, if the father was married at the time the minor was conceived or at any time after conception, the minor is his child by adoption, or he has otherwise legitimated the minor under the laws of the state

Alaska Statutes, § 20.15.040 (1974)

Section 50 referred to above says, *inter alia multa*, that consent is not required of a parent who has abandoned a child without affording means of identification. *See* Alaska Statutes § 20.15.050 (1974). Section 20.15.050 also states that consent need not be obtained from the parent of a child in the custody of another if the parent has failed for at least a period of a year to communicate meaningfully with the child or to provide for the care and support of the child as required by law.

If we compare the prior 1966 Alaska law with the new post-*Stanley* 1974 amendments, one may conclude that despite the new statutory revisions on the matter in Alaska the rights to notice of the unwed father who has not legitimated his child have not been appreciably increased in Alaska despite the new post-*Stanley* legislation. It is true that the new Alaska termination of parental rights statute provides for "notice of hearing on the petition and opportunity to be given" for the parents of the child. Alaska Statutes § 20.15.180 (1974). However, since adoption can be effected in Alaska without a prior termination decree, the crucial

With respect to the broad view of *Stanley,* Wisconsin's new statute is of particular interest. It is not surprising that the Wisconsin legislature decided to take a broader view of the reach of *Stanley* than have the states whose new legislation I have already discussed. In 1972, the Supreme Court remanded "in the light of *Stanley*" a Wisconsin case where the state courts had rejected an unwed father's attempt to challenge a perfected adoption which had not been preceded by notice to the unwed father.[12] On remand, the Supreme Court of Wisconsin held that the natural father had been improperly denied a hearing with respect to termination of parental rights.[13] The Supreme Court of Wisconsin held that Wisconsin statutes which permitted adoption of minor illegitimates on the sole consent of the mother and without consent of the father could not be given legal effect under *Stanley.* The Supreme Court of Wisconsin observed in *Rothstein* that the Wisconsin Children's Code was being revised in order to redraft "those provisions of the Children's Code which are in conflict with the *Stanley* and *Rothstein* decisions."[14]

The revision of the Wisconsin Children's Code in 1973 addressed itself specifically to complying with the notice requirements of *Stanley.* According to the new statute the notice of the termination of parental rights should be served on the parents.[15] If personal

---

features of the new post-*Stanley* legislation in Alaska are the minimal duties imposed on the state with respect to obtaining consent from and furnishing notice to the unwed father with respect to a petition to adopt his child.

12. Rothstein v. Lutheran Social Service of Wisconsin and Upper Michigan, 47 Wis. 2d 240, 178 N.W.2d 56 (1970), *vacated* 405 U.S. 51 (1972).

13. State *ex rel.* Lewis v. Lutheran Social Services of Wis., 207 N.W.2d 826 (Wisc. 1973).

14. Note 13, *supra*, n. 4.

15. The full text of the Wisconsin notice provisions are as follows:

48.42. Procedure in terminating parental rights. (1) The termination of parental rights under 48.40 shall be made only after a hearing before the court. The court shall have notice of the time, place and purpose of the hearing served on the parents personally at least 10 days prior to the date of the hearing. If the court is satisfied that personal service, either within or outside the state, cannot be effected, then such notice may be given by registered mail sent at least 20 days before the date of the hearing to the last-known address of the parent. If notice by registered mail is not likely to be effective, the court may order notice to be given by publication at least 20 days before the date of the hearing. If notice is given by publication, the name of the mother shall be included in such notice only if the court following a hearing on the need for inclusion of the mother's name determines in any termination proceeding that such inclusion is essential to give effective notice to the natural father. In determining whether such inclusion is essential, the court shall consider the mother's right to privacy. Publication shall be in a newspaper likely to give notice to the county of the last-known address of the parent, whether within or without the state, or if no address is known, in the county where the termination petition has been filed. Publication within the state shall be as a class 1 notice, under ch. 985. Publication outside the state shall be in a manner which the court finds to be comparable to a class 1 notice. A

service or registered mail is not likely to be effective, the statute directs that service by publication should be used. At this point we come to an interesting feature of the new Wisconsin statute—a provision that the mother's name may be included in the notice by publication. But inclusion of the mother's name may be had only "if the court following a hearing on the need for inclusion of the mother's name determines . . . that such inclusion is essential to give effective notice to the natural father." The statute then goes on to provide: "In determining whether such inclusion is essential the Court shall consider the mother's right to privacy."[16]

The words of the Wisconsin legislature regarding the inclusion of the mother's name deserve attention: the interest in the right of privacy of the mother must be considered but the legislature does not make that interest determinative. This is a sensible resolution of the problem. It should never be forgotten that although the due process rights of the parents in termination proceedings should be recognized, the best interests of the child is, after all, also a vital aspect of such proceedings. The due process rights of the parents should not extend to a point where the focus on procedural rights of notice to the unwed father undervalue and jeopardize the full extension of the child's constitutional rights of life and liberty. It is clear, on the other hand, that the new Wisconsin statutes display a greater concern to give notice to the unwed father so that he may protect his parental rights than do the statutes of South Dakota, Michigan, Minnesota and Colorado. Wisconsin is trying to reach the unwed father insofar as that most unrealistic of legal communications vehicles, notice by publication, will permit. Not only may the Wisconsin court, if it wishes, include the mother's name in the notice by publication, but the court may inquire of the mother as to the identity of the father.[17]

---

parent who consents to the termination of his parental rights under s.48.40(1) may waive in writing the notice required by this section; if the parent is a minor or incompetent his waiver shall be effective only if his guardian ad litem concurs in writing.

Wis. Children's Code, 48.42 (1973).

16. Note 15, *supra*.

17. The new Wisconsin statutory provision on the point is as follows: "48.425. Hearings and Findings. § (1) *If no person has previously been adjudged to be the natural father of the child, the court shall make inquiry of the mother as to the identity of the natural father.* The parental rights of a person who has been adjudged in a court proceeding to be the natural father of a child born out of wedlock and not subsequently legitimated or adopted shall be terminated only in accordance with s. 48.43." Wis. Children's Code § 48.425 (1973). (Emphasis supplied.)

Although Wisconsin has obviously made more of an affirmative effort to notify and identify the unwed father than the other jurisdictions I have mentioned, it should be stressed that its new statute does not compel the mother to testify as to the whereabouts and identity of the father.[18] In this respect, other post-*Stanley* legislative developments have gone farther than Wisconsin. Thus, the Uniform Parentage Act not only requires the court to inquire of the mother concerning the identity of the natural father in order to identify him,[19] but permits the court to compel the mother's testimony on this point. Section 10(b) of the Uniform Parentage Act explicitly provides that if any witness including a party refuses to testify, such refusal shall constitute a civil contempt. Thus, under the section 25(b) statutory scheme of the UPA, the court is required to inquire of the mother concerning the identity of the father and section 10(b) of the act compels every witness including a party, *i.e.*, the mother, to testify.[20] On the issue of compelling

18. Another state which has enacted post-*Stanley* legislation which attempts to cope directly with the problem of notifying the unknown unwed father, and which attempts to involve the mother in that effort, is Florida. Thus a new Florida statute provides:

> No consent (to adoption) shall be required from the father of a child born out of wedlock when the mother of the child does not know the identity of the father and a reasonable search would not reveal his identity. In this event, the mother shall execute an affidavit under oath that she does not know either the (identity) or the location of the father. FLA. STAT. ANN. § 63.062 (1973).

The usefulness of this statute seems questionable since the mother may know the identity of the father but be unwilling to disclose it. In such a case, she, of course, would hardly be in a position to file an affidavit that she did not know the identity of the unwed father. In that situation, would the unwed father's consent to adoption still be required? Would notice to such a father of the adoption hearing be required? In my view, the answer to both questions is probably in the negative. A new Florida statute, for example, describes the "parent" to whom notice of the hearing on the petition to adopt must be given as follows:

> (c) The parent who, by written sworn acknowledgement or court proceeding, has been established to be the parent of the minor or who has provided the child with support in a repetitive, customary manner. FLA. STAT. ANN. § 63.122 (1973).

The above-quoted language would appear to relieve the state from any obligation to notify the unknown unwed father.

19. 24(e) of the Uniform Parentage Act provides:

> If, after the inquiry, the court is unable to identify the natural father or any possible natural father and no person has appeared claiming to be the natural father and claiming custodial rights, the court shall enter an order terminating the unknown natural father's parental rights with reference to the child. Subject to the disposition of an appeal upon the expiration of [6 months] after an order terminating parental rights is issued under this subsection, the order cannot be questioned by any person, in any manner, or upon any ground, including fraud, misrepresentation, failure to give any required notice, or lack of jurisdiction of the parties or of the subject matter.

20. Section 10(b) of the Uniform Parentage Act provides:

> Upon refusal of any witness, including a party, to testify under oath or produce evidence, the court may order him to testify under oath and produce evidence concerning all relevant facts. If the refusal is upon the ground that his testimony or evidence might tend to incriminate him, the court may grant him immunity from all criminal liability on account of

the mother's testimony, Prof. Krause has written of the Uniform Parentage Act:[21]

> [The Act's] guiding principle is full equality for all children, legitimate and illegitimate, in their legal relationship with both parents (§§ 1, 2). Moreover, the Act emphasizes the right in question is the right of the child (§§ 6(a), 9)—not the right of his mother as current state laws insist. Accordingly, the mother may not stand in her child's way and, if necessary, may be compelled to testify as to the father's identity and whereabouts—just as any other witness (§ 10(b)).

Both the Uniform Parentage Act and the Wisconsin Children's Code present problems. The Wisconsin statute does make an effort to furnish notice, but it is possible that notice by publication may merely result in delaying the termination process, and thus the adoption process. Notice by publication is unlikely to reveal the identity of very many natural fathers. Yet the Uniform Parentage Act procedure, focused as it is on securing the identity of the father from the mother, may involve severe infringements of human dignity and privacy. Moreover, the Uniform Parentage Act notice procedure, at least contrasted with Wisconsin's which provides for the possibility of the inclusion of the mother's name in notice by publication to the father, may be inadequate to show that reasonable search for the natural father which the notice requirement of *Stanley* requires.

Clearly, there is a major problem in providing due process to the natural father since service by publication in termination presents even more difficulties than, for example, in divorce proceedings. Reliance on service by publication to the unwed father for notice of a termination proceeding is obviously foolish and futile when the name and whereabouts of the natural father are unknown. It is therefore not surprising that there is currently debate on whether the mother may be compelled to provide this information. Does such a requirement unconstitutionally infringe the mother's right of privacy? On one side the Attorney General of Vermont has answered the question in the affirmative:[22]

> The father's parental rights and the mother's right of privacy are each recognized as fundamental human rights, and it would be cruel and unseemly

---

the testimony or evidence he is required to produce. An order granting immunity bars prosecution of the witness for any offense shown in whole or in part by testimony or evidence he is required to produce, except for perjury committed in his testimony. The refusal of a witness, who has been granted immunity, to obey an order to testify or produce evidence is a civil contempt of the court.

21. Krause, *Uniform Parentage Act*, 8 Fam. L.Q. 1 (1974).

22. Vermont Att'y Gen. Op. No. 997, December 12, 1972, at 6.

for the Department to compel a woman to be subjected to possible personal trauma in order to give the father his right to appear as a parent, where the mother does not seek legal relief for herself.

A recent case on a related matter which involves the question of compelling the mother of a child to identify the father is *Doe v. Norton.*[23] In that case, unwed mothers brought suit challenging the constitutionality of a Connecticut statute whereby any unwed mother might be compelled both to disclose the name of a child's putative father and to institute a paternity action. A three judge federal court upheld the statute, on the ground, *inter alia multa*, that compelling disclosure of the identity of the father would not invade any "zone of privacy" of the mother. Quoting from *Roe v. Wade,*[24] the court declared that since the fact of pregnancy is visible, the "woman's privacy" was "no longer sole" and "any right of privacy she possesses must be measured accordingly."[25] *Roe* had distinguished pregnancy in this regard from "marital intimacy, or bedroom possession of obscene material, or marriage, or procreation, or education. . . ."[26] The court said that "[v]iewed from the perspective of the class denied the privilege of remaining silent the 'embarrassing' information has in large part been widely disclosed before any inquiries are made."[27] The court reasoned further:[28]

> . . . the inquiry focuses on identity of the father, not on the mother's misconduct. The question asked of the unwed mother is, 'Who is the father of your child?' The object of the inquiry is to enforce a familial monetary obligation, not to interfere with personal privacy. There is no intrusion into the home nor any participation in interpersonal decisions among its occupants. . . . The only restriction it imposes upon either the unwed mother or the biological father to do as they please or make any decisions they wish in whatever relationship they desire to maintain is that the father satisfy his legal obligation to support his own child and that the mother provide what information she possesses useful toward that end.

Professor Krause in his helpful article on the Uniform Parentage Act described *Doe v. Norton* as having "answered effectively" the constitutional right of privacy questions arising from state compulsion of the mother's testimony for purposes of expediting termination of the father's parental rights.[29]

---

23. 365 F. Supp. 65 (D. Conn. 1973).
24. Roe v. Wade, 410 U.S. 113 (1973).
25. Quoted in Doe v. Norton, *supra*, at 77, n. 19.
26. *Id.*
27. *Id.* at 77.
28. *Id.* at 77-78.
29. Krause, note *21*, *supra*.

Certainly, from the viewpoint of validating section 10(b) of the Uniform Parentage Act compelling the mother's testimony with respect to identifying the father, *Doe v. Norton* was a helpful precedent. On the other hand, the interests in *Norton* and in a termination proceeding are different. Support from the state to mother and child is not necessarily involved in the termination context. Moreover, in *Norton* it was stressed that identifying the father related only to a matter of support and did not affect the "interpersonal" decisions of the parties. But it would seem that it is at least arguable that a state determination depriving parents of parental rights interferes with "interpersonal" decision-making (and therefore, the right of privacy) in the most fundamental way.

A final blow to whatever helpfulness might have been derived from the three judge court opinion in *Doe v. Norton, supra*, occurred on June 24, 1975: the Supreme Court in *Roe v. Norton* vacated the judgment in that case and remanded for consideration in light of Pub. L. No. 93-647, and if a relevant criminal proceeding is pending, also for consideration in light of *Younger v. Harris*, 401 U.S. 37.[30] Pub. L. No. 93-647,[31] which made a variety of amendments to the Social Security Act, was enacted after the three judge court decision in *Doe v. Norton*. After the enactment, counsel for the plaintiffs in *Doe* filed a supplemental brief to the three judge federal court. Plaintiffs argued that Pub. L. No. 93-647 provided in essence that if a mother refused to cooperate with the state in establishing the paternity of a child born out of wedlock the mother should lose her welfare payments. Counsel for the plaintiffs then argued, unsuccessfully, that this penalty for non-cooperation on the part of the mother was exclusive and that, therefore, the Connecticut statute was pre-empted by the new and exclusive federal statutory penalty. The Supreme Court in *Roe* obviously was sufficiently impressed with this argument to vacate the three judge court judgment and to remand to order consideration of the matter in the light of Pub. L. No. 93-647.

The constitutional question of whether compelling the mother to identify the father for purposes of a termination proceeding violates the right of privacy was not illuminated by the Supreme

30. Roe v. Norton, 95 S. Cit. 2221 (1975).
31. Pub. L. No. 93-647, 93rd Cong., H.R. 17045, January 4, 1975.

Court order in *Roe*. It can, of course, be argued that compelling the mother to identify the father in the context of whether the mother should be deprived of governmental funds is altogether different from the termination context where the mother's refusal to identify the father may so hamper the child's opportunities for adoption as to critically prejudice the child's future happiness and development. But as a legal matter, the three judge federal court opinion in *Doe* that the Connecticut statute compelling the mother to identify the father did not violate the mother's constitutional right of privacy was not passed on by the Supreme Court. We are still without guidance from that Court on the validity of such provisions.

Aside from the unresolved right of privacy question aside, what in general has been the post-*Stanley* legislative response to the problem of providing notice to the unwed father? It is noteworthy that the majority of states have yet to enact legislation which directly responds to this problem with respect to a termination of parental rights and/or adoption proceeding. The legislation on this issue enacted by a minority of states divides between states which have attempted to make some new and diligent effort to give notice to the unwed father and those which do not. A few of the states have now bound themselves by statute to assume at least some affirmative obligation to give notice to the unwed father. Most states which have enacted post-*Stanley* legislation, on the other hand, have taken the implicit position that *Stanley* does not impose upon them any duty to notify the unwed father unless he is either known, identified by the mother, or has acknowledged the child; they have elected a narrow construction of what is required of them with respect to giving notice of termination or adoption to the unidentified natural father of an illegitimate child.

III. Some Conclusions

It is quite clear that legislation in the post-*Stanley* era must implement two important social policies: (1) the constitutional duty to give the unwed father notice of a pending termination of parental rights decree; and (2) the establishment of a statutory structure for termination and adoption which will not result in long delays before children can be freed for adoption. The challenge is to make sure that the implementation of one policy does not destroy the other, that an accommodation is reached between the twin goals of satisfying the due process rights of the unwed father and the just necessities of a sensible and sensitive termination and adoption procedure. Children who are obviously and ultimately going to be adopted must not be kept for unpardonably long periods of time in agency custody or unsatisfactory private arrangements because of a mindless adherence to unwise, time-consuming and largely futile legal formalisms.

In the light of these goals, how should the law respond to the problem of notice to the unwed father in the context of the termination proceeding? What policies should be served by the notice in a state termination of parental rights statute? I believe that four important issues must ultimately be faced by any "notice" pro-

First: should the mother be compelled to identify the father for purposes of notifying the father of a termination proceeding? Policy and constitutional considerations would seem to argue against compulsion. In such situations the right of privacy of the child as well as of the mother may be involved. (Suppose, for example, the mother declines to identify the father because the child is the product of an incestuous relationship?) The Supreme Court in *Roe v. Norton*,[32] discussed earlier, did not pass on the validity of compelling the mother to identify the father in a slightly different context. As a constitutional matter, therefore, that question is still open. But whether or not such compulsion is unconstitutional, there are strong policy considerations which militate against compulsion. A legal obligation on the mother to testify concerning the identity of the father, punishable by contempt, might well incline a mother unable to provide adequate care for her child nevertheless to refuse to relinquish her child for adoption solely out of unwillingness to identify the father. The due process rights of the unwed father in a termination proceeding should not be interpreted to result in a situation where a mother is compelled to identify the unwed father against her will.

A second important question raised by the notice to the unwed father is how broad the category of unwed fathers reached by *Stanley* should be. Should the notice requirement, for example,

32. Note 30, *supra*.

be limited only to those unwed fathers whose paternity has been acknowledged or adjudicated? Some states, as mentioned earlier, have given a narrow definition to the class of unwed fathers reached by *Stanley*. Some law review support has been accorded to this position:[33]

> The Illinois approach of requiring a father's consent in all adoptions, or making him a party defendant and thus requiring notice, is an over-reaction to *Stanley* which has substantially interfered with adoptions in that state and caused long delays in child placement. . . . It is quite clear that *Stanley* does not permit a state to ignore the father's interest in his child merely for administrative operating convenience. However, it is equally clear that *Stanley* does not mandate that the interests of the child in as rapid an adoption as possible be sacrificed while the state seeks to notify an elusive or unknown father.

It seems clear, however, that *Stanley* requires something more than notice to those unwed fathers who have in fact already identified themselves through acknowledgement or adjudication. Although I believe that the Court in *Stanley* intended the states to make a good faith effort to furnish notice of termination to all unwed fathers, this conclusion was reached with full awareness of and full sympathy for the Court's qualifying language in a subsequent post-*Stanley* case. In *Rothstein v. Lutheran Social Services of Wisconsin and Michigan*, the Supreme Court vacated and remanded a Wisconsin decree which refused to interfere with a natural father's request to upset a perfected adoption order.[34] The Supreme Court vacated in the light of *Stanley* but then, very importantly, instructed the Wisconsin courts to consider the case in the light of *Stanley* "and the fact that the child has apparently lived with the adoptive family for the intervening period of time."[35] Taking a generous view both of *Stanley* and the sensible language protective of the adoptive parents and of the adoptive children in *Rothstein*, it becomes clear that the problem of notice to the unwed father is perhaps best resolved by the court's wise use of discretion in the termination proceeding.

---

33. Comment, *Stanley v. Illinois, What It Portends for Adoptions in Montana*, 36 MONTANA L. REV. 137 at 144-145 (1975).

34. Note 12, *supra*.

35. *Id.*

It should be noted that even a retroactive application of *Stanley* with respect to the unwed father is unlikely to upset a perfected adoption. Thus, in the *Rothstein* case, although the unwed father won the right to be heard with respect to the termination of his parental rights, the Wisconsin county court judge nevertheless terminated the unwed father's parental rights.

The Supreme Court of Wisconsin affirmed the order terminating the unwed father's parental rights. State *ex rel.* Lewis and Rothstein v. Lutheran Social Services of Wisconsin

Such a resolution may well apply also to the third issue—the question of whether, if at all, the mother's name should be included in the notice of service by publication on the unwed father. It may well be that the determination of whether the circumstances in a given case warrant the inclusion of the mother's name in the notice of publication to the father, should be left, as the new Wisconsin statute provides,[36] as a matter for the exercise of the court's discretion after hearing. In other words, the mother's name may be included in the notice of service by publication even though she may not consent to such inclusion, provided that the court in its best judgment thinks such inclusion is warranted.

This approach would strike a balance between those jurisdictions which make no effort to identify the unknown unwed father and those which go as far as compelling the mother to identify the father. Whenever we talk about making a good faith effort to reach the largest number of unwed fathers possible with respect to termination proceedings, we are really talking about service by publication. Even though this mode of communication may merit all the harsh things that have been said of it,[37] it should be stressed

---

and Upper Michigan, Supreme Court of Wisconsin, Slip Opinion, filed April 10, 1975. The Supreme Court of Wisconsin explained its affirmance in part as follows:

> The facts in this case compel the conclusion that Rothstein abandoned the child before it was born. The trial court concluded:
>
> That his repeated denials of paternity, lack of concern for or interest in the support, care and well-being—including pre-natal care—of the child, and the disregard for the well-being of the child's mother from the date of the pregnancy was announced to approximately the birthdate of the child manifested a clear intent on the part of petitioner, Rothstein, to disassociate himself from responsibility for the birth and care of the child.
>
> Rothstein's refusal to accept responsibility required Miss Lewis (the mother) to decide whether to keep the baby or put it out for adoption after it was born. She chose the latter course, making her decision in the best interests of the child. She was not required to wait until the last minute to make this decision. She was entitled to act in reliance on Rothstein's actions and statements prior to and during the spring of 1968.
>
> Since we have concluded Rothstein abandoned the child, the question becomes whether Rothstein should be permitted to avoid the effects of his abandonment because of his subsequent change of heart. . . .We are persuaded that the best interests of the child in this case will be served by terminating Rothstein's parental rights because of his abandonment of the child prior to its birth. Accordingly, we affirm that portion of the county court's order which terminates the parental rights of Jerry D. Rothstein.

36. Note 15, *supra*.

37. At this juncture, it is worth recalling some comments of Mr. Justice Jackson for the Court in Mullane v. Central Hanover Bank & Trust Company, 339 U.S. 306 (1950). In *Mullane*, Mr. Justice Jackson made two observations which have relevance to the subject of this paper. First, he pointed out that service by publication would hardly guarantee that people would learn that their rights were before the courts. Second, he pointed out that, nevertheless, where missing or unknown persons were involved, service by publication was constitutional.

that such notice is better than no notice, and that it is more useful to work to make service by publication more effective than simply to disparage it altogether. To make service more effective in the termination context, something must be included in the notice which gives some reasonable prospective of alerting the unwed father to the imminence of a termination proceeding.

Already discussed in this paper have been the reasons against an absolute requirement for the mother to identify the father by name against her will. On the other hand, inclusion of the mother's name in such a notice at the discretion of the court does give some hope of reaching the unwed father. A provision for inclusion of the mother's name, if circumstances warrant, would also indicate that the state has made some reasonable effort to identify and notify the unwed father.

There is still one final issue to consider with respect to satisfying the notice requirements of *Stanley* in a termination proceeding. Is a court, consistent with these notice requirements, ever justified in dispensing altogether with notice by publication to an unwed father? The answer to this question is: "Yes." The Supreme Court in *Stanley* seems to have encouraged and anticipated flexibility and a rule of reason where notice to the unwed father in the context

---

Mr. Justice Jackson's comments on the inadequacies of service by publication are as follows:

> It would be idle to pretend that publication alone as prescribed here is a reliable means of acquainting interested parties of the fact that their rights are before the courts. It is not an accident that the greater number of cases reaching this Court on the question of adequacy of notice have been concerned with actions founded on process constructively served through local newspapers. Chance alone brings to the attention of even a local resident an advertisement in small type inserted in the back pages of a newspaper, and if he makes his home outside the area of the newspaper's normal circulation the odds that the information will never reach him are large indeed. *The chance of actual notice is further reduced when as here the notice required does not even name those whose attention it is supposed to attract, and does not inform acquaintances who might call it to attention. In weighing its sufficiency on the basis of equivalence with actual notice we are unable to regard this as more than a feint.* (Emphasis supplied.)
> 339 U.S. 306 at 315.

Mr. Justice Jackson's comments on the constitutional validity of service by publication as a means of informing missing or unknown persons are as follows:

> This court has not hesitated to approve of resort to publication as a customary substitute in another class of cases where it is not reasonably possible or practicable to give more adequate warning. *Thus it has been recognized that in the case of persons missing or unknown employment of an indirect and even a probably futile means of notification is all that the situation permits and creates no constitutional bar to a final decree foreclosing their rights.* Cunnius v. Reading School District, 198 U.S. 458, 25 S. Ct. 721, 49 L. Ed. 1125, 3 Ann. Cas. 1121; Blinn v. Nelson, 222 U.S. 1, 32 S. Ct. 1, 56 L. Ed. 65, Ann. Cas. 1913B, 555; and *see* Jacob v. Roberts, 223 U.S. 261, 32 S. Ct. 303, 56 L. Ed. 429. (Emphasis supplied.) 339 U.S. 306 at 317.

of adoption and custody was concerned. The question of whether notice by publication should be required or dispensed with should, therefore, be left to the sound discretion of the court which, in a hearing, has inquired into the matter. This is the approach taken by the Uniform Parentage Act.[38] Such a procedure is sound because it gives proper weighting to the due process rights of the natural parent and to the practical necessities of the adoption process.

In sum, the constitutional duty of notice to the unwed father with respect to the termination of his parental rights requires a good faith effort by the state to notify him of a termination proceeding, even if such a father is unknown. It is nonetheless permissible for a state to terminate parental rights if the court concludes that the process of searching for the unwed father is a futile one.

---

38. Uniform Parentage Act, § 24(f), provides:
[If no person has been identified as the natural father or a possible father, the court, on the basis of all information available, shall determine whether publication or public posting of notice of the proceeding is likely to lead to identification and, if so, shall order publication or public posting at times and in places and manner it deems appropriate.]

The Impact of *Roe v. Wade* on Paternal Support Statutes: A Constitutional Analysis

MARTIN R. LEVY* and ELAINE C. DUNCAN†

Synopsis

This article considers the question of whether current paternal support statutes are constitutional in the face of legalized abortion after *Roe v. Wade.*[1] Such statutes are subject to constitutional attack under the Equal Protection and Due Process Clauses of the Fourteenth Amendment.[2] In order to impose the duty of support upon a limited group of people, the classification must comply with the Equal Protection Clause. The minimum equal protection standard generally requires that there be a rational relationship between the class affected by the statute and the constitutionally permissible objective of that statute.[3] The purpose of parental support statutes is to place the burden of support on those responsible for the birth, and therefore, a rational relationship or nexus between the father's act of intercourse and the birth of the child is an implicit requirement if such paternal support statutes

*Assoc. Prof. of Law, University of Louisville.

†J.D., University of Louisville.

[1]Roe v. Wade, 410 U.S. 113 (1973). *See* text *infra.*

[2]"No state shall . . . deprive any person of life, liberty, or property, without due process of law; nor deny to any person within its jurisdiction the equal protection of the laws." U.S. CONST. *amend.* XIV, § 1.

[3]P. BREST, PROCESSES OF CONSTITUTIONAL DECISIONMAKING 558 (1975).

are to be consistent with equal protection.[4] Paternal support statutes which impose a duty of support on the father irrebuttably presume this nexus.

In illegitimacy situations where a woman consciously decides to bear, rather than abort, however, it can be argued that the required nexus is broken by the mother's intervening decision to bear.[5] Following this view, the reason a woman decides to bear, rather than abort, is a proper subject of judicial inquiry to determine whether the woman acted volitionally in choosing to bear, and therefore whether the nexus exists. Current paternal support statutes, however, do not require the courts to review the individual circumstances of each case. Under this analysis, the statutes should, therefore, be held unconstitutional under the due process clause as relying on an irrebuttably presumed nexus. It would then be necessary to revise paternal support statutes to provide for inquiry into why a woman decides to bear an illegitimate child, and to use the outcome of that inquiry as the basis for placing the burden of support. The question is whether such revisions are constitutionally mandated.

I. Introduction

The support of a growing child, including its education and nurture and the medical expenses arising from its birth, are factual real-life requirements for its survival. In the absence of permitting children to die, the duty of support must fall either on one or both parents, social welfare agencies, or the state. Where the child is illegitimate, the possibility that the burden of support will fall on the institutions or on the state greatly increases. Neither the agencies nor the state is responsible for the birth of the child, and therefore, the burden of support should fall on them only when the responsible parties—the parents—*cannot* meet the needs of the child. For this reason, the

---

[4]In order to legally take the property of the father to support the child, there must be some basis for holding the father responsible for the birth of the child; simple biology supplies such a basis. Thus, "[a] father's duty to support his child rests upon not only moral law but legally upon the voluntary status of parenthood which the father assumed." Niesen v. Niesen, 38 Wis. 2d 599, 601, 157 N.W.2d 660, 662 (1968). Voluntary intercourse provides the volitional act. See also note 14 *infra.*

[5]While the putative father may, in fact, be the biological father, it may be argued that he has no longer voluntarily assumed the status of parenthood; that choice is the mother's alone. See text *infra.*

duty of support has been statutorily imposed upon the parents—primarily on the father.[6] Such paternal support statutes do not serve as a punishment for the parents' (parent's) indiscretion,[7] but rather as a means of insuring parental, rather than state, support of the illegitimate child.[8]

Under the early common law, no duty of support was imposed upon the father of an illegitimate child.[9] Absent a contract between the parties, the father's only duty of support is that created by statute.[10] Most jurisdictions have now enacted statutes which establish paternity proceedings, and require the person adjudged to be the father to support the child.[11] The purpose of these statutes was primarily to free the state from the duty of support, and only secondarily to provide for the welfare of the child.[12] Paternal support statutes, thus, relieve the state of its duty under the doctrine of *parens patriae,*[13] and place the duty of support on one of the parties responsible for the birth of the child.[14]

In 1973, the responsibility of the father for the birth of the child

---

[6]"The primary obligation of maintaining the children was on the husband and father. The foundation of this superior obligation rests upon the general fact that he is most capable of discharging it." Fulton v. Fulton, 52 Ohio St. 229, 232, 39 N.E 729, 732 (1895). *Accord* Dunbar v. Dunbar, 190 U.S. 340 (1903).

[7]Bielawski v. Burke, 121 Vt. 62, 64, 147 A.2d 674, 676 (1959).

[8]Kowalski v. Wojtkowski, 19 N.J. 247, 250, 116 A.2d 6, 9 (1955).

"The purpose of paternity proceedings under our statute is to secure the support and education of children born out of wedlock." Howard v. Howard, 122 Vt. 27, 31, 163 A.2d 861, 865 (1960).

[9]Kowalski v. Wojtkowski, 19 N.J. 247, 251, 116 A.2d 6, 10 (1955); Mays v. Commonwealth, 363, S.W.2d 110, 111 (Ky. 1962).

[10]Note, *Illegitimates—Father's Duty to Support,* 28 N.C. L. Rev. 119, 120 (1949).

[11]10 Am. Jur. 2d *Bastards* § 68 (1963).

An example of one such statute is Ky. Rev. Stat. Ann. § 406.011 (Supp. 1974) which states:

"The father of a child which is or may be born out of wedlock is liable to the same extent as the father of a child born in wedlock, whether or not the child is born alive, for the reasonable expense of the mother's pregnancy and confinement and for the education, necessary support and funeral expenses of the child."

[12]Kowalski v. Wojtkowski, 19 N.J. 247, 251, 116 A.2d 6, 10 (1955).

[13]"The duty of parents to provide necessary support, care, and maintenance for their children, although arising out of the fact of their relationship, may be rested also upon the interest of the state as parens patriae of children and of the community at large in preventing them from becoming a public burden, and is, therefore, a duty not only to the children themselves, but to the public as well." 59 Am. Jur. 2d *Parent and Child* § 51 (1971).

[14]"A sufficient reason for holding parents to be under a legal obligation, apart from any statute, to support their legitimate child while it is too young to care for itself, is that the liability ought to attach as a part of their responsibility for having brought it into being . . . it does not in the least depend for its force upon the fact that the parents were married to each other, but is equally persuasive when that is not the case." Doughty v. Engler, 112 Kan. 583, 584, 211 P. 619, 620 (1923).

came into question with the Supreme Court's decision in *Roe v. Wade.*[15] *Roe* challenged the Texas abortion statutes[16] which prohibited abortions, except where necessary to save the life of the mother. The Court, basing its conclusion on the woman's right to privacy,[17] held that the decision to have an abortion, at least in the first trimester, is strictly a matter between the patient and her physician.[18]

Beyond the obvious effect of invalidating the various state abortion statutes, *Roe v. Wade,* by placing the abortion decision solely on the mother and her physician, also raised doubts about the validity of paternal support statutes. According to the *Roe* opinion, the decision to bear a child is unilateral; it is the female's decision alone.[19] The question then arises as to whether that decision preempts conception as the cause of birth, or acts as an intervening causation of birth, thus making the mother solely responsible for the actual birth of the child. This question raises a second question as to whether, at least in illegitimacy situations, it violates equal protection to require the father to support a child whose birth results solely from the mother's decision to bear; or, alternatively, whether statutes which require such support irrebuttably presume a nexus between intercourse and birth, and are, therefore, unconstitutional under the Due Process Clause.

II. A Statement of the Issues

The impact of *Roe v. Wade* on paternal support statutes was considered in: *Abortion on Maternal Demand: Paternal Support Liability Implications,*[20] which was concerned only with the validity

---

The parents' duty of support is " '. . . an obligation laid on them not only by nature herself, but by their own proper act, in bringing them into the world. . . . By begetting them, therefore, they have entered into a voluntary obligation to endeavor, as far as in them lies, that the life which they have bestowed shall be supported and preserved.' " Wells v. Wells, 227 N.C. 614, 616, 44 S.E.2d 31, 33 (1947), *quoting* 1 W. Blackstone, Commentaries 419 (Lewis' Ed. 1897).

[15]410 U.S. 113 (1973).

[16]Tex. Penal Code art. 1191-1194, 1196 (repealed).

[17]*Id.* at 152-56.

[18]410 U.S. at 164.

See also Doe v. Bolton, 410 U.S. 179 (1973). In *Doe,* Georgia abortion statutes were held unconstitutional as not being rationally related to the objectives sought. 410 U.S. at 195.

[19]*Roe* held that the decision to abort is between the mother and the physician. The father's rights in an abortion case, if any exist, were not at issue, and thus, were not considered in either *Roe* or *Doe.* 410 U.S. at 165, n.67. See notes 35-47, and text, *infra.*

[20]Swan, *Abortion on Maternal Demand: Paternal Support Liability Implications,* 9 Valparaiso U. L. Rev. 243 (1975).

of contractual, tort, and criminal parallels for support statutes. In that article the author challenged the notion that the father is liable for the support of the child due to his responsibility for its birth. In light of *Roe v. Wade,* the author argued that "[n]o longer can a court seriously allege that the 'nature of the connection' between father and child has 'brought it into being.' Legally, the person—perhaps arguably the life itself—was created independently of the father's act or omission. A father is now a 'progenitor' who has 'brought life into this world' only in some zoological sense. His legal status relative to his unborn children is that of a helpless by-stander."[21] Serious questions arise from this argument: What are the constitutional consequences of this point of view? Is this point of view constitutionally mandated?

In order to sustain a father's duty of support under the Equal Protection Clause of the Fourteenth Amendment, it is necessary to presume that there is a nexus between intercourse and birth.[22] The question then becomes whether such a presumption, in light of *Roe v. Wade,* creates a fiction which is not sustainable on the facts. If so, statutes which rely on this irrebuttable presumption should be declared unconstitutional under the Due Process Clause as relying on an irrebuttable presumption,[23] or under the Equal Protection Clause, as being overinclusive.[24]

The class to which the duty of support is assigned must be appropriate under the Equal Protection Clause. Accordingly, there must be a rational relationship between the class of persons regulated by the statute and the purpose of the statute. It has been stated that "[a] reasonable classification is one which includes all persons who are similarly situated with respect to the purpose of the law."[25] In *Reed v. Reed,*[26] the Supreme Court held that the minimum rationality standard of equal protection requires that the classification rest upon ". . . some ground of difference having a fair and substantial relation to the object of the legislation, so that all persons similarly circumstanced are treated alike."[27] If the

---

[21] *Id.* at 256.

[22] See notes 3-4, and text, *supra.*

[23] See notes 48-54, and text, *infra.*

[24] See notes 25-31, and text, *infra.*

[25] Tussman & tenBroek, *The Equal Protection of the Laws,* 37 CALIF. L. REV. 341, (1949).

[26] Reed v. Reed, 404 U.S. 71 (1971).

[27] *Id.* at 76.

father is not responsible for the birth of the child, the class charged is overinclusive.

Paternal support statutes seek to place the duty of support upon that class of persons who are responsible for the birth of the child.[28] The effect of these statutes is to create an irrebuttable presumption of nexus between intercourse and birth. This presumption of nexus was valid so long as abortion was illegal, since courts could justifiably ignore the abortion option. However, statutes which irrebuttably presume a nexus violate the Due Process Clause, as discussed hereinafter.

It is not presumed that the expectant mother always makes a conscious choice to bear or to abort the child. It is obvious that there are cases in which the mother is unable to abort the child due to physical, emotional or religious reasons.[29] However, given a mother physically, emotionally or religiously capable of making the decision to abort, the responsibility of bearing the child rests *solely* on the expectant mother.[30] Though society may condemn the relationship which leads to illegitimate births, the putative father, like the mother, has constitutional rights.[31] In one view, these rights are violated by paternal support statutes which force the father to support a child where the nexus between the father's act of intercourse and the birth of the child is broken by the mother's conscious decision to bear and not to abort.

A second view, however, and one supported by these authors, is that the father's act of intercourse is sufficient to bring him within the class of persons on which the duty of support is visited. Furthermore, the mother's conscious decision to bear is not sufficient to break the required nexus, and thus to relieve the father of the duty to support the resulting child.

---

[28]*See* notes 13-14 and accompanying text, *supra.*

[29]In the majority of paternity actions, the relationship between the parties is not harmonious. The mother wants no further contact with the father except that of support for the child, and the father desires no contact with either the mother or the child. Thus, we are not concerned here with the case where the father desires a continuing relationship with the mother but refuses to support the offspring of that relationship; nor are we concerned with the case where the putative father desires to assert his paternal rights under *Stanley v. Illinois,* 405 U.S. 645 (1972).

[30]The decision whether to bear or abort is solely between the mother and her physician. *Roe v. Wade,* 410 U.S. 113, 164 (1973).

[31]Under the Due Process Clause, the father, like all citizens, has the right not to have his property taken from him without due process of law. U.S. Const. *amend.* XIV, § 1.

III. Arguably—A Break in the Nexus

A. *Irrebuttable Presumptions and Equal Protection*

In view of *Roe v. Wade,* it may now be argued that the nexus between conception and birth can no longer be presumed; it has become a proper subject of judicial inquiry. The courts must, then, consider: (1) Why did the mother choose to bear?; (2) Was it a voluntary and conscious choice? Under this argument, if the choice was voluntary and conscious, then the responsibility for child support is removed from the father.

Roe provides the woman who has conceived with the option of aborting or bearing the child. This decision is solely that of the woman and her doctor.[32] The woman who consciously chooses *not* to correct the mistake of conception[33] by aborting, *unilaterally* decides to bear the child. It is argued that the male is no more a "parent" in such a situation than is a sperm donor in a case of artificial insemination.[34] The nexus is *broken,* and the man, therefore, should not be bound by an irrebuttable presumption of his responsibility for the child because the mother's voluntary and conscious decision to bear intervenes between intercourse and birth.

Recent decisions[35] depriving the father of a voice in the abortion decision do support this contention. In *Jones v. Smith,*[36] a Florida

---

[32]See notes 15-19, and text, *supra.*

[33]In cases where a paternity action is brought against the putative father, the relationship between the parties is usually such that a conception is a mistake. See note 29 *supra.*

[34]*See* People v.Sorenson, 66 Cal. Rptr. 7, 437 P.2d 495 (1968). In this case the husband consented to the artificial insemination of his wife, and treated the resulting child as his own. Subsequently, the parties were divorced, and the husband was found guilty of having violated the Penal Code by failing to pay child support. He appealed, claiming the child was not his. The court held that he was the lawful father of the child, and thus, liable for its support. The court stated: ". . . the term 'father' as used in [the Statute] cannot be limited to the biologic or natural father as those terms are generally understood. The determinative factor is whether the legal relationship of father and child exists." 66 Cal. Rptr. at 10, 437 P.2d at 498. The court also stated that the sperm donor cannot be considered the natural father. 66 Cal. Rptr. at 10, 437 P.2d at 498.

Therefore, a party who is the biological father but has no further contact with the child nor responsibility for its birth is not liable for its support. In the situation considered by this article, the putative father likewise has no further contact with the child, or responsibility for its birth, and thus, under the "break in the nexus" theory, should not be held responsible for its support.

[35]Doe v. Bellin Memorial Hosp., 479 F.2d 756 (7th Cir. 1973); Coe v. Gerstein, 376 F. Supp. 695 (D. Fla. 1973), *cert. denied,* 94 S. Ct. 2246 (1974); Doe v. Rampton, 366 F. Supp. 189 (D. Utah 1973); Jones v. Smith, 278 So. 2d 339 (Fla. Ct. App. 1973), *cert. denied,* 415 U.S. 958 (1974); Doe v. Doe, 314 N.E.2d 128 (Mass. 1974).

[36]278 So. 2d 339 (Fla. Ct. App. 1973), *cert. denied,* 415 U.S. 958 (1974).

court held that a putative father has no right to enjoin the natural mother from terminating the pregnancy.[37] The court reiterated the Supreme Court's holding that the abortion decision is solely between the mother and her physicians.[38] The court further stated: "The right of privacy of the mother with respect to a termination of pregnancy as delineated by the decisions of the United States Supreme Court is a right separate and apart from any act of conception."[39] Federal courts[40] have also held that the consent of the putative father is not required since the right to privacy is an individual right[41] which should not be subjected to the consent of others.[42]

In *Doe v. Doe,*[43] a Massachusetts Court held that a husband has no constitutional right to object to his wife's decision to have an abortion.[44] In view of the *Roe v. Wade* decision, the court found that the ". . . recognition of an enforceable right in the husband to prevent the abortion would raise serious constitutional questions."[45] A federal district court has held that a Florida statute requiring the husband's consent to an abortion is unconstitutional.[46]

Most recently the U.S. Supreme Court[47] has struck down a Missouri statute requiring prior written consent of the spouse of a woman seeking an abortion during the first twelve weeks of pregnancy unless the abortion is certified to be necessary to preserve the life of the mother. The Court said that the state cannot "delegate to a spouse a veto power which the state itself is absolutely and totally prohibited from exercising during the first trimester of pregnancy."[48] These decisions emphasize that the

---

[37]*Id.* at 344.

[38]*Id.* at 341.

[39]*Id.* at 343.

[40]Doe v. Bellin Memorial Hosp., 479 F.2d 756 (7th Cir. 1973); Doe v. Rampton, 366 F. Supp. 189 (D. Utah 1973).

[41]Doe v. Bellin Memorial Hosp., 479 F.2d 756, 758-59 (7th Cir. 1973).

[42]Doe v. Rampton, 366 F. Supp. 189, 193 (D. Utah 1973).

[43]314 N.E.2d 128 (Mass. 1974).

[44]*Id.* at 130.

[45]*Id.* at 132.

[46]Coe v. Gerstein, 376 F. Supp. 695, 698 (D. Fla. 1973), *cert. denied,* 94 S. Ct. 2246 (1974).

[47]Planned Parenthood of Central Missouri v. Danforth, 2 Fam. L. Rep. 3039, (June 29, 1976).

[48]This itself is a direct quotation from the law court decision at 392 F. Supp. 1362, 1375 (1975).

father no longer has a voice in the decision to bear the child,[49] and support the argument that he should not be burdened with the financial results of that decision, where the option to abort is available and the decision to bear is consciously made.

If this argument is carried to its logical conclusion, the courts must look to recent Supreme Court decisions which have held that statutes which rely on irrebuttable presumptions that deny fundamental rights are unconstitutional. In *Cleveland Board of Education v. LaFleur,*[50] the Court considered the concept of irrebuttable presumptions in situations involving fundamental rights. This case concerned a school board rule which required pregnant school teachers to take a maternity leave without pay beginning five months before the expected birth of the child. A teacher taking such a leave was not allowed to return to work until the next school semester following the date when the child is three months old.[51] The court found that this rule was based upon an irrebuttable presumption that pregnancy has so impaired the teacher at that time that she could not continue employment, even where the medical evidence was to the contrary.[52] The Court held that the right to bear a child is a fundamental liberty protected by the Due Process Clause of the Fourteenth Amendment.[53] As such, it cannot be burdened with an irrebuttable presumption and the school board must determine the fitness of the pregnant teachers on a case by case basis.[54]

In *Vlandis v. Kline,*[55] the court struck down an irrebuttable presumption relating to non-residency in school tuition cases. An irrebuttable presumption relating to an unwed father's competency to raise his children was declared unconstitutional in *Stanley v. Illinois.*[56]

---

[49]In cases where the mother is physically, emotionally and religiously capable of aborting, the decision to bear is not made at the moment of conception but rather at the moment when the mother decides whether to bear or abort. The father has no right to participate in that decision. *See* text *supra,* and *see* note 19 *supra.*

[50]Cleveland School Board v. LaFleur, 414 U.S. 632 (1974).

[51]*Id.* at 634-35.

The school board made no promise of re-employment after the required leave was completed, and failure to comply with the rule was grounds for dismissal. *Id.* at 635.

[52]*Id.* at 645-46.

[53]*Id.* at 639-40.

[54]*Id.* at 646-47.

[55]Vlandis v. Kline, 412 U.S. 441 (1973).

[56]Stanley v. Illinois, 405 U.S. 645 (1972).

So long as there is a causal unbroken nexus between intercourse and birth, the requirements of equal protection are satisfied. However, if *Roe v. Wade* permits a break in the nexus in certain situations, the class of persons to which the duty of support is assigned is no longer rationally related to the purpose of the statute, and the statute is in violation of the Equal Protection Clause as being overinclusive, and alternatively, of the Due Process Clause under the theory of irrebuttable presumptions. If one accepts the argument that the nexus between intercourse and birth is broken by a woman's decision to bear, then it follows from the *Cleveland, Vlandis* and *Stanley* opinions that a judicial inquiry on a case by case basis is necessary to protect the constitutional rights of the father. Such a judicial inquiry should include a consideration of several factors, including the woman's emotional and physical ability to abort, and the relationship between the parties.

B. *The Legitimacy—Illegitimacy Distinction*

The argument that the nexus between intercourse and birth is broken in certain cases by the mother's failure to abort in light of *Roe v. Wade* leads to the obvious conclusion that paternal support statutes must be revised. Such revisions must include a legitimacy-illegitimacy distinction. In order to preserve the marriage relationship and the responsibilities which are attached to that formal relationship, it is necessary to place an absolute obligation of support upon the father of the offspring of that relationship. Thus, the revised paternal support statutes would necessarily distinguish between legitimate and illegitimate children by continuing to place an obligation of support upon the fathers of legitimate children, and at the same time requiring the fathers of illegitimate children to support those children only where the opportunity to abort is not available. It is the authors' view that unless this distinction is made, the inevitable results of the "break in the nexus" view lead to the conclusion that there be no paternal support liability even in the marriage relationship for a child born to a mother over the father's objections where the mother was physically, emotionally and religiously free to abort. Such a result would tend to destroy the marriage institution and is untenable.

Recent Supreme Court decisions[57] have struck down state statutory distinctions between legitimacy and illegitimacy where no rational basis was found for the distinction or the statutes were not rationally related to the purpose for which they were enacted. The necessary revisions must, therefore, provide different criteria for paternal support for legitimate children and illegitimate children, in order to overcome the rational basis test.

Arguably, the legitimacy-illegitimacy distinction arises from a finding of an implicit acquiescence, arising from the marriage relationship, to support legitimate children. Furthermore, this classification will not affect all illegitimate children; it will affect only those born to a mother who was consciously free to abort but chose not to do so. This implicit acquiescence provides a rational basis for the difference in criteria here offered between the duty of a father of an illegitimate child and the father of a legitimate child where the mother freely and consciously chooses to bear rather than abort while at the same time preserving the due process rights of such fathers. The distinction would seem to draw support from the *Labine* holding as discussed hereinafter. However, for this argument to prevail, the issues in *Gomez v. Perez,*[58] which were decided contrary to this thesis, must be reconsidered in light of *Roe v. Wade.*

The Supreme Court, in *Gomez v. Perez,*[59] was confronted with the question of the validity of a Texas statute[60] wherein legitimate children were given a right of support from their fathers, but illegitimate children were denied this right. The Court, in declaring the law unconstitutional, stated: "We therefore hold that once a state posits a judicially enforceable right on behalf of children to needed support from their natural fathers there is no constitutionally sufficient justification for denying such an essential right to a child simply because its natural father was not married to its mother."[61]

---

[57]Levy v. Louisiana, 391 U.S. 68 (1968); Glona v. American Guarantee Co., 391 U.S. 73 (1968); Weber v. Aetna Casualty and Surety Co., 406 U.S. 164 (1972); and Gomez v. Perez, 409 U.S. 535 (1973).

[58]409 U.S. 535 (1973).

[59]*Id.*

[60]TEX. FAM. CODE, § 4.02 (1970).

[61]409 U.S. at 538.

The proposal based on the "break in the nexus" theory requires a distinction which is in part contrary to *Gomez v. Perez.* However, it may be significant to note that *Gomez* was decided *prior* to *Roe v. Wade.*[62] The Court, in *Gomez,* was concerned only with the child's right to receive necessary support, and was not faced with a due process argument on behalf of the father. Thus, the Court failed to distinguish between the child's right to support and the rights of those on whom the duty of support was imposed.[63] Equal protection requires this duty to be placed on that parent or parents who are responsible for bringing the child into the world. In light of *Roe v. Wade,* arguably, this will not always include the biological father. It follows then that the issues in *Gomez* should be reconsidered.

Without the *stare decisis* effect of *Gomez v. Perez,* one must look to other cases involving the legitimacy-illegitimacy distinctions to determine whether such a distinction can stand in the face of constitutional attack. Proponents of the father's right will turn for support to *Labine v. Tubrix Vincent, Administrator.*[64] In *Labine,* the appellant challenged a state law[65] whereby an illegitimate child, although recognized by the father, may not inherit in the absence of a will.[66] The Court held that the statutory scheme is constitutional,[67] but the dissent found the Court's reasoning to be unclear.[68] The Court seems to have based its decision on the fact that the child was not absolutely precluded from inheriting since the child could have inherited if the father had so provided in a will.[69] The Court was further persuaded by the fact that matters of intestacy are traditionally left to state regulation.[70]

---

[62]*Gomez* was decided Jan. 17, 1973 and *Roe* was decided on Jan. 22, 1973.

[63]The dissent in *Gomez* notes that the issues were not adequately briefed, and that the parties ". . . failed to provide [the] Court with a sufficient understanding of Texas law with respect to such matters as custodial versus noncustodial support obligations, legitimation, [and] common-law marriage, ..." 409 U.S. 538, 539 (Justice Stewart's dissenting opinion).

[64]Labine v. Tubrix Vincent, Administrator, 401 U.S. 532 (1971).

[65]LA. CIV. CODE art. 206 (1870).

[66]Louisiana has a complex family law scheme based on French, Spanish, and Roman civil law. See 401 U.S. at 541, 545 (Justice Brennan's dissenting opinion).

[67]401 U.S. at 539-40.

[68]See 401 U.S. at 541, 548-51 (Justice Brennan's dissenting opinion).

[69]401 U.S. at 539.

[70]*Id.* at 537-39. *See also* Weber v. Aetna Casualty and Surety Co., 406 U.S. 164, 170 (1972).

Reliance on *Labine,* however, is open to attack in light of other cases which have struck down such distinctions. In *Levy v. Louisiana,*[71] the Court struck down a Louisiana statute[72] which prevented illegitimate children from recovering for the wrongful death of their mother. The Court termed the classification invidious, and refused to deny the children the right to recover simply because they were born out of wedlock.[73] The mother had cared for and nurtured the children, and ". . . they were indeed hers in the biological and in the spiritual sense . . ."[74]

In *Glona v. American Guarantee Co.,*[75] a companion case to *Levy,* the Court upheld the right of a parent of an illegitimate child to recover for the wrongful death of that child. Again, the Court found that the Louisiana statutory classification would not prevent illegitimacy, and thus, served no rational purpose.[76]

A Louisiana workman's compensation law[77] which distinguished between legitimate and illegitimate children in allocating recovery for the death of a parent was held unconstitutional in *Weber v. Aetna Casualty and Surety Co.*[78] Under the statute, illegitimate children could recover only if the maximum benefits were not exhausted by awards to legitimate children. The Court, in analogizing to *Levy* and *Glona* held that the classification had no rational relationship to the purpose of the statute.[79]

In each of these cases, the Court struck down classifications which discriminated against those parent-child relationships which had not been formally sanctioned by the marriage ceremony, but were, in fact, actual parent-child relationships in both ". . . the biological and . . . the spiritual sense. . ."[80]

Whereas *Levy, Glona,* and *Weber* each concerned statutorily assigned rights, from which illegitimates were excluded, the statute

[71]391 U.S. 68 (1968).
[72]LA. CIV. CODE ANN. art. 2315 (Supp. 1967).
[73]391 U.S. at 72.
[74]*Id.*
[75]391 U.S. 73 (1968).
[76]*Id.* at 75.
[77]LA. REV. STAT. § 23:1232 (1967).
[78]406 U.S. 164 (1972).
[79]*Id.* at 175.
[80]Levy v. Louisiana, 391 U.S. 68, 72 (1968).

in *Labine* did not involve any rights assigned to either legitimate or illegitimate children. Rather in *Labine,* the sole issue of importance was the father's right to dispose of his property at death. The state inheritance statute gives the father complete discretion to determine to whom his property will pass at his death. In the absence of formal parental action, that of making a will, the statute merely presumes that the father has chosen not to dispose of his property in such a manner as to benefit his illegitimate child.

Thus, the Court, in *Labine*, held that a state statutory classification based on legitimacy may stand where such classification may be refuted by the positive action of the parent and the matter is one traditionally left to state law.[81] In comparison, the statutory classification of different criteria for paternal support statutes based on legitimacy may also be refuted by the parent's positive action, i.e., the father may choose to marry the mother, or choose to support the child, or the parents may be married when the child is conceived. Further, this is an issue traditionally left to state law. Therefore, the paternal support statutes which distinguish between legitimate and illegitimate children *may* find support in the *Labine* holding absent the *Gomez* decision.

Further support for such a distinction may be found in the dissenting opinion in *Glona.* The *Levy, Glona,* and *Weber* decisions expound on the theme of biological parentage rather than legal relationships;[82] *Gomez v. Perez,* although not based on this premise, is also in line with this theory.[83] However, Justices Harlan, Stewart, and Black, in dissent,[84] found this theme to be fallacious, and argued that the states have the right to make classifications based on the relationship of the parents, even where the resulting classifications based on the relationship of the parents, even where

[81]Mr. Justice Black in the opinion of the Court notes that "[t]here is not the slightest suggestion in this case that Louisiana has barred this illegitimate from inheriting from her father." The child could have inherited if the father had . . . "bothered to follow the simple formalities of executing a will." 401 U.S. at 539.

[82]Levy v. Louisiana, 391 U.S. 68, 70-71 (1968); Glona v. American Guarantee Co., 391 U.S. 73, 75-76 (1968); Weber v. Aetna Casualty and Surety Co., 406 U.S. 164, 168-170 (1972).

[83]Gomez v. Perez, 409 U.S. 535, 536 (1973).

[84]Glona v. American Guarantee Co., 391 U.S. 76 (1968) (Justice Harlan's dissenting opinion; Justices Black and Stewart also dissented).

the resulting classification is based on legitimacy.[85] Arguably, this view may be accepted in light of the due process implications following naturally from the "break in the nexus" theory. While the father may be the "biological" parent of the child, he no longer has a part in the actual decision to bear the child. However, the fact remains that paternal support statutes which recognize this new "status" of the father, and make appropriate distinctions, would have difficulty in being upheld as constitutional in light of *Gomez v. Perez.*

C. *Equal Protection and Due Process Requirements Are Satisfied*

The constitutionality of paternal support statutes depends upon whether *Roe v. Wade* does in fact, permit a break in the nexus between conception and birth. These authors believe it does not. While it may be conceded that the Supreme Court's decision in *Roe v. Wade* has reduced the father's role in the birth of the child, it has not totally excluded him. The mother's decision to bear, rather than abort, does not break the connection between intercourse and birth. That decision is, in effect, a passive act or inaction. The issue may be analyzed from a tort, contract and criminal liability standpoint. Swan, in his aforementioned article,[86] makes such an analysis, without considering the constitutional ramifications, and concludes that the nexus is broken. However, if one looks more closely at each of these types of liability, it may be readily seen that although the nexus between conception and birth may be weakened, it is not broken by the impact of *Roe v. Wade.*

---

[85]391 U.S. at 76-82. Mr. Justice Harlan notes that the statutory scheme for wrongful death recovery is actually based on legal relationships rather than personal relationships, i.e., a man may recover for the wrongful death of parents he did not love; a child cared for and nurtured by friends or neighbors may not recover for their wrongful death. "In short, the whole scheme of the Louisiana wrongful death statute . . . makes everything the Court says about affection and nurture and dependence altogether irrelevant." 391 U.S. at 78. ". . . [N]either a biological relationship nor legal acknowledgment is indicative of the love or economic dependence that may exist between two persons." 391 U.S. at 80. Justice Harlan ". . . could not understand why a State which bases the right to recover for wrongful death strictly on family relationships could not demand that those relationships be formalized." 391 U.S. at 82.

[86]Swan, *Abortion on Maternal Demand: Paternal Support Liability Implications,* 9 VALPARAISO U. L. REV. 243 (1975), [hereinafter cited as Swan].

1. THE TORT ANALOGY

Swan treats the father as an innocent bystander in a tort liability case; this bystander is not liable for the child's support since he is free to assume, under the doctrine of shifting responsibility, that the mother will provide for the child's support.[87] However, in tort actions, it is generally held that ". . . when the defendant has negligently created a risk of harm to the plaintiff, the failure of a third person to intervene and take some action to prevent the risk from being realized, that is, to prevent the harm, will not affect the liability of the defendant when it in fact occurs."[88] By analogy, it may be argued that the father can foresee that a possible result of his act of intercourse is the birth of the child. Therefore, the mother's decision to bear where the abortion option is available is not sufficient to shift the burden of support to the mother. The question of whether the defendant is relieved from liability by the subsequent event has generally ". . . been determined by asking whether the intervention of the later cause is a significant part of the risk involved in the defendant's conduct, or is so reasonably connected with it that the responsibility should not be terminated."[89] Here, the birth of a child is an obvious part of the risk involved in the father's action. Thus, he should not be relieved of liability.

Once a person is placed in a position of having a duty of care toward another person, there must be some act which intervenes before that duty can shift to another person. Under Swan's analysis, that act is the mother's conscious decision to bear the child.[90] At first glance, it may seem that the Tenth Circuit Court of Appeals[91] supports Swan's analysis: ". . . the doctrine of proximate cause requires a continuous and unbroken sequence of events to establish liability, and . . . where the original wrong only becomes injurious in consequence of the intervention of some distinctive intervening negligent act by others, the proximate cause of the injury will be imputed to the second wrongdoer."[92] It may be

[87] *Id.* at 261.
[88] W. Prosser, & J. Wade, Cases and Materials on Torts 341 (5th ed. 1971).
[89] W. Prosser, The Law of Torts 272 (1971).
[90] Swan, *supra* note 86, at 261.
[91] U.S. v. First Security Bank, 208 F.2d 424 (10th Cir. 1953).
[92] *Id.* at 429.

argued that the act of the father becomes "injurious" *only* when the negligent act of the mother, that of bearing the child, intervenes, and that, therefore, the proximate cause of the "injury" should be imputed to the mother. However, the Tenth Circuit further states: "This is a correct statement of the abstract law, but to be applicable it must be shown that the intervening act would have caused the injuries independently of the original wrong."[93] In the situation discussed herein, such a notion is untenable!

Similarly, the Eighth Circuit Court of Appeals,[94] in an earlier decision, held that "[t]he intervening cause that will insulate the original wrongful act or omission from the injury and relief of liability for it must be an independent, intervening cause which interrupts the natural sequence of events, prevents the ordinary and probable result of the original act or omission, and produces a different result which could not have been reasonably anticipated."[95] The mother's decision to bear does not interrupt the natural sequence of events but rather allows the natural sequence of events to take place. Thus, the mother's decision to bear is not a sufficient intervening cause to shift the burden of support from the father to the mother.

Swan further cites the doctrine of last clear chance in support of his tort argument.[96] He argues that since the mother had the last clear chance to avoid the "injury" she should be required to indemnify the father.[97] However, this argument disregards the fact that, whereas the proximate cause analogy is applicable regardless of whether the act in question is a right or wrong, the doctrine of last clear chance is premised upon a duty to avoid which implies that what is avoided is a wrong. The analogy thus fails on two points: 1) The case which has dealt with the question, *Zepeda v. Zepeda,*[98] has held that birth is not a wrong for which recovery may be had; and 2) If the mother is held to have a duty to avoid, this implies a contract to abort. Such a contract is in violation of public

[93] *Id.*
[94] City of Winona v. Botzet, 169 F. 321 (8th Cir. 1909).
[95] *Id.* at 329.
[96] Swan, *supra* note 86, at 263.
[97] *Id.*
[98] Zepeda v. Zepeda, 41 Ill. App. 2d 240, 190 N.E.2d 849 (Ct. App. 1963).

policy, and will be more fully discussed under the contract analogy, *infra.* Without the assumption that birth is a wrong, the doctrine of last clear chance is inapplicable.

It may be further argued that the doctrine of last clear chance is actually the doctrine of proximate cause,[99] or shifting responsibility wherein the father again attempts to shift liability to the mother. As has been shown earlier, the parents' act of intercourse remains the proximate cause of the birth of the child regardless of any subsequent decision on the part of the mother. Thus, the last clear chance doctrine is not applicable.

The father's act of intercourse is sufficient to create a chain of causation between the initial event and the resulting effect; the mother's passive action or inaction may weaken that chain of causation but is not sufficient to break the chain. Without the broken chain or nexus, proponents of the father's rights are unable to successfully challenge the paternal support statutes under the *Roe v. Wade* analysis.

2. THE CONTRACT ANALOGY

Swan also uses contract law to support his argument that the nexus is broken by *Roe v. Wade.* He argues that the child can no longer be considered a third-party beneficiary of the contract between the parents since the ". . . procreation and nurture of children is . . ." no longer ". . . expressly contemplated by one sexual partner . . ."[100] Will public policy permit foreclosing the birth of a child as a foreseeable result of illicit intercourse? In order to relieve the father of his duty, it becomes necessary to imply a contract between the parties wherein the mother agrees to abort any child which may result. Such a contract would appear to be void as a violation of the public policy by implying an illicit relationship as a part of the contract.[101]

Swan further argues that if ". . . infants are free to sue fathers as well as mothers for maintenance, society's pregnant mothers will be more financially free to create future 'harms' (the 'harm' meaning

---

[99]Louisville & N.R. Co. v. Patterson, 77 Ga. App. 406, 408, 49 S.E. 2d 218, 220 (Ct. App. 1948).

[100]Swan, *supra* note 86, at 257.

[101]Doty v. Doty, 118 Ky. 204, 208, 80 S.W. 803, 807 (1904).

the maintenance need of children). If, conversely, infants are allowed only to sue mothers for maintenance, society's future mothers will be discouraged from producing infants in need of support. They instead will be encouraged to exercise their constitutional abortion rights."[102] Such an argument is highly coercive in nature. By using the threat of damages, the courts would, in effect, force the mother to give up her fundamental right to bear a child. Some parties may go still further and argue that specific performance is the only appropriate remedy. However, the Supreme Court has held that: "[t]o compel the specific performance of contracts still is the exception, not the rule, and courts would be slow to compel it in cases where it appears that paramount interests will or even may be interfered with by their action."[103] Whether the remedy be damages or specific performance, it is apparent that it is not merely a paramount interest which will be interfered with by such an argument, it is a paramount civil right. In *Skinner v. Oklahoma,*[104] a case involving a state statute requiring the sterilization of habitual criminals, the Supreme Court stated: "We are dealing here with legislation which involves one of the basic civil rights of man. Marriage and procreation are fundamental to the very existence and survival of the race."[105] Similarly, in *Griswold v. Connecticut,*[106] Justice Goldberg in his concurring opinion stated that "[t]he entire fabric of the Constitution and the purposes that clearly underlie its specific guarantees demonstrate that the rights to marital privacy and to marry and raise a family are of similar order and magnitude as the fundamental rights specifically protected . . ."[107] It is impossible for the courts to grant specific performance, or to award damages without jeopardizing the mother's fundamental right to give birth.

Furthermore, *Roe v. Wade* specifically limits the abortion decision to the mother and her doctor.[108] While *Roe* does prevent

[102]Swan, *supra* note 86, at 259.
[103]Beasley v. Texas & P.R. Co., 191 U.S. 492, 497 (1903).
[104]Skinner v. Oklahoma, 316 U.S. 535 (1942).
[105]*Id.* at 541.
[106]Griswold v. Connecticut, 381 U.S. 479 (1965).
[107]*Id.* at 495.
[108]410 U.S. at 164.

the state from prohibiting abortions during the first trimester, it does not shift to the other side of the coin to allow the state to compel abortions; *Roe* simply prohibits the state from interfering in the decision.[109]

As long ago as 1887, the Supreme Court of Georgia stated: "No one would contend for a single moment that a contract, agreement, or understanding, founded upon a consideration, in whole or in part, for the commencment or continuance of meretricious intercourse between the sexes, would not be directly contrary to law or public policy and the best interests of society."[110] Thus, the father continues to have a duty of support for the third-party beneficiary, the child, of the contract with the mother.

Since the third-party beneficiary contract may still be implied by a test of foreseeability, a father can escape liability under a contract analogy only by contracting with the mother to abort any resulting child. Such a contract would be void and/or unenforceable. Thus, the father remains liable.

3. THE CRIMINAL LAW ANALOGY

Finally, the argument can be made that the father is a mere bystander who could not be held liable as a criminal defendant.[111] Swan is willing to make only limited concessions on this point: "Even assuming that the physical cause-and-effect of impregnation makes the father's original act one cause among others resulting in the child, the father cannot be held liable in a criminal analogy for more than limited consequences of his act."[112] Such an argument brings us once more to the doctrine of proximate cause. In an analysis of proximate cause, Professor Joseph Beale of Harvard Law School stated: "Though there is an active force intervening after defendants' act, the result will nevertheless be proximate if the defendants' act actively caused the intervening force. In such a case the defendants' force is really continuing in active operation, by

---

[109]During the first trimester, the state may not interfere. 410 U.S. at 164. After the first trimester, the ". . . State may regulate the abortion procedure to the extent that the regulation reasonably relates to the preservation and protection of maternal health." 410 U.S. at 163.

[110]Smith v. DuBose, 78 Ga. 413, 418, 3 S.E. 309, 314 (1887).

[111]Swan, *supra* note 86, at 264.

[112]*Id.*

means of the force it stimulated into activity. . ."[113] In the situation considered here, the intervening act, that of the mother's decision to bear, does not and cannot arise without the father's act of intercourse. Thus, it may be said that the father's act continues in active operation by way of the mother's decision to bear.

One authority has stated that "[i]n order to sustain a conviction, the state must establish that the alleged conduct of the actor was the cause which, operating in natural and continuous sequence, was unbroken by any superseding or independent intervening cause, that it produced the result complained of, and that without such conduct the result would not have occurred."[114] It is obvious that without the conduct of the father, the birth of the child would not have occurred. Furthermore, under this authority's analysis only "independent" intervening causes can ". . . break the causal connection between the actor's initial conduct and the harm or injury suffered by the victim."[115] As a dependent intervening cause or one which the father could foresee, the mother's decision to bear does not break the chain of causation.

The Alabama Court of Appeals[116] has held that the fact that the victim had an equal opportunity of seeing the approaching danger and avoiding it is no defense.[117] A recent Englsh case[118] involved a stabbing victim who, as a Jehovah's Witness, refused to allow the doctors to give her a blood transfusion. The court held that: "It has long been the policy of the law that those who use violence on other people must take their victims as they find them. This in our judgment means the whole man, not just the physical man. It does not lie in the mouth of the assailant to say that his victim's religious beliefs which inhibited him from accepting certain kinds of treatment were unreasonable. The question for decision is what caused her death. The answer is the stab wound. The fact that the victim

---

[113]Beale, *The Proximate Consequences of an Act,* 33 HARV. L. REV. 633, 646 (1920), as cited in Commonwealth v. Almeida, 362 Pa. 596, 601, 68 A.2d 595, 600 (1949), *cert. den.*, Almeida v. Commonwealth, 339 U.S. 924 (1950), *rehearing den.*, 339 U.S. 950 (1950); *cert. den.*, Commonwealth ex rel Almeida v. Baldi, 340 U.S. 867 (1950).

[114]M. BASSIOUNI, CRIMINAL LAW AND ITS PROCESSES 75 (1969).

[115]*Id.*

[116]Broxton v. State, 27 Ala. App. 298, 171 So. 390 (Ct. App. 1936).

[117]*Id.*, 171 So. at 392.

[118]R. V. Blaue, [1975] 3 All E.R. 446 (C.A.).

refused to stop the end coming about did not break the causal connection between the act and death."[119]

Swan further argues that the father's act is too remote in time to hold him liable: "The mother's failure to abort during the long period of pregnancy makes the childbirth result not proximate to but remote from the father's role."[120] This argument ignores the fact that *Roe* has not legalized abortion for the entire term of the pregnancy but merely for the first trimester,[121] which makes the father's act only slightly more remote from the result than the mother's. The remoteness argument should therefore be discarded.

Thus criminal law analogy leads us once again to the question of causation. It is evident that the father cannot escape liability under this theory.

4. THE NEXUS IS NOT BROKEN

Upon examining the nexus between conception and birth from a tort, contract and criminal law analogy, it becomes clear that the nexus is not broken by the impact of *Roe v. Wade.* Without a broken nexus, there can be no valid challenge to paternal support statutes under the Equal Protection Clause since there is a rational relationship between the class affected and the objective of the statute.

Proponents of the father's rights may then argue that the equities lie with the father: "To saddle a man with twenty years of expensive, exhausting child support liability on the basis of a casual vicissitude of life seems to shock the conscience."[122] It seems unlikely that any court would accept such an argument. A more likely argument on the father's behalf is that since the act of intercourse provides the rationality for imposing a duty of support, that duty should be imposed equally upon both parents. This argument is already being made under the Equal Protection Clause.[123]

---

[119] *Id.* at 450.
[120] Swan, *supra* note 86, at 264.
[121] 410 U.S. at 163.
[122] Swan, *supra* note 86, at 265.
[123] *See* Fisher and Saxe, *Family Support Obligations: The Equal Protection Problem,* 46 N.Y.S.B.J. 441 (1974).

IV. Conclusion

The Supreme Court's decision in *Roe v. Wade* has greatly affected the parent-child relationship. The mother now has the opportunity to consciously decide whether to bear or abort the child; the father has no right to participate in this decision. Under one view, the irrebuttable presumption of nexus in paternal support statutes should be refutable and statutes which place the duty of support on the father in situations where the child is illegitimate and the mother has consciously decided to bear rather than abort, should be declared unconstitutional. This article argues to the contrary: that the mother's decision to bear does not refute the rational basis for holding fathers at least equally liable with mothers for the support of children resulting from the parents' sexual union. Current paternal support statutes deriving from this basis should be upheld.

Life With Father: 1978

HENRY H. FOSTER*
DORIS JONAS FREED†

Introduction

The noted English historian and jurist, Sir James Bryce, once asserted that in patriarchal societies there was an evolutionary change in the status of wives from a position of subordination to a level of equality.[1] Although the history of Roman law supported Bryce's thesis, English history makes it doubtful.

It is true that at one time evolutionary change in the status of wives did take place in England, so that under Anglo-Saxon law a wife was free to repudiate a marriage and to leave with her children and half the property.[2] But the establishment of the feudal order and the power of the church changed all that. There was an atavistic return to a status of subordination for almost 900 years until the women's movement of the nineteenth century brought a mutation which produced a measure of equality. As long as feudalism or its relics remained, the wife was not a legal person in the eyes of the

---

*Professor of Law Emeritus, New York University; immediate past Chairman, Family Law Section of the American Bar Association.

†Member, New York and Maryland Bars; Secretary, Family Law Section of the American Bar Association.

1. Bryce, *Marriage and Divorce Under Roman and English Law,* II STUDIES IN HISTORY AND JURISPRUDENCE 470 (1901), reprinted in III SELECT ESSAYS IN ANGLO-AMERICAN HISTORY (1909).

2. The *Dooms of Aethelbert* indicate that the wife had freedom to repudiate the marriage, saying that "if she wish to go away with her children, let her have half of the property. If the husband wish to have them, (let her portion be) as one child. If she bears no child, let paternal kindred have the 'fich' and the 'morgengyfe.'" *Dooms,* Nos. 79-81, reprinted in I ANCIENT LAWS AND INSTITUTIONS OF ENGLAND (1840).

law, and her role as mother merely entitled her to respect but not to authority.[3]

The English tradition was that the father was the natural guardian of the children and controlled their education and religious training.[4] He had the primary right to association with and the services of his children. In return, initially under the Elizabethan Poor Laws, and later by common law and statute, he was liable for their support and maintenance.[5] Thus, it was the father who could maintain an action for the seduction of a daughter or the enticement of a son who left home.[6] Since the seduction or enticement deprived him of services or earnings, such economic harm was actionable. Moreover, the father's authority had been abridged, and hence deserved vindication.

In general, today it is more accurate to speak of parental as distinguished from paternal authority, even though vestiges of feudalism survive. For example, the New York court in *Roe v. Doe,*[7] held that a twenty-year-old co-ed was obligated to comply with the reasonable regulations of her father if she was to receive his bounty. Moreover, the reasonableness of the regulations was viewed from the vantage point of the father, not that of the daughter. Presumably the same result would have been reached if it had been the mother instead of the father who had been footing the bills, although some of the language in the court's opinion indicates a specific identification with the peculiar problems of fathers.[8] As a caveat, it should be noted that *Roe v. Doe* does not necessarily control if a disobedient child seeks public assistance.[9]

So far as is known, to date no appellate court has considered the

---

3. *See* I BLACKSTONE, COMMENTARIES ON THE LAW OF ENGLAND 453.

4. *See* Andrews v. Salt, (1873) 8 Ch. App. 622. Subject to certain exceptions, the father had absolute right both at common law and in equity to determine the form of his children's education and religious training and his wishes had to be respected even after his death.

5. *See* Foster, *Dependent Children and the Law,* 18 U. PITT. L. REV. 579 (1957).

6. *See* Foster, *Relational Interests of the Family,* 1962 ILL. L. FORUM 493, 497-505.

7. 29 N.Y.2d 188, 324 N.Y.S.2d 71, 272 N.E.2d 567 (1971).

8. *Id.* at 29 N.Y.2d 194. "The father has the right, in the absence of caprice, misconduct or neglect, to require that the daughter conform to his reasonable demands. Should she disagree, and at her age that is surely her prerogative, she may elect not to comply; but in so doing, she subjects herself to her father's lawful wrath. Where, as here, she abandons her home, she forfeits her right to support."

9. *See* N.Y. Soc. Serv. Law § 101, and for a recent case, *see* Sevrie v. Sevrie, 394 N.Y.S.2d 389 (Fam. Ct. Rensselaer Co. 1977). *Compare,* Matter of Bickford v. Bickford, 371 N.Y.S.2d 782 (Fam. Ct. Schenectady Co. 1976). *See* decision by New York Court of Appeals, *Parker v. Stage* 43 N.Y.2d 128, 400 N.Y.S.2d 794 (1977).

common law tort liability of a religious cult that entices a minor child away from home to enter its order. Assuming no charitable immunity, on common law principles, the cult or its leaders are liable for interfering with the parent-child relationship,[10] although it may be argued that First Amendment principles preclude judgment or provide justification for the interference.[11] *Wisconsin v. Yoder*[12] may not provide an answer to this question, and the extent to which children's rights supersede parental authority when they are in conflict has yet to be determined.[13]

The current ferment in Family Law is such that virtually no tradition or precedent is secure. There is a real conflict of interests. And there is a children's movement as well as the women's movement. The traditional prerogatives of husband and father may now be regarded as historical anachronisms; everyone in the family is entitled to do his (or her) thing; and like the members of the Swiss navy, they are all admirals. But the death of paternalism and the diminution of authority is not a complete loss. The husband-father of 1978 has won some battles even though he may have lost the war. His gains have been principally in the areas of child support and child custody. If he can adapt, in the final analysis, he may be better off.

Since 1970 the majority of new state laws make child support the obligation of both parents,[14] rather than the primary obligation of the father, with the mother only secondarily liable if he is dead or cannot be found. Although this development may have occurred as a backlash to the women's movement, nonetheless it is fair and equitable to base the child support obligation upon the respective abilities to pay. The Uniform Marriage and Divorce Act goes further and takes the child's resources into account in setting the

---

10. *See* Foster, *Relational Interests of the Family*, 1962 ILL. L. FORUM 493, 498. The classic case is Tavlinsky v. Ringling Bros. Circus, 113 Neb. 632, 204 N.W. 388 (1925). *See also*, State v. Macri, 498 P.2d 355 (Utah 1972), which deals with the problem of liability for harboring runaway minors.

11. *Compare*, United States v. Ballard, 322 U.S. 78 (1944).

12. 406 U.S. 205 (1972).

13. Bartley v. Kremens, 402 F. Supp. 1039 (E.D. Pa. 1975), held that the consent of the minor was essential for involuntary commitment and that parental consent was insufficient. The case posed a conflict between parental authority and the autonomy of minors regarding hospitalization in a mental facility. The Supreme Court assumed jurisdiction to hear the case but later dismissed it as moot because of statutory changes in Pennsylvania law.

14. *See* Freed and Foster, 3 FAM. L. REP. 4052 (1977).

amount of child support.[15] Without the aid of statutory change, some states, such as New York, by decision, or perhaps by judicial legislation, have made child support the mutual obligation of both parents.[16] There appears to be a definite trend in that direction.

Child support has gone through several periods of transition.[17] At common law, there was no right to sue for child support by either the mother or the child. Under the poor laws, however, the parish might seek reimbursement from an errant father, or the mother might charge necessaries for herself and the children. The father's liability to creditors of his children for necessaries is a comparatively recent development, and, of course, the doctrine of parental immunity for many years precluded the child from suing as such for support. Today, in most states, there is a statutory hodge-podge of civil, criminal, and quasi-criminal statutes which impose a legal duty to support children and in some cases stepchildren.[18] Moreover, federal legislation and regulations now make federal resources available for the collection of child support, parent locator services are in operation in Washington and the several states, and no longer is it easy to evade support orders.[19] The only safe escape is death, since fathers, except in Louisiana and Oregon, are free to disinherit their children, a loophole which should be closed by remedial legislation.[20]

Although child support is an economic concern for many fathers, and an obligation that is increasingly difficult to shirk, it is in the area of custody and visitation that the father has the greatest emotional involvement. Here too, as a possible backlash from the women's movement, the legal status and the practical disadvantage of fathers are changing. It is this phenomenon we will discuss in more detail, and, borrowing a phrase, will consider in terms of the rise and fall of the "feminine mystique."

---

15. Uniform Marriage and Divorce Act § 332.

16. Although the N.Y. Family Court Act §§ 413 and 414 clearly impose a primary duty of child support on the father and only a secondary duty on the mother if the father is dead or cannot be found, § 415 imposes a duty on a *parent* if the child is or is about to be a recipient of public assistance. Despite the specific statutory language, the Appellate Division recently found that the duty of child support was mutual. *See* Carter v. Carter, 58 A.D.2d 438, 397 N.Y.S.2d 88 (2d Dept. 1977), and Lea v. Lea, N.Y.L.J., Nov. 14, 1977, p. 1, col. 6, p. 13, cols. 1-3 (1st Dept. 1977).

17. *See* Foster, *Dependent Children and the Law*, 18 U. PITT. L. REV. 579 (1957).

18. *Ibid.*

19. *See* Foster, Freed, and Midonick, *Child Support: The Quick and the Dead*, 26 SYRACUSE L. REV. 1157 (1975).

20. *Id.* at 1180 *et seq.*

Child Custody: The Rise and Fall of the Feminine Mystique

Feudalism and the church combined to make the husband the *paterfamilias* at common law. His dominance, under the law, was well nigh absolute, and if one were to arbitrarily set the date at which his control was relaxed, it would be 1817. In that year the poet Percy Bysshe Shelley lost the custody of his children after Harriet's suicide because of his atheistic beliefs and profligate conduct.[21] Lord Eldon in effect held Ariel unfit as a parent, thus qualifying the father's absolute right to custody.

Before *this* rule in Shelley's case, Blackstone had stated the law to be that the father had a natural right to his children and the mother "is entitled to no power [over her children], but only to reverence and respect."[22] Although this broad statement in general was true, possible exceptions were noted by that careful craftsman, Lord Mansfield, who was cautious enough to recognize that there might be limits to a father's absolute power or *potestas* over his children.

In *Rex v. Delaval,*[23] a girl of about 18 was freed from apprenticeship when the musician to whom she was bound by her father turned the girl over to Delaval for the purposes of prostitution. Initially, Lord Mansfield was of the impression that the father was in on the conspiracy, but he was found not to have been involved, and the girl was "discharged from all restraint" and was set "at liberty to go where she will." Lord Mansfield was prepared to act in a *parens patriae* capacity to protect the girl from the conspirators and even from her father if necessary. The Chancellor or the bishop will protect the working girl.

In *Blisset's Case,*[24] Lord Mansfield denied a writ of habeas corpus sought by the father, and, while conceding that he had a natural right to his child, held that, since the father was bankrupt,

---

21. Shelley v. Westbrooke, 37 Eng. Rep. 850 (Ch. 1817). Shelley was the son of a Whig aristocrat and M.P. and was expelled from Oxford for writing a pamphlet on "The Necessity of Atheism" which he improvidently mailed to all of the bishops and heads of colleges. Subsequently Shelley eloped with Harriet, and later left her with one child and another on the way, to take up life with Mary, the daughter of William Godwin and Mary Wollstonecraft and later the author of *Frankenstein.* Harriet committed suicide and Shelley sought to obtain custody of their two children. After being deprived of their custody, he spent his last four years in self-exile in Italy.

22. 1 Blackstone, Commentaries on the Law of England 453.

23. 3 Burr. 1413 (1763).

24. Loft's Rep. 748 (1773).

contributed nothing to the child or the family, and had engaged in improper conduct, "the court will not think it right that the child should be with him," and further, "if parties are disagreed, *the court will do what shall appear best for the child.*" [emphasis supplied]

Thus, while there were broad statements as to the custodial entitlement of the father, and ordinarily his paternal rights were enforceable, the above cases indicate that his claimed absolute right was conditioned upon his fitness as a parent. Such was consistent with the obligations that status imposed under the feudal system and in keeping with the traditions of Chancery and the ecclesiastical courts. *Noblesse oblige.* Moreover, Lord Mansfield in *Blisset's Case* even anticipated the subsequent "best interests" rule.

Whether the father had an absolute right to the custody of his children, or alternatively his right was "absolute" only when he was a *fit* custodian, is largely a matter of academic interest since in fact the father usually prevailed even in unlikely situations. For example, Lord Ellenborough ordered the return of a nursing infant to a French father, who was an enemy alien, even though the father's cruelty had driven the mother and the children from his home.[25] Considering English distaste for the French, the decision is remarkable, and in light of the circumstances it may have been unconscionable.

After Shelley's case, Parliament by a series of statutes, culminating in Justice Talfourd's Act in 1839,[26] diluted the rights of the father and extended the claims of the mother so that chancery was permitted to award custody to the mother if the children were less than seven years old. This latter statute was the origin of the "tender years doctrine" in England and may have influenced some American decisions.

It is doubtful that the father's right to child custody ever was absolute in the United States. Early decisions, although sometimes referring to the father's "natural rights,"[27] reckoned with the cir-

25. King v. De Manneville, 3 East 221, 102 Eng. Rep. 1054 (1800). *See also. Ex parte* Skinner, 9 Moore 278 (1824), where the court of Chancery denied the mother custody even though the father had caused the separation and was sharing custody of the child with his mistress who visited him in jail.

26. 2 and 3 Vict. c. 54.

27. *For example, see* United States v. Green, 26 F. Cas. 30 (D.R.I. 1824) No. 15,256; Commonwealth v. Addicks, 5 Binn. 519 (Pa. 1813); McKim v. McKim, 12 R.I. 462 (1879);

cumstances of the particular case. By a process of evolution, perhaps reflecting a change in social attitudes, the mother eventually came to be the preferred custodian of young children and daughters, if, but only if, she were a "fit" mother.[28] If the mother was divorced for her adultery, she might lose custody of her children if their father claimed them;[29] so too if she was addicted to liquor or had "loose morals."[30] Vice was its own reward.

Some of the better known nineteenth century American custody decisions reached the same result that one would expect today. A New York court in 1816 refused to disturb the de facto custody of maternal grandparents who continued to raise the child after the mother's death, although the separated father did receive liberal visitation rights, "taking it for granted that he will not attempt to take her [the child] away from the custody of her grandparents."[31] The court said:

> *The case of Commonwealth v. Addicks and Wife* (5 Binney's Rep. 520) is very much in point, and a strong corroboration of the principle, that it is a matter resting in the sound discretion of the court, and not a matter of right which the father can claim at the hands of the court. *It is to the benefit and welfare of the infant to which the attention of the court ought to be directed;* and this can be much better guarded and protected by the court of chancery, under its peculiar jurisdiction, than by this court, upon habeas corpus. . . .[emphasis supplied]

The same reasoning and result was reached by a Rhode Island court in a case involving a famous New York architect.[32] A four-year-old daughter was left with her mother and maternal grandparents who lived in Newport, even though the father was found to be a fit parent, the court saying

> The welfare of the child, considering her tender age, her sex, and the delicacy of her constitution, will . . . be best subserved by leaving her for the present with her mother; and indeed we think that for the present, to take her from her mother is too hazardous an experiment for us to try. . . .

Commonwealth v. Briggs, 16 Pick. 203 (Mass. 1834); People *ex rel.* Olmstead v. Olmstead, 27 Barb. 9 (N.Y. 1857); and *In re* Waldron, 13 Johns. 417 (N.Y. 1816). *Compare,* People *ex rel.* Barry v. Mercein, 3 Hill 399 (N.Y. 1842).

28. For an excellent recent article, *see* Roth, *The Tender Years Presumption in Child Custody Disputes,* 15 J. FAM. L. 423 (1977). Cases are collected from some 37 states adopting the tender years doctrine, often despite "equalization" acts.

29. *See* Simpson, *The Unfit Parent,* 39 U. DET. L.J. 347 (1962); Foster & Freed, *Child Custody*, 39 N.Y.U. L. REV. 423, 429-31 (1964); and Comment, *Effect of Adultery on Custody Awards,* 16 WASH. & LEE L. REV. 287 (1959).

30. *Ibid.*

31. *In re* Waldron, 13 Johns. 418 (N.Y. 1816).

32. McKim v. McKim, 12 R.I. 462 (1878).

Although the child's welfare was emphasized in the above cases, a mother who separated from her husband without justification was vulnerable. Chief Justice Shaw in 1834 wrote the opinion in *Commonwealth v. Briggs,*[33] saying that

> the Court ought not to sanction the unauthorized separation of husband and wife, by ordering the child into the custody of the mother, thus separated and out of the custody of the father.

Even though the "good of the child is to be regarded as the primary consideration" in determining the custody of a child of tender years, the unauthorized separation of the mother, without any apparent justifiable cause, was a "strong reason why the child should not be restored to her." In effect, public policy regarding the obligations of marriage, or a desire to punish an errant wife, superseded concern over the child's best interests.

Such moral activism also was evident in *People ex rel. Olmstead v. Olmstead,*[34] where the New York court punished a wife who had been brainwashed by her mother and without good cause left the marital home. This classic case of an intermeddling mother-in-law probably overstated legal doctrine when the court said that

> The paramount legal right of the father to the custody and education of his child can be interfered with by a court of equity only when he has been at fault in bringing about the separation. It has never been dreamed that, when the mother has been at fault in the occurrences preceding the separation, she should be rewarded for her faults by the interposition of the courts.

The court rejected the contention that the "true test" was the ultimate good of the child and held that it was more important to protect the family from attacks such as had been made by the mother-in-law.

The fault of the father also was a crucial factor in numerous custody decisions in the last century. *Brinster v. Compton*[35] is a good example of a father whose conduct forfeited his claim to custody. The father in question had abandoned two motherless sons in their infancy, made no provision for their support, and for eight years failed to let them know where he was or that he was alive. When the boys were nineteen and fourteen years old, and were serving as ap-

---

33. 16 Pick. 203 (Mass. 1834).

34. 27 Barb. 9 (N.Y. 1857). *See also,* People *ex rel.* Barry v. Mercein, 3 Hill 399 (N.Y. 1842), where the mother without justification took her child and left her husband, moving back into her father's home. The father obtained a writ of habeas corpus even though he had agreed in writing that the mother should have custody of their four-year-old daughter.

35. 68 Ala. 299 (1880).

prentices, the father brought habeas corpus for their custody. In denying the writ, the court noted that it had discretion which should be exercised "for the benefit of the infant primarily," and that if the father was reasonably suitable and able to maintain and rear his children, he should be preferred, but if "he be unsuitable or unable properly to care for his offspring . . . [and especially if the children are of sufficient age and prefer not to return to him], the court should grant no relief in the premises. . . ."

The rules and principles applicable to custody cases which were developed in the last century form the matrix for the law today. But the priorities are different and the emphasis is not the same.

In this century, at the conclusion of the Victorian period, conduct which formerly provoked automatic disqualification came to be considered as mere factors to be weighed and balanced in the exercise of judicial discretion. Today, for a claimant to custody to be disqualified, usually the "unfitness" must be directly related to child care, although rural courts may enforce a more inflexible sense of morality. Sophisticated judges, on the other hand, assume that a bad spouse may be an excellent parent, and that even a poor parent may be better than a stranger or institutionalization.[36] The course of development perhaps may best be seen if we examine the evolution of the so-called tender years doctrine.

The Tender Years Doctrine

In the United States, as we have seen, custodial rights from the beginning have been conditioned upon parental fitness. For either parent to prevail, he or she must be deemed "fit." The caution of Lord Mansfield and the indignation of Lord Eldon, plus the policy behind Justice Talfourd's Act of entrusting young children to their "fit" mother, were expressed in early American decisions. It has been reported that the first pronouncement of the tender years doctrine,[37] or the rule as to maternal preference, was the decision in *Helms v. Franciscus.*[38] The Maryland court in 1830, after stating

36. *Id.* Today, concern over an adulterous parent having custody has been diverted to the problem of whether or not a homosexual parent is entitled to custody or visitation. In effect, Texas says "no"; Washington "yes"; and California "it all depends."

37. *See* Kurtz, *The State Equal Rights Amendments and Their Impact on Domestic Relations Law,* 11 FAM. L.Q. 101, 137 (1977).

38. 2 Bl. Ch. (Md.) 544 (1830).

that the father is the sole and legal guardian of all of his infant children, and that generally, no court can take them from him and give them to his wife, went on to say by way of dicta,

> yet even a court of common law will not go so far as to hold nature in contempt, and snatch helpless, puling infancy from the bosom of an affectionate mother, and place it in the coarse hands of the father. The mother is the softest nurse of infancy, and with her it will be left in opposition to this general right of the father.

Obviously, the Maryland court had not heard of Lord Ellenborough's decision.

At least inferentially, an even earlier case, *United States v. Green,*[39] opened the door for the tender years doctrine. Mr. Justice Story, on circuit, assumed *federal* jurisdiction over a habeas corpus action brought by the father to obtain custody from the maternal grandfather. Considering that eventually federal courts adopted a "hands off" attitude regarding jurisdiction over domestic relations cases, the assumption of habeas corpus jurisdiction was surprising. As Lord Mansfield had done before him, Justice Story conceded that generally a father had the right to the custody of his children, and then said,

> But this is not on account of any absolute right of the father *but for the benefit of the infant,* the law presuming it to be for his interest to be under the nurture and care of his natural protector, both for maintenance and education. When, therefore, the court is asked to lend its aid to put the infant into the custody of the father, and to withdraw him from other persons, *it will look into all of the circumstances and ascertain whether it will be for the real permanent interests of the infant; and if the infant be of sufficient discretion, it will also consult its personal wishes. . . .It is an entire mistake to suppose the court is at all events bound to deliver over the infant to the father, or that the latter has an absolute vested right to the custody. . . .* [emphasis supplied]

It is interesting to note that in the hands of judges of the caliber of Lord Mansfield and Justice Joseph Story, the entitlement of the father was qualified by the child's best interests. Their decisions sound contemporary. Lesser judges, however, spoke uncritically in terms of absolutes.[40] In another famous child custody decision, later Justice Brewer spoke for the Kansas court in declaring that the

39. 26 F. Cas. 30, 31 (D.R.I. 1824) No. 15,256.

40. *For example, see* King v. De Manneville, and *Ex parte* Skinner, *op. cit. supra* note 5; and People *ex rel.* Barry v. Mercein, 3 Hill (N.Y.) 399 (1842), which rejected an agreement that the mother have custody, saying that the wife had no separate identity recognized by law, and that, "By the law of the land the claims of the father are superior to those of the mother."

paramount question in custody cases was what would best promote the welfare and interest of the child;[41] and in *Finlay v. Finlay,*[42] then Judge Cardozo emphasized the state's role as *parens patriae* and the need to protect children as the basis for custody jurisdiction.

At least in some measure, the central problem has been, and still is, that in custody cases there is no substitute for hard and meticulous fact-finding by the trial court. The great jurists who have had something to say about child custody have recognized this and have avoided over-generalization and absolutes. Less sensitive and knowledgeable judges have found it convenient to apply presumptions, doctrines, or rules of thumb. *Painter v. Banister*[43] is a judicial example of over-reaction to the parental rights doctrine, and the slender volume, *Beyond the Best Interests of the Child,* is an academic example of over-reacting and replacing inflexibility with rigidity.[44] Hard doctrines make hard doctrines.

The law's use of fictions and substantive rules of law disguised as presumptions is probably as old as our art and craft. These fictions and rules have been useful devices to avoid difficult fact-finding and provide a means of adapting the law to a myriad of unforeseeable circumstances so that the law may appear to be what it is not: secure and certain. In our world of legal make-believe it is a wonder that *Alice Through the Looking Glass* has been cited less frequently than Blackstone, or A. P. Herbert's *Uncommon Law* less often than *Prosser on Torts.*

The tender years doctrine comes in different forms. It may serve as a mere preference or "tie breaker" when other factors are equal, or it may require that the father introduce rebuttal evidence.[45] In some cases it serves in lieu of evidence, as in the famous "Baby Lenore" case,[46] where the New York court gratuitously presumed

---

41. Chapsky v. Wood, 26 Kan. 650, 40 Am. R. 321 (1881).

42. 240 N.Y. 429, 148 N.E. 624 (1925).

43. 140 N.W.2d 152 (Iowa 1966). *See* Foster, *Adoption and Child Custody: Best Interests of the Child?,* 22 BUFFALO L. REV. 1, 4-7 (1972).

44. *See* Foster, *A Review of Beyond the Best Interests of the Child,* 12 WILLAMETTE L. REV. 545 (1976).

45. *See* Kurtz, *op. cit. supra* note 37 at 138, and, in general, *see* Roth, *op. cit. supra* note 28 at 441, where he states: "Some courts claim that the preference for a mother is merely that—a preference—and not a legal presumption, but in the practical effect, it would seem that the father still has the burden to persuade that she is unfit."

46. People *ex rel.* Scarpetta v. Spence-Chapin Adoption Service, 28 N.Y.2d 185, 321 N.Y.S. 65, 269 N.E.2d 787 (1971), discussed by Foster, *op. cit. supra* note 29 at 7-10. *See*

that the child's best interests would be served by returning it to the natural mother. Recent decisions, however, seem to accord lesser weight to the tender years doctrine, and where it still exists it may function mainly as a "tie breaker" when other factors are equal. It should be noted, however, that factors are rarely equal if there is a meticulous investigation and evaluation of the facts.

There also is uncertainty as to just what are "tender years." Generally it is agreed that preschool age children so qualify, but there is a conflict in the cases as to older children.[47] It may be that there is a maternal preference for daughters to an older age than that for sons. There also is some evidence that there is a recent trend to reduce the operative age for the tender years doctrine.[48]

A recent check of the American jurisdictions indicates that the tender years doctrine has lost ground so that in 1978 it is either rejected or relegated to the role of "tie breaker" in most states. The doctrine itself remains "gospel," but may be subordinated to the assumed best interests of the children in some fourteen states.[49] In at least twelve states there is a preference for a "fit" mother, other factors being equal.[50] And in twenty-two states the tender years doctrine is rejected by statute or court decision.[51] It has a doubtful status in three states.[52] Of necessity this tabulation is only approximate because of conflict in the language and in the decisions.

One of the amazing things about the tender years doctrine is that it has often persisted even in the face of "equalization" statutes or state Equal Rights Amendments (ERA). For example, New York for many years has provided by statute that neither parent has a

---

also S. Katz, *The Adoption of Baby Lenore: Problems of Consent and The Role of Lawyers*, 5 Fam. L.Q. 405 (1971).

47. *See* Clark, Law of Domestic Relations 585 (1968).

48. The authors were informed at a program attended in 1974 at the University of Kentucky that by court decision the tender years doctrine had been lowered from adolescents to preschool children.

49. Alabama, Arkansas, Florida, Kentucky, Louisiana, Maryland, Mississippi, New Jersey, Rhode Island, South Carolina, Tennessee, West Virginia, Wisconsin, and Wyoming.

50. The so-called "tie breaker" jurisdictions appear to be: Idaho, Minnesota, Missouri, Montana, Nevada, New Mexico, North Dakota, Oklahoma, Pennsylvania, South Dakota, Utah, and Virginia. Other factors being equal, preference may be given to the mother where young children are involved.

51. Jurisdictions which appear to reject the tender years doctrine appear to be: Alaska, Arizona, California, Colorado, Connecticut, Delaware, District of Columbia, Georgia, Hawaii, Illinois, Indiana, Iowa, Maine, Massachusetts, Michigan, Nebraska, New Hampshire, New York (lower court decision), North Carolina, Ohio, Texas, and Washington.

52. The three doubtful states are Kansas, Oregon, and Vermont.

prima facie or preferred right to child custody.[53] Nonetheless, until quite recently the mother prevailed in at least 90 percent of the cases where she sought custody, and ordinarily she lost only upon a showing of parental unfitness. The New York experience was not unique.

In the seventeen states presently having ERA provisions,[54] the tender years doctrine is alive and well in eight states,[55] and has supposedly been discarded in nine states.[56] Although considering the wording of ERA provisions, and the intent and purpose back of them, it is difficult to see how the tender years doctrine could survive in a state having ERA, courts wanting to do so have found ways around the law. One way is to stress the best interests of the child and then to assume that ordinarily the child's welfare will be best served by being with the mother.[57] The Utah court in *Arends v. Arends,*[58] did just that when it rejected a father's claim to parity with the observation that his claim might have merit "if the father was equally gifted in lactation as is the mother," thus imposing an insurmountable burden upon him even in these silicon days. As has been noted, sexual stereotyping of the loving, tender, and self-sacrificing mother makes any other choice as to custody a more detrimental alternative.[59] Uncritical sentimentality toward mothers in general came to be as unsupportable as the feudalistic premises

53. *See* N.Y. Dom. Rel. L. §§ 70 and 240. "In all cases there shall be no prima facie right to the custody of the child in either parent, but the court shall determine solely what is for the best interest of the child, and what will best promote its welfare and happiness, and make award accordingly." "In all cases there shall be no prima facie right to the custody of the child in either parent."

54. The ERA states are: Alaska, Colorado, Connecticut, Hawaii, Illinois, Louisiana, Maryland, Massachusetts, Montana, New Hampshire, New Mexico, Pennsylvania, Texas, Utah, Virginia, Washington, and Wyoming.

55. Louisiana, Maryland, Montana, New Mexico, Pennsylvania, Utah, Virginia, and Wyoming.

56. Alaska, Colorado, Connecticut, Hawaii, Illinois, Massachusetts, New Hampshire, Texas, and Washington.

57. *See* Kurtz, *op. cit. supra* note 12 at 135-43.

58. 30 Utah 2d 328, 517 P.2d 1019 at 1020 (1974). *See also.* Funkhouser v. Funkhouser, 216 S.E.2d 570 at 574 (W. Va. 1975), which claims that "a mother's love, affection and care of a child of tender years [here 4 years] is essential to the welfare of the child." *Compare.* Rayer v. Rayer, 512 P.2d 637 at 640 (Colo. 1973), holding that the mere fact of motherhood was insufficient to give the mother any special standing or preference and the child's welfare was the prime criterion. *See also,* Eviston v. Eviston, 507 S.W.2d 153 (Ky. App. 1974), upholding award of 6-year-old son to father; and McCray v. McCray, 56 Wash. 2d 73, 350 P.2d 1006 at 1008 (1960), which held that the tender years doctrine was inapplicable to school children but that "prior to the bottle feeding vogue" the mother's care was "well nigh indispensable."

59. Kurtz, *op. cit. supra* note 32 at 138.

that the father-husband was lord and master by natural right.

Today, while some courts cling to the tender years doctrine despite statutes and ERA provisions, other courts, with or without the aid of statutes, have condemned the doctrine as sex discrimination. New York, in *State ex rel. Watts v. Watts,*[60] specifically rejected the doctrine as violative of the due process and equal protection provisions of the federal Constitution. Iowa, by court decision, held that the doctrine must be discarded,[61] and decisions from ERA states such as Illinois[62] have held that a preference for the mother violated its ERA.

One of the difficulties in eliminating the maternal preference is that the older literature on child development supported it, and there have been but few studies on the effect of paternal, as distinguished from maternal, deprivation on child development.[63] More recently, a growing number of experts on child development have recognized that a father may be the one with whom children have the most affectionate relationship and hence he should be awarded custody.[64] Presumably the age and sex of the child, and the closeness of its associations are considerations that should be reckoned with in determining custody and visitation. The Michigan custody statute[65] stresses psychological parenthood, as does the Uniform Marriage and Divorce Act to a lesser degree.[66] Other states, however, may have a predilection if not an overt preference for the mother as custodian. Although Dr. Salk in New York won the custody of his two children, and the case purports to have been decided on a best interests basis,[67] it is not safe to assume that even a child psychologist would have prevailed in New York if the children in question had been puling babies or toddlers.

---

60. 77 Misc. 2d 178, 350 N.Y.S.2d 285 (Fam. Ct. 1973).

61. *In re* Marriage of Bowen, 219 N.W.2d 683 (Iowa 1974) "We do not think either parent should have a greater burden than the other in attempting to obtain custody. . . .It is neither necessary nor useful to infer in advance that the best interests of children [here 10-year-old boy and 1-year-old girl] will be better served if their custody is awarded to their mothers instead of their fathers. We previously emphasized the weakness of the inference, we now abandon it."

62. *See* King v. Vancil, 341 N.E.2d 65 (Ill. App. 1975), and discussion by Kurtz, *op. cit. supra* note 12 at 139-40.

63. *See* Roth, *op. cit. supra* note 28 at 449-57 for a recent discussion of the literature.

64. *Ibid.*

65. MICH. COMP. LAWS ANN. § 722.73 (Cum. Supp. 1977-1978).

66. *See* Uniform Marriage & Divorce Act § 402.

67. Salk v. Salk, 393 N.Y.S.2d 841 (1977).

In the *Watts* case,[68] and also in *In re Marriage of Bowen*,[69] the respective courts of New York and Iowa subjected the tender years doctrine to its most searching analysis. In *Watts* the New York court concluded that the tender years presumption

> is actually a blanket judicial finding of fact, a statement by the court that, until proven otherwise by the weight of substantial evidence, mothers are always better suited to care for young children than fathers. This flies in the face of the legislative finding of fact . . . that the best interests of the child are served by the court's approaching the facts of the particular case before it without sex preconceptions of any kind.[70]

It also was noted that "the trend in legislation, legal commentary, and judicial decisions is away from the 'tender years presumption.' "

The court cited Margaret Mead and other authorities who have acknowledged and asserted that both female and male parents are equally able to provide care and to perform child-rearing functions. The court concluded that

> The "best interests" of the child might well qualify as . . . a compelling state interest if, in fact, it were served by the "tender years presumption." But since . . . the presumption does not in fact serve the child's best interests, it does not constitute a compelling state interest justifying the different treatment of parents on the basis of sex. Thus the "tender years presumption" in addition to its other faults, works an unconstitutional discrimination against the respondent.[71]

The *Bowen* case involved a thirty-nine-year-old mother of six children who had extra-marital affairs with teen-age boys. Applying the tender years presumption, the trial court awarded her custody of the minor children. The appellate court abandoned the doctrine; rejected any hard and fast rule; and said that the issue is ultimately [to be] decided by determining upon the whole record which parent can minister more effectively to the long-range best interests of the children.

> It is wrong to treat a parental custody decision as merely an adjudication of parental rights. Children are innocent victims of marital bankruptcy. Their welfare is paramount. Custodial claims of contending parents are subservient to the rights of their children to grow to maturity in a proper environment.[72]

Instead of following the *Watts* declaration that the tender years

---

68. 77 Misc. 2d 178, 350 N.Y.S.2d 285 (Fam. Ct. N.Y. Co. 1973).
69. 219 N.W.2d 683 (Iowa 1974). *See also, In re* Wahl, 3 FAM. L. REP. 2077 (Iowa 1977).
70. 350 N.Y.S.2d at 287-88.
71. 350 N.Y.S.2d at 291.
72. 219 N.W.2d at 688.

doctrine was unconstitutional as a violation of equal protection principles, the Iowa court merely held that the doctrine was *unwise.*

> It is simply not justified as an *a priori* principle. It tends to obscure the basic tenet in custody cases which overrides all others, the best interests of the children. The real issue is not the sex of the parent but which parent will do better in raising the children. Resolution of that issue depends upon what the evidence actually reveals in each case, not upon what someone predicts it will show in many cases. If past decisions teach us anything, "it is that each case must be decided on its own peculiar fact. . . ."[73]

Because the father had maintained a wholesome and constructive relationship with the children, and had placed their interests first, and provided a stable and loving home, it was held that the prospects for the children were better with him than with their mother.

Instead of abandoning the tender years doctrine, Wisconsin now holds that there is a "slight" maternal preference.[74] Texas appears to have a modified version of the doctrine,[75] and in Maryland[76] and Missouri,[77] recent decisions limit the doctrine to a "tie breaker" function. However, Idaho[78] and Louisiana[79] are among the states that still adhere to the maternal preference philosophy, and seem to be unaffected by its demise elsewhere.

Other recent decisions have weighed and balanced the adulterous or immoral conduct of a mother along with the needs of the children and the custodial claims of the father. Thus, in *Moore v. Smith,*[80] the Arkansas appellate court reversed the trial court's award of a twelve-year-old son to the mother, citing as reasons the son's preference for life with father; the fact that the mother had been married and divorced five times; and could not control her son; twisted his hair; and the fact that the son did better in school when living with his father who also took him to Sunday school. The court also found that the mother had a boy friend who lived with

---

73. *Ibid.*

74. *See* Scolman v. Scolman, 66 Wis. 2d 761, 226 N.W.2d 388 (1975).

75. Erwin v. Erwin, 505 S.W.2d 370 at 372 (Tex. Civ. App. 1974), held that as a general rule a mother should be awarded custody of children of tender years when she is found to be fit and all other factors are equal, but the general rule states no more than a preference for the mother and not a legal presumption.

76. Cooke v. Cooke, 319 A.2d 841 (Md. App. 1974).

77. L.D.H. v. T.P.H., 492 S.W.2d 857 (Mo. App. 1973).

78. Barrett v. Barrett, 94 Idaho 64, 480 P.2d 910 (1971).

79. Whatley v. Whatley, 312 So.2d 149 (La. App. 1975) (mother preferred unless she is shown to have forfeited her right to custody by being shown to be morally unfit or otherwise unsuitable).

80. 499 S.W.2d 634 (Ark. 1973).

her, and that the father did not curse nor drink, while the mother was a visitor to local night clubs. Although the maternal preference was not rejected by the Arkansas court, it did note that the doctrine had less force the older the child and that the primary concern was which one would make the better parent.

The Kansas court, as Iowa had done in *Bowen*, condemned sexual affairs by a middle-aged mother with teen-aged boys, and held that an award of custody of two young boys to her was an abuse of discretion.[81] The rule announced was that "Almost, but not quite of necessity, is custody of small children to be placed with the mother." Florida reached the same result in a case involving a three-year-old where it was found that the adulterous conduct of the mother adversely affected the child.[82] Michigan, however, under its comprehensive custody statute, held that moral fitness of each parent was merely one factor to be considered, and affirmed the placement of the child with the mother even though the father was found to be "more fit," morally speaking.[83] The mother had been guilty of adultery but was a concerned parent who maintained close contact with school teachers and the family doctor, kept the children clean, well dressed, and adequately fed, and did not leave them unattended. She had "a closer, more intimate relationship with the children than defendant." In another case, Illinois rejected the mother's argument that she had lost custody because of judicial bias against her lifestyle.[84] She claimed that the court was influenced by the fact that she drove a motorcycle, had smoked marijuana, had continued in college after her child was born, occasionally swore, had gay friends, and wanted to pursue her career and to raise an independent child. The court held that the best interests of the child required that custody be awarded to the father.

There is one situation where a strong maternal preference is likely to remain even though otherwise the tender years doctrine has been abolished or downgraded. The natural mother of a child born out of wedlock traditionally has been favored over the natural father and only recently has he been accorded even visitation rights. None

81. Dalton v. Dalton, 214 Kan. 805, 522 P.2d 378 (1974).
82. Bone v. Bone, 344 So.2d 142 (Fla. App. 1976).
83. Feldman v. Feldman, 55 Mich. App. 147, 222 N.W.2d 2 (1974).
84. Anagnostopoulos v. Anagnostopoulos, 22 Ill. App. 3d 479, 317 N.E.2d 681 (1974).

other than Abraham Lincoln, Esquire, in an 1845 Illinois case,[85] stated the common law rule that as between the mother and father of an illegitimate child the mother's right of custody is superior and the father's right secondary. In *People ex rel. Irby v. Dubois,*[86] Lincoln's common law rule was abandoned, and it was held that no presumption favoring either parent would be indulged in, since the modern woman often was employed and authorities assert that "fathering" can be as important as "mothering" for both boys and girls. "The factual basis, if there was one, for the so-called 'tender years doctrine' is gone." This result was reinforced by the ERA amendment in Illinois.

The leading recent decision relegating the tender years presumption to a limited role as a "tie breaker" is from Virginia.[87] The court asserted that the doctrine

> has nothing to do with the respective rights of the two parents. Rather, it has to do with the right of the child. The "presumption" is, in fact, an inference society has drawn that such right is best served when a child of tender years is awarded to the custodial care of its mother. . . .The courts, acting in the interest of society at large, apply that inference irrespective of the rights of the parents. And that inference controls unless, in a particular case, it is overcome by evidence that the right of the child will be better served by awarding the child to the custodial care of its father. By definition, the inference controls only when the evidence shows that the mother is fit and "other things" affecting the child's welfare are equal.[88]

Since the trial court concluded that "other things" were not equal, and the appellate court agreed, the custody of children four and five years old remained with the father who was found to have performed both the mother and father roles in the particular family, while the mother was more concerned about her career and an affair with her supervisor than she was over her children.

Those states which have enacted the Uniform Marriage and Divorce Act,[89] or other recent statutory revisions,[90] make no reference to a maternal preference. The new states of Alaska[91] and

85. Wright v. Bennett, 7 Ill. 587 (1845).

86. 41 Ill. App. 3d 609, 354 N.E.2d 562 (1976).

87. McCreery v. McCreery, 3 FAM. L. REP. 3181 (Fairfax Co., Va. 1977).

88. 3 FAM. L. REP. 3181-82.

89. *For example, see* Georgia v. Georgia, 27 Ariz. App. 271, 553 P.2d 1256 (1976); Rayer v. Rayer, 512 P.2d 637 (Colo. App. 1973); Eviston v. Eviston, 507 S.W.2d 153 (Ky. App. 1974) (if placed with father, child would live in customary home); and *In re* Tweeten, 3 FAM. L. REP. 2500 (Mont. 1977).

90. *For example, see* Nelson v. Murray, 211 A.2d 842 (Del. 1965); Ray v. Ray, 502 P.2d 397 (Ore. 1972). *See also,* Folsom v. Folsom, 228 Ga. 536, 186 So.2d 752 (1972).

91. King v. King, 477 P.2d 356 (Alaska 1970); and Johnson v. Johnson, 3 FAM. L. REP.

Hawaii[92] also reject the tender years doctrine, and Ohio[93] has declared that custody must be awarded on the basis of the best interests of the children, rather than because of any preference for mothers.

Considering the gross sentimentality which long has been associated with the rule of maternal preference and the changes which have occurred in the modern American family, it is difficult to justify retention of this rule. However, if courts believe it is necessary to go on record in favor of mother love, as legislators feel compelled to do regarding sin, the restricted use of the tender years doctrine as a "tie breaker" may be a step forward. The Maryland decision in *Cooke v. Cooke*[94] illustrates the point.

In that case the trial judge rested his decision upon an application of the tender years doctrine to the facts before him. The appellate court affirmed, not on the basis of the doctrine but because of the facts. The father had abducted the child from the mother and had tried to use the child as a hostage in order to force the wife to return to live with him. The evidence showed that the father was unpredictable, highly volatile, and impulsive, while the mother had been the stabilizing influence and the main financial support of the family. The court upon appeal criticized the trial court's reliance upon the tender years doctrine and noted that Maryland had both an ERA amendment and an equalization statute. The court said:

> The child's best interest, the "cardinal principle" and the "paramount consideration" . . . is not a "principle to be placed upon the balance scales" but rather is the measure by which all else is to be decided. No factor will be given weight that is not homogeneous with that "cardinal principle."[95]

The court further noted that "Every statement of the preference is hedged about by the context, 'all else being equal.' The presumption is obviously intended to serve the limited function of a 'tie-breaker.'"[96] It also was noted that it was unlikely that litigants will

---

2501 (Alaska 1977) ("the mother's argument that the presumption is justified based on the 'greater probability that a mother will better supply mothering' is unpersuasive in view of the fact that the doctrine is 'not an appropriate criterion' for a determination of the best interest of a child.").

92. Turoff v. Turoff, 527 P.2d 1275 (Hawaii 1974) (each parent has an equal right to an award of custody and crucial question is child's best interests).

93. McVay v. McVay, 44 Ohio App. 2d 370, 338 N.E.2d 772 (Ohio App. 1974).

94. 319 A.2d 841 (Md. App. 1974).

95. 319 A.2d at 843.

96. *Ibid.*

have parental qualities so equally balanced that resort to the maternal preference is necessary, and that its use should be reserved for those limited instances where it was impoossible to decide the case upon the evidentiary facts. Only when the scale was still in a state of equipoise was the doctrine relevant. "The appealing procedure of applying formulae as ready answers atrophies the judicial process, which is, of necessity, a sometimes tedious preoccupation with detail."[97]

We have come full circle in our discussion of child custody. Obviously there have been pendulum swings, back and forth, as to which parent is the sentimental favorite in the application of vague principles and loose standards. But at the same time able jurists have stressed the importance of fact-finding. Currently, in addition to the demise of the tender years doctrine there has been a renewed interest in joint custody awards.

Joint Custody

Prior judicial experience with joint custody awards led to disapproval of such a custodial arrangement, but the principle of sexual equality has moved a few courts to try experimental decrees.[98] If custody proceedings are viewed as contests between parents, a joint award has a certain appeal. Neither or both parents are winners. The trouble is that a joint award may be a judicial "cop out" in order to avoid complex and difficult fact-finding. Moreover, unless the circumstances are unusual, a joint award ordinarily is not to the best interests of the children. It may place the child in a "double bind" and it may constitute a threat to the stability, continuity, and security that a child needs for healthy development.[99] Unless the divorced and separated parents are reasonable and cooperative, shared authority is apt to breed contention.

This is not to say that joint custody never will work, but merely that overwhelming odds are against it and that it should not be tried

97. 319 A.2d at 844.

98. New York appears to have had a recent increase in joint custody awards. *See* Levy v. Levy, N.Y.L.J., Jan. 29, 1976, p. 11, col. 3, p. 12, cols. 1-6 (Sup. Ct. N.Y. Co. 1976); Perotti v. Perotti, 355 N.Y.S.2d 68 (Sup. Ct. Queens Co. 1974); Woicik v. Woicik, 66 Misc. 2d 357, 321 N.Y.S.2d 5 (Sup. Ct. N.Y. Co. 1971); Ross v. Ross, 4 Misc. 2d 399, 149 N.Y.S.2d 585 (Sup. Ct. Erie Co. 1956); and Schack v. Schack, N.Y.L.J., Aug. 21, 1974, p. 15, cols. 4-6, p. 17, col. 1 (Co. Ct. 1974).

99. *See* S. Katz, When Parents Fail 146 (1971).

save under optimal conditions. One factor which may lead a court to award joint custody is the need of a child to have the companionship of his father.[100] Another important factor is where the parents have agreed to joint custody. Such factors, however, ordinarily may be served by a grant of liberal visitation, and there may be no need to stipulate a divided authority. If the focus is on the child's welfare, rather than on a battle of the sexes, an award of joint custody will rarely seem justified. The fact that custody awards are always subject to modification upon a showing of substantial change in the circumstances should not lure courts into reckless experimentation with children.

Conclusion

It may be more meaningful not to view child custody as a battle of the sexes, but as an illustration of legal craftsmanship. As we have seen, able jurists sift the facts and eschew hyperbole and absolutes. The complexity and diversity of custody issues are such that there should be no "automatics" or rules of thumb. Psychiatrists and psychoanalysts as well as lawyers should accept the inherent difficulties of custodial decisions and forget about panaceas as well as presumptions.

The law of custody also serves to illustrate how the law adapts and changes in reaction to changing values which achieve consensus or a near consensus. It is not surprising that the common law preference for the father was secure as long as feudalism flourished but disintegrated with the advent of the industrial revolution, nor that the tender years doctrine lost its luster at a time when sex discrimination was "bad form" if not unconstitutional. Eventually the law adapts to social change. The unique thing some of us have learned from the women's movement, if not beforehand, is that sexual stereotyping should be taboo in modern society. We must look at the particular facts to see which custodian probably is the more fit parent and discard our prejudices, whether they exist in the form

100. *See* Note, *Divided Custody of Children After Their Parents Divorce*, 8 J. FAM. LAW 58 (1968), which points out that the first recorded example of joint custody was when Jupiter divided the custody of Prosperina between a custodian in hell and another on earth, and says that at the beginning of this century there was "almost a total judicial prohibition of joint custody." Only North Carolina by statute provides for joint custody. *See* N.C. GEN. STAT. § 50-13. Many American cases have condemned it. *Id.* at 62-65, and only a small minority of cases have approved it. *Id.* at 65.

of legal presumptions or unexamined assumptions. This area of law formerly was known as *The Law of Domestic Relations and Persons.*[101] We need to emphasize the concept of "persons," perceive that the Emperor wore no clothers, and admit that children are people.

101. *See* MADDEN, THE LAW OF DOMESTIC RELATIONS AND PERSONS (1931).

APPENDIX

State	A Is Tender Years Doctrine in Effect?	B Relevant Statutes 1. Parental Rights Statute 2. Statute Specifying Criteria 3. State E.R.A.	C Significant Decisions
Alabama	Yes, but only rebuttable presumption. Statute states court should consider "moral character and prudence of the parents, the age and sex of the children." Ala. Code Ann. tit. 34, § 35 (Recompiled 1958).		*Thompson v. Thompson,* 326 So.2d 124, *cert. denied,* 326 So.2d 129 (Ala. Civ. App. 1976); *Linderman v. Linderman,* 275 So.2d 342 (Ala. App. 1973); *Rowe v. Rowe,* 231 So.2d 144 (Ala. App. 1970); *Turner v. Turner,* 242 So.2d 397 (Ala. App. 1970); *Tyler v. Thompson,* 276 So.2d 610 (Ala. App. 1973) ("tender years" doctrine not violative of F's rights to equal protection under law).
Alaska	No. See statute equalizing rights of parent, col. B and Alaska cases, col. C.	1. Statute equalizing parental rights. "As between parents adversely claiming custody neither parent is entitled to it as of	*Sheridan v. Sheridan,* 466 P.2d 821 (Alaska 1970); *Turner v. Pannick,* 540 P.2d 1051 (Alaska 1975); *Johnson v. Johnson,* 3

	A	B	C
STATE	IS TENDER YEARS DOCTRINE IN EFFECT?	RELEVANT STATUTES 1. Parental Rights Statute 2. Statute Specifying Criteria 3. State E.R.A.	SIGNIFICANT DECISIONS
Alaska (*continued*)		right." Alaska Code Civ. Proced. tit. 09.55.205. 2. Criteria specified (Laws 1977, ch. 63). 3. Alaska Const. Art. I § 3.	F.L.R. 2501 (Sup. Ct. Alaska, May 20, 1977) ("tender years" presumption at odds with Alaska's statutory prohibition against a preference to either party); *King v. King*, 477 P.2d 356 (Alaska 1976).
Arizona	No, not since 1973 amendment to law by Ariz. Rev. Stat. § 25-332.	2. Specified criteria for court's determination of custody as in Uniform Marriage and Divorce Act, § 402: 1. The wishes of the child's parent or parents as to his custody. 2. The wishes of the child as to his custodian. 3. The interaction and interrelationship of the child with	*Orezza v. Ramirez*, 507 P.2d 1017 (Ariz. 1973); *Morales v. Glenn*, 560 P.2d 1234 (Ariz. 1977); *Georgia v. Georgia*, 553 P.2d 1256 (Ariz. 1976) (Stat. A.R.S. § 25-332 [A, B], provides controlling test which requires custody award according to best interests of child).

		his parent or parents, his siblings, and any other person who may significantly affect the child's best interests. 4. The child's adjustment to his home, school and community. 5. The mental and physical health of all individuals involved. Ariz. Rev. Stat. Ann. § 25-332, added Laws 1973, ch. 139, § 2.	
Arkansas	Maternal preference exists but limited by age and sex of child.		*Weber v. Weber,* 508 S.W.2d 725 (Ark. 1974); *Moore v. Smith,* 499 S.W.2d 634 (Ark. 1973).
California	No; maternal preference abolished (Laws 1972, ch. 1007, p. 1855, § 1).	1. Statute equalizing parental rights. Court awards custody "To either parent according to the best interest of the child. . . ." (Laws 1972, ch. 1007, p. 1855 § 1, deleted provision re maternal preference).	*In re Reyna,* 126 Cal. Rptr. 138, 55 C.A.3d 288 (1976); *In re Marriage of Urband,* 137 Cal. Rptr. 433, 68 C.A.3d 796 (1977).

	A	B	C
STATE	IS TENDER YEARS DOCTRINE IN EFFECT?	RELEVANT STATUTES 1. Parental Rights Statute 2. Statute Specifying Criteria 3. State E.R.A.	SIGNIFICANT DECISIONS
Colorado	No. Welfare of children held prime criterion and no maternal preference. See *Rayer v. Rayer,* col. C. But earlier cases upheld maternal preference. See col. C.	1. Statute equalizing parental rights. 2. Criteria specified as in U.M. & D.A. Colo. Stat. Ann. § 14-10-124 (Colo. Uniform Dissolution of Marriage Act, 1973. 3. Colo. Const. Art. II § 29.	*Rayer v. Rayer,* 512 P.2d 637 (Colo. 1973); *Evans v. Evans,* 314 P.2d 291 (Colo. 1957); *Smith v. Smith,* 474 P.2d 619 (Colo. 1970) (no preference to a parent because of sex).
Connecticut	No.	1. Statute equalizing parental rights. The court "may assign the custody of any such children to either parent, . . . according to its best judgment upon the facts of the case . . . the court shall be guided by the best interests of the child, . . . provided that in making such initial order the court may take into consideration the causes for dissolution	*Raymond v. Raymond,* 345 A.2d 48 (Conn. 1974).

		of the marriage. . . .(Conn. Gen. Stat. Ann. § 46-42 (as amended P.A. 1973, 73-373, § 15; P.A. 74-169, § 8. 3. Conn. Const. Art. I § 20.	
Delaware	No.	1. Desexing statute. "The Court shall not presume that a parent, because of his or her sex, is better qualified than the other parent to act as custodian for a child. . . ." Dela. Code tit. 13 722(b), as amended 59 Del. Laws ch. 569, § 4 (1975 Cum. Supp.). 2. Specified criteria in Dela. Code, tit. 13, § 722(a) as in U.M. & D.A.	*Nelson v. Murray,* 211 A.2d 842 (Del. 1965).
District of Columbia	No.	1. Custody desexed. Custody awarded "without conclusive regard to the . . . sex, . . ., in and of itself, of the other party." D.C. Code Ann. § 16-911 (as amended, Oct. 1, 1976, D.C. Law, No. 1-87, § 14 (1977 Cum. Supp.)).	No cases found since statutory revision; prior cases held maternal preference in effect. *Rzeszotarski v. Rzeszotarski,* 296 A.2d 431 (D.C. App. 1972); *Monacelli v. Monacelli,* 296 A.2d 445 (D.C. App. 1972); *O'Meara v. O'Meara,* 355 A.2d

	A	B	C
STATE	IS TENDER YEARS DOCTRINE IN EFFECT?	RELEVANT STATUTES 1. Parental Rights Statute 2. Statute Specifying Criteria 3. State E.R.A.	SIGNIFICANT DECISIONS
District of Columbia (*continued*)		2. Criteria specified as in U.M. & D.A. (D.C. Code Ann. § 16-911, as amended Act, 1976, D.C. Law No. 1-87 § 14 (1977 Cum. Supp.)).	561 (D.C. 1976).
Florida	Yes, all things being equal.	1. Statute equalizing parental rights. "Upon considering all relevant factors, the F of the child shall be given the same consideration as the M in determining custody." (Fla. Stat. Ann. § 61.13, amended Laws 1975, chs. 75-99, § 1, eff. June 12, 1975) (1976 Cum. Supp.). 2. Criteria specified, more detailed than in U.M. & D.A. § 61.13 (1976 Cum. Supp.).	*Goodman v. Goodman,* 291 So. 2d 106 (Fla. App. 1974); *Snedaker v. Snedaker,* 327 So. 2d 72 (Fla. App. 1976); *Bone v. Bone,* 334 So. 2d 142 (Fla. App. 1976); *Ross v. Ross,* 321 So. 2d 443 (Fla. App. 1975) ("tender years" doctrine applies despite parental equalizing statute).

Georgia	No.	1. Statute equalizing parental rights. Statute provides that the F has no prima facie right to custody but the court in its discretion awards custody in the best interests of the children's welfare and happiness. A child of 14 may select parent with whom he wishes to live, and this selection is controlling if parent selected is fit. Ga. Code Ann. § 74-107, amended Laws 1976, pp. 1050, 1053, eff. July 1, 1976 (1977 Cum. Supp.).	*Folsom v. Folsom,* 186 S.E.2d 752 (Ga. 1972); *Allsop v. Allsop,* 225 S.E.2d 284 (Ga. 1976).
Hawaii	No.	1. Statute equalizing parental rights. "Custody should be awarded to either parent according to the best interests of the child." Hawaii Rev. Stat. § 1571-46 (Rev. Laws 1965, ch. 83, § 1) (1968). 3. Hawaii Const. Art. I, §§ 4, 21.	*Turoff v. Turoff,* 527 P.2d 1275 (Hawaii 1974).
Idaho	Yes, but only where all other things are equal.		*Barrett v. Barrett,* 480 P.2d 910 (Idaho 1971).

	A	B	C
STATE	IS TENDER YEARS DOCTRINE IN EFFECT?	RELEVANT STATUTES 1. Parental Rights Statute 2. Statute Specifying Criteria 3. State E.R.A.	SIGNIFICANT DECISIONS
Illinois	No, abandoned after state E.R.A.	2. Specific criteria as in U.M. & D.A. (Ill. Marriage and Divorce Act, § 602, eff. Oct. 1977). 3. Ill. Const. Art. I § 18.	*King v. Vancil,* 341 N.E.2d 65 (1975); *Carlson v. Carlson,* 225 N.E.2d 130 (Ill. App. 1967); *Randolph v. Dean,* 327 N.E.2d 473 (Ill. App. 1975); *Irby v. Dubois,* 354 N.E.2d 562 (Ill. 1976) (presumption abandoned).
Indiana	No.	1. Statute equalizing parental rights. "In determining the best interests of the child, there shall be no presumption favoring either parent." Burns Ind. Stat. Ann. § 31-1-11.5-21 (added by Arts. 1973, P.L. 297, § 1, p. 1585) (1974 Cum. Supp.). 2. Criteria same as in U.M. & D.A. (31-1-11.5-21).	*Franks v. Franks,* 323 N.E.2d 678 (Ind. App. 1975).

Iowa	No, presumption abandoned.		*Winter v. Winter,* 223 N.W.2d 165 (Iowa 1974); *Blessing v. Blessing,* 220 N.W.2d 599 (Iowa 1974); *Re Marriage of Bowen,* 219 N.W.2d 683 (Iowa 1974) (maternal preference explicitly abandoned); *Schoonover v. Schoonover,* 228 N.W.2d 31 (Iowa 1975).
Kansas	Cases in conflict.		*St. Clair v. St. Clair*, 507 P.2d 206 (Kan. App. 1973); *Patton v. Patton*, 524 P.2d 709 (Kan. 1974); *Moudy v. Moudy*, 505 P.2d 764 (Kan. 1973); *Berry v. Berry*, 523 P.2d 342 (Kan. 1974); cf. *Dalton v. Dalton*, 522 P.2d 378 (Kan. 1974).
Kentucky	Yes, but not controlling or conclusive.	2. Criteria specified as in U.M. & D.A. See Ky. Rev. Stat. § 403.270 (Acts 1972, ch. 182, § 7 (1973 Cum. Supp.)).	*Brown v. Brown,* 510 S.W.2d 14 (Ky. App. 1974); *Parker v. Parker,* Ky., 467 S.W.2d 595 (1971); *Eviston v. Eviston,* 507 S.W.2d 153 (Ky. App. 1974).

	A	B	C
STATE	IS TENDER YEARS DOCTRINE IN EFFECT?	RELEVANT STATUTES 1. Parental Rights Statute 2. Statute Specifying Criteria 3. State E.R.A.	SIGNIFICANT DECISIONS
Louisiana	Yes, if "fit" (despite statute, and despite state E.R.A.).	1. Statute equalizing parental rights. "In all cases of separation and divorce, children shall be placed under the care of the party who shall have obtained the separation or divorce unless the judge shall, for the greater advantage of the children, order that some or all of them shall be entrusted to the care of the other party." (La. Civ. Code, Art. 157A (amended by Acts 1970, No. 436, § 1) (1977 Cum. Supp.)). 3. La. Const. Art. I § 3.	*Whatley v. Whatley,* 312 So. 2d 149 (La. 1975); *Hudson v. Hudson,* 295 So. 2d 92, *cert. denied,* 295 So. 2d 446 (La. App. 1974); cf. *Murphy v. Murphy,* 293 So. 2d 909 (La. App. 1974); *Caraway v. Caraway,* 321 So. 2d 405 (La. App. 1975).
Maine	No.		*Dumais v. Dumais,* 122 A.2d 322 (Me. 1956); *Lovelett v. Lovelett,* 98 A.2d 546 (Me. 1953);

			Grover v. Grover, 54 A.2d 637 (Me. 1947); *Roussel v. State,* 274 A.2d 909 (Me. 1971).
Maryland	Yes, but only where all else equal (despite state E.R.A.).	3. Md. Const. Declaration of Rights, Art. 46.	*Cooke v. Cooke,* 21 Md. App. 376, 319 A.2d 841 (1974); *Kirstukas v. Kirstukas,* 286 A.2d 535 (Md. App. 1972).
Massachusetts	No, but no recent cases found.	1. Statute equalizing parental rights. "In making an order or decree relative to the custody of children . . . the rights of the parents shall, in the absence of misconduct, be held to be equal and the happiness and welfare of the children shall determine their custody or possession." Ann. Laws Mass. ch. 208 § 31 (1969).	*Stevens v. Stevens,* 151 N.E.2d 166 (Mass. 1958).
		3. Mass. Const. Declaration of Rights, Art. I.	
Michigan	No.	2. Ten criteria specified. (Mich. Comp. Laws Ann. § 722.73 (PA 1970, no. 91, sec. 2, eff. April 1, 1971) (1977-1978 Cum. Supp.);	*Pyle v. Pyle,* 188 N.W.2d 641 (Mich. 1971); *Feldman v. Feldman,* 222 N.W.2d 2 (Mich. App. 1974).

	A	B	C
STATE	IS TENDER YEARS DOCTRINE IN EFFECT?	RELEVANT STATUTES 1. Parental Rights Statute 2. Statute Specifying Criteria 3. State E.R.A.	SIGNIFICANT DECISIONS
Michigan (*continued*)		see also § 722.25 (providing for custody according to best interests of child).	
Minnesota	Yes, other things being equal, despite 1974 desexing statute and criteria specified.	1. Statute desexing child custody. "In determining the parent with whom a child shall remain the court shall consider the best interests of the children, and shall not prefer one parent over the other solely on the basis of the sex of the parent." Minn. Stat. Ann. § 518.17 (subd. 2) (as amended by Laws 1974, c. 330, § 2) (1977 Cum. Supp.). 2. Criteria specified similar to but more elaborate than that in U.M. & D.A. (§ 518.17 (subdiv. 1)).	*Erickson v. Erickson,* 220 N.W.2d 487 (Minn. 1974); *Ryg v. Kerkow,* 207 N.W.2d 701 (Minn. 1973); *Davis v. Davis,* 235 N.W.2d 836 App. dism'd, *cert. denied,* 96 S. Ct. 3160 (Minn. 1975); *Hoffman v. Hoffman,* 227 N.W.2d 387 (Minn. 1975).

Mississippi	Yes, where M is fit.		*Sistrunk v. Sistrunk,* 245 So. 2d 845 (Miss. 1971).
Missouri	Yes, all else being equal despite criteria specified.	2. Criteria specified are same as those in U.M. & D.A. See Ann. Mo. Stat. § 452-375, as amended L. 1973, p. 189, eff. Jan. 1, 1974 (1977 ed.).	*Downing v. Downing,* 537 S.W.2d 840 (Mo. App. 1976); *Johnson v. Johnson,* 526 S.W.2d 33 (Mo. App. 1975).
Montana	Yes, but not controlling or conclusive.	2. Criteria specified as in U.M. & D.A. (Rev. Codes Mont. (Uniform Marriage and Divorce Act) § 48-322, amended Laws 1975, ch. 536, sec. 32 (1975 Cum. Supp.). 3. Mont. Const. Art. II § 4.	*Love v. Love,* 533 P.2d 280 (Mont. 1974); *Libra v. Libra,* 484 P.2d 748 (Mont. 1971); *In re Tweeten,* 3 F.L.R. 2500 (Mont. 1977) (each case to be decided on facts, not by "controlling or conclusive" presumption).
Nebraska	No.	1. Custody desexed. "In determining with which of the parents the children . . . shall remain, the court shall not give preference to either parent based on the sex of the parent and no presumption shall exist that either parent is more fit to have custody than the other." Rev. Stat.	*Young v. Young,* 195 Neb. 163, 237 N.W.2d 135 (1976); *Boroff v. Boroff,* 250 N.W.2d 613 (1977); *Knight v. Knight,* 241 N.W.2d 360 (1976).

	A	B	C
State	Is Tender Years Doctrine in Effect?	Relevant Statutes 1. Parental Rights Statute 2. Statute Specifying Criteria 3. State E.R.A.	Significant Decisions
Nebraska (*continued*)		Neb. § 42-364 (2) (1976 Cum. Supp.). 2. Criteria specified. Rev. Stat. Neb. § 42-364(1) (1976 Cum. Supp.).	
Nevada	Yes, other things being equal.		*Peavy v. Peavy*, 85 Nev. 571, 460 P.2d 110 (1969).
New Hampshire	Yes, unless M is unfit.	1. Desexing statute. The court makes such order relative to the rights of the children as shall be most conducive to their benefit. "In making any order relative to custody, the court shall not give any preference to either of the parents . . . because of the parent's sex. . . ." N.H. Rev. Stat. Ann. (1968) § 458.17 (as	*Del Pozzo v. Del Pozzo*, 113 N.H. 436, 309 A.2d 151 (1973); *Lemay v. Lemay*, 247 A.2d 189 (N.H. 1968).

		amended 1975) (1975 Cum. Supp.). 3. Const. Pt. I, Art. 2.	
New Jersey	Yes, if M fit.	1. Statute equalizing parental rights. ". . . [I]n making an order or judgment relative to the custody of the children . . . the rights of both parents" in the absence of misconduct, shall be held to "be equal." N.J. Stat. Ann. § 9-2-4 (1976).	*Vannucchi v. Vannucchi,* 113 N.J. Super. 40, 272 A.2d 560 (1971); *DiBianco v. DiBianco,* 105 N.J. Super. 415, 252 A.2d 735 (1969); *Esposito v. Esposito,* 41 N.J. 143, 196 A.2d 295 (1963).
New Mexico	Doctrine used as an aid to court in determining custody.	3. N.M. Const. Art. II, § 18.	*Ettinger v. Ettinger,* 72 N.M. 300, 383 P.2d 261 (1963); *Gholson v. Gholson,* 483 P.2d 1313 (N.M. 1971); *Csanyl v. Csanyl,* 483 P.2d 292 (N.M. 1971).
New York	No.	1. Statute equalizing parental rights. Dom. Rel. L. §§ 70, 240: "there shall be no prima facie right to the custody of the child in either parent. . . ."	*Watts v. Watts,* 77 Misc. 2d 178, 350 N.Y.S.2d 285 (1973) ("tender years" presumption violative of U.S. Const. and Dom. Rel. L. §§ 70, 240); *F.F. v. F.F.,* 37 A.D.2d 893, 325 N.Y.S.2d 291 (1971).

STATE	A IS TENDER YEARS DOCTRINE IN EFFECT?	B RELEVANT STATUTES 1. Parental Rights Statute 2. Statute Specifying Criteria 3. State E.R.A.	C SIGNIFICANT DECISIONS
North Carolina	Doubtful, but probably doctrine not followed.	1. Statute equalizing parental rights. "Provided, between the M and the F . . . there is no presumption as to who will better promote the interest and welfare of the child." Gen. Stat. N.C. (§ 50-13.2, as amended by Laws 1977, sec. 2).	*Griffith v. Griffith,* 81 S.E.2d 918 (N.C. 1954) (preference for M subordinate to child's best interests). No cases found since 1977 statute equalizing parental rights.
North Dakota	Probably, if other things are equal.		*Ferguson v. Ferguson,* 202 N.W.2d 760 (M.D. 1972); *Silseth v. Levang,* 214 N.W.2d 361 (N.D. 1974); *Matson v. Matson,* 226 N.W.2d 659 (1975); *De Forest v. De Forest,* 228 N.W.2d 919 (N.D. 1975); *Kottsick v. Kottsick,* 241 N.W.2d 842 (N.D. 1976).

Ohio	No.	1. Statute equalizing parental rights. Parents "shall stand upon an equality as to the care, custody and control of such offspring as far as parenthood is involved." Ohio Rev. Code Ann. § 3109.03 (1976 Cum. Supp.) 2. Criteria specified. (Ohio Rev. Code Ann. § 3109.04 (1976 Cum. Supp.).	*McVay v. McVay,* 44 Ohio App. 2d 370, 338 N.E.2d 772 (Ohio App. 1974).
Oklahoma	Yes, all things being equal.		*Earnst v. Earnst,* 418 P.2d 351 (Okla. 1966); *Irwin v. Irwin,* 416 P.2d 853 (Okla. 1966); *Duncan v. Duncan,* 449 P.2d 267 (Okla. 1969).
Oregon	Unsettled.		*Deardorff v. Deardorff,* 2 Or. App. 117, 467 P.2d 137 (1970); *Ray v. Ray,* 502 P.2d 397 (Or. App. 1972).
Pennsylvania	Yes, other things being equal. No mention in cases of state E.R.A.	3. Pa. Const. Art. I § 28.	*Commonwealth ex rel. Parikh v. Parikh,* 449 Pa. 105, 296 A.2d 625 (1972); *Commonwealth ex rel. Lucas v. Kreischer* 450 Pa. 352, 299 A.2d 243 (1973); *Com-*

STATE	A IS TENDER YEARS DOCTRINE IN EFFECT?	B RELEVANT STATUTES 1. Parental Rights Statute 2. Statute Specifying Criteria 3. State E.R.A.	C SIGNIFICANT DECISIONS
Pennsylvania (*continued*)			*monwealth ex rel. Grillo v. Shuster*, 226 Pa. Super. 229, 312 A.2d 58 (1973).
Rhode Island	Yes.		*Loebenberg v. Loebenberg*, 85 R.I. 115, 127 A.2d 500 (1958).
South Carolina	Yes, if M fit, and custody to her serves best interests of child.		*Ford v. Ford*, 242 S.C. 344, 130 S.E.2d 916 (1963); *Peay v. Peay*, 260 S.C. 108, 194 S.E.2d 392 (1973); *Powell v. Powell*, 231 S.C. 283, 98 S.E.2d 764 (1957); *Pullen v. Pullen*, 253 S.C. 283, 169 S.E.2d 376 (1969).
South Dakota	Yes, all things being equal.		*Hershey v. Hershey*, 85 S.D. 85, 177 N.W.2d 267 (1970).
Tennessee	Yes.	1. Parental equalizing statute. ". . . court may . . . award the care, custody and control of such	*Bevins v. Bevins*, 53 Tenn. App. 403, 383 S.W.2d 780 (1964); *Mollish v. Mollish*, 494 S.W.2d

		child or children to either of the parties to the suit. . . ." Tenn. Code Ann. § 36-828.	145 (1972).
Texas	No.	1. Custody desexed. "In determining which parent to appoint as managing conservator [of child], the court shall consider the qualifications of the respective parents without regard to the sex of the parent." Vernon's Family Code, § 14.01(b) (1974). 3. Tex. Const. Art. I § 3a.	*Erwin v. Erwin,* 505 S.W.2d 370 (Tex. Civ. App. 1974) (maternal preference effectively destroyed by desexing statute passed after decision in case); cf. *Spitzmuller v. Spitzmuller,* 429 S.W.2d 557 (Tex. Civ. App. 1968).
Utah	Yes, all things being equal, despite state E.R.A.	1. In the case of divorce, the court shall consider ". . . the natural presumption that the M is best suited to care for young children." Utah Code Ann., § 30-3-5 (1969). 3. Const. Art. IV § 2.	*Arends v. Arends,* 30 Utah 2d 328, 517 P.2d 1019 (1974) (F's reliance on state E.R.A. discounted by court); *Hyde v. Hyde,* 22 Utah 2d 429, 454 P.2d 884 (1969); *Cox v. Cox,* 532 P.2d 994 (Utah 1975).
Vermont	Unsettled, but welfare of child paramount consideration.	2. Criteria specified. Vt. Stat. Ann. tit. 15 § 557 (1974).	*Lafko v. Lafko,* 127 Vt. 609, 256 A.2d 166 (1969); cf. *Savery v.* Savery, 360 A.2d 58 (Vt. 1976).

	A	B	C
STATE	IS TENDER YEARS DOCTRINE IN EFFECT?	RELEVANT STATUTES 1. Parental Rights Statute 2. Statute Specifying Criteria 3. State E.R.A.	SIGNIFICANT DECISIONS
Virginia	Yes, all things being equal, despite state E.R.A., and parental rights statute.	1. Statute equalizing parental rights (Va. Code § 20-107 (1975 Cum. Supp.). 3. Va. Const. Art. I, § 11.	*Rowlee v. Rowlee,* 211 Va. 689, 179 S.E.2d 461 (1971); *Moore v. Moore,* 212 Va. 153, 183 S.E.2d 172 (1971) (no mention of state E.R.A.); *McCreery v. McCreery,* 3 F.L.R. 3181 (Va. 1977) ("tender years" presumption, if all things equal, is valid despite Virginia statute equalizing parental rights).
Washington	No, probably not.	2. Criteria specified as in U.M. & D.A. See Rev. Code Wash. Ann. § 26.09.190 (1974 Cum. Supp.). 3. Wash. Const. Art. 31, § 1.	*McCray v. McCray,* 56 Wash. 2d 73, 350 P.2d 1006 (1960); *Silverton v. Silverton,* 427 P.2d 1001 (Wash. App. 1967); *Brauhn v. Brauhn,* 518 P.2d 1089 (Wash. App. 1974).
West Virginia	Yes, when other things are equal.		*Funkhouser v. Funkhouser,* 216 S.E.2d 570 (W. Va. 1975).

Wisconsin	Yes, all things being equal.	1. Custody desexed. "In determining the parent with whom a child shall remain, the court . . . shall not prefer one parent over the other wholly on the basis of sex." Wis. Family Code, § 247.24(3) (1976 Cum. Supp.).	*Koslowsky v. Koslowsky,* 41 Wis. 2d 275, 163 N.W.2d 632 (1968); *Scolman v. Scolman,* 226 N.W.2d 388 (Wis. 1975) (desexing statute did not eliminate maternal preference); *Masek v. Masek,* 228 N.W.2d 334 (Wis. 1975).
Wyoming	Yes, but presumption in favor of M rebuttable in best interests of child.	3. Wyo. Const. Art. 1, § 3.	*Butcher v. Butcher,* 363 P.2d 923 (Wyo. 1961) (case decided after state E.R.A.); *Wilson v. Wilson,* 473 P.2d 595 (Wyo. 1970).

Le Vice Anglais?—Wife-Battering in English and American Law*

MICHAEL D. A. FREEMAN†

Madam Giroud, the French Minister for Women's Affairs, recently referred to wife-battering as "an English malaise."[1] Like many politicians she must have been unaware as to what was going on about her, for some seven months later an article in *Le Monde*[2] indicated that women in Paris were organizing around the issue of wife-battering. The article informed us that that lady of many battles, Simone de Beauvoir, was president of the *Ligue du droit des femmes* which operates the *S.O.S. femmes—alternative* hotline finding battered women emergency housing. Nor was this the only group. The *Librairie des Femmes* maintained a phone service and moves were afoot to promote a refuge for battered women in Paris. Of course the problem is not uniquely English, any more than it is a problem of the 1970s. It is a world-wide phenomenon and an age-old problem. It is true, though, that a reawakening of concern for the plight of battered women appears to have hit the public conscience in England before it spread elsewhere. That it did is largely due to the crusading efforts of Erin Pizzey[3] in establishing the now world-famous hostel in Chiswick in London.

*This article is an amended version of a paper delivered at the Second World Conference of the International Society on Family Law in Montreal in June 1977. The issues explored in this article are dealt with at greater length in the author's forthcoming book, VIOLENCE IN THE FAMILY—A SOCIO-LEGAL STUDY, to be published in 1978.

†Lecturer in Law, University College London; Gray's Inn Barrister.

1. Reported in The Daily Express, 21 April 1975.
2. FRAPPAT, UN FLEAU SOCIAL: LES FEMMES BATTUES, 4 November 1975.
3. *See* her SCREAM QUIETLY OR THE NEIGHBOURS WILL HEAR, Penguin 1974.

This article is about legal responses to the problem. It concentrates very largely on the achievements and deficiencies of English law. Some comparative material is also included. Violence in the home cannot be eradicated by legislation. It is salutary to remember this, for the 1970s are not the first occasion that the plight of battered women has surfaced to public attention. In an article in *The Sunday Times* of August 24, 1851, John Stuart Mill listed some of the cruelties inflicted by husbands and lovers: a bulldog set at the heels of a wife, attempted murder by hanging, stabbings, blows with a poker, murder in a fit of drunkenness. Dickens's novels *Bleak House* and *Oliver Twist* and the novels of Mrs. Gaskell[4] are replete with similar brutalities. The solution was thought to lie in the introduction of separation orders which could be obtained simply and speedily in magistrates' court. The case was put by Frances Power Cobbe in a pamphlet called *Wife Torture.*[5] She rejected the expedient of flogging the culprits for "after they had undergone such chastisement . . . the ruffians would inevitably return more brutalized and infuriated than ever, and again have their wives at their mercy."[6] It should be remembered that contemporaneously with the English reform the legislature of Maryland[7] passed legislation to whip wife beaters, and an attempt was made to copy this example in Pennsylvania.[8] The English reform may have helped some women. Certainly, the problem thereafter is no longer perceived as such,[9] though men clearly continued to batter their wives and mistresses. Today's solutions must, therefore, be treated cautiously.

Solutions presuppose an understanding of the problem. Legal responses cannot operate *in vacuo.* Successful solvents require more than willingness to act. What is required is a thorough cognizance

---

4. MARY BARTON and NORTH AND SOUTH.

5. *See also* ROMEIKE, THE WIFE-BEATER'S MANUAL 1884 and STEAD, MAIDEN TRIBUTE OF MODERN BABYLON.

6. *See* her LIFE vol. 2, pp. 220-1, Bentley 1894.

7. In 1883.

8. *See* STEINMETZ AND STRAUS, VIOLENCE IN THE FAMILY, Dodd, Mead 1974, p. 45.

9. In the nineteenth-century it was considered a working-class problem: the solution was seen as two-fold (i) an improvement in working-class conditions so that the women could make "homes" and their husbands respond by not beating them and (ii) a speedy, accessible remedy which resulted in the development of non-cohabitation orders. On (i) *see* BASCH, RELATIVE CREATURES, Allen Lane 1974: on (ii) *see* FINER REPORT ON ONE-PARENT FAMILIES vol. II, pp. 104-108 (McGregor and Finer).

of the aetiology of wife battering. Hasty measures passed in moral panics in reaction to the latest folk-devil,[10] whether that be football hooligans, squatters, brutal husbands or parents or whoever, are unlikely to grasp the problem by its roots. Of course, interim measures may be necessary. But one must then recognize them for what they are, and not expect them to emerge as panaceas.

Why Do Men Batter Their Wives?

The House of Commons Select Committee on Violence In Marriage reported in 1975 that "hardly any worthwhile research into either causes or remedies has been financed by the Government."[11] To put it more boldly, there has been hardly any worthwhile research.[12] We do not know how much violence there is in marriage nor whether it is increasing. For even if we concentrate on indictable offenses official statistics only tell us about what the police and courts do,[13] not about the incidence of male violence to women and, outside of homicide, statistics are not available on the sex of the victim.[14] More interesting data were collected by the Dobashs in Scotland in 1974.[15] They examined the initial charge sheets for all offenses in all precincts in Edinburgh and one in Glasgow. Violence and its threat accounted for only 11.1 percent of the offenses reported to these police stations. More of this (6.31 percent) was non-family violence than violence within the family (4.79 percent). Within the family, wife assault accounted for 47.25 percent of the offenses. Of non-family violence only 13 percent was directed by men against women, lending support to the view that to marry or cohabit is to increase the risk of physical attack. But the Dobashs' research cannot tell us how much violence is perpetrated on women

10. *Cf.* S. COHEN, FOLK DEVILS AND MORAL PANICS, McGibbon and Kee, 1972.

11. REPORT FROM THE SELECT COMMITTEE ON VIOLENCE IN MARRIAGE 1974-5 H.C. 553-i, ¶ 5.

12. The most useful are R. GELLES, THE VIOLENT HOME, Sage Publications, 1972, and R. AND R. DOBASH, VIOLENCE AGAINST WIVES: A CASE AGAINST THE PATRIARDRY, Free Press, 1977 (forthcoming). Other research of note is referred to in the course of this paper.

13. *Cf.* KITSUSE AND CICOUREL, SOCIAL PROBLEMS 11, 131 (1963).

14. The annual Home Office publication, CRIMINAL STATISTICS: ENGLAND AND WALES published by H.M.S.O. is singularly unhelpful on such questions.

15. THE NATURE AND EXTENT OF VIOLENCE IN MARRIAGE IN SCOTLAND, Scottish Council of Social Service, 1976.

in the home. So much depends upon the woman's reaction[16] and the response of the police to her cry for help. She can perceive the phenomenon of her husband's violence in a number of ways.[17] She can optimize and hope that his behavior will improve.[18] She can accommodate to it in a way that obscures it.[19] She can normalize it and regard it as but a special case of normal behavior.[20] Only if she pessimizes, accepts the worst, considers his deviance to be basically irreversible, is she likely to alert control agencies. Her motivation to report is attenuated by her knowledge that the police traditionally do not interfere in domestic disturbances.[21] The police reluctance to arrest wife batterers is reflected in official statistics and research such as that conducted by the Dobashs: we cannot pretend that either gives us a true picture of the extent of the problem. In default we are forced to reply on speculation. Jack Ashley M.P., a champion of the cause of battered women, has suggested that between 20,000 and 50,000 women a year may be involved.[22] Marsden and Owens estimated the true incidence in Colchester (population 72,000) to be 1 in 200 wives/cohabitees or even 1 in 100.[23] Much depends on how we define battering.

But we do know that a woman is more likely to be killed by someone she knows than by a total stranger.[24] This applies to rape[25] as well, and doubtless to other crimes of violence. We have some evidence that as the degree of violence decreases, the percentage of strangers committing the offense goes up.[26] McClintock, in a study

16. *See* Biderman, When Does Interpersonal Violence Become Crime?, paper delivered to International Sociological Association Conference. Cambridge 1973, and Block, Criminology 11,555 (1974).

17. *See* E. RUBINGTON and M. WEINBERG, DEVIANCE—THE INTERACTIONIST PERSPECTIVE, MacMillan 1973, p. 31.

18. A good illustration of this is to be found in the initial reactions of the wife in Yarrow *et al, The Psychological Meaning of Mental Illness in the Family*, J. OF SOC. ISSUES, 11, 12 (1955).

19. See, for example, Sampson *et al.*, *Family Processes and Becoming a Mental Patient*, AM. J. OF SOCIOLOGY, 68, 88 (1962).

20. *See* Gelles, *op. cit.*, note 12, p. 58ff and Jackson, *The Adjustment of the Family to the Crisis of Alcoholism*, Q. J. OF STUDIES ON ALCOHOL, 15, 564. (1954).

21. *See* Parnas, WIS. L.R. 914 (1967).

22. H.C. DEBATES vol. 895, col. 982.

23. New Society, 8 May 1975, p. 333.

24. GIBSON AND KLEIN, MURDER 1957 TO 1968. H.M.S.O.

25. *See* AMIR, PATTERNS OF FORCIBLE RAPE, U. of Chicago Press, 1971.

26. *See* Mulvihill, Tumin and Curtis in Crimes of Violence: STAFF REPORT TO NATIONAL COMMISSION ON CAUSES AND PREVENTION OF VIOLENCE, vol. 11. 1969.

in London, accounted for 30 percent of homicides as domestic disputes.[27] Similar evidence is available from the United States,[28] Portugal,[29] Denmark[30] and Eire[31] and doubtless other countries as well. We know less about assault but there seems to be a basic similarity between patterns of assault and patterns of homicide. We also know that violence is often cited as a cause for marital unhappiness and divorce. Chester and Streather's[32] analysis of divorce petitions bears this out as does O'Brien's study.[33] He found spontaneous mention of overt violence in 25 of the 150 interviews of "divorce-prone families" he carried out. Eighty-four percent of the reports of violence emanated from women. Levinger[34] found that physical abuse was an important factor in one-fifth of middle-class divorces and twice as many involving working-class couples. There wives complained of physical abuse eleven times more frequently than did husbands.

There is thus more violence in marriage than many people suppose.[35] But, as Goode[36] has pointed out, all families are characterized by some degree of conflict. All conflictual situations do not, however, lead to violent behavior. The factors leading to a conflictual family situation which ends in violence may not be radically different from those which lead to other conflictual situations in the

27. CRIMES OF VIOLENCE, Macmillan, 1963.

28. Boudouris, J. MARR. FAM. 33,667 (1971) (Detroit), Voss and Hepburn, J. CRIM. LAW, CRIMINAL, POLICE SCI. 59,499 (1968) (Chicago), WILLIE, REVISTA INTER-AMERICANA DE PSICOLOGÍA 4, 131 (1970) (Michigan), WALFGANG, PATTERNS IN CRIMINAL HOMICIDE, Wiley, 1958 and Psychology Today 3, 54, 72 (1969).

29. MALDONADO, BOLETIM DA ADMINISTRACAO PENITENCIARIA E DOS INSTITUTOS DE CRIMINOLOGIA 23, 5. (1968).

30. SICILIANO, ANNALS INTERNATIONALES DE CRIMINOLOGIE, 7, 403 (1968).

31. McCarthy in (eds.) DE WIT AND HARTUP, DETERMINANT AND ORIGINS OF AGGRESSIVE BEHAVIOUR, De Mouton, The Hague 1974. *See* Lystad, AM. J. ORTHOPSYCHIAT. 45, 328.

32. *Cruelty in English Divorce: Some Empirical Findings* J. MARR. FAM. 34, 706 (1972).

33. *Violence In Divorce Prone Families*, J. MARR. FAM. 33,692. (also in STEINMETZ AND STRAUS *op. cit.*, note 8).

34. *Sources of Marital Dissatisfaction among Applicants for Divorce*, AM. J. ORTHOPSYCHIAT. 36, 803 (reprinted in STEINMETZ AND STRAUS, *op. cit.*, note 8 and GLASSER AND GLASSER, FAMILIES IN CRISIS, Harper and Row).

35. Gelles found violence in 37 percent of his control group (THE VIOLENT HOME p. 49); Straus, *Leveling, Civility and Violence In the Family*, J. MARR. FAM. 36, 15 found that college students reported that 16 percent of their parents used physical violence against one another in the previous year; the Western Michigan School of Social Work, SPOUSE ASSAULT: ITS DIMENSIONS AND CHARACTERISTICS IN KALAMAZOO COUNTY (1975) estimates 10 percent in that county.

36. *Force and Violence In the Family*, J. MARR. FAM. 33,624.

domestic setting. The concern is, therefore, with why some husbands respond violently to situations of conflict: indeed, why some, probably a minority, act violently when there appears to be no disagreement between themselves and their wives.

We do not know the answer. True, a number of myths have grown up as putative explanations of the phenomenon. These are a form of defense mechanism which have been constructed to protect the family as a social institution. They are well-described by Steinmetz and Straus[37] in the introduction to their collection of essays, and will not be rehearsed here. As they say, each of the myths contains a scintilla of truth. None of them, however, adequately explains the phenomenon.

There are a number of theories as to why violence occurs in marriage. The dominant view emphasizes individual pathology: particular characteristics are isolated, they are found to exist in statistically significant numbers in husbands who have battered their wives and the battering is then attributed to possession of the particular pathological characteristic in question. This view individualizes the problem and locates its source in behavioral characteristics of "official" deviants.[38] Thus, one commonly hears that battering husbands are alcoholics or have "personality disorders" or that they are psychopaths. Violent behavior is said to be "irrational" rather as other deviant behavior is labeled as "mindless" or "meaningless" or "stupid."[39] Erin Pizzey subscribes to this view.[40] In a forthright article in *The Spectator* she wrote: "no one likes the word 'psychopath,' everyone is afraid of it, but that is exactly what he is—aggressive, dangerous, plausible and deeply immature."[41] And in her evidence to the House of Commons Select Committee she wrote:

---

37. VIOLENCE IN THE FAMILY *op. cit.*, note 8.

38. *Cf.* S. BOX, DEVIANCE, REALITY AND SOCIETY ch. 1, Holt, Rinehart and Winston (1971).

39. Good illustrations of this are to be found in COHEN, IMAGES OF DEVIANCE, Penguin Books (1971), particularly the chapters on industrial sabotage, blackmail and football hooliganism.

40. *Op. cit.*, note 3, *passim.* RYAN, in BAMING THE VICTIM (revised edition, 1976), has referred to this emphasis as applying "exceptionalist" explanations to "universalistic" problems. I am critical of the individualistic approach in a paper prepared for a Ford Legal Workshop in London in July 1977 (*Child Welfare: Law and Control*).

41. *Violence Begins at Home*, 23 November 1974.

> In a democratic society laws are made for reasonable men. . . . These men are outside the law; they have been imprinted with violence from childhood, so that violence is part of their normal behavior. All the legislating and punishment in the world will not change their methods of expressing their frustration. I believe that many of the children born into violence grow up to be aggressive psychopaths, and it is the wives of such men we see at Chiswick. I feel that the remedies lie in the hands of the medical profession and not in the court of law, because the men act instinctively, not rationally.[42]

Gayford's view is not far removed from this. When questioned by the Select Committee he spoke of husbands' "pathological jealousy" produced by alcohol and not susceptible of being removed by "logical reasoning."[43] He has emphasized also pathological features of the women, notably the fact that their disastrous marriages were often "undertaken precipitately by a desire to leave home," short courtships and early and unplanned pregnancy.[44]

Such positivistic interpretations lead to suggestions of treatment-oriented solutions; more refuges, better medical provision, more social workers, etc. The "therapeutic state"[45] takes over and deviance is medicalized. Where this form of positivistic criminology differs from the usual is that it rarely examines the deviant.[46] Nearly all the research, and Gayford's is a good example, has concentrated on the wife-victims and has not examined the husband-batterers.[47] Conclusions about his pathology are often thus drawn from what his wife says about his personality and disposition.

A second view is to attribute violence to frustration, stress and blocked goals. Such a view is not novel and can be traced, in different contexts, to Durkheim[48] and Merton.[49] It stresses social structural factors. The British Association of Social Workers in a discussion document put it like this:

---

42. Minutes of Evidence, p. 2.
43. *Idem.*, p. 43.
44. Br. Med. J. 1975, 194 (25 January 1975).
45. *Cf.* N. Kittrie, The Right to Be Different, Johns Hopkins Press 1971.
46. A point made cogently by Martin, Battered Wives, Glide 1976. Good examples are Gayford's work (*op. cit.*, note 44), Snell *et al. The Wifebeater's Wife*, Archives of General Psychiatry 11, 107 (1964), and, to a lesser extent, Gelles, *op. cit.*, note 35. Positivistic criminology explained only "official" deviants: most of this research concentrates on the victims of "official" batterers.
47. It is, of course, more difficult to interview the husbands.
48. The Division of Labour in Society, Free Press 1964; Suicide, RKP 1952.
49. *Social Structure and Anomie*, Am. Soc. Rev. 3, 672 (1938) and in Social Structure and Social Theory, Free Press 1957. *See also* Horton, Br. J. of Sociology (1964).

> [E]conomic conditions, low wages, bad housing, overcrowding and isolation; unfavorable and frustrating work conditions for the man; lack of job opportunities for adolescent/school leavers, and lack of facilities such as day care (e.g., nurseries), adequate transport, pleasant environment and play space and recreational facilities, for mother and children were considered to cause personal desperation that might precipitate violence in the home.[50]

To the Dobashs "numerous factors of a structural and interactional nature . . . might be considered as amplifying the potential for violence between spouses. Some of the structural elements which should be seen as important include socialization into a subculture of violence; limited access to and achievement of status within the larger social system; lack of effective sanctions on the part of the immediate social audiences and of relevant social agencies, and the general status of women."[51]

Gelles's researches led him to the conclusion that "violence is an adaptation or response to structural stress. Structural stress produces frustration, which is often followed by violence (expressive violence). Structural stress also produces role expectations (particularly for the husband) which, because of lack of resources, only can be carried out by means of violence (instrumental violence). The second major precondition . . . is socialization experience. . . . If an individual learns that violence is an appropriate behavior when one is frustrated or angry . . . then this will be the adaptation to stress employed."[52] In his study of eighty families he found that violence was more likely to occur in the lower socioeconomic groups. But this can only partially be attributed to a subculture of violence. There is lack of privacy in lower-class families with the result that temporary escape from the other's clutches is more difficult and the violence more visible. It is also a fact that the poorer sections of the population tend to call in social control agencies like the police where the middle classes resort to social support institutions such as marriage guidance clinics and psychologists.[53] The effect this has on statistics, and through this

50. *Discussion Document on BASW Working Party on Home Violence*, SOCIAL WORK TODAY 6, 409 (1975).

51. Violence between Men and Women within the Family Setting, Paper presented to VIII World Congress of Sociology, Toronto, August 1974.

52. *Op. cit.*, note 35, p. 185.

53. *Cf.* BOTTOMLEY, DECISIONS IN THE PENAL PROCESS, Robertson, 1973.

on theory, cannot be underestimated.

More significantly it is the lower socio-economic classes who are most likely to suffer the anomie described in the Dobashs and in Gelles. This is developed by Goode into a resources theory. He recognizes that "most people do not willingly choose overt force when they command other resources because the costs of using force are high."[54] He therefore hypothesizes that the greater the other resources an individual can command, the less he will use force in an "overt manner."

> The husband in the middle or upper class family commands more force, in spite of his lesser willingness to use his own physical strength, because he possesses far more other social resources. His greater social prestige in the larger society and the family, his larger economic possessions, and his stronger emphasis on the human relations techniques of counter-deference, affection and communication give him greater influence generally, so that he does not have to call upon the force or its threat that he can in fact muster if he chooses.[55]

Some of Goode's ideas are developed in the research of O'Brien.[56] His assumption is that the family is a social system in which dominance patterns are based on social categories of age and sex. We find violence, he argues, where the male-adult-husband fails to possess superior skills, talents, or resources on which his superior status is supposed to be legitimately based. So he expected violence to be prevalent in families in which the husband-father was deficient in relation to the wife-mother on achieved status characteristics. What he found, in a large population in a midwest standard metropolitan area largely devoid of the poor and blacks, was that husbands in his violent subgroup showed evidence of underachievement in work roles as well as being deficient in achievement potential: they were, for example, dissatisfied with their job or education dropouts. In 84 percent the husband's income was the source of serious and constant conflict. O'Brien's interpretation of his research is in terms of status inconsistency where superior ascribed status category fails to live up to achieved status characteristics. Violence, he suggests, results from a reassertion of male dominance. O'Brien's research is open to a number of inter-

54. *Op. cit.*, note 36, p. 628.
55. *Idem.*
56. *Op. cit.*, note 33.

pretations. Thus, as well as that suggested by O'Brien himself, his research may give support to those who see violence as a response to frustration, in this case of a low status job.

As the development of the Women's Movement has been a primary factor in sensitizing our consciences to the plight of the battered woman,[57] it is not surprising that theories as to the aetiology of male violence towards women should have developed within the ideology of their liberation politics. The Women's Movement sees battering as an adjunct of women's generally oppressed position. "The challenge of Women's Aid," states Weir, "is that it demands a fundamental change in the way in which women are defined."[58] No one has shown better than Kate Millet[59] how the patriarchal bias has operated in culture and is reflected in literature. The view is thus presented that the purpose of male violence is to control women. Nor is it a view unique to militant women. Whitehurst, whose own frame of reference is within social-structural theories of strain, admitted that a survey of his had shown that "threats of violence are frequent among husbands as a means of controlling wives."[60] He describes a case where a husband catching his wife *in flagrante delicto* "set upon the two of them in a jealous rage." Whitehurst interprets this in terms of "the husband's own need to control his wife and feel superior," and explains that this was "too much of an emotional burden for him to handle without recourse to violence."[61]

In Jalna Hanmer's recent piece[62] this control thesis has evolved into a complete theory incorporating the whole state apparatus. In her view the state represents the interests of the dominant group who in this case are men. Thus, she says, "It is consistent that in domestic disputes the status of the victim determines the response

---

57. Is this why their plight also came to public attention in the latter part of the nineteenth century? It is a plausible part-explanation.

58. In (ed.) MAYO, WOMEN IN THE COMMUNITY, RKP, 977 ch. 11, p. 119. On this question generally see BULLOUGH, THE SUBORDINATE SEX (1973).

59. *Sexual Politics*, Hart Davis, 1969, particularly pp. 43-46 and in her critique of Henry Miller, ch. 6 and comparison of Ruskin and Mill (pp. 99 ff).

60. STEINMETZ AND STRAUS in *Violence in Husband-Wife Interaction:* VIOLENCE IN THE FAMILY *op. cit.*, note 8, 75, 80.

61. *Idem.*, p. 81.

62. Violence and the Social Control of Women, Paper presented to British Sociological Association Annual Meeting, Sheffield, March 1977.

of that section of the state given the task of controlling violence. That men unknown to the woman (the policemen) would back up the man known to her (the husband) in pursuit of their joint state-defined interest is to impartially enforce the law, for the state defines women as less equal."[63] Certainly the policies of the welfare state induce dependency. As Hanmer says: "[L]aw and law enforcement, housing policies, income maintenance, employment and earnings, interlock to trap the woman in dependence."[64] And it was the House of Commons Select Committee who asked the pertinent but rhetorical question in relation to a battering husband: "Why should it be the wife and children who have to leave, and not the husband? . . . Why should we not create hostels to receive the battering husband?"[65]

If male violence to women is to be seen in this way then there are no straightforward solutions, for what is being demanded is nothing less than a complete social revolution. This is recognized both by Whitehurst and Hanmer. Whitehurst has put the case for "alternative family structures,"[66] families which contain more people than the traditional nuclear family, such as communes and group marriages. He rejects the hierarchical structure of the traditional family and looks to greater interpersonal openness. But, as Steinmetz and Straus recognize, there is no evidence that such families would be free of violence.[67] There are anthropological findings that male violence to women antedates monogamy.[68] Hanmer recognizes that "male violence to women is not an unfortunate vagary of human nature called forth by class oppression."[69] Hanmer herself is less ambitious. She calls for women to challenge the use of force by males. She demands that "the problem of men"

---

63. *Idem.*, p. 18.
64. *Idem.*, p. 19.
65. Minutes, p. 190. Of course, if she succeeds in obtaining an injunction, that is likely to be the end result.
66. In a piece specially written for the Steinmetz and Straus collection (*op. cit.*, note 8), 315.
67. *Op. cit.*, note 8 at p. 315 (introduction to Whitehurst).
68. *See* Delmer *Looking Again at Engels's Origin of the Family, Private Property and the State* in Oakley and Mitchell (eds.), THE RIGHTS AND WRONGS OF WOMEN, Penguin Books, 1976, p. 271.
69. *Op. cit.*, note 62, p. 10.

be "raised theoretically and with it the question of the extent to which men can be re-educated."[70]

Four explanations have thus been put forward to gain an understanding of the phenomenon of wife-battering. Most attention has been given to the pathological explanation, and insofar as measures to reduce violence have been taken they have been directed towards the problem so conceived. This is hardly surprising. It is always easier to individualize a problem and, to many, preferable to psychologize it. It is comforting to think that violence in the family is abnormal. But so long as we think this way we are unlikely to solve the problem. On this pessimistic note I turn to consider how English law and English institutions have conceived the problem and what solutions have been offered.

Married Women In English Law

The Christian conception of man and wife as one flesh is the foundation of much of the common law on husband and wife.[71] And, as has been said, to the Pauline conclusion English law added the rider: "and I am he."[72] The very being of the married woman was suspended during coverture. Most of the disabilities have now been removed though significant vestiges remain: a married woman living with her husband, for example, (indeed any woman living with any man) is not entitled to apply for supplementary benefits in her own right.[73] The strength of the *Volksgeist*[74] in expressive relationships has often been commented upon:[75] law reform in family law does not guarantee a change in the mores.[76] This needs to be understood in this context.

---

70. *Idem.*, p. 24.

71. Graphically described in volume 1 of BLACKSTONE'S COMMENTARIES ON THE LAW OF ENGLAND. A good accout of this is DE CROW, SEXIST JUSTICE (1974). *See also* KANOWITZ, WOMEN AND THE LAW—THE UNFINISHED REVOLUTION (1969).

72. *Per* O.R. McGregor quoted in FLETCHER, THE FAMILY AND MARRIAGE IN BRITAIN Penguin, 1973, p. 103.

73. Because of the cohabitation rule.

74. The expression is Savigny's (SYSTEM OF MODERN ROMAN LAW 1840).

75. *See Dror, Law and Social Change*, TUL. L.R. 33, MASSELL 2 LAW AND SOCIETY REVIEW 179 (1867), AUBERT, ACTA SOCIOLOGICA 10, 99 (in AUBERT, SOCIOLOGY OF LAW, Penguin 1969, p. 116. *See* generally FREEMAN, THE LEGAL STRUCTURE, Longman 1974, ch. 3.

76. *Cf.* EEKELAAR, FAMILY SECURITY AND FAMILY BREAKDOWN, Penguin Books, 1971, p. 44.

For centuries husbands had the right to chastise their wives. Thus, Hawkins would allow a man to exercise "moderate correction," upon his wife as he would "correct his apprentices or children."[77] In Bacon's Abridgment of 1736 a husband is said to have the right to "beat" his wife.[78] Blackstone, in words reminiscent of contemporaries who believe wife-batterers to be confined to a working-class subculture, believed that the right was obsolete, having been doubted in the politer reign of Charles II, but that "the lower rank of people who were always fond of the old common law still claim and exert their ancient privilege and courts of law still permit a husband to restrain a wife of her liberty in case of any gross misbehavior."[79] In an aside he explained that this was for women's "protection and benefit . . . so great a favorite is the female sex of the laws of England!" The right was "finally abolished"[80] in 1891 in *R v. Jackson:* the Master of the Rolls doubted whether "it ever was the law"[81] and the Lord Chancellor referred to "quaint and absurd dicta."[82] There are, however, dicta as late as 1840 supporting a general right.[83]

More recently judges have supported the right of a husband to correct his wife. In 1946 Henn Collins, J in *Meacher v. Meacher*[84] held a husband was within his rights in assaulting his wife because she refused to obey his orders not to visit her relations. The Court of Appeals reversed him. In 1959 a judge held that it was cruelty when a husband gave his adulterous wife the "hardest smacked bottom she had ever had" but added that if he had punished her as one punishes a naughty child it would not have been cruel.[85] Only two years ago a sheriff in Scotland, on fining a husband for hitting his wife in the face, remarked: "It is a well-known fact that you can

77. 1 Hawkins P.C.130.

78. Quoted in BLACKSTONE'S COMMENTARIES.

79. 1 COMMENTARIES 445.

80. *Per* Graveson, in GRAVESON AND CRANE, A CENTURY OF FAMILY LAW, Sweet & Maxwell, 1957, p. 16.

81. 1891 1 Q.B. 671, 682.

82. *Idem.*, p. 679.

83. Cochrane's Case 8 Dowl. 630. Coleridge J said there was "no doubt of the general dominion which the law of England attributed to a husband over his wife."

84. [1946] p. 216.

85. McKenzie v. McKenzie, TIMES, 5 June 1959, commented on in BIGGS, THE CONCEPT OF MATRIMONIAL CRUELTY, Athlone Press, 1962, p. 147.

strike your wife's bottom if you wish, but you must not strike her on the face."[86] He also expressed his support for the ancient principle that "reasonable chastisement should be the duty of every husband if his wife misbehaves." Do these judicial pronouncements, isolated as they are, reflect the common consciousness of a society ruled by the ethos of male domination? Do they go some way towards explaining the oft-quoted rationalization of wife-battering that "they deserve it."[87] Gelles found women who subscribed to this view. One said: "He hit me once. It wasn't very long ago. The baby was about two months old . . . we were fighting about something. I have a habit of not keeping my mouth shut. I kept at him and at him. He finally turned around and belted me. It was my fault, I asked for it."[88] Parnas also observed occasions where wives believed that a husband should beat his wife "every once in a while."[89] The deviance has become normalized. Dunn J, though, got "a wigging from wives" when he suggested that wives in the North of England didn't mind their husbands beating them but drew the line at adultery.[90] And Faulks J confessed to having made "an ass" of himself when he insinuated that the wives of Welsh miners accepted their husbands' right to spank them.[91]

The Problem of Rape

This ideology is reflected in the attitude of English law towards rape. By definition it cannot exist within marriage, though the behavior itself, that is forced sexual intercourse, may be functionally equivalent to a comparable behavior committed outside the bounds of marriage and given the official label of rape. A husband may, however, be convicted of raping his wife if magistrates have made a noncohabitation order in favor of the wife,[92] if a decree *nisi* of divorce has been pronounced,[93] and possibly if they have agreed

86. *See No Comment* in Ms., August 1975.
87. *Cf.* PIZZEY, *op. cit.*, note 3, p. 33.
88. *Op. cit.*, note 35, p, 59.
89. *Op. cit.*, note 21, p. 952.
90. *See* The Daily Mirror 16 April 1974.
91. *Idem.*, 18 February 1974.
92. R v. Clarke [1949] 2 All E.R. 448.
93. R v. O'Brien [1974] 3 All E.R. 663.

to separate, particularly if there is a separation agreement containing a non-molestation clause.[94]

In 1972 Cairns L J opined[95] that "the notion that a husband can, without incurring punishment, treat his wife . . . with any kind of hostile force is obsolete." He held that the crime of kidnapping could thus be committed by a husband against his wife. Kidnapping and rape are not *in pari materia,* but Cairns L J's dictum is wide enough to cast doubt on the propriety of exempting husbands from prosecution for rapes upon their wives. Despite the existence of the immunity it is clear that a husband, though at liberty to have sexual intercourse with his wife, may not use force or violence to exercise that liberty. If he does he may be charged with assault or some other offense. The law rests on a fiction and is clearly inconsistent with civil law principles: a wife, for example, is not bound to submit to inordinate or unreasonable sexual demands by her husband,[96] and she may refuse sexual intercourse if he is suffering from a venereal disease.[97]

The privilege of a husband to rape his wife has been repudiated in the criminal codes of Sweden and Denmark and in the USSR and a number of other countries in the Communist bloc,[98] as well as in the state of Delaware. An attempt was made to abolish the exemption in England in 1976[99] but it ultimately failed. The logic of Soames in *The Forsyte Saga* is thus preserved: ". . . women made a fuss about it in books, but in the cool judgment of right-thinking men . . . he had but done his best to sustain the sanctity of marriage, to prevent her from abandoning her duty."[100] He had, of course, just raped Irene.

To many contemporary theorists the act of rape is a cameo of male-female relationships, forcible penetration being at one end of a spectrum of male sexual dominance.[101] Griffin refers to it as "a

94. R v. Miller [1954] 2 Q.B. 282.
95. R v. Reid [1972] 2 All E.R. 1350.
96. Holborn v. Holborn [1947] 1 All E.R. 32.
97. Foster v. Foster [1921] P. 438.
98. Livneh, *On Rape and the Sanctity of Marriage*, ISRAEL L.R. 2, 415.
99. During the committee stage in the House of Commons of the Sexual Offenses (Amendment) Bill (now Act).
100. Published in 1922, pp. 245-6.
101. *See* Greenwood and Young, *Notes on the Theory of Rape and its Policy Implications*, Paper presented to London Group on Deviancy, 1975.

form of mass terrorism."[102] Davis believes that "a primary goal of the sexual aggressor . . . is the conquest and degradation of his victim"[103] and the Schwendingers see rape as "a power trip . . . an act of aggression and an act of contempt."[104] To these writers the motivation for rape is only secondarily sexual.[105]

The Protection of the Criminal Law

What protection is afforded the battered wife by the criminal law? With the exception of rape a husband can commit all other offenses against the person on his wife. It is unnecessary to list all these offenses. Suffice it to say that any attack by a husband causing his wife any actual bodily harm constitutes a criminal offense.[106] To constitute "actual bodily harm" the harm need not be really serious.[107] Lynskey J said that it "includes any hurt or injury calculated to interfere with the health or comfort of the prosecutor.[108] This includes, so he held, a hysterical and nervous condition resulting from an assault. It seems to follow that many, if not most, acts of molestation[109] will come within the concept. A more serious offense is committed when "really serious" bodily harm is caused.[110]

If criminal proceedings are brought, the wife is a competent and compellable witness against her own husband.[111] In fact, though, if she is an unwilling witness the police may well be hard put to prove the charge. Provocation is a defense only to a charge of murder (reducing it to manslaughter)[112] so a husband may not claim that he

102. *Rape: The All-American Crime*, Ramparts (Sept. issue), 28 (1971).

103. *Sexual Assaults in the Philadelphia Prison System* in (eds.), Gagnon and Simon, THE SEXUAL SCENE, Aldine, 1970.

104. *Rape Myths*, CRIME AND SOCIAL JUSTICE, 1, 18 (1974).

105. This comes out acutely in Eldridge Cleaver's description of his rape of white women as "insurrectionary" (SOUL ON ICE (1968)). *See generally*, J & H Schwendinger, *Review of Rape Literature* in CRIME AND SOCIAL JUSTICE 6, 79 (1976).

106. Under § 47 of the Offenses Against the Person Act 1861.

107. *See* DPP v. Smith [1961] A.C. 290, 334 and SMITH AND HOGAN, CRIMINAL LAW (3rd ed., 1973), p. 297.

108. In R v. Miller [1954] 2 Q.B. 282, 292.

109. Interpreted broadly to include pestering (Vaughn v. Vaughn [1973] 3 All E.R. 449.

110. *Viz.*, wounding and grievous bodily harm under sections 18 and 20 of the 1861 Act.

111. R v. Verolla [1963] 1 Q.B. 285, R v. Lapworth [1931] 1 K.B. 117. Nokes has commented that decisions to the contrary would have constituted "a charter for wife-beaters" in GRAVESON AND CRANE, *op. cit.*, note 80, p. 148.

112. Homicide Act 1957 s. 3.

was driven to assault his wife. However, we know that juries do take account of such "defenses"[113] rather as they regard contributory negligence as a defense to a charge of rape.[114] Furthermore, the injured wife's view of her own role in the event may enter into her decision not to mobilize the criminal justice system.[115]

There have been a couple of cases in England recently of wives who killed brutal husbands. To Mabel Bangert,[116] who killed her husband by stabbing him repeatedly in the back as he went to attack their crippled son, Milmo J said: "You have lived your life with a tyrannical, violent and cruel husband. Your provocation was as severe as any I have come across." She was found guilty of manslaughter and received a suspended jail sentence. In a popular press this decision was applauded and Mrs. Bangert became a folk hero—for a day or so. Valerie Pulling[117] shot her husband when she feared another beating from him. May J told the jury it was important to assess the case without emotion, but advised an acquittal if they felt it was not Mrs. Pulling's intention to kill or seriously harm her husband. The jury did not, it seems, put emotion aside and in a perverse but arguably justifiable verdict acquitted her. It is difficult to estimate how typical these cases are; my own suspicion is that both judges and juries take a more lenient attitude in such cases than they would have done a decade ago.

In some legal systems, though not in England, wife-beating is a distinct nominate crime. Thus, in California a 1945 statute states: "[A]ny husband who willfully inflicts upon his wife corporal injury resulting in a traumatic condition . . . is guilty of a felony"[118] punishable by a jail sentence of between one year and ten. In *People*

113. A good example (though it does not involve an offense against a wife) is that of the Indian hot-dog salesman in McCabe and Purves, The Jury at Work (Oxford Penal Research Unit 1972).

114. *See* Kalven and Zeisel, The American Jury, Little Brown, 1966.

115. Reiss, The Police and the Public, Yale U.P. (1971).

116. The Times, 28 April 1977.

117. The Times, 27 April 1977. Another case is reported in *The Times*, 15 September 1977. Mrs. Newsome was given a 2-year suspended sentence after being convicted of the manslaughter of her husband who was said to have ill-treated her for 10 years. The case got minimal press coverage compared to the earlier cases.

118. Discussed in Truninger, *Marital Violence—The Legal Solutions*, 23 Hastings L.J. 259 (1971) and Martin, Battered Wives, Glide, 1976, pp. 100-101. Texas and Hawaii have a similar statutory provision.

v. Burns[119] it was held that to satisfy this provision visible bruises and injuries had to be present. Apparently, "police and district attorneys are unwilling to charge an assailant [with this offense, which is a felony] because of the higher bail and longer jail sentence involved."[120] This statutory provision is currently under a cloud. It discriminates on the basis of sex and is therefore arguably unconstitutional. Indeed, in 1975 Judge Eugene Premo of the San Jose Superior Court dismissed a charge on this very basis: he said, "a wife inflicting the same injury and trauma can be subjected to no more than misdemeanor prosecution under assault and battery sections."[121] In spite of Del Martin's forceful criticism that this decision "takes advantage of the existing male bias within the criminal justice system and denies the value of laws created to correct existing imbalances,"[122] it is difficult to see what such laws achieve. If, as is generally accepted, the criminal law is a blunt instrument in the war against domestic violence, it is dubious if the creation of specific offenses can improve the situation.

Compensation for Criminal Injury

In Great Britain since 1964 a scheme has existed whereby victims of criminal assaults can claim compensation from the state. The idea originated in New Zealand and has since spread. California was the first state in the U.S. to introduce the concept. It has cost the British exchequer £30 million. Applications are going up all the time. In 1975-76 they were 17.3 percent up on the previous year.[123] Wives who suffer personal injury at their husband's hands are, however, excluded. Paragraph 7 of the scheme reads:

> [W]here the victim who suffered injuries and the offender who inflicted them were living together at the time as members of the same family no compensation will be payable. For the purpose of this paragraph where a man and a woman were living together as man and wife they will be treated as if they were married to one another.[124]

119. 88 Cal. App. 2d 867 (1948).
120. *Per* MARTIN, BATTERED WIVES p. 100.
121. Quoted from San Jose Mercury, 5 November 1975 by MARTIN, *Idem.*, pp. 100-101.
122. *Idem.*, p. 101.
123. *See* Annual Report of C.I.C.B. 1975-76 Cmnd 6656 (12th report).
124. Reproduced in the Annual Reports. The scheme is still not statutory.

In the first twelve years of the operation of the scheme 335 applicants for compensation were ruled out of order on paragraph 7: that is 3 percent of all applications have failed because the injury was caused in a domestic setting. There were seventy-six such cases in 1975-76 (4 percent of the total number of applications). Many of these applications are made on behalf of children.[125]

The battered wife's plight was aggravated by a decision of the Divisional Court in 1972.[126] Lord Widgery held that the words "living together . . . as members of the same family" had their ordinary natural meaning and were not to be read in the light of general matrimonial law. The wife, terrified for her own safety, slept in a bedroom with her two daughters, leaving the husband to sleep on a sofa in the living room. There were no sexual relations. We do not know from the report whether meals were consumed together or whether she did his washing. But there is a good chance that he would be held to be in desertion and that they would be "living apart" for the separation provisions of the divorce legislation.[127] In view of this the decision is to be deprecated. A wife who is separated from her husband is eligible for compensation as are divorced women. Thus, where a former husband slashed his former wife's hands, lacerating tendons and ensuring that she was no longer able to work, the C.J.C.B. paid her compensation (His behavior was also sufficiently "obvious and gross" for it to be taken account of when the question of a transfer of property arose.).[128] The British system is not alone in excluding victims of family violence. According to Shank, intrafamily crime or victim participation (a category also recognized for exclusion purposes in the British scheme) may disqualify one from compensation under the California scheme.[129]

How is one to explain the exclusion from the scheme of victims of family violence? Two popular explanations would cite the dif-

---

125. A good illustration is in the 10th Report (Cmnd 5791), pp. 10-11. The origins of the exclusion are found in Cmnd 1406 ¶ 38.

126. R v. C.I.C.B. ex parte Staten, [1972] 1 All E.R. 1034.

127. *Cf.* Hopes v. Hopes [1949] P. 227, Mouncer v. Mouncer [1972] 1 All E.R. 289, Fuller v. Fuller [1973] 2 All E.R. 650.

128. *See* Jones v. Jones [1975] 2 All E.R. 12.

129. *See* 43 S. CAL. L. REV. 85.

ficulties of proof in a family situation and the "floodgates" danger argument. Neither is really a satisfactory explanation. In cases of impossibility of proof, otherwise eligible claims could be disallowed. The floodgates argument is also disingenuous as, with the number of violent crimes known to police approaching 100,000 and anyway nearly seven times more than the number of applicants for compensation, they are potentially open anyway, and it is only lack of knowledge and "legal competence"[130] which cuts access to the Board down. A better explanation is found (in another context) in Marx's recent study of violence in an Israeli township.[131] He argues that in the case of interpersonal assaults in the privacy of the home the "public interest is not at stake" with the result that "law organs tend to apply a more restricted definition of violence to them."[132] One could argue, as Hanmer does,[133] that male violence against women is in the public interest as presently defined, in the sense that it is functional to preserving male dominance. But, if that is so, it is even more likely that the state would wish to exclude battered wives from the scope of the compensation scheme. So long as husbands can legally rape their wives and some judges are prepared to concede to them a liberty to spank them, it is difficult to see how the state could compensate wives for injuries inflicted by their husbands.

The Nonenforcement of the Criminal Law

In June 1973, in answer to a question tabled by Jack Ashley M.P., a leading champion of battered women's rights, the Home Office said: "The law does not discriminate between assaults by a husband on his wife and other assaults. Any assault constitutes a criminal offense."[134] That is the theory but what happens in practice?

For a start, we know that wives are reluctant to report assaults by their husbands on themselves to the police. There are a number of reasons for this. They may expect to be degraded and humiliated.

130. Carlin and Howard, UCLA Law Rec. 12, 381.
131. The Social Context of Violent Behaviour, RKP, 1976.
132. *Idem.*, p. 18.
133. *Op. cit.*, note 62, p. 18.
134. H.C. vol. 858 written Answers cols. 149-50 *per* Mr. M. Carlisle.

They may know (or worse half-know) about police attitudes towards domestic disturbances. If they are frequent victims they may tend to refrain from reporting because the burdens of such reporting and follow-up actions may be intolerably great. They may believe that without a husband to support them, they will be worse off. They may sense that initiating police action is likely to cause them even greater distress: greater poverty, worse beatings-up, etc.

But given that they alert the police, what happens then? It is not generally realized that in cases of common assault the legal remedy is for the wife to initiate proceedings in the magistrates' court. A police officer is not entitled to act as informant on a charge of common assault,[135] unless the person assaulted is so feeble, old and infirm as to be incapable of instituting proceedings because he is not a free agent but is under the control of the person committing the assault.[136] It is arguable that some battered women come into this category but the number is probably small. In cases of more serious assault the police have the power of arrest as well as the duty to follow up and prosecute.[137]

The police attitude itself is fashioned by a number of factors. The Association of Chief Police Officers of England and Wales and Northern Ireland in their evidence to the House of Commons Select Committee cited as a consideration a factor that may well be at the root of the problem:

> Whilst such problems take up considerable Police time . . . in the majority of cases the role of the Police is a negative one. We are, after all, dealing with persons "bound in marriage," and it is important, for a host of reasons, to maintain the unity of the spouses. Precipitated action by the Police could aggravate the position to such an extent as to create a worse situation than the one they were summoned to deal with.[138]

The Association is favorable to the provision of refuges but it adds: "every effort *should be made to re-unite the family.*"[139] (their emphasis). In a similar way Parnas says of intrafamily violence that it is different from normal crime in that "preservation of family rela-

135. Nicholson v. Booth (1888) 52 J.P. 662.

136. Pickering v. Willoughby [1907] 2 K.B. 296.

137. On their reluctance to intervene *see* House of Commons, Minutes of Evidence pp. 361-391, and Dow in (ed.) BORLAND, VIOLENCE IN THE FAMILY, Manchester U.P., 1976, p. 129.

138. P. 366.

139. P. 369.

tionships may be deemed a very important social goal."[140] What is wanted is a restoration of the equilibrium with the minimum of change. It is taken as a "given" that "re-uniting" the family, "preserving" family relationships is desirable.

The attitude of the police is formed also by their training and environment. In England the police recruit learns almost nothing about the dynamics of marital conflict during his sixteen-week crash induction. Courses tend to be legalistic and the social science content is sparse. In the United States, according to Parnas,[141] what police learn about most is the danger involved in intervening in marital conflict. Certainly, this is what remains in the memory. Since over 20 percent of police deaths in the U.S. occur on domestic disturbance calls this is hardly surprising. Very few police are killed on duty in England, and to my knowledge no policeman has been killed when intervening in a domestic disturbance. But in England, too, a low profile policy is kept.

As Parnas found, it is common for the wife to go the aid of her husband so that "the danger quotient is high for both disputing parties."[142] Wives may attack the police: such a reaction being elicited by "emotional ties and habituated loyalty."[143] Furthermore, as the Metropolitan Police Memorandum to the House of Commons Select Committee points out: "[T]he wife herself [in any subsequent prosecution] is an essential witness. Experience has shown that prosecutions have failed or could not be pursued because of a withdrawal by the wife of her complaint or because of her nervous reaction to the prospect of giving evidence against her husband. A woman no matter how cruelly treated is often reluctant to see her husband imprisoned or fined."[144] This can reach the point where the police can accept marital violence as violence between "consenting adults" and hence a "private affair."[145] Even where the wife wants a prosecution to take place they may actively discourage her initiative.

---

140. 36 LAW AND CONTEMP. PROB. 539, 542 (1971).
141. WIS. L.R. 914, 920 (1967).
142. *Op. cit.*, note 138, p. 720.
143. *Idem.*, p. 921.
144. P. 376.
145. *Per* Field and Field *Marital Violence and the Criminal Process: Neither Justice Nor Peace* in SOC. SERV. REV. 47, 221, 227 (1973).

Parnas has shown that in the United States the police in the marital violence situation act as support figures rather than instruments of control,[146] and that they see their prime objective as adjustment rather than arrest. This is consistent both with general sociology of policing reserach[147] and with what has been found in England.[148] The public in England hold the police in high regard[149] and to many they are the first of the social services, acting as gatekeepers and filters to the other specialized services. No other agency is known to function for twenty-four hours in a day. Arrests, however, do take place. What are the criteria for choosing between arrest and mediation or arrest and caution?

There will undoubtedly be local variations. These will largely reflect the differences in communities. A policeman cannot be an effective peace officer, he cannot act in a social support capacity unless he understands, or better still participates in, the society he polices. Subcultural differences, also, affect patrol practices. Thus, Skolnick in his classic study of *Justice Without Trial* can write of the way the police interpret a stabbing in the white community as a "potential homicide" which in the black ghetto is "written off" as a "North Westville battery."[150]

The Association of Chief Police Officers of England, Wales and Northern Ireland in their Memorandum to the Select Committee list a number of factors which militate for or against the decision to arrest and prosecute:

(i) the seriousness of the assault;
(ii) the availability of witnesses;
(iii) the character of the alleged assailant;
(iv) age, infirmity etc., of the complainant;
(v) previous domestic history;
(vi) the wishes of the complainant; and
(vii) "if prosecution ensued against the wishes of the complainant, would the domestic situation be adversely affected."[151]

146. *See* (1967) WIS. L.R. 914.
147. *See* BANTON, THE POLICEMAN IN THE COMMUNITY, Tavistock, 1964.
148. *See* Punch and Naylor, New Society, 17 May 1973, p. 358.
149. *See* BELSON, THE POLICE AND THE PUBLIC, Harper and Row, 1975.
150. WILEY, JUSTICE WITHOUT TRIAL, 1967, pp. 171-72.
151. P. 367.

Parnas[152] divides the decision-making into two levels in both of which discretion operates.

There is, he says, an initial screening undertaken by a dispatcher.[153] Many cases get no further. Cumming *et al.*[154] found that when a complainant reported a dispute he had only a one in two chance of getting more than advice. The interpretational latitude in a communications center is great. Surprisingly, it has not been commented upon at all in an English context, though it obviously exists.

Among the factors which Parnas[155] detects in decision-making in field operations are: (a) the motivation for calling the police (does the victim want an arrest or does she rather wish to scare the offender, get him out of the house?); (b) the question whether the victim can afford to have the offender arrested (mainly the problem of support); (c) the subculture to which the disputants belong (is the conduct "not seriously objectionable to the victim?"); (d) the danger that the offender may cause more serious harm upon his return; (e) the danger that it may cause temporary or permanent termination of family relationships or harm innocent family members; (f) the knowledge that the victim may change her mind; (g) reticence in the issuance of warrants and in prosecutions by prosecuting authorities; (h) the knowledge that the victim may choose not to prosecute; (i) the knowledge of the courts' leniency in sentencing; (j) the policeman himself having had similar experiences and his feeling that a "man's home is his castle."[156]

Suggestions as to the ways in which police performance can be improved usually take two forms. One view is that if the traditional role of the police in this area is adjustment and mediation, then one should increase the effectiveness of these techniques. The work of Bard[157] and the New York Family Crisis Intervention Unit are the

152. *See* (1967) WIS. L.R. 914 and 36 LAW AND CONTEMP. PROB. 539.
153. *See* the Wisconsin article at p. 922 ff.
154. SOCIAL PROBLEMS 12, 276 (1965).
155. *See* the Wisconsin article at pp. 922, 929.
156. *Cf.* PIZZEY, *op. cit.*, note 3 at p. 30.
157. *See* Bard and Berkowitz, *Training Police as Specialists in Family Crisis Intervention: A Community Psychology Program*, COMMUN. MENTAL HEALTH J. 3, 315 (1967) and Bard in STEINMETZ AND STRAUS *op. cit.*, note 8, p. 152.

best-known examples of this philosophy. In New York, selected police officers were trained as specialists in family crisis intervention techniques. Of this Parnas has written:[158] "Domestic problems can be deemed to be significantly diverted from the criminal process only when the result of a police service call is not only restoration of order but activation of a process which at least has the potential to resolve the source of the conflict." It is difficult to assess the success or otherwise of the New York scheme.[159] The number of arrests went up as did the number of family homicides though none of these occurred in families seen by members of the F.C.I.U. The recidivism rate was high. But all these "facts" may reflect a number of unknown variables. The program fell when the Federal Grant was terminated. But it has been replicated in other cities such as Louisville and Oakland and its influence has lived on in training curricula.

It has also been suggested that the police should be encouraged to make referrals of marriages in trouble to relevant social welfare agencies. "Police contact could also be used to refer agencies to disputants."[160] As Parnas says, this would not seem to involve any violation of privacy nor any breach of confidential relationship. One of Erin Pizzey's complaints against the police is that they do not notify relevant agencies such as social services and the NSPCC.[161]

A second view is to be found in the Report of the House of Commons Select Committee. They recommended that:

> Chief Constables should review their policies about the police approach to domestic violence. Special instructions about this difficult and delicate subject should be given to all new recruits, and regular written guidance should be issued by the Chief Constable in the form of advisory leaflets.[162]

It is clear that what the Committee wanted was a more vigorous prosecution policy.

The Chief Constable of Bedfordshire, Mr. Anthony Armstrong, announced in February 1976 a tough new prosecution policy against

---

158. 36 Law and Contemp. Prob. 539, 551.

159. *See*, for comments on it, Parnas *idem.*, and Field and Field, *op. cit.*, note 145, pp. 237-8.

160. Ind. L.J. 44, 159, 180 (1969).

161. *Op. cit.*, note 3, p. 99.

162. ¶ 44.

husbands who battered their wives.[163] Under this policy violent husbands are arrested, charged and taken to court whether or not their wives are prepared to give evidence against them. If the wife withdraws her complaint by the time the case gets to court, the police invite the court to bind the husband over to keep the peace. If there are further incidents, the husband can be brought to court and dealt with for that as well as for breaking the order binding him over. At the time Bedfordshire police force set up a special advisory service to help battered wives under which senior officers based at police stations in Dunstable, Luton and Bedford, the three main centers of population, are on a 24-hour call to advise and help them.

A report has been published on the results of the new prosecution policy during its first six months.[164] During the period, 288 acts of violence in the home came to the attention of the police. In 184 of the cases (63.9 percent), following the initial intervention of a police officer and a discussion with the parties to the assault, the complainants did not wish to pursue their complaints. No further action was taken as "any injuries visible did not justify police intervention." In 104 cases, complaints were substantiated, arrests were made and proceedings commenced. In eighteen of these cases (17.3 percent), between the date the charge was preferred and the date set for the court hearing, the complainants withdrew their complaints and no further action was taken. Seventy-nine out of the remaining eighty-six cases had been disposed of by the time of the report. Only three men were given immediate custodial sentences. We are not told anything about the length of the sentences. Two hundred eighty-five men (that is nearly 99 percent) responsible for acts of violence against their wives thus remained at liberty after the wives had apprised the police. Is it any wonder that battered wives are reluctant to invoke the criminal justice system against their husbands?

It may be useful to document the decisions taken in the remain-

163. As reported in The Daily Telegraph, 28 February 1976.
164. Bedfordshire Police, Report on Acts of Domestic Violence Committed in the County between 1 February 1976 and 31 July 1976.

ing seventy-six cases. Two offenders were cautioned[165] by a senior police officer. In four cases no action was taken by the police. Five received suspended sentences and one a deferred sentence. Seventeen (that is 21.5 percent) were fined (this affects the wife and children as much as, if not more than, the husband). Another three were bound over as well as being fined. Five were put on probation. Fifteen were given conditional discharges and a further two absolute discharges. Eleven were bound over to keep the peace. A further three were bound over after the case had been dismissed and evidence heard and three more were bound over although the complaint was withdrawn. In one case a warrant was issued for arrest because the accused failed to appear. Four cases were dismissed and the men were not bound over. In total, twenty of the seventy-nine cases resulted in men being bound over to keep the peace (that is nearly 26 percent).[166]

The Role of the Courts

Erin Pizzey has asserted that "the court is not the proper place to resolve problems of the battered wife."[167] She is critical of the willingness to grant bail and the trivial sentences. She alleges that going to court is an ordeal, and that judges and officials are uncaring and unfeeling.[168] Field and Field have, however, pointed out that "the function of the criminal law is altered dramatically in the domestic-assault situation and the classical bases for the employment of the criminal process—deterrence, incapacitation, prevention, retribution or rehabilitation—do not apply in a substantial way to these cases."[169] In England this has barely been noted, and, although domestic violence has become an area for police experimentation, the traditional criminal process has remained intact. Whereas in the U.S. many attempts have been made to tailor the traditional

165. Cautioning is a variable practice, common in rural areas but less so in the metropolitan and urban areas.

166. It seems from this report that the police have not carried out their original intentions to take to court irrespective of the complainant's wishes. But the Report does not explain the change of policy.

167. *Op. cit.*, note 3, p. 129.

168. *Idem.*, p. 120.

169. *Op. cit.*, note 145, p. 227.

process to take account of the special needs of spouses at war, in England the courts adjudicate upon domestic disputes and violence as upon other criminal behavior.

In the United States there have been a number of attempts to decriminalize domestic violence.[170] In the courts of a number of cities, notably Chicago, Detroit, Milwaukee, New York and Washington, the judge has become "practically director of a welfare agency engaged in diagnostic and therapeutic rather than strictly judicial pursuits."[171] This has met with nearly universal approval. Parnas writes that "persons and institutions best equipped to deal [with domestic disturbances] are not those trained primarily in the law—but in the workings of the mind itself and the conflicts peculiar to marriage."[172] There is thus a premium on counselling, there are cooling-off periods and pretrial conferences, there is pretrial screening with unenforceable peace bonds. The courts appear to be more accessible than they are in England.

We hear glowing reports of some of these experiments. They certainly appear bolder and more adventurous than anything being tried in England. Susan Maidment has "regretted that the [House of Commons] Select Committee was not more inventive and innovative in its recommendations regarding the law available to battered women."[173]

I would, however, enter a caveat against the counselling, social welfare orientation. We must ask ourselves what we are dealing with. Where we are confronted with petty violence, a couple who give as much as they take, with basically an ongoing relationship which needs sorting out, the Family Court approach may be desirable. Where the parties are in a continuous state of social propinquity, resolution by adjudication is inconsistent with continuing viable social interaction.[174] Marital relations rest upon the social assumption that parties are ready and willing to accept and deal

---

170. Discussed in Parnas, 54 MINN. L.R. 585 and in a forthcoming article by Maidment in (1977) I.C.L.Q.

171. Rheinstein, quoted in Parnas.

172. *Op. cit.*, note 170, p. 643.

173. 26 I.C.L.Q., 403, 442 (1977).

174. *Cf.* FREEMAN, THE LEGAL STRUCTURE, Longman, 1974 p. 38.

with each other: no amount of legal intervention can secure such a social basis.[175] But too often in cases of domestic violence we are face-to-face with cases of brutal violence. Can meditation[176] work in such a case?

The success of mediation depends on a number of variables, notably a common interest in having the conflict resolved. But what common interest do a brutal husband and a terrorized wife have? The standard answer is that they may have children and that it is important to stabilize the family. Mediation looks to the future whereas an adjudication measures the husband's behavior against criminal legislation.[177] Mediation looks towards a compromise solution: an adjudicator, employing traditional techniques, imposes what he regards as a just solution.[178] Once within the Family Court setting and a social welfare counselling orientation we may lose track of the fact that wife-beating may be a brutal criminal assault and not just the symptom of a troubled marriage.

The question that needs to be asked of those who see progress as lying with Family courts, counselling services, etc., is what they conceive to be the causes of wife-beating. Their goal is clear: they want reconciliation and stability, they want the family to *function as it should.* They want to preserve the family. They rarely articulate a theory of family violence but implicit is one of two assumptions: (i) that the batterer has behaved "irrationally" because he is disturbed in some way or (ii) he has problems resulting from inadequate resources. On either hypothesis the solution is seen in terms of the need for more social work intervention, courts developing welfare functions as well as better housing and improved employment prospects. But do these solutions speak to the right problem? Are they in the woman's interests? I doubt it. And even using the criterion of success employed by its proponents, I would doubt whether the counselling orientation is successful.[179]

---

175. *Cf.* Kahn-Freund, 22 CURRENT LEGAL PROB. 1, 24-25 (1969).

176. On which *see* Eckhoff, ACTA SOCIOLOGICA 10, (1966), pp. 158-66 (in AUBERT, SOCIOLOGY OF LAW, Penguin, 1969, p. 171.

177. *Idem.*, in AUBERT at p. 175.

178. *See* Aubert, J. OF CONFL. RES. 7, (1963), pp. 26-42, J. OF CONFL. RES. 11, (1967), pp. 40-50.

179. Also critical is MARTIN, BATTERED WIVES, pp. 103-104.

The Law of Tort

The act of battering constitutes the torts of assault and battery. In England until 1962 a spouse was not allowed to sue the other in tort.[180] Two reasons were given for this. First, the fiction that they were one flesh.[181] Secondly, that such litigation is "unseemly, distressing and embittering."[182] To quote Glanville Williams: "If a husband 'beats up' his wife, she cannot sue him, because to sue him would be unwifely."[183] Each of the parties to a marriage now has the same right of action in tort against the other as if they were not married. But, in order to prevent them from using the court as a forum for trivial domestic disputes, the proceedings may be stayed if it appears that "no substantial benefit"[184] will accrue to either party from their continuation.

There are no statistics as to the number of spouses who sue each other in tort or of the number of cases which are stayed. Nearly all cases will arise out of motor accidents and the spouse will be only a nominal defendant. "Nothing draws two people together like a mutual desire to get something out of one's insurance carrier."[185] While the immunity was impossible to defend it would be folly to pretend that its removal has in any way helped the battered wife. But, though rarely if ever used for such purposes, it was potentially of use prior to the passing of the Domestic Violence and Matrimonial Proceedings Act of 1976 as a way of obtaining an injunction against molestation or to exclude a brutal husband from the matrimonial home.[186]

The majority of American States have still to abrogate the doctrine of interspousal immunity.[187] California did so in the case of *Self v. Self*[188] in 1962: this case is instructive in that it arose out of

180. The Law was changed by the Law Reform (Husband and Wife) Act 1962.

181. *Cf.* McCurdy, VILL. L.R. 4, 303 (1959).

182. *Per* McCardie J in Gottliffe v. Edelston [1930] 2 K.B. 378, 392.

183. M.L.R. 24, 101.

184. This causes difficulties: how does one quantify benefit? *Cf.* STREET, THE LAW OF TORTS, Butterworths, 1976, pp. 468-9.

185. *Per* Larson, WIS. L.R. 4, 467, 499.

186. *Cf. per* Sir George Baker, A.O.C. Select Committee Minutes.

187. *See* PLOSCOWE, FOSTER AND FRIED, FAMILY LAW: CASES AND MATERIALS, Little Brown, 1972, pp. 852-4.

188. 376 P.2d 65.

an assault by a husband against his wife in the course of which her arm was broken. Again, there are no available statistics as to the use of a civil action for damages in any of the states which have abolished the immunity, but it is doubtful that it is in common use anywhere.

Matrimonial Proceedings in Magistrates' Courts: The Non-Cohabitation Clause

In England there are two types of matrimonial proceedings that can be brought. A spouse may seek the "summary, local and inexpensive relief"[189] offered by magistrates' courts. Provided an offense can be proved, the court may make an order containing a non-cohabitation clause. This relieves the complainant of his or her obligation to cohabit with the defendant. It is, however, simply a declaration and is not enforceable. If granted, it prevents the complainant from relying on the defendant's desertion subsequent to the order, so that it may have positive disadvantages to the complainant.[190] Whether such a clause is inserted depends on the discretion of the court.[191]

Gibson found that many magistrates' courts were overwilling to insert a non-cohabitation clause.[192] He noted that "in many instances the court in making a maintenance order inadvertently omits to strike out from the printed form, which is adaptable to different orders, the non-cohabitation clause."[193] He found in a survey of 1,200 orders in force in 1966 by fifty magistrates' courts that in 30 percent a non-cohabitation clause had been insured. The proportion rose to 40 percent if orders made in 1964 and 1965 only were taken into account. Further, in only 62 percent of the cases where such a clause was found was persistent cruelty either the sole ground or one ground of two or more grounds for the wife's application. In 22 percent the ground was adultery, in 11 percent desertion and in 5 percent willful neglect to maintain. Gibson also found a

189. *Per* Law Commission, Law Com. 77 (20 October 1976) ¶ 3.15.

190. Dodd v. Dodd [1906] p. 189; Harriman v. Harriman [1909] p. 123. Even if the clause was inserted without the applicant's consent: Mackenzie v. Mackenzie [1940] p. 81.

191. Corton v. Corton [1965] p. 1, Jolliffe v. Jolliffe [1965] p. 6.

192. 33 M.L.R. 63.

193. *Idem.*, p. 65.

greater propensity to insert a non-cohabitation clause in courts in the North of England. Gibson blamed justices' clerks for the over-use of the non-cohabitation clause. It is possible also that they and the magistrates react to the policies of local authorities which show a greater willingness to transfer council tenancies where the wife has such an order.[194]

Many magistrates will not make a non-cohabitation order where a wife is still living with her husband. Others expect the impossible: that, although remaining in the matrimonial home, she lead a separate life from her husband. Magistrates have as yet no power to evict husbands, though the Law Commission has recommended[195] that such a power should be conferred on them, where they are satisfied that the wife or a child of the family is in danger of being physically injured by the husband and that he has used violence against the wife or a child of the family, or he has threatened violence against the wife or a child of the family and also has used violence against some other person, or he has disobeyed a personal protection order.

Magistrates do not dissolve marriages. Only the superior courts, divorce country courts and the High Court can grant a license to remarry. So non-cohabitation orders do not affect status and the wife is left in a state of limbo. But something like 50 percent of the magistrates' court matrimonial orders remain the final orders for that marriage, leaving spouses neither properly married nor free to remarry.[196] Women in such cases invariably rely on state assistance and can form no regular sexual relationships unless the man concerned is ready and able to support them and their children, for the cohabitation rule (one of the best examples of the way in which the state controls women) prevents the payment of benefit where a woman lives with a man *as* his wife.[197]

The magistrates' courts "deal exclusively with what used to be called the lumpen proletariat . . . the poorest, the least literate, the

---

194. On which *see* SHAC, VIOLENCE IN MARRIAGE, 1976; GRANT, LOCAL AUTHORITY HOUSING: LAW, POLICY AND PRACTICE IN HAMPSHIRE, 1976, Ch. 5; NWAF, AND STILL YOU'VE DONE NOTHING, 1976.

195. *Op. cit.*, note 18, ¶¶ 3, 40.

196. *See* MCGREGOR *et al.*, SEPARATED SPOUSES, Duckworth, and Finer, pp. 90-106 and Appendix 7.

197. Supplementary Benefits Act 1976, Schedule 1, paragraph 3.

worst informed section of the population."[198] Indeed, the domestic jurisdiction of the magistrates' courts was designed for this very population. Magistrates' courts domestic jurisdiction is now under a cloud: attacked by McGregor *et al.* in *Separated Spouses*,[199] Marsden in *Mothers Alone*[200] and most notably in the Finer Report.[201] There has been a considerable decline in recent years in the numbers of those using the courts for domestic proceedings. Finer recommended family courts,[202] but the Government "sees no prospect of accepting [this] recommendation."[203] The Law Commission's recent proposals for change take this into account and make suggestions for change in the substantive law within the existing structure of courts.[204]

The Law Commission proposes[205] that a magistrates' court should have power, if it is satisfied by evidence of violent behavior or threat of violent behavior on the part of the respondent against the complainant or a child of the family to make one or both of the following orders: (i) an order that the respondent shall not use or threaten violence against the complainant; (ii) an order that the respondent shall not use or threaten violence against a child of the family. It also recommends the power to make exclusion orders. There is also power to make emergency orders, though a sitting of a full court is required for this.

A number of criticisms may be made of the Law Commission's proposals. They propose extending protection to husbands and wives but not to those who live together outside lawful wedlock. Since legislation has just been passed enabling the county courts to do just this,[206] it is difficult to defend their exclusion from magisterial domestic jurisdiction. Secondly, protection is extended

198. *Per* McGregor, in Proceedings from Conference on Matrimonial Jurisdiction of Magistrates, Institute of Judicial Administration, Birmingham 1973, quoted in Seago and Bissett-Johnson. Cases and Materials on Family Law, Sweet and Maxwell, 1976, pp. 104-105.

199. *Op. cit.*, note 196, *passim.*

200. Penguin Books, 1973, ch. 10.

201. In §§ 5-11.

202. In §§ 13 and 14.

203. H.C. Debates vol. 898, cols. 51-60. *See also* H.L. Debates vol. 366, cols. 1560-1 *per* Lord Chancellor.

204. *See* criticism of this by Maidment, 7 Fam. Law 50, 52.

205. *See* Law Com. No. 77 pt. III.

206. *Viz.*, the Domestic Violence Act 1976 § 1(2).

to children of the family. This includes children "treated" as such by a nonparent. But while it may be reasonable to limit the provision of financial support to such children, it is difficult to see why a personal protection order should not extend to children who have not been "treated" in this way. Thirdly, while the new legislation refers to "molestation," and in the arrest provision, to "actual bodily harm," the Law Commission's proposals are more circumscribed in their references to "violence." Superior court judges thus have jurisdiction to make injunctions where husbands (or wives) merely pester, and can attach a power of arrest where psychological harm is perpetrated. But the Law Commission defends its rejection of granting magistrates jurisdiction in this terrain by arguing that "adjudication on an allegation of psychological damage is a very difficult matter which may involve the assessment of evidence by psychiatrists. This is a highly skilled task which we do not think can appropriately be placed on judges."[207] It is difficult to accept this reasoning. Many magistrates will be better equipped to tackle psychiatric evidence than most judges. Fourthly, the Law Commission has, in my opinion, given insufficient attention to the question of enforcement of the orders it proposes. It points out correctly the present deficiencies and then assumes that monetary sanctions and ultimately committal will ensure compliance with the new orders. Financial penalties, however, are unlikely to have an impact on the clientele of the domestic courts because quite simply the money is not there. If the system the Law Commission proposes is implemented, the woman will have to go back to the court to ask it to enforce the order. It is not proposed to give magistrates the power to attach a power of arrest to the orders they make. Finally, it is suggested that the power to make emergency orders could be widened so that a single magistrate (or even a justice's clerk) might make a protection order out of court hours.[208]

The existing system is not satisfactory. The Law Commission's proposals will effect some improvement but are of limited value.

---

207. *Op. cit.*, note 188, ¶ 3.12.
208. *See also* THE TIMES, 27 May 1977 for similar suggestion of Brian Harris.

Divorce

Another remedy open to a battered wife is to seek dissolution of her marriage. Not that with this accomplished, she will then necessarily live in peace. The Law Reports are replete with instances of post-dissolution batteries. Indeed, as will be shown later in this paper, a divorced woman is at a disadvantage in seeking an injunction.

There is little doubt, however, that a woman battered by her husband can divorce him. Like many other systems, English law now bases divorce on the concept of irretrievable breakdown. Unlike some systems,[209] however, it does not leave the question at large but specifies facts,[210] proof of any of which raises a strong presumption that the marriage has broken down irreparably. One of these facts is "that the respondent has behaved in such a way that the petitioner cannot reasonably be expected to live with the respondent."[211] The courts consider not only the behavior of the respondent but "the character, personality, disposition and behavior of the petitioner."[212] The question asked is "can this petitioner, with his or her personality, with his or her faults and other attributes, good and bad, and having regard to his or her behavior during the marriage, reasonably be expected to live with this respondent?"[213] Bagnall J gave as an example the following: "A violent petitioner can reasonably be expected to live with a violent respondent."[214] There are reported cases where wives have obtained decrees where husbands have treated them with violence.[215] In one case (*Bradley v. Bradley*)[216] the Court of Appeal accepted that a wife could not reasonably be expected to live with her husband "even though she [was] in the same house with him—and in fact living with him," as she had "no alternative open to her, nowhere else to go." It was "not reasonable to expect her to live there, but

---

209. *E.g.*, California, Australia.

210. The Law Commission thought the proposals of PUTTING ASUNDER which would have left the question at large impracticable. *See* discussion of this in FREEMAN, (1971) CURRENT LEGAL PROBLEMS 178, 183-5.

211. In § 1(2)(b) of the Matrimonial Causes Act 1973.

212. *Per* Bagnall J in Ash v. Ash [1972] 1 All E.R. 582, 585.

213. *Idem.*, p. 585.

214. *Idem.*, pp. 585-86.

215. Ash v. Ash, *op. cit.*, note 211 and Bradley v. Bradley [1973] 3 All E.R. 750 are but two reported examples.

216. [1973] 3 All E.R. 750.

albeit unreasonable, she [had] no option but to be there."[217] Mrs. Bradley had seven children living with her, and two non-cohabitation orders for persistent cruelty; but the council would not rehouse her until she secured a divorce against her husband. The case is thus particularly instructive.

It should be noted that one may only petition for divorce after three years of marriage.[218] A judge may, however, allow the presentation of a petition within this period if he considers the case one of exceptional hardship suffered by the petitioner or of exceptional depravity on the part of the respondent.[219] In determining the application the judge is to have regard to the interests of any child of the family and to whether there is a reasonable probability of reconciliation within the three years. This provision was first introduced forty years ago and has been consistently defended by official committees[220] though it finds little support in academic literature.[221] It has never existed in Scotland or in most of the rest of the world. Its effect is to delay divorce, which in England reaches its peak after four years. As women who are going to be battered often find that this begins shortly after marriage, the bar to divorce is potentially a serious inconvenience. In the past the courts have construed serious cruelty coupled with physical injury as exceptional depravity.[222] In considering exceptional hardship the courts have considered what effect the facts have had on the particular petitioner. So, if a nervous wife suffered a breakdown because of her husband's conduct she might well get leave to petition within the three-year period.[223] Because of such interpretations battered women should not suffer unduly from the bar. They did, however, suffer under the old law of injunctions when it was held that under a summons asking for leave to petition within three years the courts could not exclude the husband from the matrimonial home where this was in his name,

217. *Idem.*, p. 752.

218. M.C.A. 1973 § 3(1).

219. M.C.A. 1973 § 3(2).

220. *See* Royal Commission on Marriage and Divorce (Morton Commission) Cmnd 9678, ch. 5. (1956); PUTTING ASUNDER, S.P.C.K., 1966, ¶ 78; Law Commission, FIELD OF CHOICE, Cmnd 3123, ¶ 19.

221. *See* Hayes, 4 FAM. LAW 103; Miller, 4 ANGLO-AM. L.R. 163, MORTLOCK, THE INSIDE OF DIVORCE, Constable 1972, pp. 11-15.

222. *See* Bowman v. Bowman [1949] P. 353, 356-7 *per* DENNING L.J.

223. *See* Hiller v. Hiller [1958] P. 186.

although they could grant an injunction against molestation.[224] This is no longer the case since the passing of the Domestic Violence Act of 1976.

A further problem for the battered wife, and one which may have far-reaching implications, is the recent withdrawal of legal aid from undefended divorces.[225] She can still seek legal advice and assistance but she will have to negotiate the mechanics of the divorce herself.

Divorce is an obvious remedy and is usually efficacious. But it is final. Many women, distraught, bruised, and battered, and doubtless endowed with beliefs about the necessity of trying to "make a go of it" will lack the mental composure to consider the long-term decision of divorce. As Baroness Phillips said in the House of Lords in July 1976: "[A]t the time of probably having been beaten, assaulted and thrown out of the house, bruised and frightened, the last thing a woman wants to do is start the complications of a divorce or separation proceedings."[226] Nor must one forget her "romantic delusions,"[227] the "Beauty and the Beast syndrome,"[228] how she can reform him and preserve the marriage for the sake of the family. Perhaps she also considers the alternatives; accommodation problems, living on state assistance, employment prospects, day-care facilities for children, etc. These may be the real reasons why she stays and does not seek divorce: the romanticism may be merely rationalization. It may be predicted that divorce applications will increase as the alternatives to married life improve.

The Injunction Weapon

The injunction is the battered wife's best legal weapon. It is also the most popular legal remedy. In November 1975 there were 252 ap-

224. McGibbon v. McGibbon [1973] Fam. 170. McCleod v.McCleod (1973) 117 Sol. Jol. 679 is sometimes cited as an authority to the contrary but there the *wife* was the *tenant*.

225. As from 1 April 1977. It is still available to seek an injunction. On the withdrawal *see* Freeman, 6 FAM. LAW 255, and Davis and Murch, 1 FAM. LAW 71.

226. H.L. Debates vol. 373, col. 1438. *See also* H.C. vol. 905, col. 858 *per* Miss J. Richardson.

227. *Per* Truninger, 23 HASTINGS L.J. 259, 260 (1971).

228. *Per* PIZZEY, *op. cit.*, note 3, p. 41.

plications, three-quarters of them in large cities.[229] According to the Lord Chancellor, speaking in the House of Lords in July 1976, "practically all of them involved physical violence to the person, and the very large majority related to couples who were still married."[230] This means that about 3000 applications are made a year. When the President of the Family Division, Sir George Baker, gave evidence to the House of Commons Select Committee he noted that applications in the long vacation for injunctions had increased in London. In 1972 there had been 339 applications, in 1973, 468 and in 1974, 502. But outside London there was no evidence of increase.[231] With the introduction of the Domestic Violence and Matrimonial Proceedings Act 1976 the spiral may be expected to continue.

The High Court's power to grant injunctions is contained in the Supreme Court of Judicature (Consolidation) Act of 1925. Section 45 of this states that an injunction may be granted "in all cases in which it appears to the court to be just or in which it appears to the court to be just or convenient to do so." The jurisdiction of county courts is contained in section 74 of the County Courts Act of 1959 and is in every way as full as that of the High Court. The courts, however, cut down their jurisdiction. They decided that there had to be a sufficient nexus between the subject-matter of the main action and the relief sought by injunction.[232] It followed that an application for an injunction had to be ancillary to other proceedings. In theory these needed to be nothing more than an action for assault claiming £2 damages. In practice it tended to mean divorce proceedings. The courts also decided, though they hardly needed to, that an injunction could only be granted to support a legal right.[233] They then set about repairing some of the damage by holding that the wife's personal right to remain in the matrimonial home is such a right,[234] though this right ceased on termination of the marriage.[235] What jurisdiction they had they exercised most

229. *See* LAG Bulletin, June 1976, p. 125.
230. H.L. Debates vol. 373, col. 1441.
231. P. 462.
232. Des Salles d'Epinoix v. Des Salles d'Epinoix [1967] 2 All E.R. 539.
233. Montgomery v. Montgomery [1965] p. 46.
234. Jones v. Jones [1971] 2 All E.R. 737.
235. Robinson v. Robinson [1965] p. 39; Brent v. Brent [1974] 2 All E.R. 1211.

sparingly. The general attitude adopted until very recently was that to exclude a husband from the matrimonial home was a drastic step to be taken only in extreme circumstances. Thus, in *Hall v. Hall,*[236] the Court of Appeal said it would not order a husband out unless it was proved to be impossible for the spouses to live together. And in *Mamane v. Mamane,*[237] the Court of Appeal said it would only make an order where it was "imperative and inescapable." An order was refused despite the fact that the husband was given to unbalanced emotional outbursts and acts of violence and there were two young children.[238]

The question of jurisdiction has been radically remolded by the Act of 1976. There is also evidence from the landmark decision of *Bassett v. Bassett*[239] that the way the court exercises its discretion has been liberalized.

The 1976 Act[240] provides that a county court shall have jurisdiction to grant injunctions against molestation and to exclude a spouse from the matrimonial home, whether or not any other relief is sought and irrespective of whether the man and woman involved are husband and wife or cohabitees. The jurisdiction of the High Court is not altered by the Act but this required only an amendment to Rules of Court, and this has been made. The relevant section (sec. 1) refers to applications "by a party to a marriage" and gives jurisdiction to grant an injunction against "the other party to the marriage." Husbands as well as wives can, therefore, apply for an injunction. So can cohabitees "living with each other in the same household as husband and wife" (sec. 1(2)). But former spouses cannot. This means that a county court which formerly had jurisdiction to issue injunctions restraining molestation of former spouses can no longer do so.[241] Further, county courts had been known to exclude former husbands from the former matrimonial

236. [1971] 1 All E.R. 762.
237. 4 FAM. LAW 87 (1974).
238. A digest of recent cases is in LAG Bulletin, June 1976 p. 137.
239. [1975] Fam. 76.
240. On the Act *see* Freeman, 127 NEW L.J. 159, and *Man's Inhumanity to Wife* in M.L.R. (forthcoming). There is also a detailed legal commentary in CURRENT LAW STATUTES ANNOTATED 1976 (Sweet and Maxwell). *See also* Masson, 7 FAM. LAW 29, and Maidment, 7 FAM. LAW 50.
241. *See* Ruddell v. Ruddell (1967) 111 S.J. 497. For another interpretation see Lane, 127 L.J. 298.

home where they considered it necessary to protect children.[242] Such jurisdiction was dubious but there is no doubt it was exercised. County courts will no longer be able to do so. The High Court, in exercise of its inherent jurisdiction to protect children, will continue to be able to exclude husbands from their property where the marriage is already dissolved, when it is necessary to protect the welfare of children.[243]

Since injunctions may only be sought against "the other party to the marriage" (or cohabitation), wives cannot exclude mistresses and husband's relatives from the matrimonial home, unless they have a proprietary interest in it, for otherwise they have no legal rights against such intruders.[244] An injunction not to molest is valueless if the offending party cannot be ejected. Courts in the past have certainly ordered mistresses out of the matrimonial home.[245] On the plain language of the 1976 Act they will no longer be able to do so. This may not be of much practical significance since most mistresses will follow their lovers out of the matrimonial home, but problems could arise.

Another problem is that the Act is limited to, and does not define, the matrimonial home. English law is still founded upon separation of property.[246] A vindictive husband could thus on being excluded from the matrimonial home remove *his* furniture and leave the wife to a miserable existence.[247] As the Act does not define "matrimonial home" there must be considerable doubt as to whether a wife could exclude her husband from a home where she has never lived with him.[248] He may have sold the matrimonial home over her head and be threatening violence if she enters the house he has now bought. She could get an injunction against molestation but it is dubious if she could exclude him from the

---

242. *See* Phillips v. Phillips [1973] 2 All E.R. 423.

243. *See* Stewart v. Stewart [1973] 1 All E.R. 31; Phillips v. Phillips [1973] 2 All E.R. 423.

244. *See* Adams v. Adams (1965) 109 S.J. 899.

245. *Idem.* and Jones v. Jones [1971] 2 All E.R. 737. *See also* Bowens v. Bowens, The Guardian, 10 August 1973.

246. The Law Commission has rejected community of property, though it is currently considering the conveyancing complications of what it calls "a matrimonial home trust." *See* LAW COM. No. 52.

247. *See* W v. W [1951] 2 TLR 1135 in the light of Pettitt v. Pettitt [1970] AC 777.

248. *Cf.* the facts of Nanda v. Nanda [1968] p. 351.

house. She certainly cannot do so under the Matrimonial Homes Act of 1967, even as amended by sec. 3 of the 1976 Act.[249]

The Act is silent on the criteria for the exercise of jurisdiction. Its sponsor, Miss Jo Richardson, thinks "the court will exercise its discretion along the lines of the policy it has already developed."[250] The courts were formerly most reluctant to order a man out. But in *Bassett v. Bassett*[251] the Court of Appeal took a more practical approach to the problem. Ormrod L J accepted that ordering a spouse to leave was a drastic order but he suggested that "to refuse to make such an order may have no less drastic results, if the consequences of refusing to make an order is to inflict severe hardship on the unsuccessful spouse."[252] He thought that, particularly in cases where the marriage has already broken down, the court "should think essentially in terms of homes, especially for the children, and then consider the balance of hardships."[253] He believed that the husband would find it easier to secure accommodation for himself than the wife with a baby would. This is not necessarily so: local authorities are more willing to help mothers with young children than single men. Ormrod L J's reasoning could, therefore, rebound.

Another decision which is particularly favorable to the wife is *Hunt v. Hunt.*[254] The wife made allegations of repeated violence on her by her husband. She left the home and wished to return. She sought an interlocutory order to exclude him on the ground that his violence made her fear for her safety and for that of the children who were also emotionally upset by the violence. The allegations were not substantiated. The Court of Appeal took the view that it didn't have to be satisfied that the wife's allegations were true, merely that they might be true, and that the truth could be ventilated at the full hearing. But supposing the husband does not defend, for example, for reasons of cost?[255]

The courts are showing a much greater willingness to exclude a

249. *See* Matrimonial Homes Act 1967 § 1(8).
250. H.C., vol. 905, col. 859.
251. *See* note 239.
252. [1975] Fam. 76, 82.
253. *Idem.*, p. 84.
254. 5 Fam. Law 21 [1975].
255. *Cf.* 125 N.L.J. 493.

husband from the matrimonial home. The tendency is to think in terms of homes rather than property rights.[256] But how easy is it to get an injunction and of what value is it once obtained?[257] First, the woman has to know how to set about getting it. She will almost certainly need a solicitor and legal aid. Finding a solicitor willing to act is not easy. If legal aid is required it will be needed urgently, so that emergency legal aid will have to be applied for. Many solicitors do not touch injunction cases and, if they do, will not get a legal aid certificate quickly enough. Pizzey reports that neighborhood law centers also usually exclude matrimonial matters, as these are allegedly served adequately by the private profession, though there is evidence of a greater willingness to help battered women secure injunctions than there was only a couple of years ago.[258] If these barriers can be overcome, matters can proceed very swiftly and an injunction can be obtained quickly. In the November 1975 survey 88 percent of the orders were made within a day of the application and 58 percent within an hour. Eighty-four percent of the applicants obtained an interim injunction, although twenty cases were stood over to allow the respondent to attend.[259] Sir George Baker assured the House of Commons Select Committee that at "the very worst" applications for injunctions were heard within fourteen days.[260]

The "Saga of Mrs. D" which the N.W.A.F. submitted to the Select Committee[261] is concrete demonstration of the value attached to an injunction. Things may be changing, as the Domestic Violence Act now gives a judge for the first time power to attach a power of arrest to an injunction.[262] Hitherto, many injunctions have not been worth the paper on which they were written. They are frequently broken and up till now this meant the woman's returning to the court. The court could imprison or fine for breach of an injunc-

256. Even outside cases of violence. *See* Browne v. Pritchard [1975] 3 All E.R. 23, Williams v.Williams [1977] 1 All E.R. 28, Martin v. Martin 7 FAM. LAW 80.

257. *See generally*, PIZZEY, *op. cit.*, note 3, p. 118 ff., TRACEY, BATTERED WIVES, Bow Group 1974; Women's Aid, *Battered Wives*, June 1973.

258. *See op. cit.*, note 3.

259. LAG Bulletin, June 1976 p. 125. *But see* now Ansah v. Ansah [1977] 2 All E.R. 638, and Maisich v. Maisich, THE TIMES July 14, 1977.

260. P. 463.

261. Taken from H.O.C. Minutes p. 62.

262. *See* § 2.

tion. It rarely did either. Pizzey tells us of "Joan"[263] who took her husband before judges on eleven occasions before he was committed to prison. The police have looked to the civil authorities, bailiffs and tipstaffs, who work office hours and not weekends, to enforce an injunction after further proceedings to establish a breach.[264] Margaret Gregory tells us of "one case where the man contrived to avoid being served with the warrant for breach of injunction for six months, continuing all the time to commit further breaches."[265] Even when men are committed to prison for breach of an injunction their contempt can be purged relatively quickly, and the process starts all over again.

The reluctance of the police to get involved is as evident here as it is in the area of the criminal law. In answer to the sort of suggestions that led to Section 2 of the 1976 Act, the Metropolitan Police in their evidence to the House of Commons Select Committee argued that: "the civil and the criminal law have always been separated for good reasons, and it would be wrong both constitutionally and practically to extend the criminal law to enable police to exercise powers to enforce orders made within the civil jurisdiction of the courts."[266] Section 2 has not extended the criminal law but it has brought the police into the enforcement of one aspect of the civil law. The Lord Chancellor could not "claim that this will make the job of a policeman easy, but it may well make it easier than it is now."[267] It is difficult to see the force of this argument: the policeman, contrary to what the Lord Chancellor thought, will have to exercise his own judgment. The statute says (Section 2(3)): "[A] constable *may* arrest." How he will exercise his discretion remains to be seen.

Section 2 provides the police with powers of arrest for breach of injunctions in cases of domestic violence. It gives a judge power to attach a power of arrest to an injunction where (a) he grants an injunction containing a provision restraining the use of violence against the applicant or a child or makes an exclusion order and (b)

---

263. *Op. cit.*, note 3, p. 119.
264. *Idem.*, p. 118.
265. In (ed.) BORLAND, VIOLENCE IN THE FAMILY (1976) p. 117.
266. P. 378.
267. H.L. Debates vol. 373, col. 1443.

he is satisfied that the addressee of the injunction has caused actual bodily harm to the applicant or the child and (c) he considers he is likely to do so again. The police are given the power of arrest without warrant where there is reasonable cause for suspecting breach of the injunction by reason of use of violence or entry into the excluded premises or area. Persons so arrested must be brought before a judge within 24 hours.[268] The police are not allowed to bail a person so arrested.[269]

This new provision may prove valuable. But one must not read too much into it. It does little, at least directly, to alter current police attitudes towards intervention in situations of domestic violence. It applies only to the situation where there has been an injunction and it has been disobeyed. One must not lose perspective: most people, even violent husbands, obey the law.[270] Police operations at preinjunction stage are not affected. There are also practical problems. How are the police to know about orders made in civil courts? There are perhaps 3,000 injunctions issued each year. It is impossible to tell as yet how many of them will have powers of arrest attached to them. Because of their policy of non-intervention they may not have been concerned hitherto in the spouses' domestic problems at all. Is there to be a register of matrimonial injunctions and are individual constables to be conversant with its details? The effective operation of this provision requires a centralized data bank. Is one to be set up? If not, how else are the police to know whether a particular alleged assailant is in breach of an injunction to which a power of arrest has been attached when the couple concerned come from a distant part of the country? She may have fled for refuge and he may have tracked her down, but how are the police to know the details of the injunction?

Hitherto, injunctions have not been a particularly effective weapon. But with the passing of the Domestic Violence Act and the

---

268. Most domestic violence takes place at weekends. Friday nights is very common. Are the police then to release the man on Saturday evening? The alternative is for duty judges to operate a weekend roster. This has been promised. *See* se the man on Saturday evening? The alternative is for duty judges to operate a weekend roster. This has been promised. *See* Shaw, The Daily Telegraph, June 1, 1977.

269. In striking contrast to the Bail Act 1976 which has created a statutory presumption in favor of bail.

270. A point made by Mr. I. Percival, H.C. Debates vol. 905, col. 879.

line of cases beginning with *Bassett v. Bassett* it may be that the injunction will prove useful protection for the battered wife. The Act could have been better drafted and some of its practical implications better thought through but it is still a distinct improvement on the existing situation.

The Problem of Accommodation

We have seen how English law in a rather ham-fisted way sets about protecting the battered wife. The law sees protection as a primary need, for its ultimate goal is to keep her within the family and rehabilitate it. The concern is less with rescue and refuge than with providing alternative accommodation, alternative life-styles. A good example of this ideology at work is the action taken in the mid-1960s over Part III accommodation.[271]

Until 1966 such accommodation, which is provided by local authorities for homeless families, was open only to wives and children. Husbands were not admitted. "Battered women" did not "exist" in 1965 but it was known that many of the women living in Part III accommodation were there because of their husbands' violence. But the campaign in 1965-66 to secure the entry of husbands into such accommodation was expressed in terms of the inhumanity of separating wives and husbands.[272] Of course, for many of these wives being separated from their husbands was not desirable. But for many more it was a prime objective for coming to the accommodation. In the interests of the "family," battered women were thus deprived of refuge. One wonders whether it is just coincidence that the concept of battered wives was to emerge in the four or five years following the opening of Part III accommodation to husbands.

A woman who leaves a husband is, it is frequently argued, not technically homeless. The existing law on homelessness provides that it is the duty of every local authority to provide residential accommodation for persons who by reason of age, infirmity or other circumstances are in need of care and attention which is not otherwise available to them, and to provide temporary accommodation

271. Discussed in R. BAILEY, THE SQUATTERS, Penguin, 1973.
272. Particularly in the confrontation over the King Hill Hostel in Birmingham.

for persons who are in urgent need of it, where the need has arisen in circumstances which could not reasonably have been foreseen.[273] A joint Department of the Environment/D.H.S.S. Circular in 1974 made the following recommendation:

> Homelessness which results often very suddenly from the break up of family relationships can present particular difficulties for authorities in deciding what to do for the best. Accommodation for the mother and children may be required while the future of the relationship is in doubt, particularly when the future of the marriage itself has to be resolved.[274]

It is thus not mandatory on local authorities to make provision for battered women. There is considerable variation in the provisions that are made. Aylesbury claims that battered women are voluntarily homeless: it refuses to accept that she is homeless if her husband will have her back, regardless of her own choice and any danger she may face in returning.[275] Epping wants evidence that she will not be accepted back before they will even consider accepting her on the housing list.[276] Indeed, only twenty of seventy authorities where the N.W.A.F. has a group accepted battered women as homeless.[277] A new Act, the Housing (Homeless Persons) Act 1977, which comes into force on 1 December 1977, might improve the housing situation of the battered woman considerably. But an amendment to single out the battered woman as having "a priority need for accommodation" was lost during the Bill's passage. The Act also develops the concept of "intentional homelessness" and this is unlikely to assist women who flee from the matrimonial home.[278]

Local authorities adopt different attitudes toward the rehousing of battered women.[279] Some require that she has taken out legal proceedings against her husband. Some are satisfied that proceedings have been initiated, others insist that the divorce be completed. A number now do not require a battered wife to start proceedings before granting temporary accommodation. A common and reasonable requirement is that the children be in the woman's

---

273. *See* National Assistance Act 1948 § 21.
274. 18/74, ¶ 24.
275. NWAF, AND STILL YOU'VE DONE NOTHING, 1976, p. 2.
276. *Idem.*
277. *Idem.*
278. *See* §§ 2 and 7.
279. *See* SHAC, VIOLENCE IN MARRIAGE; GRANT, LOCAL AUTHORITY HOUSING; NWAF *op. cit.*, note 275.

care. But this can lead to a Catch-22 situation when a woman is refused custody of her children because she is homeless and the local authority refuses to rehouse her as she does not have children in her care. Some impose residency qualifications. Some operate the 24-hour ruling under which the local authority ceases to have any responsibility toward rehousing when the person concerned has been out of the area for twenty-four hours. Both Cardiff and York apply this stringent rule.[280] In London an agreement operates between boroughs (the London Boroughs Association Agreement) under which it is recommended that "the authority in whose area the applicants were in residence the preceding night is the authority primarily responsible for the reception."[281] SHAC found that most boroughs fulfilled at least some part of this agreement but some do not. In Redbridge, for example, the woman is referred to the "responsible Borough."[282] Similar agreements operate outside London. N.W.A.F. found that twenty-eight out of the seventy authorities under study operated this type of scheme.[283]

Many battered women will have been living in council accommodation. There is an increasing tendency, at least in London, for this to be rented in joint names.[284] The majority of council tenancies are, however, still in the husband's name, and many local authorities do not grant joint tenancies at all—Bexley, for example.[285] On a divorce the courts have a power to transfer council tenancies to the wife, though they are reluctant to exercise their powers unless the local authority is cooperative.[286] This is understandable. The attitude of most London boroughs (and it is representative of the country as a whole) is to transfer tenancies to the wife's name where she has obtained custody of the children. As most of them require also that the wife has obtained a separation order or divorce before the tenancy transfer is effected, it implies

---

280. *Op. cit.*, note 275, p. 4.
281. *See* SHAC report, *op. cit.*, note 279.
282. *Idem.*
283. *Op. cit.*, note 272, p. 9.
284. *See* SHAC report, *op. cit.*, note 279. It is less common in Hampshire; *see* GRANT, *op. cit.*, note 279.
285. *See* SHAC report, *op. cit.*, note 279.
286. *See* Thompson v. Thompson [1975] 2 All E.R. 208, Regan v. Regan [1977] 1 All E.R. 428.

that an interim custody order pending the divorce hearing will not of itself be sufficient. But final orders of custody can be obtained only at the stage of a decree *nisi* and then only in cases where the custody is not contested. Where it is, or where the divorce itself is contested, the entire case can take up to six months. Even an uncontested case may take three months.

Where is the battered woman to live during this period? Unless she has successfully excluded her husband from the matrimonial home by injunction, she will either have to live with him or with relatives or friends or in temporary accommodation or in a refuge. Another possibility is squatting but the courts have already held that "necessity" is no defense,[287] and that reasonable force may be used to eject squatters.[288] The legislature is on the point of turning squatting into a criminal offense.[289] If she is on the streets with children and nowhere to go, the children can be received into care (more children are in care because of parental homelessness than for any other reason).[290] Local authorities' social services departments have a discretion to make payments to a parent to diminish the need to receive their children into care.[291] Some local authorities make generous provision (ironically but not surprisingly those where the population as a whole is comparatively wealthy) and others hold the purse strings very tightly.[292] Some councils will pay to keep families or mothers and children in bed and breakfast accommodation. They are now cutting back on this and the courts refuse to control the way they choose to make provision so long as it remains a lawful exercise of discretion. Thus Dorset County Council declines to accept or continue bed and breakfast commitments where there is only one child.[293] But, however generous authorities are, bed and breakfast accommodation in cheap hotels is no substitute for a home.

---

287. L.B. of Southwark v. Williams [1971] Ch. 734.

288. McPhail v. Persons Unknown [1973] 3 All E.R. 393.

289. Criminal Law Act 1977 pt. II.

290. Under § 1 of Children Act 1948. The play *Cathy Come Home* stirred up national conscience on this issue.

291. Under § 1 of Children and Young Persons Act 1963.

292. *See* HEYWOOD AND ALLEN, FINANCIAL HELP IN SOCIAL WORK Manchester U.P. 1971, and EMMETT, UNDER THE SAFETY NET (1976), CPAG.

293. *See* Roberts v. Dorset C.C., TIMES, 30 July 1976. *See also* House of Commons Report, ¶ 26.

Many women thus fall back on the hostels established by Women's Aid or the National Women's Aid Federation. There were hostels before Erin Pizzey established one in Chiswick. There was one in Pasadena, California in 1965: this was established by women from Al-Anon, a self-help group for families of alcoholics.[294] But the establishment of Chiswick Women's Aid in 1971 was the starting point for the current trend to create refuges specifically for battered women. Today there are more than 100 in Great Britain and shelters also exist in the U.S., Canada, the Netherlands (the one in Amsterdam is called "Blijf van m'n Lijf"—stay away from my body), France, West Germany, Denmark, Australia and India, and doubtless in many other countries as well.[295]

The House of Commons Select Committee recommended that "the Department must ensure that refuges are provided by local authorities and/or voluntary organizations."[296] There should be "one family place per 10,000 of the population,"[297] it recommended. The N.W.A.F. thinks that 15,500 family places or over 1,000 refuges will be needed to meet the Select Committee's "initial target." In its report *And Still You've Done Nothing* published in 1976 it stated that there were only 504 family places in seventy-three refuges and that often the provision was inadequate.[298] By December 1976 the government was estimating that there were over one hundred.[299] But whichever figure is correct, by House of Commons Select Committee's standards Great Britain is at least 900 refuges short of the recommended "initial" provision. The Select Committee also recommended that local authorities make available to voluntary groups some of the larger houses they own or may acquire and stipulated that this should be regarded as a "priority category for local authority expenditure and acquisition and improvement."[300] Many local authorities have disregarded these

294. *See* MARTIN, BATTERED WIVES, p. 197.
295. A detailed source of reference is MARTIN, *idem.* Ch. 10.
296. Report, ¶ 29.
297. *Idem.*
298. *Op. cit.*, note 275 pp. 13-14.
299. *See* its Observations on the Select Committee Report, Cmnd. 6690, and TIMES 10 December 1976.
300. ¶ 30.

recommendations and some, Hull, Leeds[301] and Great Yarmouth[302] being three notorious examples, have positively obstructed attempts to set up refuges. The government which has helped the spread of refuges by channeling in Urban Aid money has now announced that it cannot provide any more money for projects concerning battered wives. "Increased expenditure on services for the victims of violence in marriage can in practice take place only by a redeployment by the bodies concerned of resources already available to them."[303]

Perhaps the biggest blow and certainly the most insulting gesture came when the London Borough of Hounslow prosecuted Erin Pizzey for knowingly failing to comply with the requirements imposed on her by the 1961 Housing Act fixing thirty-six as the maximum number of individuals permitted to occupy the Chiswick refuge at any one time. At the date of the alleged offense the number of residents was seventy-five and it often exceeds one hundred. Pizzey's policy is never to turn away women who come for shelter. The House of Lords held,[304] with considerable regret, that, as the law now stood, the occupier of a house of refuge for battered mothers and their children was not a single household, so that when the residents at any time exceeded thirty-six, the occupier of the house could be prosecuted. Erin Pizzey is now awaiting sentence. Lord Hailsham clearly indicated that the magistrates should exercise restraint and mercy in sentencing her and doubtless they will. But the prosecution raises a number of important questions. Where were the other forty persons to go on the night of January 14, 1976? Would the London Borough of Hounslow have provided alternative accommodation? What is a "single household"? Certainly in 1961 Parliament did not have the problem of battered women in mind when it passed the statute. Is this perhaps an area where the decision to prosecute should be entrusted to another body? Perhaps it could be reserved to the Attorney-General.[305] As yet, the effects of the decision cannot be ascertained but with money cut and limits

301. *See* Minutes of Select Committee, pp. 67-68.
302. *See* NWAF Report *op. cit.*, note 275, p. 15.
303. *See op. cit.*, note 299.
304. *See* Simmons v. Pizzey, [1977] 2 All E.R. 432.
305. *Cf.* Harper, 127 N.L.J. 479, 503.

enforced on numbers admitted, the plight of the battered woman could indeed become grave. It is to be hoped that other local authorities will put their efforts into establishing hostels, not into prosecuting energetic individuals who do so.

Advice

The complications in the law and the difficulties of securing accommodation point indubitably to one conclusion. To the battered woman it is "one vicious circle of a very large perimeter, with the woman in the middle and the husband and bureaucracy hitting out from all points."[306] What she needs above all else is advice to enable her to cope with her problems. This was recognized by the Select Committee of the House of Commons. It recommended the setting up of "well-publicized family crisis centers open continuously to which wives, husbands, and children can turn."[307] The centers would, it argued, have three primary roles:

> Firstly, they should provide an emergency service, hence the 24-hour requirement. This means that they will need to develop very close liaison with the local medical, social, legal and police services. A very important link will be with the refuges. . . . Secondly, they should be specially responsible for the coordination of the local arrangements already available to women and children in distress. We have been impressed by the fact that one of the prime problems for the family in stress is the need to consult with several different professionals, in different places, employed by different agencies, very often not relating together very effectively. . . . The third and non-emergency role we see for the family crisis centres is the development of specialist advisory services, education and publicity programmes, group support and meetings for women with similar problems.[308]

There is currently a multiplicity of organizations which give advice and assistance to battered women. But one is struck, as the Select Committee was, by lack of coordination and by the fact that most advice is given when it is too late. For, just as many seek legal aid when had they sought legal advice earlier the need for aid would not have arisen, so too few battered women take advice as a preventive measure. That they do not do so stems partly from their own lack of competence but as much from the lack of provision of such

306. *Per* PIZZEY, *op. cit.*, note 3, p. 28.
307. Report, ¶ 20.
308. *Idem.*

advice. The Select Committee's proposal is, therefore, to be supported. But nothing has come of it. The Domestic Violence Act has been passed, the Law Commission has reported, but neither the Act nor the proposed measures can prevent much violence and neither does anything to provide alternatives to the woman in danger.

Of course 24-hour crisis centers would cost a lot of money just as would implementing Finer's recommendation of a guaranteed maintenance allowance.[309] But then the Silver Jubilee has cost a lot too. It is a matter of getting priorities right.

We are not going to get 24-hour crisis centers. We should, therefore, consider whether improved advisory services could be worked into existing structures. To that end the proposal of SHAC deserves consideration. It recommends the establishment of a "Primary Advisory Service" for battered wives.[310] Unlike crisis centers, the PAS would not necessarily require a fixed center but could be based in a particular local authority department, or in a Citizens' Advice Bureau or Housing Aid Center. This would cut down on the cost of establishing centers in separate premises. SHAC recognizes the need to publicize such a service widely. To be successful there would have to be duty officers available on a round-the-clock basis like that in social service departments. A number of voluntary experimental schemes are beginning in different parts of the country (Andover, Leicester, Stoke and Ormskirk) but it is premature as yet to assess their impact.

Coordinated, expert and sympathetic advice is crucial if many of the women who suffer are to be relieved of their fears and feelings of impotence. At present in Great Britain it is the absence of such advice which should cause anxiety and disquiet.

Conclusion

There are no simple solutions to this problem. What is required is nothing less than a complete redefinition of the status of women in society. So long as women are perceived as inferior, so long also as preservation of existing family units is seen as the overriding con-

309. FINER REPORT, p. 289 ff., on which *see* EEKELAAR, PUBLIC LAW 64 (1976).
310. *Op. cit.*, note 279.

sideration, force will be used to control women. So long as force and control are acceptable, violence will also occur. At root the problem, like so much else, is one of education and socialization.

In the meanwhile everything must be done to protect women from violence in the home. They must have ready access to sympathetic and integrated advice; there must be a proliferation of refuges; it must be made easier for wives to leave husbands. Current social policy is geared toward rehabilitation of the family. In many contexts that is right. But not here. Women stay, they do not report domestic violence because there are often no alternatives. We need improvements in child care facilities, better employment prospects for women with children, guaranteed income maintenance and alternative accommodation. Fewer women will then be battered.

At present, man's inhumanity to man is matched only by his inhumanity to wife.

Alimony and Assignment of Property: The New Statutory Scheme in Massachusetts*

MONROE L. INKER †
JOSEPH H. WALSH ‡
PAUL P. PEROCCHI §

I. Introduction

Critics of divorce laws have long contended that the extant statutory provisions on alimony and property division are rooted in archaic concepts.[1] Reforms, spurred by the facts that currently one out of three marriages ends in divorce[2] and that alimony and property orders are most often challenged on appeal,[3] have been reflected in recent statutory changes by a number of states to provide improved systems of adjusting the financial aspects of the marital relationship upon divorce.

Chapter 565 of the Massachusetts Acts and Resolves of 1974,[4]

---

*Reprinted with minor changes from SUFFOLK UNIVERSITY LAW REVIEW, Volume X, Number 1, Fall, 1975. The authors gratefully acknowledge the assistance of Carol Rotenberg in the preparation of this article.

†Member, Massachusetts Bar.

‡Member, Massachusetts Bar.

§Member, Massachusetts Bar.

1. *See Symposium on Alimony*, 6 LAW & CONTEMP. PROB. 183 (1939).

2. Hatten & Brown, *Impressions of a Domestic Relations Judge,* 13 S. TEX. L.J. 250, 253 (1972). In 1939 when the first cries for reform of the economic incidents of divorce were voiced, only one marriage in six resulted in divorce. Kelso, *The Changing Social Setting of Alimony Law,* 6 LAW & CONTEMP. PROB. 186, 190 (1939).

3. Bradway, *Proposed New Techniques in the Law of Divorce*, 28 IOWA L. REV. 256, 259 (1943).

4. Act of July 19, 1974, ch. 565, [1974] Mass. Acts & Resolves 544 (codified at MASS. GEN. LAWS ANN. ch. 208, § 34 (Supp. 1975), *formerly* MASS. GEN. LAWS ANN. ch. 208, § 34 (1958)). In order to prevent confusion between the law as amended and the prior statute, the authors

which amends the law relative to alimony and property division, is a significant reform in this area. Unlike its predecessor, section 34 of chapter 208 of the Massachusetts General Laws,[5] Chapter 565 is not limited to awards traditionally denominated as "alimony" or "in the nature of alimony," but changes the historical basis underlying alimony awards and grants the court jurisdiction to adjust the division of all property of the spouses.[6] This article focuses primarily on four concepts: (1) the basis and purposes of property division embodied in the new Massachusetts statute; (2) the effect of Chapter 565 on the historical basis of alimony awards;

---

will henceforth refer to the amended statute as Chapter 565. It provides as follows:

> Upon a divorce or upon petition at any time after a divorce the court may order either of the parties to pay alimony to the other. In addition to or in lieu of an order to pay alimony, the court may assign to either the husband or wife all or any part of the estate of the other. In determining the amount of alimony, if any, to be paid, or in fixing the nature and value of the property, if any, to be so assigned, the court, after hearing the witnesses, if any, of each party, shall consider the length of the marriage, the conduct of the parties during the marriage, the age, health, station, occupation, amount and sources of income, vocational skills, employability, estate, liabilities and needs of each of the parties and the opportunity of each for future acquisition of capital assets and income. The court may also consider the contribution of each of the parties in the acquisition, preservation or appreciation in value of their respective estates.

Chapter 565, originally House No. 285, was effective October 19, 1974 and was sponsored by Representative Paul Maurice Murphy of Brockton on petition of the Massachusetts Bar Association. House No. 285 (1974). Its legislative history is sketchy.

> H. 285 (Judiciary) Bill providing for alimony and the assignment of property in divorce actions. Based in part on House 4496. Reported in House, May 14, ord. 3d, May 15; amended and eng. May 28; rec'd in Senate, May 29; recommitted, June 5; report, ought not to pass, June 20; Senate refused to reject the bill; ord. 3d, June 26; eng. July 1; to Gov. July 8; signed July 19. Chap. 565.

Legislative Record, August 3, Massachusetts General Court of 1974.

During its passage, House No. 285 was amended three times. House of Representatives, Calendar, May 15, 1974, at 16 (amendment providing that the guidelines set out be applicable to alimony as well as property division); Journal of the Senate, July 1, 1974, at 01349 (amendment of title of act to "An Act further regulating the payment of alimony and the assignment of property in libels for divorce"); Mass. H.R. Jour. 1833-34 (1974) (amendment striking out in line ten the word "may" and inserting in place thereof the word "shall"). The latter amendment is significant. *See* text accompanying notes 74-80 *infra.*

5. MASS. GEN. LAWS ANN. ch. 208, § 34 (1958), *as amended,* MASS. GEN. LAWS ANN. ch. 208, § 34 (Supp. 1975) provided:

> Upon a divorce, or upon petition at any time after a divorce, the court may decree alimony to the wife, or a part of her estate, in the nature of alimony, to the husband.

6. Like its predecessor, the new statute is not triggered until a divorce has been entered. Kinosian v. Kinosian, 351 Mass. 49, 52, 217 N.E.2d 769, 771 (1966); Weidman v. Weidman, 274 Mass. 118, 121, 174 N.E. 206, 207 (1931); Parker v. Parker, 211 Mass. 139, 141, 97 N.E. 988, 989 (1912); Adams v. Adams, 100 Mass. 365, 373 (1868). This in turn limits the operation of the statute to cases where a valid marriage previously existed. Kelley v. Kelley, 161 Mass. 111, 112, 36 N.E. 837, 838 (1894) (no alimony in void marriages); Norcross v. Norcross, 155 Mass. 425, 428, 29 N.E. 506 (1892) (no divorce granted where no valid marriage). The same principle is applicable to petitions for separate support. Limoges v. Limoges, 287 Mass. 260, 261, 191 N.E. 639 (1934) (no power to order support where no valid marriage); Murphy v. Murphy, 249 Mass. 552, 555, 144 N.E. 394, 395 (1924) (no power to order support where no valid marriage).

(3) modification of alimony awards; and (4) the effect of the new statute on appellate review of assignments of property and alimony awards.

II. Property Division

The courts have observed that the strong drive for economic independence by women will have significant effects on the setting of alimony awards.[7] Coupled with the changing economic status of women is the social reality that marriage is a joint enterprise and shared undertaking, based on a division of labor, which should entitle each spouse to a share of the family assets upon divorce.[8]

In a great number of marriages the husband still provides for the economic needs of the family while the wife devotes herself to the family's physical, mental, and social well-being. It is she who makes the daily decisions on child discipline, the running of the home, and other vital arrangements. With these aspects of private life handled by the wife, the husband is free to conduct the economic affairs of the family. It is because of this that the wife should be entitled to an equitable share of marital assets when the marital partnership is dissolved by divorce.

In recognition of the marital partnership concept, a number of noncommunity property states, including Massachusetts, have enacted legislation that empowers courts to divide the property of the spouses upon divorce.[9] With the enactment of Chapter 565, the

---

7. Surabian v. Surabian, 362, Mass. 342, 348 n.7, 285 N.E.2d 909, 913 n.7 (1972) (enhanced desire and ability of women to care for themselves, a proper consideration in determining whether self-termination provision in separation agreement is equitable); D'Amico v. D'Amico, 1 Mass. App. Ct. 561, 562, 303 N.E. 2d 737, 738 (1973) (duty of support not invariably imposed on husband as wife was always gainfully employed).

8. *See, e.g.*, Rothman v. Rothman, 65 N.J. 219, 229, 320 A.2d 496, 501 (1974); Vier v. Vier, 62 Wis. 2d 636, 641, 215 N.W.2d 432, 434 (1974); Lacey v. Lacey, 45 Wis. 2d 378, 382, 173 N.W.2d 142, 144 (1970). The idea that marriage is a partnership in one form or another has been advanced by legal scholars for many years. *See, e.g.*, J.S. Mill, *The Subjection of Women*, in ESSAYS ON SEX EQUALITY 168 (Rossi ed. 1970); Daggett, *Division of Property Upon Dissolution of Marriage*, 6 LAW & CONTEMP. PROB. 225, 230 (1939); and more recently, H. CLARK, LAW OF DOMESTIC RELATIONS IN THE UNITED STATES 450-51 (1968) [hereinafter cited as CLARK]; Foster & Freed, *Marital Property Reform in New York: Partnership of Co-Equals?*, 8 FAM. L.Q. 169, 176 (1974) [hereinafter cited as Foster & Freed].

9. Some statutes empower the courts to award statutorily defined marital property. *See, e.g.*, COLO. REV. STAT. ANN. § 46-1-13 (1971); ME. REV. STAT. ANN. tit. 19, § 722A (1972); MINN. STAT. ANN. § 518.54(5) (Supp. 1974); TENN. CODE ANN. § 36-825 (Supp. 1974). The community property states are Arizona, California, Idaho, Nevada, New Mexico, Texas, and Washington. Other statutes provide that the court may divide joint property and award separate property of the spouses. *See, e.g.*, ALASKA STAT. § 09.55.210 (1973); CONN. GEN.

Massachusetts probate courts, upon entry of a decree of divorce,[10] now have the power to make a fair and just assignment of the spouses' property.[11] The assignment authorized is grounded on neither the court's equity powers nor its power to award alimony. The new statute provides that all or any part of the estate of one spouse may be assigned to the other in addition to, or in lieu of, an order to pay alimony.[12] The use of the words "in lieu of" clearly indicates that something other than alimony was intended.[13] Furthermore, the enumeration of factors on which any property assignment is to be based establishes that the statute is not a codification of the court's equity powers.[14] Chapter 565 may be more fully understood by reference to the Uniform Marriage and Divorce

---

STAT. ANN. § 46-50 (Supp. 1975); HAWAII REV. STAT. § 580-41 (Supp. 1973); KAN. STAT. ANN. § 60-1610(b) (Supp. 1974); OKLA. STAT. ANN. tit. 12, § 1278 (1969); OREGON REV. STAT. §§ 107, 105(c) (1971); S.D. COMPILED LAWS ANN. § 30-3-5 (1967); WIS. STAT. ANN. § 247.26 (Supp. 1974); WYO. STAT. ANN. § 20-63 (1959). *See generally* Freed & Foster, *Economic Effects of Divorce*, 7 FAM. L.Q. 275 (1973).

10. The new statute provides that "[u]pon a divorce or upon petition at any time after a divorce" the court may award alimony and assign property. MASS. GEN. LAWS. ANN. ch. 208, § 34 (Supp. 1975). Petitions *after* divorce however may be maintained only where the right to an award of alimony or assignment of property has not been previously adjudicated. *See* notes 101-03 *infra* and accompanying text. Since one of the primary purposes of property assignment is to effect as full and complete a financial settlement between the parties as is possible, the court should always specifically determine and adjudge the property rights of the parties, thereby precluding by the doctrine of res judicata a petition after entry of the final decree. *See* Chadbourne v. Chadbourne, 245 Mass. 383, 384, 139 N.E. 532, 533 (1923). In the absence of a specific judgment, nothing would preclude a party from returning to court "upon petition . . . after a divorce" and requesting an assignment of an inheritance, lottery winnings, or any other form of subsequently acquired wealth. In short, the assignment authorized is premised on the existence of a marital partnership, and the assignment should take place upon dissolution of the partnership. Certainly no basis exists on which to justify an assignment of property acquired after entry of the final decree of divorce.

11. Case law provides that the assignment of property is a matter of judicial discretion but that the disposition must be fair, just, and reasonable. *See, e.g.*, Crow v. Crow, 49 Hawaii 258, 262-63, 414 P.2d 82, 85 (1966); Colley v. Colley, 460 S.W.2d 821, 826 (Ky. 1970); Vier v. Vier, 62 Wis. 2d 636, 638, 215 N.W.2d 432, 435 (1974); Morris v. Morris, 13 Wis. 2d 92, 93, 108 N.W.2d 124 (1961).

12. MASS. GEN. LAWS ANN. ch. 208, § 34 (Supp. 1975).

13. Reed v. Albanese, 78 Ill. App. 2d 53, 60, 223 N.E.2d 419, 423 (1966) ("in lieu of" denotes instead of); State *ex rel.* Jones v. Johnson Circuit Court, 243 Ind. 7, 16, 181 N.E.2d 857, 861-62 ("in lieu of" by definition marks an alternative); Glassman Constr. Co. v. Baltimore Brick Co., 246 Md. 478, 481, 228 A.2d 472, 474 (1966) ("in lieu of" means *instead* of or in substitution of). Clearly if the assignment provided for is an alternative to, or a substitute for, alimony, it is something other than alimony.

14. For example, "length of the marriage," conduct of the parties during the marriage," and contribution to one's own estate have no relevance in determining who owns the property in question. Indeed the fact that one spouse's entire estate may be awarded to the other spouse based on such noneconomic factors is indicative that equity principles are not always involved in the assignment. *See, e.g., In re* Dietz, 19 Ore. App. 334, 340, 527 P.2d 427, 429 (1974) (source of an asset is relevant but not controlling); Bloom v. Bloom, 150 Mont. 511, 515, 437 P.2d 1, 3 (1968) (property acquired may be divided regardless of whether title is in either or both of the parties).

Act, Section 307, Alternative A, which is substantially similar to the Massachusetts law.[15] The official comment to Alternative A states that all assets of the spouses, however acquired, are considered marital assets available for distribution upon "dissolution of a marriage."[16] The intent to provide for a "fair and just" assignment of property is evident from the express language of the statute, its similarity with Alternative A and, finally, from the memorandum submitted by the sponsor of the bill in support of its enactment.[17] The broad and expansive power accorded the courts by the new statute becomes apparent when it is compared with the preexisting power of the courts to award alimony and to exercise equity jurisdiction over property.

A. *Assignment of Property: New Powers*

The distinction between the former and present authority accorded the probate courts is significant. It has long been held that there is jurisdiction in equity over suits between husband and wife to secure

---

15. UNIFORM MARRIAGE AND DIVORCE ACT § 307, Alternative A [hereinafter cited as U.M.D.A.] utilizes almost identical language:

> (a) In a proceeding for dissolution of a marriage . . . the court . . . shall . . . finally equitably apportion between the parties the property and assets belonging to either or both however and whenever acquired, and whether the title thereto is in the name of the husband or wife or both. In making apportionment the court shall consider the duration of the marriage . . . the age, health, station, occupation, amount and sources of income, vocational skills, employability, estate, liabilities, and needs of each of the parties, custodial provisions, whether the apportionment is in lieu of or in addition to maintenance, and the opportunity of each for future acquisition of capital assets and income. The court shall also consider the contribution or dissipation of each party in the acquisition, preservation, depreciation, or appreciation in value of the respective estates . . .

See also CONN. GEN. STAT. ANN. § 46-50 (Supp. 1975) (makes provision for assignment of property in language that is almost identical to Chapter 565); McAnerney & Schoonmaker, *Connecticut's New Approach to Marriage Dissolution,* 47 CONN. B.J. 375, 395 (1973) (recognizing that the Connecticut statute provides for equitable distribution of property interests).

16. U.M.D.A. § 307, Alternative A, Comment provides in pertinent part:

> Alternative A . . . proceeds upon the principle that all the property of the spouses, however acquired, should be regarded as assets of the married couple, available for distribution among them, upon consideration of the various factors enumerated in subsection (a).

U.M.D.A. § 307, Alternative B, on the other hand, implicitly exempts from division, *inter alia,* property acquired prior to the marriage, property acquired by gift, bequest, devise or descent, and the increase in value of property acquired prior to the marriage. Alternative B is intended to provide a definition of marital property which is consistent with the existing definition in community property states. U.M.D.A. § 307, Alternative B, Comment.

17. Memorandum in Support of House Bill No. 285 from Monroe I. Inker to the Members of the Joint Committee on the Judiciary of the Massachusetts General Court, at 2-4, April 16, 1974 [hereinafter cited as Inker Memorandum]. A letter recommending that the bill be amended to make the guidelines applicable to alimony as well as to "assignment of property" accompanied the memorandum. The proposed amendment was later adopted. House of Representatives, Calendar, May 15, 1974, at 16.

separate property, to prevent fraud, to relieve from coercion, to enforce trusts, and to establish other conflicting rights concerning property.[18] Division of property pursuant to the equity power of the court was, and is, both a recognition and an implementation of the separate property concept.[19] In separate property cases emphasis is placed on the means of acquisition, the furnishing of consideration, and the intent at the time of taking title.[20] Before the enactment of Chapter 565, Massachusetts was one of the common law jurisdictions emphasizing the importance of how title was held. Although the courts, aside from their equity jurisdiction, had no power to divide property upon a divorce,[21] they have always had jurisdiction to order a conveyance of property in lump sum as alimony.[22] Since alimony, however, is that amount necessary for

---

18. *See, e.g.*, Patuleia v. Patuleia, 127 F. Supp. 60, 62 (D. Mass. 1955); Zwick v. Goldberg, 304 Mass. 66, 70, 22 N.E.2d 661, 663-64 (1939); Gahm v. Gahm, 243 Mass. 374, 376, 137 N.E. 876, 878 (1922). *See also* MASS. GEN. LAWS ANN. ch. 215, § 6 (Supp. 1975) (granting probate courts original and concurrent jurisdiction in equity with the supreme judicial court and superior courts of all matters cognizable under general principles of equity jurisprudence.)

19. *See, e.g.*, Yurkanis v. Yurkanis, 321 Mass. 375, 376, 73 N.E.2d 598, 600 (1947); Swenson v. Swenson, 320 Mass. 105, 108, 67 N.E.2d 746, 748 (1946); Matek v. Matek, 318 Mass. 677, 679-80, 63 N.E.2d 583, 584-85 (1945).

20. *See, e.g.*, D'Amico v. D'Amico, 1 Mass. App. Ct. 561, 562, 303 N.E. 2d 737 (1973) (joint bank account in the names of husband and wife divided according to their respective economic contributions); Krasner v. Krasner, 362 Mass. 186, 189, 285 N.E.2d 398, 399–400 (1972) (property in wife's name was held upon a resulting trust for the benefit of her husband where he purchased it with his own funds—presumption of gift to wife rebutted); MacLennon v. MacLennon, 311 Mass. 709, 713–14, 42 N.E.2d 838, 840 (1942) (husband alleged wife held her interest in stock certificates upon an oral trust for his benefit where stocks were purchased with his funds and were in the names of husband and wife jointly).

21. The powers of the court involving support and maintenance obligations between husband and wife devolve exclusively upon statute. Gediman v. Cameron, 306 Mass. 138, 140, 27 N.E.2d 696, 697 (1940). By statute the probate courts have been empowered only to award alimony. MASS. GEN. LAWS ANN. ch. 208 § 34 (Supp. 1975). The contention that the courts have had the power to make an "equitable" division of property has been consistently rejected. Ober v. Ober, 1 Mass. App. Ct. 32, 34, 294 N.E. 2d 449 (1973) (award in the nature of alimony for support and maintenance and not for the purpose of dividing property); England v. England, 329 Mass. 763, 764, 107 N.E.2d 30, 31 (1952) (alimony for support and maintenance, not for the purpose of an equal division of property); Coe v. Coe, 313 Mass. 232, 235, 46 N.E.2d 1017, 1019 (1943) (alimony is for support and maintenance and not for the purpose of division); Topor v. Topor, 287 Mass. 473, 475, 192 N.E. 52, 53 (1934) (alimony award for support and not based on the theory of an equitable division of property).

22. Dembro v. Dembro, 362 Mass. 884, 289 N.E.2d 866 (1972) (court ordered conveyance of wife's interest in real estate); Blitzer v. Blitzer, 361 Mass. 780, 784, 282 N.E.2d 918, 921 (1972) (court ordered conveyance of husband's interest in marital home); Kahn v. Kahn, 353 Mass. 771, 233 N.E.2d 902, 903 (1968) (court ordered conveyance of husband's interest in real estate); Klar v. Klar, 322 Mass. 59, 60, 76 N.E.2d 5, 6 (1947) (court ordered transfer of marital home and bonds in husband's possession). *See* Surabian v. Surabian, 362 Mass. 342, 348, 285 N.E.2d 909, 913 (1972). *See also* MASS. GEN. LAWS ANN. ch. 208, § 34A (Supp.

support and maintenance, the courts were thereby limited.[23] The emphasis placed on the separate property concept, coupled with the limitation of separate property awards only for support and maintenance, severely narrowed the avenues available to the courts in effecting justice on marital dissolution.

The effect of the new statute on judicial powers can be demonstrated by a simple illustration. Assume *H* and *W* are married. *H,* a successful business executive, is the sole wage earner and has an income of forty thousand dollars per year. Title to the family home, the automobile, and the savings account are in his name. He pays all the bills, including the mortgage on the home and the installment payments on the car. Despite his income, *H* is frugal. The family lives in a modest two-family dwelling and maintains a standard of living far below what *H*'s income would permit. *W* is a dedicated and hardworking homemaker and childrearer. There are three children by the marriage, which breaks down after thirty years. The parties are divorced. At the time of the divorce there is two hundred and fifty thousand dollars in the husband's bank account and both the home and automobile have been paid for.

Massachusetts law regards the bank account, the home, and the automobile as belonging to the husband. On the facts stated, there is no basis for the court to exercise its equity jurisdiction. *W,* of course, may be awarded periodic alimony or a conveyance of property or both as lump sum alimony.[24] The alimony award in this case, however, would very likely amount to only a trifle since: (1) alimony is the amount necessary to support the wife in the manner of living to which she has been accustomed; and (2) the parties, because of the husband's penuriousness, have maintained a very modest lifestyle.

By virtue of Chapter 565, however, the court is empowered to make a fair and just assignment of "all or any part of the estate of the other" having regard to the factors set out in the statute. In short, in addition to alimony, the court may award to the wife a

1975) (decree providing for conveyance of real estate creates an equitable right of enforcement thereof). *But cf.* Gould v. Gould, 359 Mass. 29, 32, 267 N.E.2d 652, 655 (1971) (probate court without authority to order sale of realty owned by husband and wife and to divide proceeds).

23. *See* cases cited note 43 *infra* (alimony based on husband's common law duty to support his wife).

24. *See* note 21 *supra* and accompanying text.

portion of the husband's separate estate in recognition of the vital and substantial, although nonmonetary, contribution which she has made to the marital partnership. The equities of making such an assignment in the present case are as clear as are the inequities under the former statute which allowed the wife only an award of alimony for support and maintenance.

Thus, while Chapter 565 does not repudiate the separate property concept,[25] the severity of that doctrine is mitigated by the provision that the separate property of one spouse may be assigned to the other, not by way of support and maintenance, but by way of property division. Both the nature and value of the property to be assigned by the court are determined with reference to the guidelines set out in the statute.

B. *Operation of Guidelines*

While all the enumerated factors are relevant to property division, the nature and value of the property must be distinguished if the statute is to be applied intelligently. The value of the property to be assigned is dependent on those circumstances which warrant division of property in recognition of the marital partnership concept: "the length of the marriage," " the conduct of the parties during the marriage," and "the contribution of each of the parties in the acquisition, preservation or appreciation in value of their respective estates."[26]

Length of the marriage is a critical consideration in assignment of property.[27] The equities of assigning to one party a portion of the other's estate are clearly diminished where the marriage is of only brief duration.[28] The inequities are even clearer where the estate in question was acquired prior to a short-lived marriage.[29] Often,

25. The new statute makes reference on three occasions to separate property: "estate of the other," "estate of each of the parties," and "their respective estates." MASS. GEN. LAWS ANN. ch. 208, § 34 (Supp. 1975).

26. *Id.* These are the guidelines set out in the statute which directly bear on a spouse's right to share in the partnership assets upon divorce. Contribution has previously been defined. *See* text accompanying notes 8-9 *supra.*

27. *See, e.g.,* Carson v. Carson, 50 Hawaii 182, 187, 436 P.2d, 10-11 (1967) (marriage of six years of sufficient length to require reversal of lower court's failure to award portion of husband's separate estate of $250,000); Plageman v. Plageman, 79 S.D. 221, 225-26, 110 N.W.2d 337, 338-39 (1961) (short-term marriage to which wife did not contribute by her industry).

28. *See* Lacey v. Lacey, 45 Wis. 2d 378, 382, 173 N.W.2d 142, 144-45 (1970) (recognizing that in a marriage of brief duration an alimony award of one-third of the property to the wife may be too liberal an allowance).

29. *Id.*, 173 N.W.2d at 145.

however, the quality and length of the marriage are such that the estate of one partner is enhanced by the direct, or indirect, contributions of the other spouse.[30] Certainly, in that instance, the property should be subject to assignment.

The parties' conduct is a factor frequently considered, and persuasive arguments have been advanced to eliminate fault from consideration in property division.[31] While assignment of property is neither a prize for virtue nor a punishment for wrongdoing,[32] the court, if it is to be fair to the parties, must review the whole situation and balance all the equities. If contribution is to be considered, failure to contribute must also be acknowledged. Fault may be one indicium of noncontribution. That one party, whether male or female, is the achiever, while the other is adulterous, disloyal, dishonest, cruel, or otherwise objectionable may well be relevant. It is not suggested that consideration of fault in property divisions necessitates a judicial determination that only one party to the marriage is at fault, since in many cases both parties are responsible for the breakdown.[33] However, the courts should determine comparative fault and adjust the assignment of property accordingly.[34] Conduct therefore should not be arbitrarily and abstractly assigned either a high or a low priority in property division. The nature, effect, and extent of the parties' conduct as it bears on their estates, both joint

---

30. *See, e.g.*, Rothman v. Rothman, 65 N.J. 219, 229, 320 A.2d 496, 501-02 (1974) (if property division is to be equitable, the economic contribution must be considered). *See generally* Foster & Freed, *supra* note 8, at 176; Glendon, *Is There a Future for Separate Property,* 8 FAM. L.Q. 315, 316-17 (1974).

31. Note, *The Economics of Divorce: Alimony and Property Awards,* 43 U. CIN. L. REV. 133, 141-45 (1974) [hereinafter cited as *Economics of Divorce*]; Cooey, *The Exercise of Judicial Discretion in the Award of Alimony,* 6 LAW & CONTEMP. PROB. 213 (1939); Draggett, *Division of Property Upon Dissolution of Marriage,* 6 LAW & CONTEMP. PROB. 225 (1939).

32. Britz v. Britz, 95 Ariz. 247, 249, 389 P.2d 123, 124 (1964); Honig v. Honig, 77 Ariz. 247, 251, 269 P.2d 737, 739 (1954); Caldren v. Caldren, 9 Ariz. App. 538, 541, 454 P.2d 586, 589 (1969); Knutson v. Knutson, 15 Wis. 2d 115, 121, 111 N.W.2d 905, 909 (1961); Beckle v. Beckle, 422 P.2d 205, 208 (Wyo. 1969). *Cf.* Barrock v. Barrock, 257 Wis. 565, 570, 44 N.W.2d 527, 530 (1950).

33. *See* Clark, *Divorce Policy and Divorce Reform,* 42 U. COLO. L. REV. 403, 409-12 (1971); Hayes, *California Divorce Reform: Parting is Sweeter Sorrow,* 56 A.B.A.J. 660-61 (1970); Note, *Alimony—The Next Step,* 9 J. FAM. L. 200, 202 (1969).

34. Baer & Davis, *Merit In No Fault Divorce,* 60 ILL. B.J. 766, 769-70 (1972). Since the only grounds for divorce in Massachusetts are fault based, the trial court must consider fault in every proceeding. It would be better if consideration of fault were mandated, thereby requiring the trial judge to include its consideration in his report of material facts where there is an appeal from the decree, while concomitantly according the appellate courts an opportunity to review whether fault was overemphasized in the lower court's assignment of property.

and separate, are the factors to consider in weighing the importance of conduct in a particular case.

With regard to the value of the property to be assigned each of the spouses, it has been suggested that there should be a presumption that upon divorce each spouse be assigned one-half of the marital property.[35] In some states, there is a judicially generated rule of thumb that the wife should be awarded one-third to one-half of the marital property.[36] There is no basis for any such presumption in the present Massachusetts statute, and accordingly, simple formulas should be rejected and each case examined on its own merits. Obviously, the wide discretion afforded the courts in property division carries with it a heavy burden of responsibility. However, the fact that divorce evokes a myriad of human situations, none identical, calls for flexibility in the court's authority if it is to provide for just and equitable resolutions.[37]

Other guidelines enumerated in the statute are relevant to the nature of the property to be assigned. One of the primary purposes of property division is to effect as full and complete a settlement of financial obligations between the parties as is possible, and, therefore, the court must be cautious not to assign property to the prospective alimony recipient which by its nature is more of a liability than an asset.[38] Concomitantly, the court should, to the extent possible, award income-producing property to the prospective alimony recipient, thereby mitigating the obligations of the payor-spouse, and perhaps eliminating altogether the necessity for an award of alimony.[39] It follows that division of property should

---

35. *See* House No. 4496 (1974), which was sponsored by the Boston Bar Association, but failed to pass.

36. *See, e.g.*, Kramer v. Kramer, 171 Neb. 123, 131, 105 N.W.2d 741, 744 (1960) (awards generally from one-third to one-half, depending on circumstances); Strandberg v. Strandberg, 33 Wis. 2d 203, 207, 147 N.W.2d 349, 351 (1967) (award generally one-third, but varies to an extent depending on circumstances).

37. Rothman v. Rothman, 37 N.J. 219, 232-33, 320 A.2d 496, 503 (1974) (reject formulas and balance equities in each case); Lacey v. Lacey, 45 Wis. 2d 378, 380, 173 N.W.2d 142, 145 (1970) (all relevant factors necessary for equitable division of property considered).

38. Scott v. Scott, 331 Mich. 273, 49 N.W.2d 175, 176 (1951) (division of property wherein husband received home and wife (with custody of child) received business of greater value, requiring her full-time employment, set aside as not being in best interest of the parties); Pinney v. Pinney, 47 Mich. App. 290, 292, 209 N.W.2d 467, 468 (1973) (wife's challenge to award denied whereby property awarded to husband was valued at $116,000, but was heavily encumbered).

39. *See, e.g.*, Cool v. Cool, 203 Kan. 749, 754-55, 457 P.2d 60, 64-65 (1969) (where sufficient income-producing property was awarded to the wife thereby negating any necessity for an award of alimony).

precede the alimony award, as the needs of each spouse will be affected by the property assignment.

Finally, it is important that the courts do not blur the distinction between alimony and property division. Alimony is an award for support and maintenance and has historically been based on the common law duty of the husband to support his wife. Property division, on the other hand, is based on the joint contribution of the spouses to the marital enterprise. Tied to, and justified by, the theory of marital partnership, it rests on the concept that non-economic contributions can enhance the partnership. In short, property division recognizes the essential supportive role played by a spouse, acknowledging that as a homemaker and childrearer that spouse is entitled to a share of the family assets. Since alimony and property division spring from different considerations, the courts must recognize the distinction if a uniform application of the law is to be achieved. Furthermore, because of the difference in tax consequences, the distinction between alimony and property division should be clarified in both separation agreements and divorce decrees.[40] Finally, the distinction is important for modification purposes, since alimony is generally modifiable, while property division, once made, is final.[41]

III. Alimony

A. *Alimony in Massachusetts— The Traditional Concept*

Prior to October 19, 1974,[42] Massachusetts courts followed the tradition that alimony was based on the common law duty of the

40. Alimony is includible in the wife's income and may be deducted by the husband if the payments qualify as periodic. INT. REV. CODE § 71(a)(1), 215(a). Where property is conveyed as part of a settlement upon divorce the transfer is treated as a sale. The transferor is taxed to the extent that the fair market value of the property exceeds its adjusted basis. The transferee takes as his or her adjusted basis the fair market value of the property on the date of the transfer. United States v. Davis, 370 U.S. 65, 73, *rehearing denied,* 371 U.S. 854 (1962).

41. *See, e.g.,* Arakaki v. Arakaki, 54 Hawaii 60, 63, 502 P.2d 380, 383-84 (1972) (decree not modifiable since it was in the nature of final property division rather than support and miaintenance); Walters v. Walters, 409 Ill. 298, 302, 99 N.E.2d 342, 344-45 (1951) (settlement agreement incorporated in decree providing for a gross sum as alimony, payable in installments, held to be property division and not modifiable); Pierson v. Pierson, 351 Mich. 637, 643, 88 N.W.2d 500, 504 (1958) (court decree that one spouse had right to sell home and divide proceeds not modifiable). *See generally* Annot., 48 A.L.R.2d 270, 302 (1956).

42. For text of the amended statute see note 4 *supra.*

husband to support his wife.[43] This attitude is implicit in early decisions defining alimony as an award to be made to the wife from the husband's separate estate.[44] It is also reflected in the distinction drawn by Chapter 565's predecessor between awards made to the wife, denominated as alimony, and awards made to the husband, which were "in the nature of alimony."[45]

This theory of alimony had its origin in common law property and divorce concepts.[46] Under traditional property law, a married couple was considered to constitute an indivisible unit in which all property was held by the husband.[47] While a wife had certain equitable and inchoate claims in the property during coverture, legal title to all property was vested in the husband.[48] In addition, since at common law the unit was considered insoluble,[49] the only divorce available was *a mensa et thoro* which left the marital bond unimpaired.[50] In view of this continuation of the marital bond it was logical that the marital duty of the husband to support his wife should also continue.[51] Moreover, an award of alimony as a matter of right seemed essential to avoid leaving propertyless divorcees destitute.

---

43. England v. England, 329 Mass. 763, 764, 107 N.E.2d 30, 31 (1952); Coe v. Coe, 313 Mass. 232, 235, 46 N.E.2d 1017, 1019 (1943); Topor v. Topor, 287 Mass 473, 475, 192 N.E. 52, 53 (1934); Rollins v. Gould, 244 Mass. 270, 138 N.E. 815, 816 (1923); Brown v. Brown, 222 Mass. 415, 416, 111 N.E. 42, 43 (1916). *See also* Limoges v. Limoges, 287 Mass. 260, 261, 191 N.E. 639 (1934) (alimony is not granted if the marriage is void, implying that in a void marriage the husband has no duty to support); Farrington v. Boston Safe Deposit & Trust Co., 280 Mass. 121, 125, 181 N.E. 779, 780 (1932) (duty to pay alimony ceases upon husband's death, since duty of support would end then); McIlroy v. McIlroy, 208 Mass. 458, 464, 94 N.E. 695, 698 (1911) (wife's return to husband does not permanently destroy her right to enforce alimony decree); Kelley v. Kelley, 161 Mass. 111, 119, 36 N.E. 837, 841 (1894) (in absence of a statute, equity court lacks power to decree alimony *pendente lite*).

44. Burrows v. Purple, 107 Mass. 428, 432 (1871) (alimony to be awarded "out of husband's estate"); Holbrook v. Comstock, 82 Mass. (16 Gray) 109, 110 (1860) (alimony not considered separate property of wife but that portion of the husband's estate which is allowed her for her subsistence and livelihood).

45. *See* Buckman v. Buckman, 176 Mass. 229, 230 (1900). MASS. GEN. LAWS ANN. ch. 208, § 34 (1958) provided that "alimony" may be awarded to the wife, but if an award is made to the husband, it can only be "in the nature of alimony." The statute itself, then, reflected the view that alimony could be awarded only to wives.

46. *See generally* CLARK, *supra* note 8, at 420-22; *Economics of Divorce, supra* note 31, at 140.

47. *Economics of Divorce, supra* note 31, at 146.

48. *Id.*

49. CLARK, *supra* note 8, at 420; *Economics of Divorce, supra* note 31, at 141.

50. This was a divorce from bed and board, and it is equivalent to the modern separation. *See* CLARK, *supra* note 8, at 420. *See also* Buckman v. Buckman, 176 Mass. 229, 230 (1900) (by 1900 the court had recognized divorce from bonds of matrimony as well as from bed and board).

51. *See* CLARK, *supra* note 8, at 420.

However, with the advent of married women property acts, permitting women to own separate property though married,[52] and absolute divorces, dissolving the bonds of marriage,[53] the rationale and purpose of alimony became less clear.[54] Where a woman had sufficient property in her separate estate to support herself, no reason existed why she should be entitled to alimony. Where the wife did not have such property, a right to alimony was more palatable as a necessity to avoid leaving her destitute. Nevertheless, despite the apparent equity of an alimony award in these circumstances, no sound justification was advanced to show why alimony, based as it was on the husband's duty to support his wife, should continue once the husband/wife bond was severed by a divorce absolute.[55]

This tension between the concept of traditional alimony on the one side and the development of separate property rights for married women and absolute divorces on the other manifested itself in numerous Massachusetts cases. For example, in *Brown v. Brown,*[56] the supreme judicial court acknowledged that alimony was based on the common law duty of the husband to support his wife.[57] However, in setting out the factors to be considered in making alimony awards, the court said:

> [Alimony] depends on the circumstances of each case, including the necessities of the wife and the pecuniary resources of the husband, the condition in life of the parties and their mode of living and the conduct of the parties.[58]

The common law duty of support contemplated an amount sufficient to satisfy the basic necessities of the wife—food, clothing, shelter—so as to enable the wife to survive.[59] The standard for

52. *E.g.,* MASS. GEN. LAWS ANN. ch. 209, § 1 *et seq.* (Supp. 1975). Chapter 209 was initially enacted in 1857. Act of Oct. 7, 1857, ch. 249, [1857] Mass. Acts & Resolves 598.

53. MASS. GEN. LAWS ANN. ch. 208, § 1 *et seq.* (Supp. 1975). *See generally* CLARK, *supra* note 8, at 420-22.

54. *See* CLARK, *supra* note 8, at 421-22.

> To the extent that alimony really is intended to provide a substitute for the common law right of support, one would expect it to be affected by the changes in the economic position of women which have occurred in the last fifty years. A woman today has far greater opportunities for employment than existed in 1900, and is therefore less dependent on her husband for support than she would have been in 1900.

55. *Id.* at 421.

56. 222 Mass. 415, 111 N.E.42 (1916).

57. *Id.* at 417, 111 N.E. at 43.

58. *Id.*, 111 N.E. at 43.

59. *Cf.* Gould v. Lawrence, 160 Mass. 232, 35 N.E. 462, 463 (1893) ("support" includes everything necessary for proper maintenance). *See generally* Coe v. Coe, 313 Mass. 232, 235, 46 N.E.2d 1017, 1019-20 (1943) (discussion of principles to be followed in determining amount of allowable support of wife).

determining alimony set out in *Brown,* including as it did such factors as the parties' social status and their accustomed mode of living, clearly contemplated something other than that intended in the concept of a husband's duty to support his wife; yet *Brown*'s progeny did not spell out a clear concept of alimony.[60] Instead, lip-service was paid to the traditional definition of alimony,[61] while awards were made according to the standards set out in *Brown.*[62] The juxtaposition of the *Brown* factors against an acknowledgement by the supreme judicial court that alimony is based on a husband's duty to support his wife, coupled with the illogic of the traditional alimony concept in light of the married women's property act and the absolute divorce, has led to confusion within the bar and in the courts concerning the modern goals of alimony and therefore the factors to be considered in making alimony awards.[63]

B. *Alimony in Massachusetts Under Chapter 565*

Chapter 565 begins by eliminating from the law the notion that alimony is based on the common law duty of the husband to support his wife.[64] Its first sentence provides:

> Upon a divorce or upon petition at any time after a divorce the court may order *either* of the parties to *pay alimony* to the other.[65]

---

60. England v. England, 329 Mass. 763, 764, 107 N.E.2d 30, 31 (1956) (alimony determined on basis of husband's duty to support wife and children but need not be based on parties' previous standard of living, depending upon discretion of trial judge); O'Brien v. O'Brien, 325 Mass. 573, 578, 91 N.E.2d 775, 777-78 (1950) (while alimony is left to discretion of trial judge, where wife's mental condition becomes grave and she is without support, husband must provide such support); Whitney v. Whitney, 325 Mass. 28, 30-31, 88 N.E.2d 647, 650-51 (1949) (no inflexible rule to be applied since alimony decree is left to trial judges' discretion; however, there is a broad power to modify said decrees where parties' conditions change); Baird v. Baird, 311 Mass. 329, 333, 41 N.E.2d 5, 7 (1942) (alimony based on sound discretion of trial judge). *Cf.* Topor v. Topor, 287 Mass. 473, 475-76, 192 N.E. 52, 53 (1934) (in awarding alimony, necessities of recipient, pecuniary resources of donor, conduct and conditions of parties must be considered); Coe v. Coe. 313 Mass. 232, 235, 46 N.E.2d 1017, 1019-20 (1943) (same principles applied in separate support cases).

61. *See* cases cited notes 43 & 60 *supra.*

62. 222 Mass. at 417, 111 N.E. at 43 (in awarding alimony, necessities of wife, pecuniary resources of husband, conditions of parties, their mode of living, and their conduct must be considered).

63. [V]ery few lawyers have been able to understand what goes through the mind of some trial judges when they make orders in certain types of cases for alimony and support, assuming they are familiar with what the Supreme Judicial Court has said and intimated in some very learned opinions based upon a pretty sound philosophy of life and economics.

2A J. Lombard, Family Law, Massachusetts Practice § 2054, at 609 (1967).

64. Chapter 565 only affects the party's rights "upon a divorce." The statute has no effect on the common law duty of a husband to support his wife while married. Mass. Gen. Laws Ann. ch. 208, § 34 (Supp. 1975).

65. *Id.* (emphasis added).

By discarding the distinction between awards of "alimony" and awards "in the nature of alimony," and by declaring that alimony may run from the wife to the husband, as well as vice versa, the statute has cut to the quick the concept that alimony is based on the husband's duty to support his wife.[66] *A fortiori,* an award of alimony from the wife to the husband could not derive from alimony based on the husband's duty to support the wife.

The rejection by Chapter 565 of the traditional basis for alimony awards is significant in several respects. First, the statute makes it clear that a court is empowered to make an award of alimony to the husband as well as to the wife.[67] Second, since alimony awards are no longer based on a "duty" to support the wife, the presumptive right of the wife[68] to an alimony allowance upon divorce is abolished. Instead, the statute places both parties[69] to the divorce on an equal footing[70] with respect to each party's right to receive alimony or obligation to pay alimony or both. By this action the General Court has avoided equal protection attacks on Massachusetts' alimony laws[71] and has recognized the independence and equality of women in today's society.[72] Finally, the statute eliminates the

---

66. *Id.*

67. Although the courts never held that the old Massachusetts statute prevented their awarding alimony to husbands, the authors are unaware of any case in which such an award was made. *Cf.* Ober v. Ober, 1 Mass. App. Ct. 32, 34, 294 N.E. 2d 449, 451 (1973) (court, although recognizing that it could make such an award, refused to do so). The traditional judicial reluctance to award alimony to the husband likely stems, at least partially, from the common law view of alimony as a means of enforcing the husband's duty to support the wife. *See generally Economics of Divorce, supra* note 31, at 140.

68. No legal presumption of a wife's right to alimony has existed in this state. *See* Brown v. Brown, 222 Mass. 415, 417, 111 N.E. 42, 43 (1916) (award of alimony discretionary with the judge). Nonetheless, in practice, a presumptive right in the wife to alimony has existed due to the basic theory of alimony and the usual marital situation which has been litigated in our divorce courts, namely the husband/breadwinner, wife/homemaker-childrearer. *See Economics of Divorce, supra* note 31, at 145-46. For a discussion of the traditional theory of alimony see notes 42-67 *supra* and accompanying text.

69. Unlike its predecessor, Chapter 565 speaks of the spouses in sexually neutral terms, as "parties," in an attempt to put them on an equal footing with respect to both alimony and property division. MASS. GEN. LAWS. ANN. ch. 208, § 34 (Supp. 1975).

70. Three purposes of the new statute were: (1) to avoid an equal protection attack on Massachusetts alimony laws based on the sexual distinction found in MASS. GEN. LAWS ANN. ch. 208, § 34 (1958), relative to awards of alimony (*see* text at notes 45 & 66 *supra*); (2) to bring Massachusetts alimony laws in line with the requirements of the pending equal rights amendment to the United States Constitution; and (3) to recognize the ability of women to be self-supporting and independent. *See* Inker Memorandum, *supra* note 17.

71. *Cf.* Stanley v. Illinois, 405 U.S. 645, 658 (1972) (violation of equal protection when unwed father is denied a hearing on his parental fitness which is granted to all other parents under an Illinois statute); Reed v. Reed, 404 U.S. 71, 74 (1971) (Idaho statute arbitrarily preferring males over females in appointment of administrators violates fourteenth amendment).

72. *See generally* CLARK *supra* note 8, at 422, *Economics of Divorce, supra* note 31, at

illogic of purporting to enforce a husband's duty to support his wife even though the marital bonds are totally dissolved.[73]

In addition to rejecting the traditional theory of alimony from Massachusetts law, Chapter 565 lists all the relevant factors to be considered in determining alimony awards. Two important facts about this list should be noted. First, the statute requires the probate judge to consider all the factors on the list.[74] However, in order to preserve flexibility in dealing with the many diverse fact situations which can arise in divorce litigation, the statute only requires that each factor be "consider[ed]" by the judge in making his award. The importance, relevance, and materiality accorded any single factor in a particular case are still left largely to the discretion of the trial judge.[75] Secondly, the list should be considered all-inconclusive.[76] Chapter 565 is a jurisdictional statute,[77] defining the constitutional power of the court to make awards of alimony, and therefore should be strictly construed.[78] In addition the statute contains an extensive list of all the factors deemed relevant in making alimony awards.[79] To permit consideration of factors

---

146-47; Note, *Interspousal Contracts: The Potential for Validation in Massachusetts,* 9 SUFFOLK U.L. REV. 185, 192-93, 200-01 (1975).

73. *See* text accompanying notes 50-55 *supra.*

74. The statute uses the mandatory language of "shall." MASS. GEN. LAWS ANN. ch. 208, § 34 (Supp. 1975).

75. Having given due consideration to the factor, the judge is free to give great, some, or no weight according to his judgment as to its relevance in the circumstances. *But cf.* text accompanying notes 113-27 *infra* (Appellate Review).

76. This fills a gap noted by the supreme judicial court in Coe v. Coe, 313 Mass. 232, 235-36, 46 N.E.2d 1017, 1020 (1943), where the court stated that due to the varied situations which arose in divorce cases, no all-inclusive list had ever been attempted.

77. Baird v. Baird, 311 Mass. 329, 331, 41 N.E.2d 5, 7 (1942) (subject to jurisdictional requirements, right to alimony governed by statute); Schillander v. Schillander, 307 Mass. 96, 99, 29 N.E.2d 686, 688 (1940) (court's power in alimony matters is solely statutorily derived); Gediman v. Cameron, 306 Mass. 138, 140, 27 N.E.2d 696, 697 (1940) (courts have no jurisdiction over alimony apart from the statute). This is due to the constitutional history of court power to award alimony. MASS. CONST. pt. 2, ch. 3 art. V (1780) provides: "All causes of marriage, divorce, and alimony . . . shall be heard and determined by the governor and council, until the legislature shall, by law, make other provision." In 1785, the legislature passed such a provision, giving competence over the enumerated questions to the courts of the Commonwealth. *See* Act of March 16, 1786, ch. 69, § 5, [1784-85] Mass. Acts & Resolves 564-67. This statute was the antecedent to the present MASS.GEN. LAWS ANN. ch. 208, § 34 (Supp. 1975). The statute, therefore, operated as a delegation of power, pursuant to the state constitution, over disputes relating to marriage, divorce, and alimony. For this reason, it was early held that alimony could be awarded only where the statute expressly permitted it. *See, e.g.,* Adams v. Holt, 214 Mass. 77, 78, 100 N.E. 1088, 1089 (1913) (alimony guaranteed only when authorized by statute).

78. *See* 2A C. SANDS, SUTHERLAND STATUTORY CONSTRUCTION § 58.03, at 465 (3d ed. 1973) [hereinafter cited as 2A SANDS] (statutes in derogation of common law strictly construed). *See also* cases cited note 7 *supra.*

79. Where a statute includes an extensive list of items, it should usually be construed to

beyond the statute would invite the conflicting and arbitrary results[80] which the statute was designed to eliminate, and which would eventually lead judges and lawyers back into the morass of confusion as to what factors are relevant to the awarding of alimony.

As to the actual process of considering the statutory factors and applying them in a particular case, Chapter 565 deliberately eschews any prescribed formulas because today there are too many different types of marriages to be dealt with by any one rule or group of rules.[81] While in the past the virtually universal marriage arrangement was one in which the husband was gainfully employed while the wife remained at home performing the chores of housekeeping and childrearing, this type of marriage, though still common, is not as pervasive as it once was. Instead, wives as well as husbands often work, some only until, others even after, the birth of children. In other marriages the wife may be the breadwinner while the husband performs the tasks of homemaking. Moreover, within any of the general categories of present-day marriages, the number of possible variations is enormous. With the traditional relationship, for instance, there is a great difference between a marriage of twenty years duration and one of only two years.[82] In each marriage the health, employability, vocational skills, and independent financial means of each party will vary almost infinitely. Binding the probate court to any rigid formula or group of formulas designed to cover all possible divorce situations would inevitably result in injustice in particular cases. By adopting the

---

exclude by implication items not on the list. This is the doctrine of *expressio unius est exclusio alterius. See* 2A SANDS, *supra* note 78, § 47.23, at 123. *See also* Ianelle v. Fire Comm'n, 331 Mass. 250, 252-53, 118 N.E.2d 757, 759 (1954) (application of the above maxim in construing a statute regarding the omission or inclusion of certain days to determine the timeliness of a hearing request).

80. By creating a clear standard to be applied in determining alimony awards, Chapter 565 will allow for more scrupulous review and appeal than was possible in the confused state of the law which existed before its enactment. *See* text accompanying notes 113-27 *infra* (Appellate Review).

81. *See* Inker Memorandum, *supra* note 17

82. Where the marriage is older, there is a greater likelihood that the spouse (usually the wife) will not readily be able to find employment without substantial training. The judge should examine this problem carefully in deciding whether to require her to prepare to fully support herself, or whether to require self-sufficiency would be fruitless or so disruptive of the recipient's life as to undermine the policy of accomplishing the divorce with a minimum of disruption. In making this determination, the judge must of course consider all the circumstances, most particularly, the financial ability of the other spouse to support the recipient.

more flexible approach of simply listing the relevant factors and leaving it to the judge to apply them to a given case,[83] the statute permits a just determination of whether the particular marriage fits into any pattern for which a preconceived formula was designed.

As with all statutes, Chapter 565 should be construed and applied to promote its intended purpose.[84] Guidelines for applying the factors involved in a particular alimony award are derived from the statute's legislative history,[85] where its goal is clearly presented, and from the factors the statute enumerates as being relevant.[86] The Memorandum in Support of House Bill No. 285[87] states that:

> [a]limony should not be thought of as a pension, but rather as an aid in supporting the receiving party in the manner to which he or she has become accustomed.[88]

Focusing on this goal, the award should attempt to balance the policy against alimony as a pension[89] with that of aiding the recipient spouse to be supported in his or her accustomed manner.

Initially the court should examine the circumstances of each party separately.[90] Since the underlying purpose of the statute is to effect the divorce with as little social and financial disruption as possible,[91] the judge should first look to the station, *i.e.*, the mode and level of living, of each party during the marriage. In attempting to leave the divorced parties in circumstances which will permit them to maintain this station, the judge should examine their

---

83. However, this discretion is now subject to more direct appellate review. *See* text accompanying notes 113-27 *infra* (Appellate Review).

84. This is simply an application of the usual rule of statutory interpretation that the legislative intent should control the construction of the statute and the statute should always be applied so as to promote its ultimate goals. 2A SANDS, *supra* note 78, § 45.05, at 15-16. *See* Meunier's Case, 319 Mass. 421, 423, 66 N.E.2d 198, 200 (1946) (legislative intent controls construction of statute); Todd v. Clapp, 118 Mass. 495, 496-97 (1875) (purpose of act should be considered and promoted when interpreting statute).

85. *See* Inker Memorandum,*supra* note 17, at 8-9.

86. *See* note 4 *supra* (text of statute). Thus, the result is the same whether the statute is construed according to its legislative intent or according to the meaning which the words in the statute import independent of the legislative intent. *See generally* O.W. HOLMES, COLLECTED LEGAL PAPERS 207 (1920) ("we do not inquire what the legislature meant; we ask only what the statute means").

87. *See* Inker Memorandum, *supra* note 17.

88. *Id.* at 6.

89. *Compare* Rader v. Rader, 126 So. 2d 189, 191 (La. App. 1961) (alimony as a pension for the wife), *with* Commonwealth v. Whiston, 306 Mass. 65, 66, 27 N.E.2d 703, 704 (1940) ("[w]e know of no law that assures the right to a life of idleness to every married woman living apart from her husband for justifiable cause").

90. By separating the needs of the parties initially from the question of ability to pay, the court should be able to assess more realistically what each party's needs are.

91. *See* CLARK, *supra* note 8, at 441-42.

independent needs, considering such factors as their age and health in order to make a realistic assessment.[92] The court should then determine how far each spouse is capable of independently satisfying individual needs and maintaining a preexisting standard of living.[93] In deciding this question, the court will be principally concerned with the spouses' occupations, amount and sources of income, and estates,[94] all factors which were held relevant under prior law.[95] Additionally, in keeping with the policy against alimony as a pension,[96] the court must also consider the vocational skills and employability of each spouse.[97] By this analysis, the court should be able to determine the actual extent to which a party can or cannot maintain his or her current standard of living without support.[98] It can then determine the most feasible way to adjust the

---

92. This article recognizes that the goal of maintaining the preexisting standard of living may not always be possible. The court will then be required to adjust the parties' rights to approximate, as nearly as possible, that standard for both parties.

93. This process of analysis is not necessarily two separate functions. The process is separated here for the purpose of clarity. In practice, the factors to be considered will continually overlap when applied to particular facts.

94. *See* note 4 *supra* (statutory language).

95. *See* cases cited notes 43, 60 *supra.*

96. *See* cases cited note 89 *supra.*

97. *See* note 4 *supra* (statute). The factors of vocational skills and employability should be used by the court to encourage self-support by awarding alimony only to the extent that the recipient is unable to support himself or herself.

98. It is submitted by the authors that "conduct of the parties during the marriage" should have little relevance in determining alimony awards, except in extreme cases. In general, "conduct of the parties during the marriage" is more appropriately considered relative to property division. *See* text accompanying notes 31-34 *supra.* However, several reasons justify its inclusion and consideration in this statute with respect to alimony. First, Massachusetts has a fault system of divorce. MASS. GEN. LAWS ANN. ch. 208 § 1 (Supp. 1975). In the usual case, the same judge who heard the evidence of fault with respect to obtaining the divorce will also make the alimony award. With the long tradition in Massachusetts of considering fault relative to alimony awards, *see, e.g.,* Graves v. Graves, 108 Mass. 314, 317 (1871), it is unrealistic to believe that the trial judge will ignore evidence of fault in making his award. By including "conduct of the parties" consideration of this factor can be made openly by the trial judge; yet the weight accorded it can be controlled by the appellate courts so as to insure a just result. Second, it would seem that in many cases, conduct of the parties during the marriage is to some degree indicative of what their conduct will be in the future. To this extent, inclusion of this factor permits the trial court to make an alimony provision based on the likelihood of its promoting the purposes of alimony. Since fault is only one factor to be considered it should be weighed only in accordance with its significance relative to the other factors and in light of the goals of the statute. For example, consider the situation where divorce is grounded upon the alcoholism of the recipient spouse. This type of conduct during marriage is relevant in determining whether an award is likely to further the purposes of the statute, since alcoholism is probative on the question of whether the spouse can be self-sufficient and what the spouse's needs are. Again, conduct which is less than that traditionally denominated as grounds for divorce may be indicative of the likelihood that an award will put the party back into the mainstream of society or ease the transition from married to single status. If one of the parties has been a spendthrift, this fact is relevant in determining the likelihood that an award will foster the goals of alimony. Also, if one of the parties, whether the potential

rights of both parties, trying to maintain as closely as possible their preexisting standard of living while not unreasonably burdening either with a support order which will make it impossible for the contributing spouse to live in his accustomed manner.

If the goals of the statute are kept in mind and the statute is carefully applied, it should afford Massachusetts courts an excellent opportunity to avoid much of the bickering and hard feelings which generally attended alimony disputes under prior law. The statute will permit divorce with much less social and financial disruption and will better enable both parties to enter single life as productive, self-supporting members of the community as soon as reasonably possible.[99]

IV. Modification of Decrees

Alimony is not a vested right.[100] Subsequent to the entry of a decree of divorce, there is often a change in circumstances which justifies a modification of the terms and conditions of the alimony award. Section 37 of chapter 208, which is the jurisdictional basis for modification, provides that a preexisting decree of alimony may be revised and altered from time to time.[101] It should be stressed that such modification has never been grounded on section 34 and therefore should not be grounded on Chapter 565's amendment of that section.[102] Chapter 565, which empowers the court to award

---

recipient or payor of alimony, has been irresponsible with respect to the marriage, that fact may bear on the likelihood that an award will promote the underlying goals. In the case of the spouse obligated to pay, past conduct evincing irresponsibility may serve as a warning to the court of the unlikelihood that that spouse will regularly perform any duties imposed by a decree of periodic alimony.

These examples are illustrative of the many possible ways in which conduct of the parties may be relevant in making alimony awards, but they should not be considered exhaustive. "Conduct of the parties during the marriage" should not, however, be allowed to take over the process of determining the financial adjustments of the parties.

99. *Cf.* Clark, *supra* note 8, at 442.

100. *See, e.g.,* Ziegler v. McKinlay, 318 Mass. 765, 767, 64 N.E.2d 15, 16 (1946) (payment of alimony subject to modification and revision; *accord,* Watts v. Watts, 314 Mass. 129, 133, 49 N.E.2d 609, 612 (1943); Southworth v. Treadwell, 168 Mass. 511, 512, 47 N.E. 93, 94 (1897).

101. Mass. Gen. Laws Ann. ch. 208, § 37 (1954) provides:

> After a decree for alimony or an annual allowance for the wife or children, the court may, from time to time, upon the petition of either party, revise and alter its decree relative to the amount of such alimony or annual allowance and the payment thereof, and may make any decree relative thereto which it might have made in the original suit.

102. Kinosian v. Kinosian, 351 Mass. 49, 52, 217 N.E.2d 769, 770 (1966) (section 34 is the jurisdictional basis for the original alimony decree); Baird v. Baird, 311 Mass. 329, 331, 41 N.E.2d 5, 6-7 (1942) (section 37 applies only after a decree of alimony has been entered pursuant to the court's jurisdiction under section 34).

alimony "upon petition at any time after a divorce," refers only to those instances where no decree for alimony has previously been entered.[103] Concomitantly, where an order for alimony has been decreed, the authority for modification of the preexisting order is governed by section 37.

Furthermore, the authority to modify pursuant to section 37 is limited to a modification of alimony.[104] Section 37 refers only to alimony, the power of the court to modify its alimony decrees, and the power to make any decree of alimony which it might have made at the time of the entry of the final decree. Since there is no provision for modification of property division, the presumption must be that the legislature did not intend to so provide.[105] This omission is particularly logical when it is considered that one of the primary purposes of property division is to effect as full and complete a settlement of financial obligations between the parties as possible.[106]

Although Chapter 565 has no direct effect on section 37, significant *indirect* effects on modification result from the new statute. It is well-established that awards of alimony, both periodic and lump sum, are subject to modification upon petition after entry of the decree. [107] The power to modify is broad and extends to arrears as well as future installments.[108] Modification is always based on a change in circumstances after the entry of the decree and is usually justified by a change in the ability of the obligor-spouse to pay or by a change in the needs of the recipient spouse.[109] A variety of occurrences, however, have been held to constitute the requisite

---

103. *See* cases cited note 102 *supra.*

104. For text of MASS. GEN. LAWS ANN. ch. 208, § 37, see note 101 *supra.*

105. *See* Wheelwright v. Tax Comm'r, 235 Mass. 584, 585, 127 N.E. 523 (1920) (new act is to be construed with preexisting sections only to the extent that it can be done consistently); Fitzgerald v. Lewis, 164 Mass. 495, 499, 41 N.E. 687, 688 (1895) (preexisting sections are construed with new sections only to the extent that it can be done consistently).

106. *See* cases cited note 38 *supra.*

107. *See, e.g.,* Whitney v. Whitney, 325 Mass. 28, 31, 88 N.E.2d 647, 650-51 (1949) (modification of periodic payments); Zeigler v. McKinlay, 318 Mass. 765, 766-67, 64 N.E.2d 15, 16 (1945) (modification of lump sum award).

108. *See* Sawyer v. Kuhnle, 324 Mass. 53, 56-57, 84 N.E.2d 546, 548 (1949) (judge may modify previous decree to determine arrears); Ziegler v. McKinlay, 318 Mass. 765, 767, 64 N.E.2d 15 (1946) (judge may, in proper situation, modify lump sum); Watts v. Watts, 314 Mass. 129, 133, 43 N.E.2d 609, 612 (1943) (court has full power to modify decrees as to both future payments and arrears).

109. Mead v. Mead, 2 Mass. App. Ct. 338, 339, 311 N.E. 2d 585, 586 (1974) (modification must be based on change in circumstances, such as change in husband's financial status); Robbins v. Robbins, 343 Mass. 247, 249, 178 N.E.2d 281, 282 (1962) (subsequent marriage of wife can be significant change in circumstances even if marriage is annulled).

change of circumstance necessary for a modification.[110] Thus it has been stated that where the court is presented with such a petition, reference should be made to the facts on which the former decree rested.[111] Chapter 565, by its comprehensive enumeration or relevant factors, establishes a framework within which the court can weigh the totality of the circumstances in determining whether a modification of the preexisting decree is justified.[112] By its thorough development of guidelines, Chapter 565 provides a base for determining the facts as they existed at the time of the former decree and a yardstick for measuring whether a change in circumstances has in fact occurred.

V. Appellate Review

The new statute will have significant impact on appellate review of both alimony awards and property divisions.[113] As was stated in *Coe v. Coe,*[114] trial judges have traditionally had broad discretion in fixing alimony.[115] "The determination of the amount [of alimony] to be allowed rests to a considerable extent in the discretion of the trial judge. . . ."[116] Trial judges were directed to make an award which was "just and reasonable upon all the circumstances of the case,"[117] and the appellate court, in reviewing alimony awards, was therefore limited to determining whether the trial

---

110. Miller v. Miller, 366 Mass. 846, 847, 314 N.E.2d 443, 444 (1974) (husband's illness which interferes with his earning power may necessitate a modification); Coe v. Coe, 320 Mass. 295, 306-07, 69 N.E.2d 793, 800 (1946) (divorced wife's illness may require increase in alimony); Southworth v. Treadwell, 168 Mass. 511, 513, 47 N.E. 93, 94 (1897) (remarriage of divorced wife prima facie cause for reducing award).

111. Sparhawk v. Sparhawk, 120 Mass. 390, 391 (1876) (court should consider facts on which original decree rested in making a subsequent modification); *see* Hinds v. Hinds, 329 Mass. 190, 192, 107 N.E.2d 319, 320 (1952) (within court's discretion to consider findings of previous decree as well as events following decree).

112. For example, the statute would provide guidelines for handling a situation such as one which confronted the court in Robbins v. Robbins, 343 Mass. 247, 178 N.E.2d 281 (1961), where it was unclear whether the wife's subsequent marriage and its annulment would constitute a change in circumstances sufficient to modify an alimony decree. The court held that, under the statute then in effect, each such case must be studied for evidence of a sufficient change of circumstances. *Id.* at 252, 178 N.E.2d at 284.

113. Prior to its amendment in 1974, the Massachusetts statute did not permit property division per se. *See* MASS. GEN. LAWS ANN. ch. 208, § 34 (1958). For further discussions of the prior statute see text accompanying note 21 *supra.*

114. 313 Mass. 232, 46 N.E.2d 1017 (1943).

115. *See* cases cited notes 43, 60 *supra.*

116. 313 Mass. at 235, 46 N.E.2d at 1020.

117. *Id.*, 46 N.E.2d at 1020. *See also* Brown v. Brown, 222 Mass. 415, 417, 111 N.E.2d 42, 43 (1916) (award of alimony depends upon a number of circumstances including the wife's needs, the husband's resources, the parties' stations in life and their conduct).

judge had abused his discretion.[118] The only real guidance given the appellate court in examining the circumstances of the case appeared in *Brown v. Brown,*[119] which listed among the factors to be considered:

> [T]he necessities of the wife and the pecuniary resources of the husband, the condition in life of the parties and their mode of living and the conduct of the parties.[120]

However, the Supreme Judicial Court of Massachusetts clearly stated that this list was not to be viewed as complete.[121] Moreover, it was never held that *all* of these factors must be considered by the trial court.[122] The trial judge was left to reach beyond these factors if he wished or to ignore them altogether. The absence of uniform criteria for making alimony awards, coupled with the confusion over the nature and purpose of alimony,[123] rendered largely illusory the abuse-of-discretion check on trial court conduct except in the most blatant cases.

Chapter 565 preserves the discretion of the trial court in applying the statutory factors to the circumstances of the case,[124] but also creates guidelines by which the appellate court can review the decision. The statute sets out a complete[125] list of factors which the trial judge must[126] consider in making any award, thus providing the appellate court with a very specific review standard. Failure by the trial court to consider all statutory factors or its consideration of nonstatutory factors will justify reversal or modification by the appellate court. In addition, depending on the degree of specificity of the record before it, the appellate court can examine the evidence and findings with respect to each factor in the statute, always according appropriate weight to the findings of the judge before whom the case was presented.[127] Finally, the statute eliminates

118. 313 Mass. at 235, 46 N.E.2d at 1020. *Cf.* Topor v. Topor, 287 Mass. 473, 476, 192 N.E. 52, 53 (1934) (portion of decree reversed because it was not supported by trial court's findings of material fact).

119. 222 Mass. 415, 111 N.E. 42 (1916).

120. *Id.* at 417, 111 N.E. at 43.

121. Coe v. Coe, 313 Mass. 232, 235-36, 46 N.E.2d 1017, 1020 (1943).

122. Both *Coe,* 313 Mass. at 236, 46 N.E.2d at 1020, and *Brown,* 222 Mass. at 417, 111 N.E. at 43, state that the relevant factors "include" those they list.

123. *See* text accompanying note 63 *supra.*

124. *See* text accompanying notes 74-75 *supra.*

125. *See* text accompanying notes 75-80 *supra.*

126. *See* text accompanying note 74 *supra.*

127. *See* Coe v. Coe, 313 Mass. 232, 235, 46 N.E.2d 1017, 1020 (1943) (reviewing court must weigh discretion of trial judge even where the grounds for his action are fully reported in the record).

confusion about the nature and purpose of alimony, substituting clear legislative intent to guide the lower court in dividing property and awarding alimony. This legislative intent provides parameters within which the trial judge may exercise his discretion and allows the appellate court to apply its abuse-of-discretion test more precisely. Chapter 565 should lead to more uniform and equitable settlements of the financial problems connected with divorce.

VI. Conclusion

The economic aspects of divorce in Massachusetts have been substantially reformed by the enactment of Chapter 565 of the Acts of 1974. By mandating that the probate courts consider both the economic and noneconomic contributions of each spouse in dividing the assets of the marriage, the new law likens marriage to the dissolution of a partnership. In addition, Chapter 565 has altered the law as it relates to the awarding of alimony by requiring that the needs of both spouses and the ability of each to be self-supporting be considered rather than any abstract "duty" of a husband to support his wife. It is the hope of the authors that Chapter 565, by bestowing upon the probate courts broad powers to effect an equitable resolution of the economic aspects of the marriage, will significantly reduce the acrimony which too frequently attended divorce under the preexisting practice.

Alimony Orders Following Short-Term Marriages

MONROE L. INKER*
JOSEPH H. WALSH†
PAUL P. PEROCCHI‡

Introduction

In the decade beginning in 1965, the United States experienced a dramatic increase in its divorce rate. Since that year the nation's divorce rate has climbed from 2.5 divorces per thousand persons to 4.6 divorces per thousand, a nearly twofold increase.[1] By 1975 the actual number of divorces and annulments was 1,026,000 annually.[2] As of 1972, one out of every three marriages ended in divorce.[3] That ratio has almost certainly increased in the six years since then.

Simultaneously, a movement toward reforming the nation's divorce laws has been developing. Numerous articles have appeared within the last ten years dealing with the changing social and economic role of women in our society and the need to reform our laws concerning alimony and disposition of assets to conform to present economic and social realities. Many states have responded

*Member, Massachusetts Bar
†Member, Massachusetts Bar
‡Member, Massachusetts Bar

1. Feldman, *A Statutory Proposal to Remove Divorce from the Courtroom,* 29 MAINE L. REV. 25, n.2 (1977).
2. *Id.*
3. Hatten & Brown, *Impressions of a Domestic Relations Judge,* 13 S. TEX. L.J. 250, 253 (1972).

to this outcry for reform, some by legislation,[4] others by case law.[5]

An inevitable by-product of the rise in the national divorce rate has been an increase in the number of "short-term marriages."[6] More and more often people seem willing to admit that their marriage is a mistake and divorce, rather than "tough it out" until "death do us part." The relatively recent phenomenon of the "short-term marriage," coming at the same time as the movement towards reform of alimony and marital property laws, has generated confusion and disagreement about the principles to be applied in determining alimony and property division after short marriages. There is no scholarly discussion of this subject, and the scattered case law rarely offers meaningful analysis and frequently reaches contradictory results.[7] Moreover, the reported cases seldom focus on the merits of the decision but simply rubber stamp the judgment by referring to the trial court's expertise on the subject, its opportunity to observe the witnesses,[8] and its broad discretion.[9]

This article is based on an examination of over 150 reported cases[10] from various jurisdictions. Its purpose is not to present a

---

4. *See, e.g.,* MASS. GEN. LAWS ANN. ch. 208, § 34 (1958), *as amended,* MASS. GEN. LAWS ANN. ch. 208, § 34 (Supp. 1977).

5. *See, e.g.,* Surabian v. Surabian, 362 Mass. 342, 348, n.7, 285 N.E.2d 909, 913 n.7 (1972); D'Amico v. D'Amico, 1 Mass. App. Ct. 561, 562, 303 N.E.2d 737, 738 (App. Ct. 1973); Lacey v. Lacey, 25 Wis. 2d 378, 382. 173 N.W.2d 142, 144 (1970).

6. *Short-term marraiges* are defined as marriages of six years or less. *See* text accompanying notes 18-23 *infra.*

7. *Compare* Nienow v. Nienow, 268 S.C. 161, 232 S.E.2d 504 (1977) (disparity of wealth and earning power between the parties held sufficient to justify an order for alimony more commensurate with the husband's ability to pay following a fourteen-month marriage) *with* Gordon v. Gordon, 335 So. 2d 321 (Fla. App. 1976) (disparity of earning capacity between the parties does not justify an order for alimony commensurate with the obligor's ability to pay following a sixteen-month marriage); *Compare* Cooper v. Cooper, 269 C.A.2d 6, 74 Cal. Rptr. 439, 448 P.2d 607 (1969) (wife who lost trust income by marriage entitled to permanent support in amount of income lost) *with* Plageman v. Plageman, 79 S.D. 221, 110 N.W.2d 337 (1961) (wife who lost social security benefits by marriage not entitled to compensation for loss).

8. *See, e.g.,* Nelson v. Nelson, 246 Iowa 760, 68 N.W.2d 746, 751 (1955) ("The parties were before the trial court, where their appearance and demeanor toward each other could be observed . . ."); Tomlinson v. Tomlinson, 352 N.E.2d 785 (1976) ("The trial court was in a position to weigh the testimony and to consider the demeanor of the witnesses. We are not.")

9. "Judicial discretion is probably nowhere more intimately connected with human relations, nor is it given freer rein, than in the field of domestic relations." Cooey, *The Exercise of Judicial Discretion in the Award of Alimony,* 6 LAW & CONTEMP. PROB. 213 (1939) [hereinafter referred to as Cooey].

10. Analyzing alimony decisions from reported cases contains inherent limitations. First, the standard for appellate review is usually whether the trial court abused its discretion in making the award in an area where the trial judge's discretion is given almost free rein.

comprehensive survey of all cases involving short-term marriages, but to select, cases which are typical (1) of the fact patterns arising in short-term marriage cases, and (2) of courts' attitudes towards such marriages. Cases are included regardless of the emphasis placed upon the brevity of the marriage by the court[11] and without regard to whether the case is from a common law jurisdiction,[12] a community property state,[13] or a jurisdiction operating under a statute governing alimony and property division.[14] This article proposes (a) to examine case law trends in order to determine the general purpose of the courts in alimony orders following short-term marriages; and (b) to analyze the factors which may affect the final alimony order. We will not discuss the relationship between short-term marriages and property division; we will discuss only alimony.

Length of Short-Term Marriages

Neither *short-term marriage* nor *short marriage* are terms of art with acquired legal meaning, and no article or case has attempted to define the term *short marriage.* Nevertheless, courts have repeatedly referred to particular marriages as being either "long"[15]

Cooey, *supra,* note 9. Furthermore, the unarticulated beliefs of the trial court will rarely be revealed:

> What has in actuality motivated the trial judge will seldom be disclosed in the appellate opinion, nor, indeed will the basis of the appellate court's action always be fully presented. What the opinion makes available is the set of factors and reasons which the court considered proper to employ in support of its decision. *Rarely* disclosed in the opinion will be the personal beliefs and biases of its author toward the marriage relation, divorce, and alimony itself, although it seems inevitable that such considerations must form the *inarticulate major premise* of many decisions in this field.

11. *Compare* Cooper v. Cooper, 269 C.A.2d 6, 74 Cal. Rptr. 439 (1969) (court mentioned the length of the marriage in its statement of facts without elaboration) *with* Grimes v. Grimes, 472 S.W.2d 477 (1971), (brevity of marriage emphasized in upholding refusal to award permanent alimony). *See also* Oppenheimer v. Oppenheimer, 22 Ariz. 238, 526 P.2d 762 (1974) (court rejected husband's argument that alimony order was too large in light of marriage of only forty months); Jernigan v. Jernigan, 344 So. 2d 778 (1977) (permanent alimony award despite court's recognition of brevity of marriage); Borowitz v. Borowitz, 19 Ill. App. 3d 176, 311 N.E.2d 292 (1974) (longer the marriage the greater the wife's claim to a right of support from husband).

12. *See, e.g.,* Ruden v. Ruden, 55 A.D. 2d 910, 390 N.Y.S.2d 451 (1977); Tomlinson v. Tomlinson, 352 N.E.2d 785 (1976); Nienow v. Nienow, 268 S.C. 161, 232 S.E.2d 504 (1977).

13. *See, e.g.,* Schulman v. Schulman, 92 Nev. 707, 558 P.2d 525 (1976); Nelson v. Nelson, 114 Ariz. 369, 560 P.2d 1276 (1977).

14. *See, e.g.,* Aguire v. Aguire, 171 Conn. 312, 370 A.2d 948 (1976); Putnam v. Putnam, 77 ASA 16 358 N.E.2d 837 (1977).

15. *See, e.g., In re* DIETZ, 1 FAMILY LAW REPORTER 2122 (Ore. Ct. of App. November 15, 1974).

or "short,"[16] without analysis of the criteria for determining which label to apply. Nor have the courts ever advanced policy reasons for characterizing marriages of six years or less as short. In cases where the courts have described a marriage as short, the length of the marriage has ranged from as little as four days[17] to as long as six years.[18] On the other hand, at least one court, when confronted with a marriage of six and one-half years, has stated: "We are of the opinion that six and a half years of a happy marriage is sufficiently long to be considered in favor of the wife."[19] Only one case was found in which a court characterized a marriage of more than six and one-half years as "short";[20] no case was found where a marriage of less than six and one-half years was characterized as "long." The courts seem to agree that "short marriages" are marriages of six years or less, and the authors are adopting this definition here.

While the courts have consistently called marriages of six years or less, short, there is disagreement over the dates to be used in measuring the length of the marriage. The courts have generally considered the date of the ceremony as the beginning of marriage:[21] this date has been used even in cases where the parties live together for a substantial period prior to marriage.[22] In *Nienow v. Nienow*, the parties began living together in August or September 1968, and married April 24, 1971. The divorce action was filed August 4, 1972. The South Carolina Supreme Court noted that the duration of the marriage was only fourteen months, giving no consideration to the two and one-half years the parties had lived together prior to the marriage.[23]

Courts have used three approaches in determining the time of termination. One approach, as used in *Carson v. Carson*,[24] looks to

16. *See, e.g.*, Jernigan v. Jernigan, 344 So. 2d 778, 780 (1977) ("[e]ven though the parties were married for only a short time . . .").

17. Hempel v. Hempel, 225 Minn. 287, 30 N.W.2d 594 (1948).

18. Berry v. Berry, 117 C.A.2d 624, 256 P.2d 646 (1953) (5 years, 11 months from marriage ceremony to filing of divorce); McEachnie v. McEachnie, 216 A.2d 169 (1966) (six-year marriage to date of separation).

19. Carson v. Carson, 50 Ha. 182, __, 436 P.2d 7, 11 (1967).

20. Underwood v. Underwood, 55 A.D.2d 1016, 391 N.Y.S.2d 213 (1977).

21. *See, e.g.*, Oppenheimer v. Oppenheimer, 22 Ariz. 238, 526 P.2d 762 (1974); Luithle v. Luithle, 23 Wash. 2d, 494, 161 P.2d 152 (1945) (four-month marriage from date of ceremony).

22. Nienow v. Nienow, 268 S.C. 161, 232 S.E.2d 504 (1977).

23. *Id.* at __.

24. Carson v. Carson, 50 Ha. 182, 436 P.2d 7 (1967).

the length of time the marriage was "happy." In *Carson*, the Supreme Court of Hawaii said: "[D]uration of the marriage, whether long or short, is not significant in itself unless it is considered in relation to whether the marriage was a happy one."[25] The court then held that six and a half years of happy marriage was a long marriage. The court specifically found that "the marriage was normal and happy; it was not mercenary and for the wife, was not a marriage of convenience."[26] *Carson* suggests that the clock stops running on the length of the marriage when the marriage ceases to be "normal and happy." But the *Carson* approach has serious problems. "Normal" and "happy" are extremely subjective standards. While a domineering husband might find the relationship quite normal and happy, his wife may not. It is also difficult to define with exactitude the point in time when a "normal and happy" marriage becomes abnormal and unhappy. The *Carson* approach is uncertain and susceptible to subjective and conflicting application.

A second approach, which seems the most favored,[27] looks to the date of physical separation.[28] Its principal advantages are that it is definite, easy to apply, and eminently practical. When marital difficulties reach the point where one of the parties leaves the other, the marriage is obviously dead. Once separation occurs, the marriage can no longer be considered a shared undertaking and neither party is likely to significantly contribute, either materially or intangibly, to the financial or emotional well-being of the other. All of the usual incidents of the marital relationship are lacking.[29]

Nevertheless, measuring the length of the marriage by reference to the date of separation has inherent weaknesses. In many cases parties continue to live together for some time before physically separating. Thus, in *Tomlinson v. Tomlinson*,[30] the court noted that the parties finally separated after "four stormy years of mar-

25. *Id.* at 187, 436 P.2d at 11.
26. *Id.* at 187, 436 P.2d at 11.
27. *See, e.g.*, McEachnie v. McEachnie, 216 A.2d 169 (1966); Putnam v. Putnam, 77-ASA 16 358 N.E.2d 837 (1977); Zeller v. Zeller, 195 Kan. 452, 407 P.2d 478 (1965).
28. *See, e.g.*, McEachnie v. McEachnie, 216 A.2d 169 (1966).
29. *Cf.* Johl v. United States, 370 F.2d 174 (9th Cir. 1967) (marriage commonly understood to mean that two people have undertaken to establish a life together and to assume certain duties and obligations).
30. 352 N.E.2d 785 (1976).

riage."[31] In *Zeller v. Zeller*,[32] the court measured the length of the marriage from the date of the wedding to the date of the separation, a period of twenty-seven months, while noting that the parties were having difficulties within a year of the marriage.[33] If one of the reasons for using the date of separation standard is that at that time the marriage can no longer be considered a shared enterprise, the court's refusal to recognize that the marriage was dead earlier dilutes the strength of that reason. Physical separation does not take into account the parties' remaining under the same roof when their emotional and physical relationship is dead. The weakness in the date of the separation test was graphically illustrated in *Ferguson v. Ferguson*.[34] The wife, a foreign resident, had placed a newspaper advertisement informing the public of her desire to marry an American. The husband had responded by letter, and the parties agreed to marry. When the wife arrived in the United States, the husband's ardor cooled, and the parties slept in separate rooms during the year they resided under the same roof. The court emphasized the lack of conjugal relations as demonstrating that the marriage was one "in name only."[35] Nevertheless, the court described the marriage as one of less than one year, noting that the parties had married in March 1952 and separated in February 1953. The description of the marriage as one "in name only" was clearly accurate. Yet the court felt constrained to find that the marriage had lasted almost a year, since the parties had physically resided together for that period, despite the absence of the usual incidents of marriage. On balance, the date of separation is a reasonable compromise between the too subjective and flexible *Carson* approach and the too rigid date of the filing test discussed below.

The third approach considers the marriage ended on the date the divorce action is filed.[36] Cases applying this standard have done so when there was no clear date of separation or where the separation

---

31. *Id.* at 787.
32. 195 Kan. 452, 407 P.2d 478 (1965).
33. *Id.* at 454.
34. 125 Ind. App. 596, 125 N.E.2d 816 (1955).
35. *Id.* at 604, 125 N.E.2d at 819.
36. *See, e.g.*, Schulman v. Schulman, Adv. 8339 Nev. __, 558 P.2d 525 (1976); Berry v. Berry, 117 C.A.2d 624, 256 P.2d 646 (1953).

and the filing occurred almost simultaneously.[37] Where the date of the separation cannot be determined, the date of the filing appears to be the logical point for marking the end of the marriage. The date of filing is objectively indentifiable, and the marriage surely is over by then.[38] However, application of this test can lead to results inconsistent with measuring the length of the marriage by its viability as a joint undertaking. The facts of the *Nelson*[39] case illustrate the possibility of harm in applying the date of filing standard. In *Nelson*, fifteen months had elapsed from marriage to separation, but the divorce was not filed until three years after the separation. Under the date of filing test, the marriage lasted five years; under the separation test, fifteen months. Thus, the filing date test, while lending certainty is, at least in some cases, contrary to the concept of measuring the marriage by its period of viability. For this reason the date of the filing test should be limited to cases where no discernible separation date can be found.

The approaches used in the short marriage cases to measure length are inconsistent. Commencement is measured from the date of ceremony, even where the parties lived together prior to marriage.[40] In determining the termination of the marriage, the short marriage cases have uniformly rejected the legal definition of marriage. None of the cases measures the length of the marriage by reference to the date of divorce, the legal end of the marriage. In light of the contemporary attitude toward and the frequency of parties living together before marriage, the courts should be more discriminating and consider examining the premarital period for evidence of a shared undertaking. Such an approach would avoid the inconsistencies evidenced by the *Nienow* case.

Relevant Factors in Determining Alimony in Short Marriages

The authors have been unable to find any case where length of the marriage, no matter how brief, was the sole predicate for an

37. *See, e.g.*, Berry v. Berry, 117 C.A.2d 624, 256 P.2d 646 (1953); Luithle v. Luithle, 23 Wash. 2d 494, 161 P.2d 152 (1945); Pinion v. Pinion, 92 Utah 255, 67 P.2d 265 (1937); (marriage measured by reference to date of filing and no separate date of separation was mentioned).

38. *Cf.* Johl v. United States, *supra*, note 32.

39. Nelson v. Nelson, 114 Ariz. 369, 560 P.2d 1276 (1977).

40. *See* Nienow v. Nienow, 268 S.C. 161, 232 S.E.2d 504 (1977).

alimony award.[41] Instead, brevity is only one of many factors considered by courts in awarding alimony. A typical recitation of relevant factors appears in *Aguire v. Aguire*[42] where the Connecticut Supreme Court summarized the Connecticut provisions:

> [The] court . . . shall consider the length of the marriage, the causes for the annulment, dissolution of the marriage or legal separation, the age, health, station, occupation, amount and sources of income, vocational skills, employability, estate and needs of each of the parties. . . .[43]

The frequency with which appellate courts cite lists of factors has led one court to conclude that in awarding alimony a trial court should consider almost everything which has a legitimate bearing on present and prospective matters relating to lives of both parties.[44]

While appellate courts have little difficulty in listing factors, they rarely comment on the weight to be given to the different factors. One commentator, reflecting upon the general failure of appellate courts to analyze the application of the factors said: "[e]xception cannot be taken to such generalities, but unless their application to the facts of specific cases is known, appraisal of the actual utilization of the factors recited is impossible."[45] The failure of the appellate courts to explain the relative importance of the criteria in short marriage cases has often led to harsh results.[46] A close examination reveals that when reviewing alimony orders, courts repeatedly stress certain factors, the most important of which is the financial circumstances of the parties. The courts have taken two approaches in analyzing the importance of financial circumstances.

---

41. At least one case has suggested that too much emphasis on the fact that the marriage is short may be an abuse of discretion. In Aguire v. Aguire, 171 Conn. 312, 370 A.2d 948 (1976), the court said:

> [T]he duration of a marriage is but one factor, and to hold that it is determinative would attach to that single factor a significance not intended by the legislature.

While in Connecticut, alimony awards are controlled by a statute modelled after the Uniform Marriage And Divorce Act § 307, Alternative A [hereinafter cited as U.M.D.A.] (*See* CONN. GEN. STAT. ANN. §§ 46-50 (Supp. 1975)), the concept expressed by *Aguire* is equally applicable to jurisdictions where alimony is to be awarded after considering a series of factors developed by case law rather than by statute.

42. Aguire v. Aguire, 171 Conn. 312, 370 A.2d 948 (1976).

43. *Id.* at 313, 370 A.2d at 949.

44. *See* Lamborn v. Lamborn, 80 C.A. 494, 251 P.943 ( ); Cooper v. Cooper, 269 C.A.2d 6, 74 Cal. Rptr. 439 (1969).

45. Cooey, *supra,* note 9.

46. *See, e.g.,* Hempel v. Hempel, 225 Minn. 287, 30 N.W.2d 594 (1948) (husband earning $7,500 per year obligated to maintain thirty year old wife of four days according to the husband's ability to pay); Astor v. Astor, 89 So. 2d 645 (1956) (wife entitled to same standard of living as husband after a marriage of six weeks which the trial court found was a marriage motivated by the wife's greed).

A. *Significance of Financial Circumstances*

1. THE MINORITY VIEW

The minority approach focuses on the relative equality of the financial circumstances of the parties. Where the financial situation of both the parties is approximately equal, no alimony will be awarded. One case adopting this approach is *McEachnie v. McEachnie*,[47] in which the court reversed an alimony order of $50 per month for the wife after a six-year marriage, noting that the wife's earnings were $279.37 per month while the husband's were $389 a month.[48] In *Howard v. Howard*,[49] the Kentucky Court of Appeals emphasized the similar circumstances of the parties in affirming the trial court's refusal to award periodic alimony after the parties lived together for seventy-six days:

> Both parties here are young [husband 27, wife 23] and in good health. Their family circumstances are similar. They have about the same amount of formal education. Both will be able to labor and earn money in the future if they so desire.[50]

The court found no abuse of discretion in a lump-sum alimony order of $400.

Where examination reveals a great disparity in the financial circumstances of the spouses, courts have held that this disparity outweighs the importance of the recipient's ability to be self-supporting. The clearest example of this reasoning is in *Nienow v. Nienow*,[51] where the trial court awarded the wife $15,000 lump sum alimony after a marriage of fourteen months. The husband, although retired, had a net worth of more than $4 million.[52] The court stated that the wife was "relatively young, in good health, and capable of self-support."[53] Nevertheless, the court held the award "unreasonable" in light of the wife's accustomed standard of living, the disparity between the parties' wealth, and their respective earning capacities,"[54] and sent the case back to the trial court for a

---

47. 216 A.2d 169 (1966).

48. *Id.* at 171. *See also* Underwood v. Underwood, 55 A.D.2d 1016, 391 N.Y.S.2d 213 (1977) (wife earned $9,000 per year and the husband earned $13,000 per year).

49. 314 Ky. 685, 236 S.W.2d 932 (1951).

50. *Id.* at 687, 236 S.W.2d at 933.

51. 268 S.C. 161, 232 S.E.2d 504 (1977).

52. *Id.* at __, 232 S.E.2d at 509.

53. *Id.* at __, 232 S.E.2d at 509. The opinion did not disclose any specific information as to either the wife's assets or her ability to be self-supporting.

54. *Id.* at __, 232 S.E.2d at 510.

determination of "reasonable alimony."[55] In *McGough v. McGough*,[56] the court affirmed an order of $300 per month permanent alimony following a four and one-half year marriage. At the time of the marriage, the husband had a net worth of $550,000, while the wife's assets amounted to $15,000. The husband earned between $24,000 and $40,000 annually while the wife only earned $15,000 a year. The court ruled that the recipient spouse was entitled to maintain the marital standard of living, stating that "a monthly alimony award of $300 was not unreasonable in light of the Defendant's substantial net worth and annual earnings."[57]

Under the minority view, where there is a significant disparity in financial circumstances the court will attempt through an alimony award to maintain the recipient spouse in the standard of living he or she has become accustomed to, irrespective of the length of the marriage.[58] The potential for abuse in using this approach is enormous. A short-term marriage even if mercenary[59] or a marriage of convenience will result in a life-time pension. Under the minority view, the recipient spouse in a fourteen-month marriage[60] is in the same position as a recipient spouse following a fourteen-year marriage who has contributed by her industry at home and by raising the children of the marriage.[61] The length of the marriage is really of little consequence and other factors such as age also seem to have little, if any, effect on the result.[62]

A persuasive argument for rejecting this minority view is expressed in *Gordon v. Gordon*[63] where the court held that an award of $1,000 per week for five hundred and twenty one weeks was an abuse of discretion after a marriage of only sixteen months. The

55. *Id.* at __, 232 S.E.2d at 511.
56. 249 N.W.2d 885 (1977).
57. 249 N.W.2d at 889.
58. *See* Hempel v. Hempel, 225 Minn. 287, 30 N.W.2d 594 (1948) (court rejected husband's argument that 30-year-old wife of four days should either support herself or be supported by him according to the standard of living of the wife before the marriage, characterizing the agreement as "brutal and degrading." Hempel, *supra,* at 292, 30 N.W.2d at 598.
59. *See, e.g.,* Astor v. Astor, 89 So. 2d 645 (1956) (trial court found the marriage to be motivated by wife's greed).
60. *See, e.g.,* Nienow v. Nienow, 268 S.C. 161, 232 S.E.2d 504 (1977).
61. *See, e.g.,* Lacey v. Lacey, 25 Wis.2d 378, 173 N.W.2d 142 (1970).
62. *Compare* Nienow v. Nienow, 268 S.C. 161, 232 S.E.2d 504 (1977) *with* McGough v. McGough, 249 N.W.2d 885 (1977) (wife was 47 years old). *See also* Hempel v. Hempel, 225 Minn. 287, 30 N.W.2d 594 (1948) (wife was 30 years old).
63. 335 So. 2d 321 (1976).

court pointed out that the wife was only thirty-three, was in good health and had employable skills,[64] and criticized disparity of wealth or income as controlling factors in awarding alimony after a short marriage:

> The husband's ability to pay (as reflected by an estimated net worth of $13,000,000) is unassailable; likewise irrefutable are the needs of the wife. . . . But there is not necessarily an ordained equality between these two factors, i.e., enormity of the ability to pay does not dictate a corresponding need to receive an amount commensurate with such ability to pay.[65] (Footnotes omitted.)

From a footnote from *Kahn v. Kahn,*[66] the court quoted the following language:

> We do not construe the marriage status once achieved, as conferring on the former wife of a ship-wrecked marriage the right to live a life of veritable ease with no effort and little incentive on her part to apply such talent as she may possess to making her own way.[67]

The court in discussing standard of living during the marriage said:

> [The] standard of living established by the parties during the (brief) marriage does not serve to bolster such an award.[68]

While the *Gordon* court offered sound criticism of the minority view, its failure to set forth the criteria which should have been applied by the lower court is unfortunate.

2. THE MAJORITY VIEW

The majority view focuses upon the ability of the demanding spouse to become self-supporting. This approach awards alimony "to give the spouse time to make a transition to a new life but prevent an able-bodied spouse from living off the labors of the former spouse."[69] The relative financial circumstances of the parties is immaterial.[70] A good example of the majority view appears in *Berry v. Berry,*[71] where the court affirmed an order of $150 per month for one year plus one-half of the husband's net earnings for two years[72]

---

64. *Id.* at 322.
65. *Id.* at 322.
66. 78 So. 2d 367 (1955).
67. *Id.* at 368, *quoted with approval in* Gordon v. Gordon, 335 So. 2d at 322 note 2.
68. Gordon v. Gordon, 335 So. 2d 321, 322 (1976).
69. Nelson v. Nelson, 114 Ariz. 369, 560 P.2d 1276 (1977).
70. *Contrast* Nienow v. Nienow, 268 S.C. 161, 232 S.E.2d 504 (1977).
71. 117 C.A.2d 624, 256 P.2d 646 (1953).
72. *Id.* at 633, 256 P.2d at 652.

following a six-year marriage. The court noted that the wife "is an able-bodied woman, 46 years of age, and a competent stenographic secretary. Before her marriage she had been steadily employed. . . ."[73]

In *Nelson v. Nelson*,[74] the court found no abuse of discretion in an alimony order of $400 per month for six months following a fifteen-month marriage.[75] Though the wife was 47 years old and her bookkeeping skills had been lost to some extent, she testified she was in good mental and physical condition, she was taking a refresher course to improve her skills, and she expected to be able to obtain employment.[76]

The courts using the majority view as exemplified by *Berry* and *Nelson* order alimony only in an amount and for a period necessary for the recipient to make the transition to an adequate single life, irrespective of the obligor's ability to pay more support[77] and irrespective of the marital standard of living.[78] In assessing the recipient's ability to become self-supporting, however, several subsidiary factors become material and may affect the court's final alimony order. Foremost among these factors is the presence of minor children.

A. *Presence of Minor Children in the Custody of the Recipient.* In *Nelson*,[79] the court said that the wife "had no child who required her presence at home."[80] In *Oppenheimer v. Oppenheimer*[81] the same Arizona court affirmed a declining alimony order[82] which was to continue until the youngest child was emancipated[83] after a marriage of only forty months. In *Oppenheimer*, the husband argued that the wife had two master's degrees, one in Spanish and one in

---

73. *Id.*
74. 114 Ariz. 369, 560 P.2d 1276 (1977).
75. *Id.* at 373, 560 P.2d at 1280.
76. *Id.*
77. *See* Berry v. Berry, 117 C.A.2d 624, 256 P.2d 646 (1953) (although facts showed the husband was the owner of three businesses and several parcels of real estate, court ordered rehabilitative alimony).
78. *Id.*
79. Nelson v. Nelson, 114 Ariz. 369, 560 P.2d 1276 (1977).
80. *Id.* at 373, 560 P.2d at 1280.
81. 22 Ariz. App. 238, 526 P.2d 762 (1974).
82. *Id.* at 240, 526 P.2d at 766. The order of the court was $475 per month for two years, $400 per month for the next thirteen years, and $200 per month for the last two years.
83. *Id.*

English, and that if she were employed, she would earn $8,000 a year.[84] The court rejected his argument:

> The trial court could well have found that [the wife's] earning potential, while great, was too speculative. Particularly is this true where the evidence indicated that [the wife] did not intend to seek full-time employment until the children were enrolled in school. . . .
>
> Admittedly, little or no time is necessary for [the wife] to acquire the education needed in her field. But no one factor is conclusive in measuring the amount of maintenance. Facts which mitigate the importance of this consideration are that [the wife] desires to stay at home with her children until they are old enough to attend school and that the job market in [the wife's] fields is limited now, not to mention what they may be in the future.[85]

Even where the minor children are not the product of the marriage but were born during the wife's first marriage, the rationale of *Oppenheimer* has been applied.[86] This result is consistent with the majority approach to self-sufficiency, since the presence of minor children in the custody of the recipient spouse is a fact with direct bearing on her employability regardless of who fathered the child.

B. *Health.* A second subsidiary factor is the demanding spouse's health. The principle case dealing with this issue is *Jernigan v. Jernigan*.[87] There, the wife suffered from a plethora of ailments:

> Prior to the marriage her left breast had been completely removed because of cancer. . . .Since the marriage she has had a cancerous growth removed from her right breast and a nerve removed from one toe. She suffers from degenerative arthritis of both knees, lymphodema of the left arm which causes swelling and requires her to wear specially made clothing, and she has high blood pressure. At the time of the trial she was about to undergo surgery to remove her gall bladder.[88]

The court noted that prior to her mastectomy the wife had been employed as a clerical worker at a hospital earning $5,000 a year, but concluded that she had not worked since the mastectomy and was now "permanently and totally disabled."[89] The court affirmed the trial court's allowance of $200 a month permanent alimony although the marriage lasted only three and one-half years:

> [*e*]*ven though the parties were* married for only a short time, [the wife] has been in poor health for most of that time and will apparently need substantial

---

84. *Id.* at 242, 526 P.2d at 766.
85. *Id.*
86. *See* Luithle v. Luithle, 23 Wash. 2d 494, 161 P.2d 152 (1945). *But see* Zeller v. Zeller, 195 Kan. 452, 407 P.2d 478 (1965) (wife received alimony for only one year).
87. 344 So. 2d 778 (1977).
88. *Id.* at 779.
89. *Id.*

> and continuing medical care in the future. She has little prospect of future employment because of her disability.[90] (emphasis supplied)

The poor health of the recipient does not mandate permanent alimony where earning capacity is not affected. In *Zeller v. Zeller*,[91] the wife, a graduate student at the University of Kansas, expected to earn a master's degree in anthropology and a doctorate in psychology. Prior to the marriage she received psychiatric treatment; after the marriage she was treated at the Menninger Clinic for psychiatric problems. The court found that she would require psychiatric care in the future and affirmed the trial court's order for alimony of $300 a month for one year;[92] although there was no evidence showing that her need for psychiatric care diminished her ability to be self-sufficient. The courts have held that a mere claim by the demanding spouse that she is "not [in] very good health" without specification[93] and corroboration[94] is illusory.

C. *Age*. A third subsidiary factor is age. No case has been found where age alone compelled an award of alimony. Courts often mention age, but its bearing on alimony in short-term marriages usually occurs when there is a claim of ill health.[95]

In *Grimes*,[96] the parties married at a late age, the marriage was a short one, and the court refused to order permanent alimony in spite of the wife's age:

> We thoroughly agree with the argument of the [husband] that the *brevity* of their marriage should be considered in determining the amount of the alimony. Especially is this so where the parties come under the category of mature citizens with no hope of having a family, where in many instances, the parties are lonely and searching for companionship.[97]

D. *Standard of Living*. The final subsidiary factor is standard of living. The majority view does not usually require the obligor to

---

90. *Id.* at 780.
91. 195 Kan. 452, 407 P.2d 478 (1965).
92. *Id.* at 461, 407 P.2d at 485.
93. *See* Pinion v. Pinion, 92 Utah 255, 257, 67 P.2d 265, 267 (1937).
94. *See* Schulman v. Schulman, 558 P.2d 525, 531 (1976).
95. *See, e.g.*, Jernigan v. Jernigan, 344 So. 2d 778 (1977) (court referred to age of the wife but the thrust of the opinion was that the wife was unemployable due to health). *See also* Borowitz v. Borowitz, 19 Ill. App. 3d 176, 311 N.E.2d 292 (1974) (court mentioned wife's age but relied on the fact that the wife was untrained for work rather than upon her age). Where the demanding spouse is young, the court is less likely to award alimony. *See* Pinion v. Pinion, 92 Utah 255, 257, 67 P.2d 265, 267 (1937) (dictum). *See also* Howard v. Howard, 314 Ky. 697, 236 S.W.2d 933 (1951) (court emphasized youth of the parties).
96. Grimes v. Grimes, 472 S.W.2d 477 (1971).
97. *Id.* at 478.

maintain the recipient at the standard of living to which she has become accustomed during the marriage.[98] In *Pinion*,[99] a four-year marriage, the court stated:

> The fact that [the parties] lived on $160 a month, plus what [the husband] spent out of his savings, gives the best idea of the standard of living. He would not be obliged *in this sort of a marriage* to keep her for the duration of her life to this standard.[100] (emphasis supplied).

The emphasized phrase from *Pinion* was a reference to the fact that the marriage lasted only four years. Forcing the obligor to continue maintenance at the marital standard of living has also been criticized in *Borowitz*,[101] a two and one-half year marriage, where the court said:

> We note that this fact [(the recent) emancipation of women socially and economically] has recently led courts to criticize the general rule that a husband is responsible for maintaining his wife at a standard of living to which she became accustomed during marriage.
>
> In *Volid v. Volid, supra*, the court commented:
>
> When the rules regarding the husband's duty of support were first enunciated, the roles of a husband and wife were more rigid and defined. The husband worked and brought income into the family while the wife maintained and managed the household. The woman generally did not seek outside employment, partly because 'her place was in the home,' and partly because few opportunities for meaningful employment were available. Married women nowadays are increasingly developing career skills and successfully entering the employment market. Where a woman is trained, healthy, and employable, and where a woman's efforts have not contributed to her husband's wealth or earning potential, the necessity for an alimony award upon breakup of the marriage is not great. (citation omitted).
>
> We are aware that these comments do not fit perfectly the situation presented in the instant case, however, there are other cases embodying a similar point of view that also articulate exceptions to the general rule that a wife should be supported at the same standard of living she was accustomed to during her marriage. *Vanderbilt v. Vanderbilt* (citations omitted) is a divorce similar to the instant case, in that there was evidence that the parties, while married, had travelled and entertained extensively, becoming accustomed to a lavish standard of living. In determining the amount of alimony to be awarded to the wife the court stated that although the wife would not be limited to only such sum as would prevent her from becoming a public charge, she was on the other hand, no longer privileged or required, as

98. *Contrast* Hempel v. Hempel, 225 Minn. 287, 30 N.W.2d 594 (1948); Nienow v. Nienow, 268 S.C. 161, 232 S.E.2d 504 (1977); McGough v. McGough, 249 N.W.2d 885 (1977) (wife entitled to be kept in the standard of living she experienced during the marriage.)

99. Pinion v. Pinion, 92 Utah 255, 67 P.2d 265 (1937).

100. *Id.* at 257, 67 P.2d at 267.

101. Borowitz v. Borowitz, 19 Ill. App. 3d 176, 311 N.E.2d 292 (1974).

> she had been while married to her husband, to accompany him on his extensive trips and voyages and in his lavish entertainment and mode of living, all of which necessitated large expenditures for her clothes, travel and hotels. The court concluded that she was not entitled to continue to be maintained in the standard of luxurious life and travel which she enjoyed during the marriage.[102]

The court then held that while the continued payment of $16,000 a year to the wife after a two and one-half year marriage was unjustified, a total termination of support was an abuse of discretion.[103]

Custody of the parties' minor children will usually mandate the marital standard of living in fixing alimony. A good illustration is *Oppenheimer*,[104] where the parties were married for only forty months but the court predicated the award of alimony on the marital standard of living.[105] The unarticulated premise of cases like *Oppenheimer* is that the court does not want the children to suffer any lessening of their standard because of the differences between their parents. Absent minor children, the courts following the majority approach do not require that the demanding spouse be maintained at the marital standard.[106] Perhaps the explanation for this attitude appears in *Borowitz*: "Obviously, the longer a woman has lived with a man and performed the functions which one normally expects from a wife, the greater is her claim to support."[107]

B. *Significance of Contribution*

A major condition frequently emphasized by appellate courts is contribution to the marriage. Evidence of a contribution may influence the court towards increasing the alimony award. The form of the contribution is generally material:[108] *Prosser v. Prosser*[109] is a

---

102. *Id.* at 182, 311 N.E.2d at 298.

103. *Id.* at 183, 311 N.E.2d at 298.

104. Oppenheimer v. Oppenheimer, 22 Ariz. App. 238, 526 P.2d 762 (1974).

105. *Id.* The court found that the trial court's order approximated the portion of the living expenses of the family during the marriage which could be allocated to the wife. *Id.* at 242, 526 P.2d at 766.

106. *See, e.g.,* Nelson v. Nelson, 114 Ariz. 369, 373, 560 P.2d 1276, 1280 (1977) (no children in wife's custody to prevent her from working).

107. Borowitz v. Borowitz, 19 Ill. App.3d 176, 311 N.E.2d 292, 297 (1974).

108. *See, e.g.,* Prosser v. Prosser, 156 Neb. 629, 57 N.W.2d 173 (1953) (supported husband during his education and helped him in his courses); Putnam v. Putnam, 77 ASA 16, 358 N.E.2d 837 (1977) (wife liable on mortgage note with husband); Tomlinson v. Tomlinson, 352 N.E.2d 785 (1976) (wife ran husband's business for one year while husband recovered from heart attack). *Cf.* Schulman v. Schulman, 92 Nev. 707, 558 P.2d 525 (1976) (wife's contribution to husband's business by designing advertisements considered by court is

classic example. At the time of the separation the wife was in her twenties and in good health; there were no children of the marriage and the wife was clearly able to support herself, having worked to support both parties during the first four years of the marriage. The trial court awarded the wife a substantial portion of the assets of the parties, but the appellate court reversed the trial court's award of $500 lump sum alimony and increased it to $6,500 payable at the rate of $100 per month for five and one-half years.[110] The appellate court emphasized the major contribution which the wife had made during the marriage. She had worked during the marriage to support the husband while he studied accounting, and the evidence also showed that she assisted the defendant in many ways with his studies and work at the university. She helped him with his job of grading papers and keeping records. She helped him with his lessons, when she could, by preparing his statistics and drawing statistical maps.[111] The court decided that by her contribution the wife had earned a claim to alimony from the husband:

> The conclusion to be drawn from the facts in the case is plain. The plaintiff had a good position at the time of the marriage. The defendant had no position or property. The parties decided that the best way to success was for the defendant to obtain a college education. This was successfully undertaken. Plaintiff worked and made the contributions herein before set forth. The defendant's earning capacity was small until he finished college and secured a position and then a partnership in an accounting firm. It is clear that plaintiff made a large investment in defendant's future with the thought no doubt that it was of joint interest to the future of both. But as the defendant's success mounted and he began to assume a higher station in the community, his interest in the plaintiff cooled and he sought the society of another. That this

---

dividing community property); Carson v. Carson, 50 Ha. 182, 436 P.2d 7 (1967) (wife's contribution consisted of being frugal, making her own clothes, refinishing second hand furniture for the house, playing a social role to help her husband in his Washington job and working without compensation in the husband's family business); Pinion v. Pinion, 92 Utah 255, 67 P.2d 265 (1937) (in dictum if the wife had contributed to the husband's accumulation of wealth, she would be entitled to a substantial portion of it.

On the other hand, by providing the wife with support or by raising her standard of living, the husband has contributed to the wife, and this contribution will be considered in the husband's favor in determining what, if any, alimony is to be given to the wife. *See, e.g.*, Billingsley v. Billingsley, 315 Mich. 417, 24 N.W.2d 96 (1946); Tomlinson v. Tomlinson, 352 N.E.2d 785 (1976) (fact that husband had improved wife's standard of living during brief marriage considered by court in determining alimony); Pinion v. Pinion, 92 Utah 255, 67 P.2d 265 (1937) (court considered fact that husband had supported wife during short marriage and she had had the benefit of expensive medical care paid for by husband in favor of husband). *See also* Underwood v. Underwood, 55 A.D.2d 1016, 391 N.Y.S.2d 213 (1977).

109. 156 Neb. 629, 57 N.W.2d 173 (1953).

110. *Id.* at 634, 57 N.W.2d at 176.

111. *Id.* at 630, 57 N.W.2d at 174.

> is true stands undisputed in this record. The evidence also shows that this plaintiff was without the semblance of fault and that the divorce was due solely to the conduct of the defendant. The latter appears to have treated the marriage as one of convenience and, when his schooling was completed and his success apparently assured, he was willing to cast her aside and bestow his affections upon one who made no contribution whatever to the success that he now enjoys. *We point out that his wife had a right to expect that in the years to come she would share in the benefits derived from the training and ability of the defendant, which she literally helped to bring about.*[112] (Emphasis supplied.)

The court also ruled that the "social standing, comforts, and luxuries of life which the wife probably would have enjoyed"[113] were to be considered in awarding alimony. The court raised the alimony order despite the fact that the recipient was clearly able to support herself without any support from her husband. The *Prosser* situation is common to cases involving young professionals.

The recipient's contribution takes different forms. In *Tomlinson v. Tomlinson,*[114] during a four-year marriage the wife did housework, and for one year she operated the husband's business for him while he was recovering from a heart attack. The appeals court found that during the marriage the net assets of the husband had increased by $12,000, and affirmed the trial court's order of $10,400 in lump-sum alimony.[115] The court reasoned that the award probably represented the trial court's judgment as to the portion of the increase in assets attributable to the wife's contribution.[116]

Failure by the recipient to contribute has also served to justify a small alimony award.[117] A good illustration is *Ferguson v. Ferguson,*[118] with a one-year marriage, where the court reversed an alimony award in the amount of $25,000 and in doing so stated:

> The [wife] in the instant case brought no property into the marriage relationship, nor does the evidence show that she contributed anything to the acqui-

---

112. *Id.* at 632, 57 N.W.2d at 175.

113. *Id.* at 633, 57 N.W.2d at 176. *Contrast* Berry v. Berry, 117 C.A.2d 624, 256 P.2d 646 (1953) (semble); Gordon v. Gordon, 335 So. 2d 321 (Fla. App. 1976).

114. 352 N.E.2d 785 (1976).

115. *Id.* at 792.

116. *Id.*

117. *See, e.g.*, Schulman v. Schulman, Adv. 8339 558 P.2d 525 (1976); Howard v. Howard, 314 Ky. 697, 236 S.W.2d 933 (1951) (no showing that the wife contributed to the accumulation of the husband's assets). *But see* Nienow v. Nienow, 268 S.C. 161, 232 S.E.2d 504 (1977) (wife made no contribution to accumulation of husband's wealth but disparity of income and assets justified alimony).

118. 125 In.A. 596, 125 N.E.2d 816 (1955).

> sition of property during the time the parties lived together as husband and wife, not even to the extent of mutually helping appellant in the normal duties of a wife during much of the short period of the marriage. The evidence bears the unmistakable imprint of a lack of conjugal relations during much of the period the parties were married, for which the court may have properly held the [husband] at fault. However, such marriage, which existed for less than a year was, for the most part, a marriage in name only.[119]

A failure by the recipient to contribute to the marital relation may influence the court in a short marriage case to reduce what she might otherwise receive as alimony. In *Plageman v. Plageman,*[120] the appellate court in affirming the trial court's award of $100 per month for one year instead of permanent alimony stated:

> As we have observed the marriage was of brief [two years, six months] duration and [the wife] did not contribute by her industry or otherwise to the accumulation of property by her husband. This is not the situation appearing in cases cited by [the wife] where property of the husband was accumulated over a period of years by the joint efforts of the parties.[121] (Citations omitted.)

C. *Significance of Financial Loss Due to Marriage*

In evaluating alimony orders following short marriages, the courts frequently deal with financial loss because of the marriage. Financial loss by the recipient usually consists of loss of income from a trust,[122] alimony from a prior marriage,[123] social security[124] or pension benefits.[125] Other forms of loss are an interruption in career,[126] the loss of skills due to separation from work,[127] and misappropriation by the obligor of the recipient's assets entrusted to him.[128]

Where the recipient can show that she has lost a right to receipt of income due to the marriage, a strong case can be made for compensating her. In *Cooper v. Cooper,*[129] a two-year marriage, the wife was the beneficiary of a trust created by her deceased first husband, prior to the marriage, which paid her $516 monthly until her death or remarriage. The trial court, finding that the husband was

119. *Id.* at 604, 125 N.E.2d at 819.
120. 79 S.D.221, 110 N.W.2d 337 (1961).
121. *Id.* at 226, 110 N.W.2d at 339.
122. *See, e.g.,* Cooper v. Cooper, 269 C.A.2d 6, 74 Cal. Rptr. 439 (1969).
123. *See, e.g.,* O'Neill v. O'Neill, 147 C.A.2d 596, 305 P.2d 1003 (1957).
124. *See, e.g.,* Plageman v. Plageman, 79 S.D. 221, 110 N.W.2d 337 (1961).
125. *See, e.g.,* Nelson v. Nelson, 246 Iowa 760, 68 N.W.2d 746 (1955).
126. *See, e.g.,* Pinion v. Pinion, 92 Utah 255, 67 P.2d 265 (1937).
127. *See, e.g.,* Nelson v. Nelson, 114 Ariz. 369, 560 P.2d 1276 (1977).
128. *See, e.g.,* McGough v. McGough, 249 N.W.2d 885 (1977).
129. 74 Cal. Rptr. 439 (1969).

aware of these facts when he married the wife and "accepted his responsibility to support,"[130] gave the wife full compensation for her loss and entered an order for $500 a month permanent alimony.[131]

On the other hand, in *Plageman v. Plageman,*[132] a two and one-half year marriage, the wife lost social security benefits by her remarriage. The court rejected the wife's claim that she was entitled to permanent alimony and affirmed an alimony order of $100 a month for one year. The court held

> that, while it was a fact to consider that the wife had voluntarily relinquished her right to payment of social security and other benefits on marriage, this fact did not obligate the husband to compensate her for her loss.[133]

As is evident form *Cooper* and *Plageman,* the courts are divided on who, upon a divorce, should bear the responsibility for financial loss due to the marriage.

D. *Marital Misconduct*

Evidence of marital misconduct, while often mentioned by the courts as a factor supporting the result, rarely actually affects the result. Rather, cases referring to the misconduct of one party usually include this factor as a make-weight element. In *Jernigan*[134] the court noted, among other items it considered in ordering permanent alimony to the wife, the misconduct of the husband. Yet the case was clearly decided not on the husband's misconduct but on the poor health and total disability of the wife. In *Prosser,*[135] while the court referred to the husband's adulterous relationship, the thrust of the court's opinion was based on the evidence of the wife's contribution to the marriage and to the husband's earning capacity. Indeed, a case may be reversed if the court feels that the order was influenced too strongly by the conduct of the parties.[136]

However, in certain situations evidence of misconduct may be material in an alimony award following a short marriage.[137] In *Pi-*

130. *Id.* at 442.
131. *Id.* at 442.
132. 79 S.D. 221, 110 N.W.2d 337 (1961).
133. *Id.* at 225, 110 N.W.2d at 337.
134. Jernigan v. Jernigan, 344 So. 2d 778 (Ala. Civ. App. 1977).
135. Prosser v. Prosser, 156 Neb. 629, __, 57 N.W.2d 173, 175 (1953).
136. *See* Putnam v. Putnam, 77 ASA 16 __, 358 N.E.2d 837 (1977).
137. At least some states prohibit consideration of conduct of the parties in making alimony orders. *See, e.g.,* Arizona, California, Colorado, Oregon, Washington and Iowa.

nion,[138] the court suggested in dictum that "[i]f there has been brutality or real cruelty, punitive elements enter and (the recipient) would be entitled to have that taken into consideration as a partial compensation for what she suffered."[139]

Conclusion

Length of the marriage is a critical consideration in awarding alimony in short marriage cases. While there is agreement that the beginning of the marriage is the date of the ceremony,[140] there is no agreement on termination date.[141] For the reasons discussed, the date of physical separation is the most logical definition of termination.[142]

After length of marriage has been determined, two principal approaches are used in making alimony awards. The minority approach, because it focuses on standard of living and financial circumstances to the exclusion of other criteria, offers too much potential for abuse.[143] The majority approach, while less mechanistic, provides sufficient flexibility in its comprehensive consideration of relevant criteria to assist in obtaining just results. A uniform approach in awarding alimony is desirable if unjustified disparity in results is to be avoided.

---

138. Pinion v. Pinion, 92 Utah 255, 67 P.2d 265 (1937).
139. *Id.* at 260, 67 P.2d at 267.
140. See text accompanying notes, 24-26 *supra.*
141. See text accompanying notes, 26-27 *supra.*
142. See text accompanying notes, 30-32 *supra.*
143. See text accompanying notes, 61-71 *supra.*

Property Rights of De Facto Spouses Including Thoughts on the Value of Homemakers' Services*

CAROL S. BRUCH†

Introduction

Unstructured domestic unions have become a widespread contemporary phenomenon.[1] People who would not have considered such a relationship ten years ago, now openly cohabit without marriage. Some have roots in countries and cultures that have long accepted informal families,[2] some prefer a personal and private commitment to the shortcomings they perceive in traditional marriage,[3] and some are no doubt influenced by the increased social acceptability of such unions. Whatever the implications for the institution of marriage, it is clear that nonmarital cohabitation

---

*This article is an outgrowth of an amicae curiae brief submitted to the California Supreme Court in the case of *Marvin v. Marvin,* discussed in note 13 *infra.* For their encouragement and considerable assistance in these efforts, the author expresses her gratitude to Professor Brigitte Bodenheimer and Robert D. Bacon of the School of Law, University of California, Davis. For their comments on the manuscript, thanks go to Professors Edgar Bodenheimer and Lenore Weitzman.

†Acting Professor of Law, University of California, Davis.

1. Estimates based on 1970 and 1960 census figures suggest that the number of unmarried couples living together increased eight-fold during the 1960s. Note, *In re Cary: A Judicial Recognition of Illicit Cohabitation,* 25 HASTINGS L.J. 1226 (1974) [hereinafter cited as HASTINGS NOTE]; 2 U.S. BUREAU OF THE CENSUS, 1970 CENSUS OF POPULATION, PERSONS BY FAMILY CHARACTERISTICS, table 11, at 4B; 2 U.S. BUREAU OF THE CENSUS, 1960 CENSUS OF POPULATION, PERSONS BY FAMILY CHARACTERISTICS, table 15, at 4B.

2. *See generally* Pinnolis, *Illicit Cohabitation: The Impact of the* Vallera *and* Keene *Cases on the Rights of the Meretricious Spouse,* 6 U.C.D.L. REV. 354, 367-69 (1973), and the authorities there cited.

3. *See* Weitzman, *Legal Regulation of Marriage: Tradition and Change,* 62 CALIF. L. REV. 1169, 1197-200, 1235-36 (1974) [hereinafter cited as Weitzman].

is both increasingly prevalent and increasingly being recognized as a theoretically defensible lifestyle.[4]

The presence of such de facto families, however, poses a serious challenge to current legal doctrine. Not only are the members of these units diverse; equally variegated are the relationships they establish and the needs that they seek to fulfill within them. Surely some of these unions are entered into with quasi-marital intent (much as is recognized in some jurisdictions through the doctrine of common law marriage);[5] others are formed by parties who do not express their long-term intentions; and yet others may entail private commitments to a permanent union outside the structure of traditional marriage. Only relatively rarely are couples sophisticated enough to enter express agreements that specify in detail their personal and economic expectations. Yet whatever the original intent, many nonmarital unions become relatively stable relationships, frequently outlasting present-day ceremonial marriages.[6] However, when any of life's misfortunes occur—loss of employment

---

4. J. Galbraith, Economics and the Public Purpose 235 (1973); *see* Weitzman, *supra* note 3, at 1235-36, and authorities there cited. A perhaps serendipitous result of the change in lifestyles is suggested by a recent Common Market study; when researchers evaluated the "general feeling of happiness" by age, sex, level of education, size of locality, income and family situation, they concluded that the most significant variable appears to be family situation, and that people "living as married" claim to be happy far more frequently than any others. Commission of the European Communities, European Men and Women 151-154 (1975). A study of 51 couples in the midwestern United States conducted by sociologists at the University of Utah, however, suggests the contrary conclusion. *Unmarried Couples Not As Happy,* San Francisco Chronicle, April 24, 1976, at 3, col. 4.

5. *See generally* Weyrauch, *Informal and Formal Marriage,* 28 U. Chi. L. Rev. 88 (1960) (noting that every state without a common law marriage doctrine has been forced to create one or more "escape strategies" to enable its courts to reach just results in individual cases). Legal recognition of common-law marriage may be making a comeback.

> In the Governor's conference on Marriage and the Family Unit in Tallahassee, Florida, of October 2 and 3, 1975, it was recommended . . .
>
> "8. In order to protect the interests of spouses and children with regard to property rights, probate and social security, common law marriage should be reinstated."
>
> The Florida Bar Committee on Family Law which, a few years ago, was instrumental in getting common-law marriage abolished, is now equally fervent in getting it reinstated.

Letter from Professor Walter O. Weyrauch to the author, January 8, 1976 on file with the author. *See* note 68 *infra* as to related legal developments in the state of Washington.

6. "[A]dults are marrying later and breaking up faster," according to statistics of the Bureau of the Census. San Francisco Chronicle, January 7, 1976, at 2, col. 3. The average age at which persons marry for the first time is increasing; between 1970 and 1975 the number of persons aged 25 to 34 who had never been married increased by 50 percent. During the same time period, the average duration of marriages terminated by divorce declined. *Id. Accord,* H. Ross & I. Sawhill, Time of Transition: The Growth of Families Headed by Women 18-21 (1976). Note the lengthy relationships in some of the reported cases in which parties to informal families request relief upon the relationship's termination by separation or death, *e.g.,* Keene v. Keene, 47 Cal. 2d 657, 371 P.2d 329, 21 Cal. Rptr. 593 (1962) (18 years); Estate of Atherley, 44 Cal. App. 3d 758, 119 Cal. Rptr. 41 (4th Dist. 1975) (22 years; terminated by death); Estate of Thornton, 14 Wash. App. 397, 541 P.2d 1243 (1975) (16 years; terminated by death).

or loss of health, accidental death, or the couple's separation—one of the partners may well find himself or herself in a highly vulnerable position that the couple did not foresee when the relationship began. For, like people who marry, many men and women who forego marriage have little idea of the economic consequences of their choice.

Despite the needs and equities present in litigation following such events, courts have often refused relief.[7] Clearly, however, the use of labels such as "meretricious" and "illicit" no longer deter large numbers of people from entering these unions in place of marriage. As a result the law can no longer plausibly ignore these relationships and the harm they may cause to one partner. Rather sound policy requires that these family forms be acknowledged to the extent necessary to prevent hardship and injustice.

The needed statutory and judicial adjustments to doctrine are in fact beginning to be made both in this country and abroad. New Hampshire, for example, relieves the problems that follow the death of one partner by providing that cohabitation for the preceding three years will allow the other party to be treated as the decedent's surviving spouse.[8] Sweden, too, follows the policy of retaining the central position of the institution of marriage in the law, but at the same time seeks to relieve hardship in cases of nonmarital cohabitation.[9] In Israel this has been accomplished through statutory provisions granting protection in specific situations to "reputed spouses."[10] Latin American countries have developed protections for partners and children of stable nonmarital unions.[11] Courts in the state of Washington have recently modified their common law doctrines to provide greater relief against unjust results in such cases,[12] and the California Supreme Court is cur-

---

7. *See* text accompanying notes 18-24 *infra.*

8. N.H. Rev. Stat. Ann. § 457:39 (1968).

9. Sundberg, *Recent Changes in Swedish Family Law,* 23 Am. J. Comp. L. 34, 38-39, 48-49 (1975).

10. Friedmann, *The "Unmarried Wife" in Israeli Law,* 2 Israel Yearbook on Human Rights 287-316 (1972).

11. Pinnolis, *Illicit Cohabitation: The Impact of the* Vallera *and* Keene *Cases on the Rights of the Meretricious Spouse,* 6 U.C.D.L. Rev. 354, 367-69 (1973), and the authorities there cited.

12. Estate of Thornton, 81 Wash. 2d 72, 499 P.2d 864 (1972), *opinion on appeal after remand,* 14 Wash. App. 397, 541 P.2d 1243 (1974); Omer v. Omer, 11 Wash. App. 386, 523 P.2d 957 (1974).

rently considering a case that raises these issues and challenges case law dating from the 1940s.[13]

The following discussion begins with an analysis of current impediments to assertions of property rights based upon nonmarital domestic relationships. Concluding that these doctrines are no longer defensible on policy grounds, the article then surveys and evaluates existing doctrinal tools in other areas of the law that might appropriately be used in the restructuring of judicial attitudes concerning de facto family relationships.[14]

Certain of the arguments advanced here have implications that extend beyond the field of nonmarital cohabitation. For example, the article is written in the context of a statutory framework like those established by community property laws or the Uniform Marriage and Divorce Act.[15] Both of these schemes treat the family

13. Marvin v. Marvin, No. L.A. 30520, ***hearing granted*** Sept. 17, 1975, ***argued*** Jan. 6, 1976 (Cal. Supreme Ct.). Michelle Triola Marvin and Lee Marvin lived together for six years. After the relationship ended Ms. Marvin sued, alleging an oral agreement under which the parties would pool property and earnings and hold themselves out as husband and wife, she would provide household services, and he would support her for life. In the alternative, she claimed property rights under a constructive trust theory. The trial court granted judgment on the pleadings to Mr. Marvin. The District Court of Appeal affirmed, in an opinion expunged from the official reports upon the Supreme Court's grant of hearing. 50 Cal. App. 3d [advance sheet] 84 (2d Dist. 1975). The court found the oral agreement unenforceable as contrary to public policy, and held that meretricious cohabitation, without more, does not create rights in the property of the other party.

The appeal questions California's longstanding doctrine established in Keene v. Keene, 57 Cal. 2d 657, 371 P.2d 329, 21 Cal. Rptr. 593 (1962), and Vallera v. Vallera, 21 Cal. 2d 681, 134 P.2d 761 (1943). Under these precedents recovery is possible only under resulting trust and express joint venture theories. Two California District Courts of Appeal recently fashioned a stronger legal remedy by adopting a strained interpretation of that state's Family Law Act. Estate of Atherley, 44 Cal. App. 3d 758, 119 Cal. Rptr. 41 (4th Dist. 1975); In re Marriage of Cary, 34 Cal. App. 3d 345, 109 Cal. Rptr. 862 (1st Dist. 1973). A justice of yet another District Court of Appeal voiced serious doubts that the doctrines of *Vallera* and *Keene* can solve today's problems in light of a clear change in social attitudes since those cases were decided. Beckman v. Mayhew, 49 Cal. App. 3d 529, 535, 122 Cal. Rptr. 604, 607-08 (3d Dist. 1975).

14. A related article that is remarkable for its continuing timeliness is Evans, *Property Interests Arising from Quasi-Marital Relations,* 9 CORNELL L.Q. 246 (1924). This article does not address tort doctrines such as deceit which may well apply if one party has made intentional misrepresentations to the other of the legal or financial consequences of a relationship. *See generally* H. VERRALL & A. SAMMIS, CASES AND MATERIALS ON CALIFORNIA COMMUNITY PROPERTY 77 (2d ed. 1971) and the cases there cited; Evans, *supra* at 249-50; *cf.* Shaw v. Shaw, [1954] 2 Q.B. 429 (C.a.) (breach of warranty where man's bigamous marriage to a putative spouse was held a warrant that he was free to marry and that she would acquire the rights of a wife).

15. UNIFORM MARRIAGE AND DIVORCE ACT § 307, Alternative A (as amended 1973), provides for the court on divorce to divide all the parties' property, including prenuptial property, regardless of the source or the form in which title is held. (The Uniform Marriage and Divorce Act, and other Uniform Laws relating to marriage and the family, are found in 9 UNIFORM LAWS ANNOTATED (West 1973 & Supp. 1975).) Indiana and Montana are to date the only states to have adopted a statute modeled on this version of the Uniform Act. IND.

as an economic unit where property acquired through the efforts of either spouse during marriage is subject to an equitable division upon termination of the marriage, regardless of the form in which title is held. In states where this is not the case, the arguments that follow might well be advanced by married homemakers who seek legislative recognition of the value of their services[16] or some share in property acquired by income-producing spouses during marriage.[17]

CODE § 31-1-11.5-11 (Burns Supp. 1975); REV. CODES OF MONT., § 48-321 (Supp. 1975).

A prior version of § 307, promulgated in 1970 and replaced in 1973, authorized the division on divorce only of property acquired by the efforts of either party during their marriage, thereby permitting a result similar to some states' community property laws. This version has been adopted in three states: COLO. REV. STAT. § 14-10-113 (1973); KY. REV. STATS. § 403.190 (Bobbs-Merrill Supp. 1974); VERNON'S ANN. MO. STATS. § 452.330 (West Supp. 1976).

16. For example, maintaining one's own household is not a form of employment covered by the Social Security system. Such a person may receive Social Security benefits only as the dependent of his or her spouse. *See* Comment, *Sex Classifications in the Social Security Benefit Structure,* 49 IND. L.J. 181, 197-99 (1973). If a couple is divorced before a wage-earner husband retires, the wife may not receive Social Security benefits on the basis of her former husband's account unless the couple had been married for at least 20 years. 42 U.S.C. § 416(d) (1970); *see* Griffiths, *Sex Discrimination in Income Security Programs,* 49 NOTRE DAME LAWYER 534, 535-36 (1974). Similar conditions exist in the social security systems of other nations. INTERNATIONAL LABOUR OFFICE, INTERNATIONAL LABOUR CONFERENCE, 60TH SESS., 1975, REPORT VII: EQUALITY OF OPPORTUNITY AND TREATMENT FOR WOMEN WORKERS 56-57 [hereinafter cited as I.L.O. REPORT].

17. *See* Foster and Freed, *Marital Property and the Chancellor's Foot—Part I,* 10 FAM. L.Q. 55 (1976). In common law property states, property acquired during marriage, including earnings, is the separate property of the spouse who acquired it. While many common law property states have made all property subject to distribution on divorce, others, including New York, have not. *See* Foster & Freed, *Marital Property Reform in New York: Partnership of Co-Equals?,* 8 FAM. L.Q. 169, 170-71 (1974) and Foster & Freed, *Economic Effects of Divorce,* 7 FAM. L.Q. 275, 278-79 & n.43 (1973) (listing states).

An example of common law courts' refusal to take household services into account in apportionment of property, even on extreme facts, is the Supreme Court of Canada's decision in Murdoch v. Murdoch, 41 D.L.R.3d 367, 13 R.F.L. 185 (Can. 1973), *noted* 20 MCGILL L.J. 308 (1974) and 6 OTTAWA L. REV. 581 (1974). Mrs. Murdoch had spent her full time for about fifteen years helping her husband operate a ranch, title to which was held in his name alone. Upon divorce, she sought a one-half interest in the ranch on a resulting trust theory, but it was denied her, the appellate court affirming the trial judge's finding that what she had done "was the work done by any ranch wife." 41 D.L.R.3d at 376, 13 R.F.L. at 194. This rule was termed "clearly anachronistic" by the Montana Supreme Court following that state's adoption of the Uniform Marriage and Divorce Act. Rogers v. Rogers, ______ Mont. ______, ______, 548 P.2d 141, 143 (1976). *See also* note 110 *infra.* A student writer has suggested finding a housewife an implied partner in her husband's business as a means of making an equitable property division in common law property states. Note, *The Implied Partnership: Equitable Alternative to Contemporary Methods of Postmarital Property Distribution,* 26 U. FLA. L. REV. 221 (1974).

The potentially inequitable results that may follow lengthy marriages in these states are possible in some community property marriages as well. In community property states where separate property may not be divided on divorce, inequitable distributions may result when the bulk of the wealth is the separate property of one spouse. *See generally* Bodenheimer, *The Community Without Community Property,* 8 CAL. WESTERN L. REV. 381 (1972).

Too, there is little in the legal or economic rationales described in this article that restricts their use to the monogamous heterosexual unit. It is true that in the context of homosexual or group living arrangements implied agreements may be somewhat less susceptible of proof, and in many states public policy may remain a defense to enforcement of established agreements. Beyond such qualifications, however, the arguments that follow apply.

I. Prior Impediments to the Use of Otherwise Standard Legal Doctrines in Cases of Nonmarital Cohabitation

Under what circumstances and theories is it appropriate to recognize property rights as between unmarried persons? Phrased in this fashion, certain aspects of the problem take on a new light. Members of an informal union historically have not enjoyed the same property rights as they would have had if there were no shared living arrangement. Instead, three major impediments have prevented the application of otherwise standard legal doctrines:

> First, cohabitation between the parties to an express or implied contract might serve to render the contract illegal and, as a consequence, unenforceable.[18]

Under California community property law, labor on one's own farm, like other labor, is held to have economic value that is by definition community property. Thus, if a married person uses his time, energy, and skill, to improve his own separate property, he has an obligation to reimburse the community for the value of the benefit he has diverted from it. Mayhood v. La Rosa, 58 Cal. 2d 498, 24 Cal. Rptr. 837, 374 P.2d 805 (1962) (*semble*), *discussed in* H. Verrall & A. Sammis, Cases and Materials on California Community Property 204 (2d ed. 1971). Similarly when the income from a farm or other business is partly the result of labor (community property) and partly the result of investment of separate property capital for the land and equipment, the income is apportioned between separate and community property, not held to be entirely separate. Estate of Neilson, 57 Cal. 2d 733, 22 Cal. Rptr. 1, 371 P.2d 745 (1962), *overruling* Estate of Pepper, 158 Cal. 619, 112 P. 62 (1910). If homemakers' services are similarly deemed to have value, a non-earning spouse in a separate property marriage ought to be credited with a community property share in the value of those services to the community. Unless the rule charging living expenses first against the community property is abandoned, however, the recognition will have little practical effect. *See* Beam v. Bank of America, 6 Cal. 3d 12, 490 P.2d 257, 98 Cal. Rptr. 137 (1971); Bodenheimer, *supra.*

Dissipation of assets poses special problems in those community property states where the husband is given management and control of his wife's earnings as well as his own. In these states a working wife's position may be more precarious if her husband is not a sound manager than if she lived in a common law property state, where her earnings would be completely under her own control. Kulzer, *Property and the Family: Spousal Protection,* 4 Rutgers Camden L.J. 195, 228-30 (1973).

18. *E.g.*, Marvin v. Marvin, 50 Cal. App. 3d [advance sheet] 84, 97-98 (2d Dist. 1975), *hg. granted,* No. L.A. 30520 (Cal. Supreme Ct., Sept. 17, 1975); Garcia v. Venegas, 106 Cal.

Second, doctrines generally applicable to arm's length business transactions were consulted, rather than those ordinarily used in noncommercial contexts.[19]

Third, courts refused to assign any economic value to the granting of personal services.[20]

Each of these factors, whatever its original merit, has produced a displacement in the development of legal doctrine in this field. As a result doctrines long since modified in the commercial field and the field of interpersonal economic transactions have remained frozen in their application to the rights of parties who cohabit without marriage.

A. *Illegality*

The most straightforward refusals to enforce express property or compensation contracts between parties to a nonmarital union reasoned that such agreements were unenforceable as illegal contracts for prostitution.[21] Although this doctrine was frequently expressed, in fact courts often strained to enforce express contracts to pool property.[22] In California, for example, until 1975 no case refused to grant relief under such an agreement on the ground that cohabitation of the contracting parties rendered it illegal.[23] Instead

---

App. 2d 364, 368, 235 P.2d 89, 92 (1st Dist. 1951) (dictum); Smith v. Smith, 255 Wisc. 96, 38 N.W.2d 12, 14 A.L.R.2d 914 (1949). *Contra,* Warner v. Warner, 76 Idaho 399, 407, 283 P.2d 931, 935-36 (1955), and cases cited. While acknowledging the general principle, the Arkansas Supreme Court granted relief on an express agreement by distinguishing cases in which the illegal relationship had terminated from those in which it was continuing. Mitchell v. Fish, 97 Ark. 444, 134 S.W. 940 (1911).

> Although a contract may be illegal, it does not follow that it is illegal or immoral for the parties to it, after its completion, to fairly settle and adjust the profits and losses which have resulted from it. The vice of the contract does not enter into such settlement.

Id. at 448, 134 S.W. at 941-42, *quoting* De Leon v. Trevino & Bro., 49 Tex. 88, 30 Am. Rep. 101 (1878). Such reasoning is no longer necessary. *See* text accompanying notes 21-30 *infra.*

19. *E.g.,* Keene v. Keene, 57 Cal. 2d 657, 664-65, 371 P.2d 329, 333, 21 Cal. Rptr. 593, 597 (1962); Garcia v. Venegas, 106 Cal. App. 2d 364, 368, 235 P.2d 89, 92 (1st Dist. 1951). *See* text accompanying notes 31-37 *infra.*

20. Keene v. Keene, 57 Cal. 2d at 668, 371 P.2d at 335-36, 21 Cal. Rptr. at 599-600. *See* text accompanying notes 38-51 *infra.*

21. *See* cases cited in note 18 *supra.*

22. *See* the cases collected at Annot., 31 A.L.R.2d 1255, 1281 (1953). *See generally* Evans, *Property Interests Arising from Quasi-Marital Relations,* 9 CORNELL L.Q. 246, 261-65 (1924).

23. Brief for Herma Hill Kay, *et al.,* as Amici Curiae at 13-23 [hereinafter cited as Kay Brief], Marvin v. Marvin, No. L.A. 30520 (Cal. Supreme Ct., *hearing granted* Sept. 17, 1975), discussing the California cases cited in note 24 *infra,* among others.

In the *Marvin* case itself, however, the trial and intermediate appellate courts concluded that the agreement between the Marvins must be distinguished because it was alleged to include among its provisions a plan for the parties to live together without the benefit of a

courts were prepared to reason that two distinct agreements had been reached by the parties: one for illicit cohabitation, the other for management by one party of all monies earned by the parties.[24]

Courts today can refuse enforcement of express compensation or pooling agreement on policy grounds only by ignoring important changes in the law concerning the regulation of adult sexual activity. Legislatures have decriminalized nonmarital sexual activity,[25] the Constitutional guarantee of sexual privacy has been extended to single people,[26] and courts have sustained parental custody rights in the nonmarital family.[27] It is clear that community mores have changed markedly in recent years and that the movement has been firmly in the direction of greater tolerance of nonmarital unions. It follows that judicial recognition of express contracts for the pooling of resources is founded upon sound policy. Just as married couples are free to delineate the nature of their ownership of property,[28] and commercial joint ventures are sustained, in states where nonmarital cohabitation is not a crime parties who choose this lifestyle should be free to regulate their financial relationships.[29]

This policy applies equally to the entire range of consensual transactions—express written and oral, implied-in-fact, and implied-in-law agreements—that may be entered into and enforced by other married and single people. Indeed, it is somewhat puzzling that the very courts that assiduously upheld express contractual

---

marriage ceremony and to hold themselves out as husband and wife. Marvin v. Marvin, 50 Cal. App. 3d [advance sheet] 84, 99-100 & n.5 (2d Dist. 1975), *hearing granted,* No. L.A. 30520, Sept. 17, 1975. The issue is now before the California Supreme Court; *see* note 13 *supra.*

24. *E.g.,* Trutalli v. Meraviglia, 215 Cal. 698, 12 P.2d 430 (1932); Barlow v. Collins, 166 Cal. App. 2d 274, 333 P.2d 64 (4th Dist. 1958); Bridges v. Bridges, 125 Cal. App. 2d 359, 360, 270 P.2d 69, 70 (3d Dist. 1954); Profit v. Profit, 117 Cal. App. 2d 126, 255 P.2d 25 (2d Dist. 1953); Garcia v. Venegas, 106 Cal. App. 2d 364, 235 P.2d 89 (1st Dist. 1951); Padilla v. Padilla, 38 Cal. App. 2d 319, 100 P.2d 1093 (1st Dist. 1940); Bacon v. Bacon, 21 Cal. App. 2d 540, 542-43, 69 P.2d 884, 885 (3d Dist. 1937); *accord,* Prieto v. Prieto, 165 La. 710, 115 So. 911 (1928), DeLamour v. Roger, 7 La. Ann. 152 (1852), and the cases cited in Annot., 31 A.L.R.2d 1255, 1297-98 (1953).

25. *See, e.g.,* Cal. Stats. 1975, ch. 71, repealing Penal Code §§ 269a and 269b, which had previously made adulterous cohabitation a criminal offense.

26. Eisenstadt v. Baird, 405 U.S. 438 (1972). *But see* Doe v. Commonwealth's Attorney, 403 F. Supp. 1199 (E.D. Va. 1975), *aff'd,* ______ U.S. ______, 96 S. Ct. 1489 (1976) (state may criminally punish sodomy between consenting adults in private).

27. *See, e.g.,* In re Raya, 255 Cal. App. 2d 260, 63 Cal. Rptr. 252 (3d Dist. 1967).

28. *E.g.,* CAL. CIV. CODE § 5103 (West 1970); ILL. ANN. STATS. ch. 68, § 6 (West 1959) ("Contracts may be made . . . by a wife . . . to the same extent and in the same manner as if she were unmarried."); NEV. REV. STAT. § 123.070 (1973); N.M. STAT. ANN. § 57-4A-2 (Supp. 1975).

29. *See* text accompanying notes 52-55 *infra.*

agreements between parties to informal domestic unions balked at the enforcement of implied agreements. Other than difficulties of proof, which are subject to the constraints of the statute of frauds in any event, the policies at stake are no different.[30] Purported policy objections should no longer preclude evenhanded enforcement of obligations arising from interpersonal transactions outside marital and commercial spheres.

B. *Application of Market-Place Concepts to Interpersonal Dealings*

Over the past thirty years the law has increasingly recognized that principles designed to deal with the legal problems of economic interaction in the commercial sphere are poorly suited to resolving the questions that arise when parties bargain outside the commercial context. Thus, as chronicled by Professor Havighurst, courts have become increasingly solicitous of contracting parties who do not fit the arm's length business model.[31] For example, traditional requirements for consideration and written promises were gradually replaced in contract law by common sense doctrines of equitable origin. The niece who cared for aging relatives only to learn after their death that the farm she had been promised in

30. To the extent that purported moral objections are in fact prompted by fear of perjury, state statutes of frauds are the appropriate tests of enforceability. For whatever the supposed difficulties of implying compensation agreements, the process is no less onerous in this context than in any other. Typically, the statute of frauds should prove no barrier as oral partnership, pooling, or compensation agreements in this setting would be capable of performance within one year. This exception to the statute for lifetime agreements or agreements of uncertain duration is well established. 2A CORBIN, CORBIN ON CONTRACTS § 446 (1950) [hereinafter cited as CORBIN]. To the extent that such an agreement would affect ownership of real property, the statute might well impose a barrier to enforcement of an oral agreement unless part performance removes the agreement from the statute. *Id.* § 420. Where one party has died, the contract is executed and thus not within the statute. *See* Garza v. Fernandez, 74 Ariz. 312, 248 P.2d 869 (1952). Implied agreements, of course, are not subject to the strictures of the statute. 1 CORBIN, *supra*, § 19.

As the California Supreme Court stated when confronted with the assertion that the parol evidence rule was necessary to protect the courts from alleged agreements that may arise in a family context, "the fear that fraud or unintentional invention by witnesses interested in the outcome of the litigation will mislead the finder of facts . . . . [could] often defeat the true intent of the parties." Masterson v. Sine, 68 Cal. 2d 222, 227, 436 P.2d 561, 564, 65 Cal. Rptr. 545, 548 (1968). Fear of the difficulties of proof of express oral agreements ought not preclude judicial enforcement. The resurrection of the statute of frauds or the parol evidence rule in nonmarital cohabitation cases by courts that have curtailed their use in more traditional family settings would be clearly inappropriate. Similarly inappropriate is a preservation of unarticulated policy objections to enforcement of oral or implied agreements between unmarried parties by courts that have no policy concerns when written or express agreements are at issue.

31. Havighurst, *Services in the Home*, 41 YALE L.J. 386 (1932) [hereinafter cited as Havighurst].

exchange for her services was willed to another was originally thought to be beyond the aid of equity.[32] Over time quasi-contractual doctrines developed that could provide equitable results and avoid the harsh preclusion of recovery otherwise imposed by commercial doctrines.[33]

This growth of the common law of contracts has sometimes been overlooked by courts faced with implied contracts for services.[34] In California, for example, courts have implied compensation agreements only when the services that were rendered were clearly commercial in nature.[35] Just as the Uniform Commercial Code recognizes the need for distinctive contract rules based upon the type of transaction and the functions of the parties to an agreement,[36] courts now recognize their obligation to tailor common law contract rules to serve the needs of family members.[37] Surely it is not premature to ask that courts treat legal problems arising in the context of nonmarital cohabitation with the same vigor and doctrinal diversity that they display in other non-commercial contexts.

C. *The Value of Personal Services*

Domestic services have economic value. Recognition of this fact in contract law has proceeded apace following the publication in 1932 of Professor Havighurst's seminal article on recovery for the value of household services rendered by one member of the household to another.[38] A recent study of British housewives indicates that weekly time spent on housework by women ranges from 48 hours

---

32. G. Gilmore, The Death of Contract *passim* (1974); L. Fuller & R. Braucher, Basic Contract Law 368-71 (2d ed. 1964) and cases cited; A. Mueller & A. Rosett, Contract Law and Its Application 16-24 (1971); L. Fuller & M. Eisenberg, Basic Contract Law 405-08 (3d ed. 1972).

33. G. Gilmore, The Death of Contract 73, 88, 90 (1974).

34. *See* Havighurst, *supra* note 31, at 397-400.

35. In *Keene v. Keene,* the California Supreme Court suggested that implied contracts might be available in litigation between parties who cohabitated but cited commercial precedents that involved hauling ore to a dump, transportation of fish from the Canal Zone to San Francisco, warehouse storage of personal effects, and the performance of real estate brokerage services. Keene v. Keene, 57 Cal. 2d 657, 664-65 n.4, 371 P.2d 329, 333 n.4, 21 Cal. Rptr. 593, 597 n.4 (1962).

36. *See, e.g.,* those provisions of Article 2 which apply only to transactions involving "merchants." The sections are cited and discussed in Uniform Commercial Code § 2-104, Comment. *See also* S. Riesenfeld, Practical Guide to the Uniform Commercial Code in Hawaii, Articles 1, 2, 6, 7 and 9, at 24 (Legislative Reference Bureau, Univ. of Hawaii, 1968).

37. *E.g.,* Masterson v. Sine, 68 Cal. 2d 222, 436 P.2d 561, 65 Cal. Rptr. 545 (1968).

38. Havighurst, *supra* note 31.

(by a housewife with a full-time job) to 105 hours.[39] Studies over the past 46 years in France, Germany and the United States have produced similar findings.[40] Yet it is only relatively recently that the value of housework and other duties undertaken in support of a spouse's career has moved beyond theoretical discussions of tax policy and imputed income to receive recognition as a function for which homemakers themselves deserve economic credit.[41] The point is of particular relevance to requests for equitable allocation of assets following the break-up of family units. Indeed an assertion of value rendered through services to the home and to personal and career needs of other family members applies whether or not both

39. A. OAKLEY, THE SOCIOLOGY OF HOUSEWORK 92-93 (1974) [hereinafter cited as OAKLEY].

40. *Id.* at 93-94. Dr. Oakley summarizes their findings as follows:

A comparison of data on housework hours

Study, and country carried out in:	*Date*	*Average weekly hours of housework*
I Rural Studies		
Wilson: United States	1929	64
US Bureau of Home Economics: United States	1929	62
Cowles and Dietz: United States	1956	61
Girard and Bastide: France	1959	67
II Urban studies		
US Bureau of Home Economics: United States	1929	51
Bryn Mawr: United States		
(i) small city	1945	78
(ii) large city	1945	81
Stoetzel: France	1948	82
Moser: Britain	1950	70
Mass observation: Britain	1951	72
Girard: France	1958	67
Oakley: Britain	1971	77

Id, at 94.

41. Weitzman, *supra* note 3 at 1185-86, n.82 (discussing the "two-person-career" in which a spouse's active support is required for professional success). *See generally* J. GALBRAITH, *supra* note 4, at 233; A. COOK, THE WORKING MOTHER 28-29 (1975) [hereinafter cited as A. COOK]; K. WALKER & W. GAUGER, THE DOLLAR VALUE OF HOUSEHOLD WORK (Cornell University Social Sciences, Consumer Economics and Public Policy No. 5, Information Bulletin 60, June 1973); K. WALKER & M. WOODS, TIME USE: A MEASURE OF HOUSEHOLD PRODUCTION OF FAMILY GOODS AND SERVICES (1976); *English Wives Want Wages,* San Francisco Chronicle, Sept. 3, 1975, at 40, col. 1; J. Galbraith, *A New Economic Role for Women?,* 155 CURRENT 41 (1973); K. Walker, *Household Work Time: Its Implication for Family Decisions,* 65 J. HOME ECON. 7 (Oct. 1973) [hereinafter cited as Walker]. *See also* Hall, *The Case of the Late Mrs. Smith, Homemaker,* 67 J. HOME ECON. 30 (Nov. 1975) (concerning preparation of expert testimony as to the value of homemakers' services).

parties were employed outside the home during their relationship.[42] Professor Cook explains:

> Virtually every society assumes that the responsibility for home and children is the woman's. The result is that when mothers work they carry two jobs. . . . Homemaking-cum motherhood often takes as many hours as does a paid job, and working mothers spend only slightly fewer hours at it than do professional housewives.
>
> . . . .
>
> . . . As the recent multinational time budget research . . . amply demonstrates, the husband spends very little more time assisting the wife and mother with household tasks when she works outside the home than when she does not.[43]

While these studies measure homemaker functions as between spouses, there is no reason to believe that allocation of such duties in nonmarital domestic units is any different. Of less certainty, given the sociological sex-role underpinnings of the practices these studies survey, is the relevance of their findings to a family in which it is the man who undertakes a full-time homemaker role.[44]

In 1962 the California Supreme Court acknowledged the value of services within the home, but concluded that when such services

---

42. The point deserves emphasis as more and more women join the work force outside the home. A. Cook, *supra* note 41, at 1-3 (1975); Weitzman, *supra* note 3, at 1217-19; I.L.O. Report, *supra* note 16, at 8 ("In the United States the percentage of women workers among all women aged 16 and over increased from 34 percent in 1950 to 43 percent in 1971 and women made up 38 percent of the total workforce in 1972 as against 30 percent in 1950.") The trend has continued. The Labor Department reported a one percent increase in the rate of working women between March 1975 and March 1976, with 46.7 percent of American women now employed. The working rate for men declined one percent during the same period to 79.8 percent. San Francisco Sunday Examiner and Chronicle, April 4, 1976, at A19, col. 1.

43. A. Cook, *supra* note 41, at 28-29, *referring to* A. Szalai, The Use of Time: Daily Activities of Urban and Suburban Populations in Twelve Countries (1972). Szalai's work grew out of studies conducted under the auspices of UNESCO by the Vienna European Coordinating Centre for Research and Documentation in the Social Sciences. Earlier reports of the study are cited in the I.L.O. Report, *supra* note 16, at 63. Accord, A. Oakley, *supra* note 39, at 135-65; I.L.O. Report, *supra* note 16, at 81; Walker, *supra* note 41, at 8-9 (Employed women spend 4-8 hours daily on household work; other women spend 5-12 hours. Employed husbands contribute an average of 11 hours per week to household work; this figure does not increase if the wife is employed outside the home).

44. It is not entirely clear that a woman who chooses to work outside the home will be as unlikely to aid in housework as a man. *See generally* J. Galbraith, *supra* note 4, at 233, 237, 239. The United Nations International Labor Organization, reporting on a study of time use by men and women conducted in 12 countries under the auspices of UNESCO, states:

> All the country studies showed that, almost without exception, married women generally worked longer hours at home than their husbands because of the traditional division of family chores and concept of sex roles. Because they were expected to conform to a certain image imposed by society women, even when working full time outside the home, had to devote a large part of their so-called 'spare' time to the care of their family.

I.L.O. Report, *supra* note 16, at 63. The extent to which parties who reverse traditional employment roles also readjust their concepts of sex roles within the family is unknown.

are rendered within a meretricious relationship their benefits must be deemed to have been granted as a gift.[45] This seems a fiction that can no longer be sustained in view of recent writings on the nature of homemakers' services. The issue transcends narrowly conceived economic analysis of the duties performed by a homemaker.[46] The implication that services provided within the home by a member of its living unit can be duplicated by the purchase of domestic services in the marketplace misses an important point. Although statistical data is unavailable, it seems safe to assume that most of the dependent parties in nonmarital unions would be both unwilling and unable to provide comparable household and career-supportive services to another family in exchange for going market wages. This is recognized by economists who reason that the societal costs of such services can be measured only by taking into account opportunity cost—that is, what homemakers would earn if they chose instead to seek employment for which they are qualified outside the home.[47] The long hours and intangible benefits[48] of services provided by a family member at home prompted

---

45. Keene v. Keene, 57 Cal. 2d 657, 668, 371 P.2d 329, 336 21 Cal. Rptr. 593 (1962). The issue is once again before that court in Marvin v. Marvin, 50 Cal. App. 3d [advance sheet] 84, (2d Dist. 1975), *hearing granted,* No. L.A. 30520, Sept. 17, 1975, described in note 13 *supra*.

46. *See, e.g.,* Office of Research and Statistics, Social Security Administration, Note No. 9, Economic Value of a Housewife (1975), which concludes that the average American housewife's services were worth $4,705 in 1972. Contrast Professor Galbraith's estimate of $13,364 as the market value of a housewife's annual services. Galbraith, *A New Economic Role for Women?,* 155 Current 41, 43 (Oct. 1973).

47. *See, e.g.,* I. Sirageldin, Non-Market Components of National Income 7-31, 74-76 (1969). *See also* H. Ross & I. Sawhill, *supra* note 6, at 42-44; Havighurst, *supra* note 31, at 403 (1932).

48. Economists describe the concept of human capital embodiment, viewing education as an investment producing a return in the form of more effective producers and consumers. *See generally, e.g.,* Schultz, *Optimal Investment in College Instruction,* 80 J. Polit. Econ. S2 (1972). Some recent economic literature has stressed the positive impact of such human capital resources on the performance of those who rendered household services, as well as to those employed producing goods and services for wages. *See* Burk, *On the Need for Investment in Human Capital for Consumption,* 1 J. Consumer Affairs 123 (1967); Benham, *Benefits of Women's Education Within Marriage,* 82 J. Polit. Econ. S57 (1974). The person maintaining the household in turn produces enhanced human capital in other members of the family, particularly young children. *Id.* at S57-58.

See also Evans, *Property Interests Arising from Quasi-Marital Relations,* 9 Cornell L.Q. 246, 252, 266 (1924).

> Assumpsit is inadequate partly because it does not permit consideration of the far more valuable features of the conjugal association: the love and affection bestowed; the society, advice, and helpfulness; the sort of services that so often cannot be purchased with money; the enlargement of the material estate because of the woman's earning or thrift, and skillful management.

Id. at 252.

Margaret Mead's comment, "It takes the work of five women to equal the work . . . a woman does in the home. . . ."[49]

Wholesale statements that all such efforts are but gifts willingly given, for which no recompense is expected, are unrealistic. As in other cases where the courts have confronted the issue of services rendered in the home, the nature of the exchange is one that can be established only by an inquiry into the particular circumstances of the parties before the court. A conclusive presumption of gift or lack of value flies in the face of reality and cannot be sustained on policy grounds, as indicated by developing contract principles.[50] Indeed, as Professor Gilmore has pointed out, exactly the opposite presumption is generally accepted:

> We are fast approaching the point [in contract law] where, to prevent unjust enrichment, any benefit received by a defendant must be paid for unless it clearly was meant as a gift . . . .[51]

II. General Legal and Equitable Doctrines of Relevance to Nonmarital Domestic Relationships

> The movement of the progressive societies has hitherto been a movement from *status to contract*—H. Maine[52]

The importance of this movement in the common law and its implications for courts faced with requests for relief by parties to informal families are suggested by recent remarks made by Professor Harry Jones of Columbia University:

> What Maine is saying here is that in primitive communities and others that have kept the character of "static" societies, what a man or woman is or does depends above all on his status, that is, on the fixed legal and social condition into which he was born or into which he, willy-nilly, has been moved. Thus to know what X's legal rights and duties are, the important question to ask is whether X be wife, child, slave, serf, feudal retainer, Brahmin, untouchable, master, servant or whatever. In "progressive" societies, as Maine characterizes them, one's legal rights and duties depend far less on caste or fixed social condition and far more on expectations created and obligations assumed by his own contracts.[53]

---

49. Sacramento Bee, Aug. 7, 1975, at A2, col. 6.

50. *See* text at notes 28-37 *supra;* L. Fuller & R. Braucher, Basic Contract Law 368-71 (2d ed. 1964) and cases cited; A. Mueller & A. Rosett, Contract Law and Its Application 16-24 (1971); L. Fuller & M. Eisenberg, Basic Contract Law 405-08 (3d ed. 1972). The value of room and board received is, of course, relevant. *See* note 86 *infra.*

51. G. Gilmore, The Death of Contract 88 (1974).

52. H. Maine, Ancient Law 141 (New Universal Library ed. 1905) (emphasis in original).

53. Jones, *The Jurisprudence of Contracts,* 44 Cincinnati L. Rev. 43, 48-49 (1975). *See generally* Note, *Marriage Contracts for Support and Services,* 49 N.Y.U.L. Rev. 1161, 1186-90 (1974).

Should this movement continue and limitations on recovery as between parties to a nonmarital union be removed, what will be the shape of things to come? Certainly courts will no longer necessarily leave the parties as they find them and harsh results can be avoided. At the same time it should not be necessary to create a doctrine of common law marriage in states where that doctrine does not already exist,[54] or to equate marriage with nonmarital cohabitation.[55] Rather, it is important to note that the degree of financial relief afforded to a dependent party in a nonceremonial relationship, whether that person is male or female, will vary according to the circumstances of the case at hand and the legal doctrine that most appropriately fits its facts. To the extent that courts are encouraged to analyze the legal import of parties' statements and actions in cases of this type as they do in all other cases that confront them, remedies will be appropriately varied.

Just as varied motives prompt the formation of informal domestic units, the expectations of parties to them will vary. And to the degree that parties have not clarified their goals, or, having clarified them, have not articulated them, the courts are faced with vital questions of interpretation and equity. For only when parties are relatively sophisticated about both their long-range intentions and the legal consequences of their relationships are they likely to verbalize their expectations.

The discussion below begins with doctrinal considerations that apply when an express agreement concerning property matters is at hand, proceeds to discuss legal and equitable theories that are appropriate when intent is not verbalized, and concludes with a discussion of remedies that apply without regard to the parties' actual intentions. While an application of any of the following doctrines can avoid hardship and inequity in some cases, the doctrines of implied partnership and constructive trust are especially well-suited to those cases of nonmarital cohabitation where an explicit agreement between the parties cannot be discerned.

A. *Express Agreements*

Unless there are policy reasons to the contrary, express property agreements are normally enforceable, as are promises that induce

---

54. *See* notes 114-124 *infra* and accompanying text. *But see* note 5 *supra*.
55. *See* text accompanying notes 109-113 *infra.*

foreseeable reasonable reliance.[56] Certainly this is the case when strangers contract and when married persons seek to adjust their financial relationships.[57] As discussed above, the same result ought to follow in the case of property agreements between unmarried persons who share a household.[58] It is irrelevant whether the contract seeks to establish a pooling agreement, a partnership, a trust, joint title to property, or an exchange of property or services.[59] So long as the contract is established by appropriate proof and is free of fraud, duress, or similar defects, public policy supports its en-

56. The doctrine of promissory estoppel, of course, expands contract doctrine by substituting reasonable, foreseeable reliance for the traditional consideration requirement, 1A CORBIN, *supra* note 26, § 194 (1963), and by omitting the requirement of a return promise. *Id.* § 195.

Because services rendered in this context confer a benefit on the defendant, when there has been a bilateral agreement the doctrine is not needed. It is however, essential when services were rendered under a unilateral promise. As to services in the home, the doctrine has also been applied to sustain recovery under a promise made for past services rendered. Henderson, ***Promises Grounded in the Past,*** 57 VA. L. REV. 1115, 1160-64 (1971) [hereinafter cited as Henderson]. But see Havighurst, *supra* note 31, at 396-97. There are no statute of frauds problems. Krauskopf, ***Solving Statute of Frauds Problems,*** 20 OHIO ST. L.J. 237, 263 (1959). As to the measurement of damages, *see* note 86 infra.

57. *See* the statutes cited in note 28 *supra* and Weitzman, *supra* note 3, at 1258-59. The general rule has not extended, however, to contracts "(1) that alter the essential elements of the marital relationship, or (2) that are made in contemplation of divorce." *Id.* at 1259. Reviewing the policies underlying this restriction, *id.* at 1259-66, Professor Weitzman suggests that courts permit recovery in many of these cases as well. *Id.* at 1266-77.

58. *See* text accompanying notes 28-30 *supra.*

59. Professor Weyrauch comments that:

> Since common law judges are traditionally property oriented it is possible that informal cohabitation may become less objectionable if it is presented in terms borrowed from the law of property rather than from the law of personal service contracts. Personal services in the sphere of intimate relationships are still often stigmatized. It is relatively easy to express the incidents of formal or informal marriage in terms of landlord-tenant relationships, co-ownerships, or perhaps even co-tenancies at will. A large part depends on the skill of the persons who draft the contract, if there is an express contract.

Letter from Walter Weyrauch to the author, Jan. 8, 1976, on file with the author.

Professor Weyrauch's comments are substantiated by the cases of Weak v. Weak, 202 Cal. App. 2d 632, 21 Cal. Rptr. 9 (3d Dist. 1962), and Cluck v. Sheets, 171 S.W.2d 860 (Tex. 1943). In ***Weak,*** a California court held that the joint tenancy title to realty held by a man and his meretricious spouse would support the finding of an enforceable express agreement to pool earnings and acquisitions. 202 Cal. App. 2d at 638-39, 21 Cal. Rptr. at 13. *Cf.* Estate of Meyron, 6 Misc. 2d 673, 164 N.Y.S.2d 443 (1957) (title taken as "husband and wife" held tenancy in common); Merit v. Losey, 194 Or. 89, 103-104, 240 P.2d 933, 939-40 (1952) (same). In ***Cluck,*** title to the land at issue was not held jointly, nor was there any evidence that the woman who worked to pay off the vendor's lien had contributed funds to the initial payment at the time title passed. *See* note 79 *infra.* However, evidence was introduced to show that the parties had inspected the land together before its purchase and the woman testified that she and the man in whose name title was held agreed that title should be taken in his name for their joint benefit. The jury found that the alleged agreement had been reached and the trial and appellate courts concluded that an express oral trust between the parties was thereby established. *Cf.* Tyranski v. Piggins, 44 Mich. App. 570, 574, 205 N.W.2d 595, 597 (1973).

forcement. Noting that a refusal to enforce express agreements "has often resulted in the male keeping the assets accumulated in the relationship and the female being deprived of what she jointly accumulated," the Oregon Supreme Court in banc recently permitted suit under an express agreement to share equally all property acquired during a relationship that had lasted nineteen years. Recovery of $100,000 was requested. Holding that a demurrer could not be sustained, the court distinguished the case from ones in which the primary or only consideration is sexual intercourse, stating that the agreement "contemplated all the burdens and amenities of married life."[60]

By the same token freely entered agreements to maintain separate earnings during cohabitation should be enforced. A state which permits even parties to the highly regulated relationship of marriage to agree to keep their property separate[61] should give no less freedom to parties to unstructured domestic relationships. In all of these cases if normal legal principles obtain, recovery in the event of litigation should be controlled by the terms of the agreement.

B. *Agreements Implied-in-Fact*

The formation and contours of an agreement may be inferred from actions taken by the parties to it.[62] As Professor Corbin has pointed out, these agreements are closely akin to express contracts, being distinguishable only by the means that the parties utilize to express their agreement.[63]

---

60. Latham v. Latham, ____ Or. ____, ____, 547 P.2d 144, 147 (1976); accord, Tyranski v. Piggins, 44 Mich. App. 570, 205 N.W. 2d 595 (1973) (enforcing an oral contract to convey realty against the administrator of a decedent's estate).

61. *See* note 28 *supra* and accompanying text.

62. RESTATEMENT (SECOND) OF CONTRACTS §§ 21, 228 (Tent. Draft Nos. 1-7 1973).

63. 1 CORBIN, *supra* note 30, § 18, at 41. A California court described conduct that would support an implied agreement to alter property rights in a case involving a transmutation of community property to separate property of the wife.

"Now, it may well have been the case that the husband could recall no conversation between them in which such an agreement was distinctly expressed . . . . And yet it might also be true that such an agreement was perfectly well understood between them. In such a case resort may be had to circumstantial evidence. . . ."

An agreement may be shown not only by words written or spoken, but by conduct. . . . [B]y an overt act, or by acquiescence in the acts of his wife, a husband may relinquish his . . . rights and permit property to be converted into the wife's . . . property.

Nevins v. Nevins, 129 Cal. App. 2d 150, 156-57, 276 P.2d 655, 659 (1954), *quoting* Kaltschmidt v. Weber, 145 Cal. 596, 599-600, 79 P. 272, 274 (1904).

The potential subject matter of such agreements is thus equally broad: Co-ownership,[64] exchange, joint venture or partnership, landlord-tenant or trust arrangements are all possible. The following discussion treats several common forms of implied-in-fact agreements.

IMPLIED-IN-FACT CONTRACTS FOR SERVICES

Most simply, an agreement to compensate may be inferred from one party's request that another perform specified services.[65] In this case, damages are determined as in the case of express contracts[66]—according to the inferable intention of the parties.[67]

IMPLIED-IN-FACT PARTNERSHIP AND POOLING AGREEMENTS

Certain trust and partnership theories are equally amenable to application in such cases. For example, in 1972 the Washington Supreme Court considered a woman's claim that an implied-in-fact partnership could be established by evidence that a couple lived together for sixteen years while the woman shared fully in the running of two farms held in the man's name and in the enhancement of the couple's economic status. Sustaining the pleadings, the court

---

64. Because of the rules of record title, if record title is held in the name of only one of the parties, co-ownership of real property is enforceable only under trust theory. D. Dobbs, Handbook on the Law of Remedies § 4.3, at 240 (1973) [hereinafter cited as Dobbs]. *See* the discussions of resulting and constructive trust, text accompanying notes 75-82, 88-91 *infra.* In theory, ownership of personality and choses in action, unless subject to recording laws, may be enforced according to implied contract theory without resort to trust doctrine. The superior remedies previously afforded under equitable theories, however, may explain the absence of cases discussing implied-in-fact co-ownership at law. *See* text accompanying notes 71-74, 93-96 *infra.*

65. Dobbs, *supra* note 64, § 4.2, at 234, 237 (1973).

66. Henderson, *supra* note 56, at 1140.

67. Utilizing such an implied agreement, a Michigan appellate court enforced against a decedent's estate an agreement to convey property to a meretricious spouse. The existence of the contract was established by testimony as well as by a change in the "tenor" of the plaintiff's life in performance of the agreement "so as to make reasonable the inference that there was such an agreement." Tyranski v. Piggins, 44 Mich. App. 570, 574, 205 N.W.2d 595, 597 (1973) (The plaintiff allegedly contributed both services and funds. The court's reasoning, however, did not turn on the contribution of funds.).

In *Warner v. Warner,* a common law wife sought divorce and property rights stemming from the time when the union between the parties was meretricious. The Idaho Supreme Court held that an implied agreement between the parties estopped the defendant husband from denying the validity of their common law marriage at the earlier time:

> While the evidence is conflicting as to what, if any, promises he made to induce her to return, it is quite evident that he did persuade her to come back. . . . It is also reasonable to conclude that she would not have returned without some inducement. . . .

Warner v. Warner, 76 Idaho 399, 407, 283 P.2d 931, 935 (1955) (emphasis added).

reversed a nonsuit against her and remanded the case for trial.[68] Had proof supported her allegations,[69] recovery in the case—a one-half interest in the farm that was held by the man at the time of his death—would have been similar to the recovery that would result in a community property situation. There is, however, an important distinction: recovery extends only to the areas contained within the implied partnership arrangement. Relief is predicated upon the model of a business enterprise in which capital may be provided by only some of the partners, with others acquiring their interests through the rendition of services.[70] Its similarity to dis-

68. Estate of Thornton, 81 Wash. 2d 72, 499 P.2d 864 (1972) (for the subsequent history of the case, see note 69 *infra*). The case is discussed in Cross, *The Community Property Law in Washington,* 49 Wash. L. Rev. 729, 736-45 (1974). In its thoughtful opinion, the court volunteered a suggestion that relief might also be possible under an implied contract to make a will or by analogy to community property. On the latter theory, the court suggested that a long-term meretricious relationship alone, during which the parties held themselves out as married, would support a property claim. Because it was not faced directly with the question, however, the court expressed its displeasure with contrary doctrine but did not reach the question of the continuing vitality of Creasman v. Boyle, 31 Wash. 2d 345, 196 P.2d 835 (1948), *criticized in* 27 Tex. L. Rev. 725 (1949), the Washington precedent which would bar recovery in such cases. The implication of its opinion and its criticism of *Creasman* have yet to bear fruit. In *Omer v. Omer,* decided two years later, the Washington Court of Appeals was equally able to avoid the issue (in this case by granting recovery under a constructive trust). 11 Wash. App. 386, 523 P.2d 957 (1974). But when the Court of Appeals was later faced with a man's claim to property acquired during a meretricious relationship of fifteen years' duration prior to the couple's marriage, it refused to follow *Thornton's* suggestion, stating that *Creasman* remains the law, and declined to recognize an implied partnership on the ground that business property was not at issue. Latham v. Hennesey, 13 Wash. App. 518, ___, 535 P.2d 838, 841-42 (1975). Should the Washington Supreme Court reach and decide the *Creasman* issue according to its reasoning in *Thornton,* the state may be en route to a common law doctrine of property rights similar to the statutory theories enunciated by California intermediate appellate courts in In re Marriage of Cary, 34 Cal. App. 3d 345, 109 Cal. Rptr. 862 (1st Dist. 1973) and Estate of Atherley, 44 Cal. App. 3d 758, 119 Cal. Rptr. 41 (4th Dist. 1975). *See* note 13 *supra.* The result may then be that courts will grant property rights, although perhaps no support rights, upon the termination of a stable meretricious union of relatively long duration. If so they may face opposition from those who seek to restrict the role of the courts in evaluating nonmarital relationships as a predicate for forcing marital status and responsibilities upon parties who wish to avoid legal pigeonholing of their relationships. *See* note 121 *infra. See generally* Weitzman, *supra* note 3, at 1272-73; Weitzman, *To Love, Honor, and Obey? Traditional Legal Marriage and Alternative Family Forms,* 24 Fam. Coordinator 531, 543-47 (1975).

69. It did not. At trial after remand, the judge concluded from the conflicting evidence that the woman was a managerial employee of the man, and that she had failed to establish the existence of an implied partnership or joint venture, a constructive or resulting trust, or a meretricious relationship in which the parties held themselves out as husband and wife. He therefore held that she was entitled to no interest in the man's estate. The appellate court found the judgment to be supported by the evidence and affirmed. Estate of Thornton, 14 Wash. App. 397, 541 P.2d 1243 (1975).

70.

> "Where, from all the competent evidence, it appears that the parties have entered into a business relation combining their property, labor, skill, and experience, or *some of these elements on the one side and some on the other,* for the purpose of joint profits, a partnership will be deemed established."

position of property at the termination of marriage under the Uniform Marriage and Divorce Act or in community property states is justified because these laws are but a recognition of the shared efforts the law supposes to exist when a man and woman become husband and wife. There seems no policy reason to ignore the actual existence of such a relationship when it occurs between parties who have not formally married. Indeed, a refusal to recognize that unmarried persons might similarly choose to consolidate their capital and efforts is to confuse a presumption of partnership in the case of marriage with the permissible inference of one in the case of persons who are unmarried. Rather, when the requisite relationship is established by proof, partnership doctrine permits an appropriate allocation of earnings or property without regard to sex or marital status, but with regard to the efforts and investments of the parties. This attribute no doubt explains the theory's popularity with those courts that have long permitted recovery of property in litigation following the termination of de facto relationships.[71]

In re Estate of Thornton, 81 Wash. 2d 72, 79, 499, P.2d, 864, 867 (1972) *quoting* Nicholson v. Kilbury, 83 Wash. 196, 202, 145 P. 189, 191 (1915) (emphasis added). "Partners are presumed equal where partnership is shown, and nothing more." Hupp v. Hupp, 235 S.W.2d 753, 756 (Tex. Civ. App. 1950). *But see* West v. Knowles, where Justice Finley of the Supreme Court of Washington cited precedent from several jurisdictions for the proposition that equal division of property is not compulsory under partnership theory, and concluded,

> I am convinced courts exist . . . to settle disputes by peaceful means, and to obviate resort to self-help and violence wherever this can be done consistently with sound public policy. In the furtherance of justice for all concerned, I think that the property of parties to a so-called meretricious relationship can and should be distributed on a fair and equitable basis. . . . A fair and equitable distribution . . . connotes a reasonable and rough approximation and appraisal of earnings and other factors, and a division of property that will in a general way be reasonable, fair, and equitable by the standards of just, tolerant, and understanding individuals.

50 Wash. 2d 311, 320, 321, 311 P.2d 689, 695 (1957) (concurring opinion).

Other courts have accomplished an equal division by declaring the parties to be tenants in common. Sousa v. Freitas, 10 Cal. App. 3d 660, 89 Cal. Rptr. 485 (1st Dist. 1970); Ross v. Sampson, 4 N.C. App. 270, 166 S.E.2d 499 (1969) (trial court judgment affirmed without discussion); West v. Knowles, 50 Wash. 2d 311, 311 P.2d 689 (1957). *See also* the tenancy in common cases cited in note 59 *supra.*

71. The cases fall into two groups: cases involving parties who in good faith believed they were married (putative spouses) and those in which the parties knew they were cohabiting without marriage (meretricious spouses). Since, historically, express partnerships between spouses were enforced without regard to the state of their belief concerning their marital status, implied recovery should similarly be equally available to the two groups. See the discussion at notes 56-61, *supra; accord,* Havighurst, *supra* note 31, at 398. The implied partnership putative spouse cases include Sousa v. Freitas, 10 Cal. App. 3d 660, 89 Cal. Rptr. 485 (1st Dist. 1970); Werner v. Werner, 59 Kan. 399, 53 P. 127 (1898); King v. Jackson, 196 Okla. 327, 164 P.2d 974 (1945) (*semble*); Lawson v. Lawson, 30 Tex. Civ. App. 43, 69 S.W. 246 (1902); Morgan v. Morgan, 1 Tex. Civ. App. 315, 21 S.W. 154 (1892); Knoll v. Knoll, 104 Wash. 110, 176 P. 22 (1918). *See also* Krauter v. Krauter, 79 Okla. 30, 190 P.

There can be similar flexibility under the rubrics of joint enterprise[72] and joint pooling of assets.[73] In these cases, courts have applied a partnership-like doctrine to agreements that focus on the pooled efforts and resources of the parties as well as on those that involve the parties' joint conduct of a business enterprise. Because of the ability of partnership, joint enterprise, and joint pooling law to allocate benefits without strict regard to the original ownership of capital,[74] these doctrines seem especially well-suited to application in cases of nonmarital cohabitation.

RESULTING (IMPLIED-IN-FACT) TRUST

As the value of a homemaker's services is increasingly recognized, however, trust theory can also provide relief when one party has contributed domestic services while the other has pursued outside employment or accrued assets in some other fashion. The implied-in-fact equitable doctrine that parallels the implied-in-fact legal doctrines discussed above is that of the resulting trust. If it is possible to conclude as a matter of circumstantial evidence that

---

1088 (1920); In re Brenchley's Estate, 96 Wash. 223, 164 P. 913 (1917); Buckley v. Buckley, 50 Wash. 213, 96 P. 1079 (1908). *See generally* Annot., 31 A.L.R.2d 1255, 1267-70 (1953). Implied partnership relief was granted to meretricious spouses in Poole v. Schrichte, 39 Wash. 2d 558, 236 P.2d 1044 (1951). ((''[I]t is immaterial whether either of these people believed they were married.'') *Id.* at 562, 236 P.2d at 1047.). *Accord,* Bracken v. Bracken, 45 S.D. 430, 188 N.W. 46 (1922) (*semble*). *See also* Buckley v. Buckley, 50 Wash. 213, 224, 96 P. 1079, 1084 (1908) (concurring opinion).

72. Joint operation of a business does not seem essential to the reasoning or scope of opinions that grant recovery on joint enterprise theory. *See, e.g.,* Garza v. Fernandez, 74 Ariz. 312, 315, 248 P.2d 869, 871 (1952) (joint enterprise may be shown where parties ''lived and cohabited together as man and wife and lent their mutual efforts toward earning a livelihood and acquiring . . . real and personal property''). The term appears to have no precise definition in this context, on occasion being used interchangeably with ''partnership.'' For example, following the state supreme court opinion in *Garza,* trial was held and recovery awarded under the joint enterprise theory. When the claim was presented to the administrator of the deceased man's estate, however, it was refused as a tardy contract claim under a statute controlling creditor claims against estates. On appeal the supreme court held that the claim was enforceable as one in partnership. Fernandez v. Garza, 88 Ariz. 214, 354 P.2d 260 (1960). *See also* Hupp v. Hupp, 235 S.W.2d 753, 754 (Tex. Civ. App. 1951) (''partnership'' and ''joint venture'' used interchangeably); Mitchell v. Fish, 97 Ark. 444, 134 S.W. 940 (1911) (same; express agreement).

73. Thus far California courts have required that such agreements be expressly entered into, Vallera v. Vallera, 21 Cal. 2d 681, 685, 134 P.2d 761, 763 (1943), yet they have labored mightily to find such express agreements. HASTINGS NOTE, *supra* note 1, at 1245-46. Other states recognize implied partnership and pooling agreements between members of informal domestic units. *See* the cases cited in note 71 *supra* (partnership); Estate of Thornton, 81 Wash. 2d 72, 499, P.2d 864 (1972) (partnership), discussed in notes 68 and 69 *supra* and accompanying text; Hupp v. Hupp, 235 S.W.2d 753 (Tex. Civ. App. 1950) (partnership); Hyman v. Hyman, 275 S.W.2d 149 (Tex. Civ. App. 1954) (pooling).

74. *See* note 70 *supra.*

property was intended by the parties to be held by one of them in trust for the other, a resulting, or implied-in-fact, trust is established.[75]

Although there may be some cases in which traditional resulting trust theory provides a basis for relief, in most states its utility has been severely limited by two requirements:[76] that intent be established by clear and convincing proof[77] and that value was provided by the beneficiary for use in the purchase price of property impressed with the trust.[78] Because many courts refuse recovery under the doctrine unless purchase funds or property passed from the beneficiary to the trustee's control at the time of acquisition,[79] the doctrine has rarely been applied to a situation in which one party grants services and the other acquires financial wealth. Yet it

---

75. Keene v. Keene, 57 Cal. 2d 657, 665, 371 P.2d 329, 333-34, 21 Cal. Rptr. 593, 597-98 (1962); DOBBS, *supra* note 64, § 4.3, at 241.

76. *See* Omer v. Omer, 11 Wash. App. 386, 390, 523 P.2d 957, 960 (1974) (dicta).

77. G. G. BOGERT & G. T. BOGERT, HANDBOOK OF THE LAW OF TRUSTS § 74, at 279 (5th ed. 1973); Moulton v. Moulton, 182 Cal. 185, 187 P. 421 (1920).

78. Sugg v. Morris, 392 P.2d 313, 316 (Alaska 1964); Keene v. Keene, 57 Cal. 2d 657, 665, 371 P.2d 329, 334, 21 Cal. Rptr. 593, 598 (1962).

79. Keene v. Keene, 57 Cal. 2d 657, 665, 371 P.2d 329, 334, 21 Cal. Rptr. 593, 598 (1962); Stevens v. Anderson, 75 Ariz. 331, 334-335, 256 P.2d 712, 714 (1953); Creasman v. Boyle, 31 Wash. 2d 345, 355, 196 P.2d 835, 840 (1948). The resulting trust cases are discussed and *Creasman* criticized in a casenote at 27 TEX. L. REV. 725 (1949). *Creasman*'s continuing validity is in doubt. *See* note 68 *supra.*

In Cluck v. Sheets, 171 S.W.2d 860 (Tex. 1943), the meretricious spouses orally agreed to purchase a parcel of land jointly, and take title in the man's name. Although the court sustained the woman's undivided one-half interest in the land upon an express trust theory, it refused to apply resulting trust theory because there was no proof that the woman had obligated herself either to repay the loan taken by the man to provide funds for the initial payment or to pay off the vendor's lien notes once title passed. In fact, however, the woman and the man jointly sawed and sold timber from the land in order to repay the notes and satisfy the lien. Cluck v. Sheets, 171 S.W.2d 857, 860 (Tex. Civ. App. 1942), *aff'd,* 171 S.W.2d 860 (Tex. 1943) ("She pulled one end of the saw and helped to haul and load the wood on the cars for shipment."). Even if resulting trust theory is not to be expanded to include relief on such facts, a court might well choose to estop the man or those claiming under him (in this case the woman he later married) from denying that the subsequently contributed funds had contributed to the purchase monies at the time of acquisition. Similar use of an equitable estoppel as a way of treating events as though they had occurred at an earlier time can be found in Warner v. Warner, 76 Idaho 399, 407, 283 P.2d 931, 935 (1955), discussed at note 67, *supra*. Less strained reasoning is displayed in the cases discussed in notes 98-101 *infra,* some of which hold parties to be tenants in common when subsequent contributions were made to pay off the mortgage. Perhaps these cases, which focus on the nature of relief without articulating the doctrinal basis for recovery, are based upon general equitable principles. Other cases display comparable disregard for statutory provisions. *See* note 13 *supra.* "But in all of them there is evinced a purpose to prevent a result so inherently wrong as to shock our common conception of fundamental justice." Ah Leong v. Ah Leong, 27 F.2d 582, 583 (9th Cir.), *cert. denied,* 278 U.S. 636 (1928). *Cf.* Estate of Ball, 92 Cal. App. 2d 93, 206 P.2d 1111 (2d Dist. 1949); Vieux v. Vieux, 80 Cal. App. 222, 251 P. 640 (2d Dist. 1926) (community property exists to the extent that community funds have paid for property acquired prior to marriage).

is clear that if services which are granted by one party to another have economic value so that the second person need not expend money to secure them elsewhere, the financial base of the second party is enhanced.[80] Sixty-seven years ago a Texas court recognized the strength of this logic in a case involving land acquired while the parties were cohabiting although not married. The court held:

> If Margreth Williams can show that the money with which the land was purchased, was acquired in whole or in part by her labor in connection with Thomas Jefferson *before* the time when the land was purchased, then she should be entitled to a share in the land in the proportion that her labor contributed in producing the purchase money . . . .
>
> It is *not* necessary that Margreth Williams should prove that she produced by her labor a part of the very money that was used in purchasing the land. If she and Thomas Jefferson were working together to a common purpose . . . she would occupy the position that a man would have occupied in relation to Thomas Jefferson under the same circumstances; each would own the property acquired in proportion to the value of his labor. . . .[81]

Such recognition of the economic worth of homemaker services will expand the reach of resulting trust theory. Even in the absence of this development relief under the doctrine can be expected to be granted more frequently in the future as women increase their access to funds through participation in employment outside the home.[82] To the extent that contributions following the acquisition of property are relied upon as a basis of ownership interest, however, other doctrines remain more suitable.

As this discussion of implied-in-fact doctrines demonstrates, where the parties to an informal domestic arrangement indicate by their actions that they expect to share the financial benefits that accrue during their life together, the firmly established legal and equitable principles described in this section support relief for the injured party.

---

80. *See* the discussion of value of household services, notes 38-51 *supra* and accompanying text; *accord,* Keene v. Keene, 57 Cal. 2d 657, 673, 371 P.2d 329, 339, 21 Cal. Rptr. 593, 603 (1962) (Peters, J. dissenting). The *Cluck* case, discussed in note 79 *supra,* demonstrates the sophistry of the rule when most or all of the payment for property occurs after the transfer of title. This is, of course, the pattern in most instances.

81. Hayworth v. Williams, 102 Tex. 308, 313-314, 116 S.W. 43, 45-46 (1909) (emphasis added). *Accord, e.g.,* Dean v. Goldwire, 480 S.W.2d 494 (Tex. Civ. App. 1972); Hyman v. Hyman, 275 S.W.2d 149 (Tex. Civ. App. 1954). For California discussions of *Hayworth, compare* Vallera v. Vallera, 21 Cal. 2d 681, 685, 134 P.2d 761, 763 (limiting the rule to "funds") *with* Keene v. Keene, 57 Cal. 2d 657, 672, 371 P.2d 329, 338, 21 Cal. Rptr. 593, 602 (1962) (Peters, J., dissenting) (correctly describing it to include services).

82. *See* note 42 *supra.*

C. *Relief Under Implied-in-Law Principles*

The relationship of implied-in-law doctrines to the just-discussed concept of implied-in-fact agreements has been described by Professors Kessler and Gilmore:

> [D]espite the common law insistence on freedom of contract and subjective intent to contract, it was early recognized (indeed it has always been recognized) that there are circumstances in which defendants may be required to compensate plaintiffs for benefits received (or for losses caused) where there was never any intention to contract or indeed any contract.[83]

Probably the prototype for this concept is the case of *Chase v. Corcoran.*[84] In *Chase* the owner of a boat that had been found adrift and repaired by another recovered it by legal process when its rescuer refused to turn it over unless the owner paid for its repair. No more clear statement could have been made that the owner had absolutely no intention to pay for the services rendered. Yet the Supreme Judicial Court of Massachusetts had no difficulty in holding that payment must be made:

> Whatever might have been the liability of the owner if he had chosen to let the finder retain the boat, by taking it from him he made himself liable to pay the reasonable expenses incurred in keeping and repairing it.[85]

CONTRACTS IMPLIED-IN-LAW: UNJUST ENRICHMENT OR QUASI-CONTRACT

The *Chase* case epitomizes the legal version of implied-in-law concepts. Known as unjust enrichment or quasi-contract, this doctrine focuses on the unseemly enhancement of one party's wealth at the improper expense of another. Damages are awarded by assessing the benefits that have accrued through the acts of the injured party.[86] Unlike implied-in-fact situations, however, recovery is not

83. F. Kessler & G. Gilmore, Teacher's Manual, Contracts: Cases and Materials 12 (1972) (quoted by permission); *accord,* Henderson, *supra* note 56, at 1140.

84. 106 Mass. 286 (1871).

85. *Id.* at 288.

86. Henderson points out that courts which state this restitutionary rule (found in Restatement of Restitution § 155(1) (1937)) "in fact award plaintiff's detriment as the measure of benefit wrongly withheld." Henderson, *supra* note 56, at 1147. This measure, Henderson notes, parallels that given in personal services cases as protection of reasonable reliance: in both cases damages are assessed at the market value of plaintiff's time and expenses. *Id.* at 1147-48. The extent to which such a measure is inadequate as to services rendered by one family member to another is discussed at notes 41 and 48 *supra* and the sources there cited. Of course an offset for the value of room, board, and other benefits received by the claimant from the defendant is required. Sanguinetti v. Sanguinetti, 9 Cal. 2d 95, 100, 69 P.2d 845, 847 (1937) (putative spouse). In this regard it should be noted that a portion of the services rendered will have been allocated to the living needs of the person supplying them. *See* Hall, *The Case of the Late Mrs. Smith, Homemaker,* 67 J. Home Econ. 30 (Oct. 1973).

predicated upon any inferable agreement between the parties. Rather, as in *Chase,* the doctrine seeks to avoid unjust results without concerning itself with the parties' intentions. Accordingly, in some instances the doctrine may be applied to facts in which an actual, implied-in-fact agreement exists, in others it provides relief although no actual thought to consequences or efforts at agreement can be discerned, and in yet others like *Chase* recovery is given in the face of express or implied hostility to that result by one of the parties.[87]

CONSTRUCTIVE (IMPLIED-IN-LAW) TRUST

Constructive trust doctrine constitutes equity's version of implied-in-law recovery. As with unjust enrichment, the parties' intentions are not the central point of inquiry. Rather the court inquires into the equities of the situation in light of all the relevant circumstances and imposes a trust if it is needed to prevent unjust enrichment by forcing restitution to the plaintiff of something that in fairness and good conscience does not belong to the defendant.[88] The degree of ownership interest in property standing in the defendant's name that is awarded to a plaintiff accordingly reflects the court's assessment of the relevant equities. As discussed in the treatment of implied-in-fact partnership theory above, a court may take into account both contributions of valuable assets and contributions of valuable services in determining the relative interests of a man and woman who acquire and enhance financial resources during their life together.[89]

When individuals who believed erroneously but in good faith that they were validly married petition courts for protection of their financial interests, constructive trust doctrine is often employed to grant relief. In some cases the courts analogize the parties' interests to those of partnership or marital property law.[90] In others,

87. A California appellate court utilized quasi-contract to sustain recovery for a woman who for twelve years mistakenly believed that her husband had abandoned divorce proceedings when they reconciled. Lazzarevich v. Lazzarevich, 88 Cal. App. 2d 708, 200 P.2d 49 (1948). *See also* Annot., 31 A.L.R. 424 (1924); Annot., 111 A.L.R. 348 (1937); Evans, *Property Interests Arising from Quasi-Marital Relations,* 9 CORNELL L.Q. 246, 251-52 (1924).

88. DOBBS, *supra* note 64, § 4.3, at 241.

89. *See* text accompanying notes 68-74 *supra.*

90. Coats v. Coats, 160 Cal. 671, 118 P. 441 (1911); Schneider v. Schneider, 183 Cal. 335, 191 P. 533 (1920); Werner v. Werner, 59 Kan. 399, 53 P. 127 (1898); Higgins v. Breen, 9 Mo. 497 (1845); Krauter v. Krauter, 79 Okla. 30, 190 P. 1088 (1920). *See generally* Annot., 11 A.L.R. 1394 (1921), and the cases there cited, and Evans, *Property Interests Arising from*

relief is granted for the value of services rendered above the value of benefits received.[91] In these cases legal theories that have long applied to interactions between persons who share no family ties are readily applied to the obligations of a man and woman whose relationship can be distinguished only in noneconomic respects. Similar relief will be given parties who knowingly cohabit without marriage once courts recognize that domestic services have monetary value to the domestic unit and realize that judicial intervention on behalf of an injured party is not equivalent to judicial sanction of unmarried liaisons.[92] Indeed, to conclude otherwise is to permit the enrichment of one whose activities bring monetary rewards at the expense of one whose efforts receive no direct financial remuneration. Such exploitation ought not be condoned under the guise of distaste for what have been until recently nontraditional lifestyles.

D. *The Scope of Relief*

Doctrinal pigeonholes that once prescribed the availability of suit and the nature of potential relief are increasingly eschewed.[93] Although for the sake of exposition this article has articulated the doctrines as distinct categories, their delineation is inevitably blurred. And in some respects the traditional lines have become less important. Since the merger of law and equity, it is possible to request any appropriate remedy once an underlying cause of action has been established.[94] Thus, an action need no longer sound in

---

Quasi-Marital Relations, 9 CORNELL L.Q. 246, 254-61 (1924). Many cases from community property states are cited in W. REPPY & W. DEFUNIAK, COMMUNITY PROPERTY IN THE UNITED STATES 59-61 (1975).

91. Sanguinetti v. Sanguenetti, 9 Cal. 2d 95, 69 P.2d 845 (1937).

92. Warner v. Warner, 76 Idaho 399, 283 P.2d 931 (1955), may well be such a case. Many of the putative spouse cases are cited. *Id.* at 407, 283 P.2d at 935-36. The court's reasoning, however, is not entirely clear, and the result may be dictated by the rules of common law marriage rather than constructive trust, given the court's imposition of an estoppel to prevent the defendant from denying such a relationship, as discussed in note 67 *supra.* Identification of constructive trust cases is hampered by the fact that courts which employ a constructive trust remedy may be giving relief upon a cause of action established under a theory other than constructive trust. *See* notes 93-96 *infra* and accompanying text. When, as in *Warner* the line between the cause of action and the remedy is not precisely articulated, it is perhaps both unwise and unnecessary to categorize the result. *Id.*

93. *See* G. GILMORE, THE DEATH OF CONTRACT 101-02 (1974).

94. DOBBS, *supra* note 64, § 2.6, at 66; A. SCOTT & R. KENT, CASES AND OTHER MATERIALS ON CIVIL PROCEDURE 193-214 (1967). In federal court, "[r]elief in the alternative or of several different types may be demanded." FED. R. CIV. P. 8(a)(3), *discussed in* 2A J. MOORE & J. LUCAS, MOORE'S FEDERAL PRACTICE ¶ 8.18 (2d ed. 1948). Of course, equitable remedies cannot be had without the traditional prerequisites—irreparable injury and inadequacy of legal remedy. 2 *Id.* ¶ 2.06, at 357 & n. 14.

equity to provide the basis for a desired equitable remedy.[95] Perhaps the most useful remedy—the imposition of a trust upon property—may accordingly be requested in a case in which trust theory does not provide the underlying cause of action.[96]

Nothing in the merger of law and equity was intended to increase the grounds for liability as between parties.[97] It was designed instead to end duplicitous litigation, first at law and then in equity, in search of appropriate relief. The merger has, however, led to a certain degree of confusion. In many cases where recovery has been allowed between parties who cohabit without marriage, courts appear to focus on the remedy and elide discussion of the underlying cause of action. Most frequently these are cases where property has been acquired through the efforts of both parties over the course of their relationship. Accordingly, any number of the express, implied-in-fact or implied-in-law doctrines described above might justify a division of property between the parties. Yet case after case is silent as to the rationale that is being employed as

---

95. *See, e.g.,* Bracken v. Bracken, 52 S.D. 252, 217 N.W. 192 (1927) (accounting and partition of realty). Relief may also include an order for transfer of title to the beneficiary. G. G. Bogert & G. C. Bogert, Handbook of the Law of Trusts § 74, at 281 (5th ed. 1973).

96.

> It is entirely appropriate to award a constructive trust as a means of forcing restitution to prevent unjust enrichment. For this purpose, it does not much matter how the unjust enrichment came about. What must give concern is not the method by which the defendant enriched himself, but the fairness and workability of the judicial decree. . . .Since the constructive trust is only a remedy, it can be administered with considerable flexibility.

Dobbs, *supra* note 64, § 4.3, at 246. The degree of ownership interest in property standing in the defendant's name that is awarded to a plaintiff reflects the court's assessment of the relevant equities. As an equitable doctrine, constructive trust recovery permits in personam orders directed to the defendant as well as other equitable enforcement techniques. For example, while the legal doctrine of unjust enrichment (quasi-contract) when considered alone authorizes the recovery of a simple money judgment, the court that imposes a constructive trust may order the defendant to transfer specific property to the plaintiff. *Id.* Similarly, the property may be traced into the hands of others and subrogation and equitable liens are recognized. *Id.* at 247-52.

97. This was the conclusion of a New York court following that state's merger of law and equity under the 1848 Field Code:

> Unless the code, by abolishing the distinction between actions at law and suits in equity, and the forms of such actions and suits, and of pleadings theretofore existing, intended to initiate, and has initiated new principles of law, by which a class of rights and of wrongs, not before the proper subjects of judicial investigation and remedy, can now be judicially investigated and remedied, the facts stated in the plaintiff's complaint in this action, do not constitute a cause of action. . . . I am not aware that any one has ever claimed for the code, or charged against the code, a mission, or purpose, so bold, novel, sweeping and dangerous. It cannot be supposed that the abolition, in words, of the distinction between actions at law and suits in equity, by the code, was intended to break up the well settled fundamental principles and limits of common law and equitable jurisdiction. . . .

Cropsey v. Sweeney, 27 Barb. 310, 311-12 (N.Y. 1858).

courts grant relief. Some may be explained as express or implied-in-fact pooling agreements (title to property being held in both parties' names),[98] others appear to qualify as implied partnership cases in which a constructive trust has been imposed upon the partnership property,[99] and others can only be explained by estoppel doctrine[100] or general equitable principles.[101] Yet, however careless the courts' articulation of the grounds for recovery, parties would be well advised to frame their claims within the context of the theories discussed in this section.

At the same time, it is important to recognize that major consequences flow from the nature of the claims set forth. First, jury trial remains available for actions and remedies drawn from common law counts[102] while equitable claims and remedies entail no such trial as a matter of right.[103] Allegations of multiple counts, some equitable and some legal in origin, therefore raise the specter of bifurcated trials, as does the combination of equitable claims and legal remedies or the converse.

While these complications are no different from those ordinarily confronted in trials since the merger of law and equity, they do pose a contrast to family law practice in many states. For example, litigation involving family matters is often treated as equitable, and jury trials are not utilized in suits requesting a dissolution or declaration of nullity.[104] In order that their case will be heard by a judge assigned to the domestic relations bench, parties who cohabit without marriage might well wish to litigate property rights in conjunction with a suit for nullity, especially if child custody and child support matters are involved. Even if the domestic relations

---

98. *See, e.g.*, Hyman v. Hyman, 275 S.W.2d 149 (Tex. Civ. App. 1954). *Cf.* Merit v. Losey, 194 Or. 89, 240 P.2d 933 (1952).

99. *See, e.g.*, Bracken v. Bracken, 52 S.D. 252, 217 N.W. 192 (1927).

100. *See, e.g.*, Warner v. Warner, 76 Idaho 399, 283 P.2d 931 (1955), discussed in note 67 *supra*; Poole v. Schrichte, 39 Wash. 2d 558, 236 P.2d 1044 (1951).

101. *See, e.g.*, Sousa v. Freitas, 10 Cal. App. 3d 660, 89 Cal. Rptr. 485 (1st Dist. 1970); Reese v. Reese, 132 Kan. 438, 295 P. 690 (1931); West v. Knowles, 50 Wash. 2d 311, 311 P.2d 689 (1957).

102. *See generally* DOBBS, *supra* note 64, § 2.6, at 69-81; 5 J. MOORE & J. LUCAS, *supra* note 94, ¶ 38.13 *et seq.*

103. Although there is no right to a jury trial in equity proceedings, the court is free to empanel an advisory jury. H. MCCLINTOCK, HANDBOOK OF THE PRINCIPLES OF EQUITY § 13 (2d ed. 1948), and authorities there cited; C. WRIGHT, HANDBOOK OF THE LAW OF FEDERAL COURTS § 92 (2d ed. 1970). *See, e.g.*, FED. R. CIV. P. 39(c).

104. H. CLARK, THE LAW OF DOMESTIC RELATIONS IN THE UNITED STATES § 13.7, at 396 (1968).

court concludes that it has jurisdiction to hear claims between members of informal families[105] it may be unable to provide a jury trial. If so, causes of action derived from common law counts must be referred to the trial court of general jurisdiction.[106] States where such restrictions on jury trial exist may well prove more receptive to equitable theories that enable judges who ordinarily deal with domestic matters to superintend litigation between parties to informal unions.

Second, tax consequences may depend upon the cause of action which is vindicated in suits between de facto spouses. However, since the characterization of recovery applied by a state is not binding as to federal taxes,[107] the results cannot be predicted with assurance.[108]

---

105. In California, even the overruling of *In re Marriage of Cary,* described in note 13 *supra,* would not necessarily preclude jurisdiction of claims between parties to informal families. The *Cary* court's grant of relief was predicated upon a questionable reading of section 4452 of the California Civil Code. Marvin v. Marvin, 50 Cal. App. 3d [advance sheet] 84, 96-97 (2d Dist. 1975), *hearing granted,* No. L.A. 30520 (Cal. Supreme Ct., Sept. 17, 1975); CALIFORNIA, REPORT OF THE GOVERNOR'S COMMISSION ON THE FAMILY 46, 76 (1966) (stating that § 4452 intended to codify existing law); Kay Brief, *supra* note 23, at 29-49, and the authorities there cited. If jurisdiction over informal families nonetheless exists (In re Marriage of Cary, 34 Cal. App. 3d 345, 353, 109 Cal. Rptr. 862, 867 (1st Dist. 1973) suggests that it does), relief under common law principles appears possible.

106. Whether quantum meruit determinations pose similar problems is unclear. Modern cases have generally treated all such claims as "legal" rather than "equitable", calling for trial by jury. DOBBS, *supra* note 64, § 2.6, at 74-79 (discussing federal law); 4 B. WITKIN, CALIFORNIA PROCEDURE, TRIAL § 75 (2d ed. 1971) (discussing California law). However, in Sanguinetti v. Sanguinetti, 9 Cal. 2d 95, 69 P.2d 845 (1937), the trial judge presiding over an annulment proceeding awarded $1,250 to the putative wife as the reasonable value of her services during the relationship and imposed an equitable lien in her favor on defendant's property. There is no discussion in the appellate opinion of the propriety of granting such relief without a jury. In Lazzarevich v. Lazzarevich, 88 Cal. App. 2d 708, 200 P.2d 49 (1948), a putative spouse was awarded a quantum meruit recovery after a non-jury trial in an action unrelated to an annulment proceeding.

107. George F. Reisman, 49 T.C. 570 (1968), *acq.* 1971-2 CUM. BULL. 3 (payments under state annulment decree treated as alimony following divorce for federal tax purposes); *cf.* Estate of Borax v. Commissioner, 349 F.2d 666 (2d Cir. 1965), *cert. denied,* 383 U.S. 935 (1966) (validity of a marriage or divorce for federal income tax purposes is a question of federal law). The Internal Revenue Service recognizes common law marriages which are recognized by the state of the parties' residence. Rev. Rul. 58-66, 1958-1 CUM. BULL. 60. The principle operative in all of these situations was expressed in *Borax:*

> This rule of validation tends to promote some measure of certainty and uniformity—important goals of the federal tax scheme. . . .

349 F.2d at 670.

108. Regardless of state law characterization, support payments pursuant to an annulment of either a void or voidable marriage, like those pursuant to a divorce or separation, are deductible to the payor and taxable to the payee. INT. REV. CODE of 1954 §§ 71, 215; Andrew M. Newburger, 61 T.C. 457 (1974), *acq.* 1974.2 CUM. BULL. 3. On the other hand, the Internal Revenue Service follows local community property law; if the state holds that a void marriage does not create community property, community property principles cannot be taken into account in filing a federal income tax return. Charles Edward Barr, Jr., 10

A more fundamental question is posed when the monetary value of recovery is compared to that available in divorce proceedings. In cases of nonmarital cohabitation, if the cause of action is designed to compensate the plaintiff for the value of services rendered or to restore to the plaintiff the value of benefits received by the defendant,[109] a substantial award may be made at the end of a lengthy relationship. If, on the other hand, a partnership interest or a constructive trust is established that recognizes a partial ownership interest in property acquired during the relationship, recovery may have no direct relationship to the duration of the union. Theoretically, a relatively brief period of cohabitation may result in an award of substantial property. More realistically, a long-standing relationship may produce an equal share of rather meager acquisitions—indeed, a share that has a market value far below the dollar recovery that would be awarded if the value of services that were rendered over the years were the measure.

Courts or legislatures faced with a choice as to the theoretical bases for recognition of property rights between de facto spouses will certainly note these possiblities and compare them to the recovery permitted following divorce.[110] While policy reasons cannot support complete denial of recovery to injured parties at the end of an informal union, they surely can preclude a measure of recovery

---

T.C. 1288 (1948) (California law; taxpayer was putative spouse, no community property recognized). These precedents suggest that marital property and support characterizations under state law of dispositions made at the termination of de facto relationships will control, while an absence of such characterization is not necessarily dispositive. *See* note 107 *supra*. If not, gift tax consequences may follow.

109. This is the case for example, in suits alleging express or implied contracts for services or requesting quantum meruit recovery in the absence of a contract. *See* notes 65-67 & 86-87 *supra* and accompanying text.

110. *See* note 17 *supra,* and authorities there cited. To the extent that the discrepancy is in favor of recovery to parties who have cohabited without marriage, it is possible that the recovery upon divorce may be too low rather than the converse. Evans, *supra* note 14, at 267. Judge Boyer dissented from a Florida opinion which held that a divorce judgment awarding $27,700 in alimony and property to the wife was inadequate as a matter of law when the couple's assets totalled $232,843:

> Alimony came about during the era that women in general and wives in particular were placed on a pedestal by male chauvinists. Women apparently found being worshipped on a pedestal to be distasteful and commenced a virtual worldwide drive to be removed from their place of superiority to a position of equality. Why one enjoying a position of superiority would intentionally seek a lower position of equality eludes the writer, but it is a fact of social history. "Success" has been marked by loss of many heretofore existing superior rights, among them being dower and alimony as a matter of right.

Brown v. Brown, 300 So.2d 719, 727 (Fla. App. 1974) (dissenting opinion). The judge appears not to recognize that for many women it is indeed possible to go up the down staircase.

that would appear to reward parties who avoid marriage by providing for greater recovery than would be possible had a ceremonial marriage taken place. The comparison can be valid only, however, if all incidents of compensation are taken into account. Most notably, spousal support has never been made available to meretricious spouses. It remains to be seen whether statutes that authorize such awards to putative spouses will be extended to persons who knowingly cohabit without marriage.[111] Unless such a development occurs, however, it is clear that an award measured by services rendered or benefits received may approximate rather than exceed the total recovery allowed upon the dissolution of long-term marriages when no substantial property exists.[112]

To the extent that partnership or constructive trust doctrines provide a division comparable to that prescribed by marital prop-

---

111. *E.g.*, CAL. CIV. CODE § 4455 (West Supp. 1976). See generally H. CLARK, *supra* note 104, § 3.5, at 137. Although property relief to putative spouses had equitable, not statutory, origins (H. VERRALL & A. SAMMIS, *supra* note 14, at 63-64), courts have not permitted spousal support under equitable analogs. There appears to be no reason for this hesitancy. The result, of course, is that neither support nor property distribution is available if parties with no acquisitions separate. Recovery quantum meruit can provide a quasi-support remedy if execution on the award is made by wage garnishment. Courts have only rarely ordered payments over time in the absence of statutory authorization. *See, e.g.*, Bensing v. Bensing, 25 Cal. App. 3d 889, 102 Cal. Rptr. 255 (1st Dist. 1972); Marriage of Juick, 21 Cal. App. 3d 421, 98 Cal. Rptr. 324 (2d Dist. 1971); Englund v. Englund, _____ Mont. _____, 547 P.2d 841 (1976); *cf.* J. DAWSON & W. HARVEY, CASES ON CONTRACTS AND CONTRACT REMEDIES 761-62 (2d ed. 1969). It would seem possible for a court to order defendant to execute a promissory note in satisfaction of a quantum meruit recovery and then merge the note into the judgement, much as is done with separation agreements and stipulations. Unless the award is denominated support, however, it may be discharged in bankruptcy, 11 U.S.C. § 35(a)(7) (1970); *cf.* § 4-506(a)(6) of the Bankruptcy Act proposed by the Commission on the Bankruptcy Laws of the United States in 1973, now pending in Congress, which would provide that property settlement obligations incurred in connection with a divorce or separation would not be dischargeable in bankruptcy. H. Doc. No. 93-137, Part II, 93rd Cong., 1st Sess. 136, 139 (1973). The present bankruptcy statute refers to support orders for the debtor's "wife," the proposed statute, the debtor's "spouse." Interpretation of these terms would be required to apply the statute to obligations arising out of putative relationships, similar to other statutory interpretation problems discussed in the text accompanying notes 114-19 *infra.* As to the tax consequences, *see* notes 107 & 108 *supra* and accompanying text. Note that such quasi-support is not necessarily inconsistent with a property division between more affluent parties so long as the value of property received is considered in the quantum meruit action. H. VERRALL & A. SAMMIS, *supra*, at 64.

112. *See* note 111 *supra.* Support statutes typically authorize a lower support award when the supported spouse has independent means such as property. H. CLARK, *supra* note 104, § 14.5, at 444-45. If alternative approaches can be preserved, the equities of a particular case may well suggest which theory of recovery is most appropriate on the facts. Those who seek to foster judicial receptivity to suits between de facto spouses should take care not to throw the baby out with the bathwater through the assertion of doctrines that lead to clearly avaricious results in one case, inviting judicial resistance that may preclude their fair use later on appropriate facts. Similar attention by courts can insure that overbroad dicta does not prematurely foreclose doctrinal growth.

erty laws, the result is readily explained. Even in the absence of community property laws, there is an increasing tendency to analyze the marital relationship as a contractual one.[113] This movement from status to contract, in accord with Maine's aphorism, supports increasingly similar treatment for those whose relationships are indistinguishable except for matters of status.

It would be both premature and unwise, however, to conclude that the relationships of parties to informal unions and of those to ceremonial marriages are or ought to become identical. Rights of support or property management during the on-going relationship are not resolved by the doctrines discussed above.[114] Although it may be possible to claim a dependency exemption for a de facto spouse,[115] the parties may not file joint income tax returns.[116] Indeed whether any governmental or statutorily-created benefits for married couples may be shared by de facto spouses depends upon the language and construction of the statutes that define them. As a result, questions of interpretation arise under intestacy, worker's

---

113. *See generally* Weitzman, *supra* note 3. Professor Weitzman suggests the law of business partnerships, particularly the Uniform Partnership Act, as "one model for contracts in lieu of marriage." *Id.* at 1255.

114. It is unlikely that courts would be any more willing to supervise an on-going family relationship in this context than in a more formal one. *See* Weitzman, *supra* note 3, at 1258-72. However, property management questions may be posed by creditors who seek to levy on the interest of a party to the union who does not hold title. Although this article does not treat the question of rights during the relationship and gives only brief attention to support rights following break-up of the family, it recognizes that developments in both of these areas may occur once courts become accustomed to entertaining suits between the parties to informal unions. *See* note 111 *supra*.

115. A dependency exemption may be claimed for a person over half of whose support was furnished by the taxpayer, and who is a member of the taxpayer's household. INT. REV. CODE of 1954 § 152(a)(9). The exemption is available unless the relationship is in violation of local law. *Id.* § 152(b)(5); Leonard J. Eichbauer, ¶ 71,133 P.H. Memo T.C. (1971). The congressional committee report on section 152(b)(5) states, however: "[T]his would make it clear that an individual who is a 'common-law wife' where the applicable State law does not recognize common-law marriage would not qualify as a dependent of the taxpayer." H. Rept. No. 775, 85th Cong., 1st Sess. (1957), 1958-3 CUM. BULL. 811, 818. This report was written at a time when nonmarital cohabitation was generally illegal. *Cf.* note 25 *supra. But see* William Thomas Hamilton, 34 T.C. 927 (1960), stating that support provided in cases of nonmarital cohabitation is remuneration for services, and hence does not qualify as "support." Therefore the dependency exemption was not allowed. The court stated that the purpose of section 152(a)(9) was to give a dependency exemption for foster children. *Id.* at 929. *Accord, e.g.,* Billy G. Newsom, ¶ 74,265 P.H. Memo T.C. (1974). Even should a dependency exemption be allowed it could not be used as the basis for obtaining "head of household" status and the lower tax rates it provides. INT. REV. CODE of 1954, § 2(b)(3)(B)(i).

116. Joseph F. Amaro, ¶ 70,208 P.H. Memo. T.C. (1970). *But see* note 107 *supra*; if common-law marriage is established, the rule is to the contrary.

compensation,[117] social security[118] and wrongful death statutes.[119]

The complexity of these issues has led to Professor Weyrauch's conclusion that great intellectual effort and innovation will be required to provide equitable results between parties who cohabit without marriage in the absence of relief under the doctrine of common law marriage.[120] While this is doubtless true, the effort may be worth it. If states return to common law marriage as a means of protecting parties from the consequences of their perhaps unthinking rejection of statutory marriage provisions, there are two possible negative ramifications. The first is a real danger that parties' freedom to experiment with newer forms of family structure will be stifled through an imposition upon them of a status they did not choose, in clear disregard of their contrary intention.[121]

---

117. In two recent cases divorced couples resumed cohabitation without remarrying in states that do not recognize common law marriage. Courts nonetheless held them "married" so as to qualify the survivor in each case for workers' compensation survivor's benefits. Burgess Construction Co. v. Lindley, 504 P.2d 1023 (Alaska 1972); Parkinson v. J. & S. Tool Co., 64 N.J. 159, 313 A.2d 609 (1974). And in West v. Barton-Malow Co., 394 Mich. 334, 230 N.W.2d 545 (1975), the Supreme Court of Michigan awarded workers' compensation death benefits to a meretricious spouse whose de facto husband was killed after a relationship of thirteen years' duration.

In contrast, two recent California cases, one state and one federal, denied survivorship benefits to surviving meretricious spouses. Powell v. Rogers, 496 F.2d 1248 (9th Cir., *cert. denied,* 419 U.S. 1032 (1974) (Federal Longshoremen's and Harbor Workers' Compensation Act, incorporating California law); Guillen v. Workers' Compensation Appeals Board, 40 Cal. Comp. Cases 470 (App., 2d Dist. 1975). The California Supreme Court granted a hearing in *Guillen,* but the case was dismissed pursuant to stipulation of the parties March 4, 1976, before a decision was rendered. Cal. Official Reports, 1976 No. 9, Minutes, at 5.

118. Social Security benefits based on marital status (*e.g.,* wives, widowers, etc.) are awarded to persons who are married according to the local law of the state of their domicile, or otherwise deemed to be a spouse under that state's intestate succession laws. 42 U.S.C. § 416(h)(1)(A) (1970). In addition, a putative spouse who married without knowledge of a legal impediment to the marriage may receive benefits as if married, unless there is a legal (de jure) spouse entitled to receive them. 42 U.S.C. § 416(h)(1)(B) (1970). *See generally* H. McCormick, Social Security Claims and Procedures §§ 222, 226 (1973). These provisions, of course, incorporate state laws relating to common law marriages as well as to ceremonial marriages. *Id.* § 231 (1973 & Supp. 1975).

119. Inequities that may result in such cases when courts zealously insist upon ceremonially valid relationships have been noted by Professor D. Currie. Currie, *Suitcase Divorce in the Conflict of Laws,* 34 U. Chi. L. Rev. 26, 65 (1966).

120. Weyrauch, *supra* note 5, at 104-10.

121. Weitzman, *To Love, Honor, and Obey? Traditional Legal Marriage and Alternative Family Forms,* 24 Fam. Coordinator 531, 543-47 (1975). Although the privacy interest is important, this objection must be qualified. Courts have long imposed restraints upon parties who would harm others if left to their own devices. *See* the discussion of quasi-contract in the text accompanying notes 83-87, *supra.* Avoiding unjust enrichment need not be equivalent to imposing marital status upon the parties. Neither the doctrine of common law marriage nor the meretricious relationship theory of the Washington courts discussed at note 68 *supra* applies to parties who indicate their choice to remain single. Of less certainty are the elements required under the statutory rationale of California's *Cary* case, should it be approved by the California Supreme Court. Weitzman, 24 Fam. Coordinator at 545-47. *See* note 13 *supra.*

The second is the equally unpleasant prospect of bigamous marriages as parties to common law marriages fail to pursue formal divorce proceedings before establishing new marital relationships.[122]

Statutory schemes have been developed that are both solicitous of the welfare of parties who cohabit without marriage and careful not to impose all the attributes of marital status upon them.[123] For legislatures that seek more than an incremental response to the issues posed by the increased number of informal families, they may provide helpful models that have been tested and refined over time.[124] To the extent that broad-scale statutory solutions are not undertaken, the equitable principles discussed in this article will depend upon legislative relief for specific problems and the growth of common law doctrine. The need for such evolution is clear.

Summary

Although the consequence of current legal treatment of parties who live together in the absence of a ceremonial marriage can be expressed in gender-neutral terms, it remains true that at present in our society it is most frequently the woman who contributes unrecompensed services and the man who acquires wealth in these situations.[125] To the extent that these roles are reversed, it is of course equally inequitable to deprive the man who remains at home of rea-

---

122. There is no "common law divorce" corresponding to common law marriage; divorce, even from common law marriages, must be decreed by a court. H. Clark, The Law of Domestic Relations in the United States § 11.3, at 302-03; Foster, *Common Law Divorce,* 46 Minn. L. Rev. 43, 67 (1961); *see* Boddie v. Connecticut, 401 U.S. 371 (1971).

The peculiar opinion in Bracken v. Bracken, 45 S.D. 430, 436, 188 N.W. 46, 48 (1922), suggested that formal divorce proceedings were not required to terminate a relationship that appeared to meet the test for common law marriage as there were no property rights to be settled. The problem is similar to that which arises when a divorce is recognized in some states but not others. *See generally* Williams v. North Carolina, 325 U.S. 226 (1945); Currie, *Suitcase Divorce in the Conflict of Laws,* 34 U. Chi. L. Rev. 26 (1966).

123. *See* notes 8-11 *supra* and accompanying text.

124. As always, care must be taken to evaluate the appropriateness of laws and institutions developed in different cultures and legal systems. R. Schlesinger, Comparative Law: Cases, Text, Materials 9 (3d ed. 1970).

125. *In re* Marriage of Cary, 34 Cal. App. 3d 345, 350, 109 Cal. Rptr. 862, 864 (1st Dist. 1973); Latham v. Latham, ___ Or. ___, ___, 547 P.2d 144, 147 (1976); Evans, *supra* note 14, at 246, 268 (1924); *cf.* West v. Knowles, 50 Wash. 2d 311, ___, 311 P.2d 689, 693 (1957) (concurring opinion):

> The rule operates to the great advantage of the cunning and the shrewd, who wind up with possession of the property, or title to it in their names, at the end of a so-called meretricious relationship. So, although the courts proclaim that they will have nothing to do with such matters, the proclamation in itself establishes, as to the parties involved, an effective and binding rule of law which tends to operate purely by accident or perhaps by reason of the cunning, anticipatory designs of just one of the parties.

sonable recovery for the increase in the woman's wealth that occurs aided by his efforts.[126]

Yet as this discussion indicates, most courts have applied only a restricted version of general legal principles in such cases. As a result they are seriously handicapped in their ability to grant relief appropriate to the particular facts of a case before them, simply because the parties have lived together in a domestic unit that is increasingly no longer illegal in either the narrow or the more general meaning of the term.

Because relationships arise in different ways, based upon different needs and assumptions, courts are faced with any number of distinctive relationships. When it can be demonstrated that the parties have expressly structured their financial responsibilities to one another, their agreement should control. Nothing in the contract, partnership, or trust law doctrines discussed above suggests any other result. And the result is the same whether the agreement is to pool some or all of their property and efforts, or whether it calls for the retention of strictly separate property rights. The only restraints on the parties' ability to control the property incidents of their relationship should be those which are imposed in any case to avoid fraud, overreaching, or some similar defect in the formation process.

Most persons, however, are undoubtedly much less sophisticated concerning financial matters than those who enter express agreements. Indeed, it is much more likely that they enter their relationship either

1. in ignorance of the legal consequences of either marriage or nonmarriage (perhaps the majority of non-lawyers believe that common law marriage exists in all jurisdictions and that protection is granted to stable nonmarital relationships),
2. under the assumption that some legal protections are available, or
3. with absolutely no thought given to the legal consequences of their relationship.

In any of these situations, expectations that exist at the time that cohabitation begins may change over time as the relationship

126. *See In re* Marriage of Mix, 14 Cal. 3d 604, 536 P.2d 479, 122 Cal. Rptr. 79 (1975).

solidifies and years go by. Courts must tailor relief to the realities of the cases presented. In doing so, they need only acknowledge that in those many cases where parties make no express agreement, normal legal and equitable principles continue to apply.

Surely it is more sensible to place the burden upon individuals to state clearly their desire to bring about inequitable results, than to impose such results upon large numbers of people who live together without marriage with no articulated division of financial responsibility. To do otherwise is to imply in law an unconscionable contract, one in which one party may render important services for a period of years only to return to the job market upon the relationship's termination with no marketable skills or financial resources while the other retains the full measure of increased wealth and increased earning power that were acquired through participation in monetarily rewarded activity outside the home. Once such inequity is rejected, Professor Bodenheimer suggests that the following principles will be available to guide the resolution of property questions raised by persons who have lived together without marriage:

> 1. If an unmarried couple enters an express contract to share property or make payments in return for property or service contributions, the agreement should be enforced according to its terms regardless of their nonmarital cohabitation.
>
> 2. If the unmarried couple agrees that their relationship should entail no property or monetary consequences, again the agreement should govern.
>
> 3. If it can be gathered from the facts and circumstances that the unmarried parties have engaged in an implied partnership or joint enterprise, or there is an implied-in-fact contract or trust, recovery should be allowed in accordance with their implied expectations.
>
> 4. But when there is no agreement one way or the other, the law should relieve inequity and hardship to one of them and prevent unjust enrichment of the other.[127]

The time has come to recognize that the standards of good faith and fair dealing required by the law in the commercial world and for most inter-personal economic transactions apply to this area as well. Whatever the causes for the development of legal taboos concerning cohabitation without marriage, the result has been palpable injustice to those whose contributions to the enrichment of others have been nonmonetary yet valuable.

---

127. Brief for Brigitte Bodenheimer, *et al.*, as Amicae Curiae at 25, Marvin v. Marvin, No. L.A. 30520 (Cal. Supreme Ct., *hearing granted*, Sept. 17, 1975).

APPLICATION FOR MEMBERSHIP
FAMILY LAW SECTION

Note: *ABA Membership is prerequisite to Section Membership*

Please Check Appropriate Box

☐ I am applying for Regular Section membership and enclose annual dues of $17.50 ($10.00 of which is a subscription to *Family Law Quarterly*).

☐ I am applying for Law Student Section membership and enclose annual dues of $5.00. I already belong to the ABA Law Student Division.

☐ I am interested in membership, but would like more detailed information before joining.

Name ____

Address ______________________________________

City____________________State__________Zip__________

Send check and completed form to:

American Bar Association
Finance Department 1031
1155 E. 60th Street
Chicago, Illinois 60637

Volumes I and II

Volume I begins with a discussion of the used and misused phrase, "the best interests of the child," and concludes with a bill of rights for children. The volume includes articles on the child in custody disputes, in foster care, the stepchild, the illegitimate, the retarded, the battered, the "stubborn," the child in need of medical treatment, the unemancipated and the juvenile court victim.

Volume II offers solutions for other contem-porary juvenile problems. The role of the ather in the legal life of the child is examin-d. Other topics discussed are subsidized adoption for children in special circumstances, the plight of children committed to institutions, the child's preference in custody proceedings, and the reputation rights of children.

These two volumes should be immensely useful to social workers. They should also be of major interest, assistance and guidance to judges, legislators, attorneys and their clients, domestic relations professors and to all those whose lives are involved in the legal lives of children.

---

rder Form

	Qty.	*Total*
oungest Minority I at $5.00 each	______	$______
oungest Minority II at $5.00 each	______	______
oungest Minority I & II at $8.50 for the set	______	______
Total for handling		$ 1.00
Total enclosed		$______

The Youngest Minority
(513-0009)

Name ______________________________

Address ____________________________

City _______________________________

State ____________________ Zip________

Please make your check payable to the American Bar Association, and mail it with this order form to *Order Billing 513, American Bar Assn., 1155 E. 60th St., Chicago, IL 60637.*